Carol and John Steinbeck

Western Literature Series

Carol & John

san Shillinglaw

Steinbeck

PORTRAIT OF A MARRIAGE

UNIVERSITY OF NEVADA PRESS
RENO & LAS VEGAS

WESTERN LITERATURE SERIES

University of Nevada Press, Reno, Nevada 89557 USA
Copyright © 2013 by University of Nevada Press
All rights reserved
Manufactured in the United States of America
Design by Kathleen Szawiola

Library of Congress Cataloging-in-Publication Data
Shillinglaw, Susan.
Carol and John Steinbeck : portrait of a marriage / Susan Shillinglaw.
pages cm. — (Western Literature Series)
Includes bibliographical references and index.
ISBN 978-0-87417-930-9 (cloth : alk. paper) —
ISBN 978-0-87417-931-6 (e-book)
1. Steinbeck, John, 1902–1968—Marriage.
2. Novelists, American—20th century—Biography.
I. Title.
PS3537.T3234Z8664 2013
813'.52—dc23
[B]   2013008777

The paper used in this book meets the requirements of American National Standard for Information Sciences—Permanence of Paper for Printed Library Materials, ANSI/NISO Z39.48-1992 (R2002). Binding materials were selected for strength and durability.

FIRST PRINTING
22 21 20 19 18 17 16 15 14 13   5 4 3 2 1

Frontispiece: Carol and John, mid-1930s. Photo from Carol's scrapbooks.

To BILL GILLY and JACK BENSON
who, in different ways,
willed this book.

And to IAN and NORA,
who, with great forbearance,
lived it.

Contents

Illustrations

Preface

ON A RECENT TOUR I led to the Red Pony ranch near Salinas, California, a woman asked me if I was related to John Steinbeck. "You are, aren't you?" No, definitely not, although when I stand on dusty Hebert Road, near the barn with the little swallows' nests still under the eaves, with the water tank behind me and the paddock before me, the white buildings of distant Salinas on the horizon, I know that I see pretty much what Steinbeck saw and I think I feel pretty much what he felt when a California vista knocks you flat. Steinbeck's soul, I sometimes think, has become a little piece of my own. I live in Pacific Grove, California, as did he and Carol, and in Los Gatos, as did they. I drive to Salinas reluctantly, as did they. And I have a husband who, like Ed Ricketts, is a marine biologist, and we met on a trip to the Sea of Cortez, digging for chocolate clams. We married on Ricketts's birthday, May 14. We teach holistic biology together at Stanford University's Hopkins Marine Station, where Steinbeck took classes in 1923. I like all these intersections. I like that I have known Steinbeck's nieces and his third wife, Elaine, and his sons, Thom and John. And I like knowing Carol's stepdaughter, Sharon Brown Bacon, who lives by the Carmel River where Mack and the boys hunted frogs. It was she who set me on this biographical road by donating Carol's scrapbooks, photographs, and poetry to San Jose State University's Steinbeck Research Center, shortly after I became director in 1987. I am profoundly grateful for her generosity and patience throughout this project. And I was guided throughout by her own love for Carol.

This "wall of background" (Steinbeck's term) helped shape this book, the story of a marriage that I have spent some twenty-five years researching and writing. Initially, I was stumped, since Carol Henning Steinbeck left no account of her life, wrote few letters, and did not confide in friends the full extent of her woe. I have worked hard to understand her role in John's life and work—work that would not have been the same without her defining presence in his life.

I am fairly certain that Carol, married to John from 1930 to 1943, never stopped loving this man who gave light and purpose to her youth. And that is part of the story I tell, how we come to be defined by the web of associations that shape formative years. During my eighteen years as director of San Jose State's Steinbeck Center, while editing the *Steinbeck Newsletter*, organizing conferences, teaching and lecturing on Steinbeck, and somehow raising two children, John and Carol's story, waiting to be told, was ever on my mind. Some of Carol's story is mine, and I hope I have plumbed her great spirit and captured a bit of it.

The list of scholars and friends who shaped my career and scholarship is a long one. Glittering at the top are Jackson J. Benson and Robert DeMott, who have counseled and inspired me for a quarter of a century. In 1987, when I became director of the Steinbeck Research Center at San Jose State, with scant qualifications for the job, I had in hand a recent PhD, a dissertation on James Fenimore Cooper, and memories of reading *The Red Pony* in junior high, a book I disliked because the pony dies. I had put Steinbeck on a back shelf with *Old Yeller, The Yearling,* and the story of Lad, a dog circling his bed for the final time. Both Jack and Bob, models of generosity, helped me catch up, sharing their rich store of Steinbeckiana. This book would not exist without them.

I also thank a woman for selecting me as director in the first place, Lou Lewandowski, chair of the English Department, who believed that a fledgling lecturer would make the grade. Two other colleagues were models of scholarly deportment and hard-won female wisdom, Ma Joads: Arlene Okerlund, provost, and Fanny Rinn, editor of *San Jose Studies.*

My heartfelt thanks to Carol's relatives: Sharon Brown Bacon; Idell Budd, Carol's sister; and Carla Budd and Nikki Tugwell, Carol's nieces. And to John's: Toni and David Heyler lifted a cover on the Steinbeck family, as did Virginia St. Jean and Steinbeck's nieces.

Without John Seelye's cheerful support, I might not have written my first two introductions for Penguin Classics—on *Cannery Row* and *Of Mice and Men;* his zest for literary studies quickened my own. He and Michael Millman, editor at Viking Penguin for many years; Eugene Winick, former president of McIntosh and Otis; Jackson Bryer, editing mentor; and Ted Hayashi, pioneering Steinbeck scholar, supported my first publications on Steinbeck. I am ever grateful.

The imprint of other Steinbeck scholars is everywhere in this book. Their friendship sustained my career. Louis Owens's work helped me to love this state of failed dreams. John Ditsky's steady output in Steinbeck was inspirational—as was his unfailing kindness. In 1996 Kiyoshi Nakayama and the Steinbeck Society of Japan invited me to lecture on Carol and John, an unforgettable journey; thanks also to Hiromasa Takamura, Osamu Hamaguchi, and Scott and Susan Pugh, who hosted me and my daughter in this country of gentle courtesies. Warren French was the dean of Steinbeck studies, a man with a lopsided tie and grin and the willingness to revise opinions on this author. Mimi Gladstein has examined Steinbeck's women steadily and well. Bob and Katherine Morsberger, Roy Simmonds, and Leland Person modeled meticulous research and unfailing grace. Katie Rodger, my former student, has often lifted my spirits—and taught me much about Edward F. Ricketts. In 1992, Susan Beegel, Wes Tiffney, and I organized a conference in Nantucket on Steinbeck and the environment that launched my study of Steinbeck as ecologist. At the Jared Coffin House, I first met ever-vibrant Elaine Steinbeck. She loved the idea of this book, but did not want my scholarship to extend to her life; I respect that boundary. Finally, Harold Augenbraum, formerly director of the Mercantile Library in New York City, was codirector of the 2002 Steinbeck Centennial, sponsored by the National Endowment for the Arts; he taught me the delights of steady collaboration.

The work of many other scholars, of course, shaped my ideas about Steinbeck, particularly John Timmerman, Chip Hughes, Chris Fink, Charlotte Hadella, Kevin Hearle, Don Coers, Cliff Lewis, Brian Railsback, Graham Wilson, and Jay Parini. I owe all these and many others a huge Steinbeckian debt of gratitude.

To those who helped me connect biographically and historically, my thanks. Anne Loftis, Barbara Marinacci, James Houston, Gerald Haslam, Kevin Starr, David Wyatt, Timothy Egan, and Morris Dickstein deepened my understanding of California history. William Wulf generously gave me access to the Henning family papers in his archive of Los Gatos history.

Of course, I also wish to thank Steinbeck's friends, the people I interviewed from 1988 on, so often quoted in this book. Many are no longer living, and as I wrote and revised this text, their kindness to me returned in waves. Ed Ricketts Jr. talked to me about his father and John and Carol more times than I can count. In Alaska and in California, his sister Nancy Ricketts has done the same as we hiked around Sitka and exchanged letters.

Bob Harmon, Jim Johnson, Art Ring, Dick Hayman, Ken and Karen

Holmes, and the late Phil Ralls and Dick Hayman, each a collector and Steinbeck enthusiast, gave me free access to their minds and collections. Jim Dourgarian, collector, took me to meet Carlton Sheffield in 1990, a memorable afternoon. Writer John Thompson introduced me to Harold Ingels, and we poured over Beth Ingels's literary past while my daughter Nora, then four, displayed "three hours of such patient charm, writing her own spontaneous scripts with her toys." Rereading John's letter of thanks twenty-two years later, I am stunned at how much I put everyone through during this long quest—especially my children Ian and Nora when my gaze was diverted from their antics to Steinbeck's.

Stanford archivist Maggie Kimball and Morgan librarian Robert Parks made research so much easier, at all stages of this project.

Nearer at hand, I warmly thank my Salinas and Monterey friends who have supported my work on Steinbeck: John Gross, director of the Steinbeck Library; Mary Gamble, archivist; and Pauline Pearson, whose spirit remains in the many interviews she conducted in the 1970s and '80s for the Steinbeck Library. More recently, Herb Behrens, archivist at the National Steinbeck Center, sent me information at regular intervals. Carol Robles's work on the Steinbeck family in Salinas is precise in ways I envy. Since 1997, directors of the center have been unstinting in their support, most recently Colleen Baily; I delight in my position there as a scholar in residence. In Monterey, hats off to Dennis Copeland and Neal Hotelling.

The work of any professor is enriched by eager students, too many to name. The high school teachers who participated in the National Endowment for Humanities Summer Institutes I have codirected, "John Steinbeck: The Voice of a Region, a Voice for America," also imprinted this narrative. I also thank my first codirector, Mary Alder, for again showing me the delights of collaboration.

Finally—and perhaps most important—a scholar is propped up by friends and family. Thanks to Betsy and Whizzer, Heather and Ian, Geri and Jim, Carol and Greg, Ginger and Doug, Susan and Vladimir—and Katie, Persis, Marianina, and Clare. Anne and Ellen Shillinglaw, my cousins, sheltered me during research trips. My very generous aunt Frances eased many burdens, financial and emotional. And in ways they scarcely know, so did my brothers, Tom and John; my sister-in-law Betsy; and my children, Ian, Nora, Clayton, and Amanda. With my husband, Gilly, they are my phalanx of believers. Add Frank and Dorothy Gilly to that mix.

This book was completed because I was granted sabbaticals at San Jose State; because my research requests were supported by directors and assistants at sjsu's Center for Steinbeck Studies—particularly Sstoz Tes and Peter Van Coutren; because I had a loving husband who served as sensitive editor; and because the University of Nevada Press and director Joanne O'Hare saw value in a California writer and his first wife, both of whose main connection with Nevada was a messy divorce from a second spouse. My heartfelt thanks to institutions and individuals alike.

This long-emerging text seems a miracle to me. Like Steinbeck, I am awed by "participation," the extensive and supportive phalanx that made this book possible.

Carol and John Steinbeck

Introduction

VIKING PRESS spent more money on the publicity campaign for *The Grapes of Wrath* than on any other book in its history. Editor, president, and sales force knew prerelease that they had a blockbuster. Sales were brisk before the novel hit bookstores on April 14, 1939, growing to a torrent after reviews came in lauding and denouncing the book that, on the one hand, so movingly depicted the Southwest migrants' poverty and, on the other, scraped nerves raw. Across the nation, fictional characters became shorthand for class fissures. *The Grapes of Wrath* was denounced and rebutted—sometimes burned and banned. The East Saint Louis, Illinois, library board ordered three copies burned in front of the courthouse. In Buffalo, New York, the city's librarian refused to purchase it for circulation. Powerful Californians were "wrathy" about the novel, and in conservative newspapers headlines screamed protests: "Native Farmers Deserve Most Pity!" Steinbeck's hometown of Salinas burned a symbolic copy, while the head librarian at the San Jose Public Library—only a dozen miles from where the author was living at the time—sniped that "a line must be drawn somewhere" and that *Grapes* was "unfit for patrons." By August of that year, the Associated Farmers of California, fuming all summer long over Steinbeck's depiction of greedy and vitriolic landowners, sent a congratulatory letter to the Kansas City school board after that body banned the book from the city's public schools. A day after posting that letter, on August 21, 1939, the Kern County Board of Supervisors banned *Grapes* throughout the county—Kern County, where John Steinbeck's Joads first stand on California soil and in glazed wonder look down on the Central Valley.

Indeed, this novel about humble migrants wanting a fresh start on California's fecund acres set off cultural wildfires in a way that is nearly inconceivable today. Articles and tracts set out to disprove everything from John Steinbeck's mathematical acumen (surely the Joads had enough money for several months in California) to the color of the soil in Sallisaw, Oklahoma

1

(not red in *that* county), from the number of tractors in Sequoyah County (a mere forty) to his depiction of California as dominated by large corporate farms. While a great many book reviewers noted the novel's fluidity of language and emotional wallop, others decried its gritty prose. Congressman Lyle Boren from Oklahoma lambasted it on the floor of Congress as a "dirty, lying, filthy manuscript . . . a lie, a black, infernal creation of a twisted, distorted mind." Steinbeck was called a communist. He was harangued by publicity requests. Mail sent to his Los Gatos home horrifed him, from death threats and warnings that his wife would be raped to pleas for money and grim accounts of suffering. He wrote woefully to Tom Collins, the man who had provided factual background: "I am getting pushed around something terrible and don't know what I am going to do." Steinbeck's dream of composing a perfectly crafted novel of social protest—so palpable when he wrote the final scene—turned into a "nightmare" only a few months later. In response, he took himself home to Moody Gulch in the Los Gatos hills and "padlocked himself against the world," admitting to Eleanor Roosevelt, who defended *The Grapes of Wrath* in a June 29th My Day column that "I have been called a liar so constantly that sometimes I wonder whether I may not have dreamed the things I saw and heard in the period of my research." Life seemed unendurable.

Someone else faced this postpublication onslaught with John—Carol Henning Steinbeck, his wife of a nearly a decade. Plucky, loyal, intensely proud of her husband, she tried to protect him from critics. When a *Los Angeles Times* reporter ventured up to their Los Gatos mountain "citadel" to write a feature on John, she chided her husband for shouting at the reporter and then brought out a stuffed gingham dog to show the visitor, "Migrant John." A gift from a destitute family, the pooch was proof, Carol thought, of the migrants' appreciation of John's book. Someone should have stitched a "Migrant Carol" mate: *The Grapes of Wrath* was, in fact, their shared creation. "To CAROL who willed this book" the dedication, in part, reads. Again and again John declared that it was truly "Carol's book," for she had been a part of its composition since gestation began nearly three years earlier; it was she who had nudged him to compose a novel about Southwest migrants. Together John and Carol had produced the manuscript—he writing, she typing and editing and coming up with the title—and together they had awaited publication of *The Grapes of Wrath* like anxious parents. When the masterpiece was buffeted unmercifully during the summer and fall of 1939, the two winced and suffered. He wrote fewer letters, fended off requests for public appearances.

She wrestled with the publicity, answered the letters, defended his prose, and also felt very much left out of the spotlight on John's book, only John's. And when he fled from the firestorm for a sojourn in Los Angeles, Carol became the lonely and besieged wife left at home.

What happens when a dream sours? This had been Steinbeck's theme for years, showing how the visions and hopes of small farmers and paisanos, bindle stiffs and migrants, shrivel in the glare of California's economic and social realities. Now, ironically, he and Carol had stepped into one of his own plots. Although not migrants, like the Joads, nor wanderers, like George and Lennie, John and Carol were similarly marooned and perplexed when the bubble of shared creativity burst. The couple paid a high price for the magisterial *Grapes*. Criticism of content and language and accuracy stung both deeply; requests for speaking engagements and for Steinbeck to solve financial woes of countless migrants distressed both; tensions and pressures of sudden money and unwanted publicity overwhelmed the couple. At this triumphal yet anguished moment, their marriage began to crumble. Step by slow step they became exiles from an Eden of their own creation. John left Carol, first emotionally, then sexually, and then through his writing. They sold their beloved ranch in the Los Gatos, California, foothills, an hour south of San Francisco. And they were divorced in 1943, when he was forty-one, she thirty-seven. The book that was dedicated to Carol, who "willed" it into being, would be both the monument to their marriage and shared creativity and also the cause of their undoing. The great dividing line between marital contentment and despair was its 1939 publication.

With its steady movement away from hierarchical and patriarchal models of home and family and toward a communal and matriarchal model, *The Grapes of Wrath* suggests much that was central to their companionate marriage. From early in their partnership, Carol and John shared a sense of themselves as outsiders and a desire to reenvision themselves apart from received assumptions. Their marriage was not bourgeois, not complacent, not rigidly defined along gender lines, not mainstream. Throughout the 1930s, John composed stories about outsiders like himself and Carol, some with the courage or pluck to envision another reality, others without that flexibility. His 1930s fiction taps into cultural stories of dispossession, loneliness, and entrapment as well as the counternarrative of possibility, articulated for generations by dreamers like Tom Joad or *Of Mice and Men*'s Lennie Small: "Tell me about the rabbits, George." Dreamers yearn for things real yet illusory: rabbits, a ranch, a little house, an orange. "A particularly American freedom," argues Arnold Weinstein, is the "imperious desire to make reality rather than to undergo it." Casting themselves out of their middle-class backgrounds, Carol and John were makers and dreamers. They were a scrappy and fiercely creative duo.

When John and Carol met in 1928, he was working at a fish hatchery in remote Lake Tahoe, adding flourishes to the novel he had rewritten countless times, *Cup of Gold,* finally published in 1929. "I learnt [my craft] with 8,000,000 words of rejection slips," Steinbeck would recall years later. During their first week together, Carol bucked his flagging confidence in the manuscript, reading it in draft and declaring it good, very good. Then he set her to work typing another manuscript, "To an Unknown God," and her own destiny was clear. In addition to creative synergy, their characters meshed. Both appreciated the offbeat. Both shunned phoniness. Both were unconventional. Even more than John, Carol was "fearless," her sister Idell remarked. She was also witty, down to earth, and practical—and a "handsome" beauty, a tall, healthy brunette with luminous skin and a clear, bold expression. Young John Steinbeck was "erotic, violent, passionate, stimulating." Their interests tallied; their energy sizzled. They brought out the best in each other.

That initial response decanted the spirit of the age, and a jolly good time it was—at least for those who could afford to thumb their noses at bourgeois complacency. In 1928 the stock market had not yet crashed, and the world seemed expansive. Both John and Carol pushed the boundaries of their parents' pieties. Together in San Francisco—Carol lured John from his Sierra Nevada retreat—they danced as joyously on the bones of straitlaced sensibilities as did Scott and Zelda Fitzgerald in New York or Ernest and Hadley Hemingway in Paris. Indeed, they were hardly distinguishable from their better-known counterparts in their determination to respond to a new cultural beat. "I think rebellion man's highest state," Steinbeck wrote a college friend in 1924. "All that we regard most highly in art, literature, government, philosophy, or even those changes which are the result of anatomic evolution had their beginnings in rebellion in an individual." Steinbeck aspired to that state.

He and Carol shook their fists at the complacencies of the world they were born to. In 1921, for example, while visiting a friend in Oakland, a nineteen-year-old John Steinbeck exploded with indignation during a church service he was attending as a guest. The long, earnest, and windy sermon intoned that the soul must be fed. "St. John," as his friend Robert Bennett called him, yelled out to the stunned congregation: "Yes, you all look satisfied here, while outside the world begs for a crust of bread or a chance to earn it. Feed the body and the soul will take care of itself!" Robert Bennett's mother was shocked and chagrined that her son's friend trampled on what most Americans still assumed were universal Protestant values. Carol's devout mother was similarly disappointed in Carol's spiritual lapses and in her daughter's disdain for convention of any kind: "I hate expediency" is Carol's earliest extant poem:

> I hate women who are afraid to love as much as they want to
> Lest their beloveds hurt them or love them less or leave them.
> I hate women who are afraid to hate—for fear of wrinkling their smooth
> beautiful faces—
> I hate children who are polite to people they intuitively dislike and distrust
> Because they have been taught that those are important ones who
> can help them.
> I hate men who are afraid to put themselves on paper for a woman friend
> Fearing that she'll turn traitor and sue them for breach-of-promise
> —or something
> And men who are afraid to love gently and tenderly lest someone
> accuse them of being effeminate—
> Oh yes—beyond all things in this uncalcuable [?] and lovely world
> I certainly do hate expediency!

Below the handwritten manuscript of this poem that is carefully pasted into an early 1930s scrapbook, Carol wrote, in pencil, "First draft 1914." That would make her eight, an enfant terrible, then and later.

Carol's life story cannot be writ small. All her dimensions, physical and mental, were oversize. Her wit made those with similar askew perspectives howl with glee. She had a warm heart and was quick to connect with children and dogs and friends who could chuckle. She made friends easily and just as easily might offend them. One acquaintance said how hard it was to capture Carol because so much of her presence was physical: her energy and wit filled a room. She was the master of the one-liner, not easy to reproduce.

That outspoken candor gave John starch when most needed. And sometimes he needed "ego bolstering," an essential boost for this powerful but sensitive, often shy man who yearned to find words for the pictures floating through his mind. John Steinbeck had a "tremendous physique and had all the macho characteristics . . . yet at the same time he had this great sensitivity," recalled one college friend. While he always was supremely confident of his eventual success as a writer, he was also plagued by self-consciousness and insecurities. In a very real sense, he grew to depend on Carol's vivid presence in the world to propel him into narratives. A year or so into their marriage, John admitted that Carol had become more real to him than he was to himself. She brought him stories, friends, and her own fine-tuned sensibilities, the fodder he needed to write.

Until recently, some of John and Carol's books remained on the shelves of the little cottage on Eleventh Street in Pacific Grove, where the couple lived in the 1930s, where his older sister Beth lived until the mid-1990s. One was Louis Paul's 1937 novel, *Hallelujah, I'm a Bum!* which was stamped on the inside cover, like so many others in their library, "This Book belongs to Carol and John Steinbeck," and was inscribed by Paul: "For John Steinbeck and Carol—my models for Resin Scaeterbun and Nina Gumbottle." After returning from World War I, Resin writes and edits a sexually explicit magazine called *Gusto;* at his trial for distributing salacious materials, Nina, an Aubrey Beardsley-like illustrator, is his indefatigable ally—much as Carol was John's:

> I love him with all my heart. Your honor, are we not all people of the world, people who have plumbed to the depths and found nature wanting, wanting, wanting what it must not ask for? Resin Scaeterbun is an artist, a genius, a great poet, whose only crime was to attempt to educate the masses in the just too simply and utterly complete joys of free, beautiful love. He worked and starved and slaved that we all might know the beauties of dynamic intercourse. I helped him in my own just simply too *humble* way, but I would gladly go to prison for him. I was as much responsible for *Gusto* as he—if not intellectually, then morally. If he is to be punished, punish me. I care not what the world thinks . . .

That's a Carol speech. And Resin is an outsized John—pornographer, bootlegger, Lothario, and "bum," a Latin- and poetry-quoting caricature. "Virgin" Nina is drawn with similar insouciance, with her *"outrageous* dreams" (which were Carol's) and bohemian notions: "Don't you think that we have been just too completely enslaved by our parents' ridiculous taboos and inhibitions, Mr. Scatterbing?" asks Nina at their first meeting. But the rebel spunk is John and Carol's, as is the love of wordplay—the silly and repeated mispronunciations of Scaeterbun's name—as is the intellectual curiosity and the sexual joie de vivre. "Hallelujah, we're bums!" might well have been the clarion call of John and Carol's early years together.

Not unlike their great collaboration, *The Grapes of Wrath,* Carol Henning Steinbeck's story has epic dimensions. Just as certainly, hers is a painfully ordinary plot, an oft-told tale of a woman who hooks herself to a man's comet. So thoroughly did Carol embrace their partnership and shared dream of artistic integrity and purpose, that it subsumed her identity. From the first weeks she and John were together, she was intellectually and emotionally bound to him. Like countless women before and since, she threw her own intelligence and considerable energies into her mate's endeavors. As Virginia Woolf observed, women may become "looking glasses possessing the magic and delicious power of reflecting the figure of a man at twice its natural size" and thus have no room of their own, no creative space that is theirs alone. Undoubtedly Carol's considerable creative drive was banked during her years with John. But she insisted that hers was not the part played by Zelda Fitzgerald, a woman embittered by the imbalance between Scott's success and her own muted triumphs: "I am not now, nor was I ever, a Zelda," Carol told Steinbeck biographer Jackson Benson. "I was not a frustrated artist, repressed by her husband. Don't see me that way." While Zelda competed with her famous husband for artistic credibility, Carol zealously supported John's writing, so much so that at least one friend from the 1930s said that Carol certainly loved John deeply but she loved his art with at least equal fervor. Friend after friend as well as her sister all said the same thing: "She really poured herself into that. If it weren't for Carol, John would not be what he was. . . . They were a team working together for a common cause," his art. Her story is, in effect, his. His greatest triumph, hers.

Carol's room was John's prose—a solution to women's subordinate roles that Virginia Woolf, no doubt, would hardly embrace. But Carol did, and did not consider her role secondary. The marriage unit was, in effect, a phalanx, larger than both individually, with art the "keying mechanism" of their marital bond. Steinbeck's theory of group man provides a clear interpretive lens to view their relationship, their artistic sensibilities grounded in a mythic fusion of artist and muse. In June 1933 he wrote: "Now in the unconscious of the man unit there is a keying mechanism. Jung calls it the third person. It is the plug which when inserted into the cap of the phalanx, makes man lose his unit identity in the phalanx. The artist is one in whom the phalanx comes closest to the conscious. Art then is the property of the phalanx, not of the individual. Art is the phalanx knowledge of the nature of matter and of life." Steinbeck intended that his art tap that deep knowledge, an intention apparent in *To a God Unknown*, composed during the first four years he knew Carol. That same urge informs the stories he wrote intermittently from 1931 to 1935, work realistic in surface texture but also plunging into the "stream underneath and the meanings I am interested in." To express the deepest human urges subsumed his identity, his ego. To write about the nature of matter—physics, biology, botany, and history—as well as a holistic sense of life itself was an ideal that took hold of Carol as well. Her role as muse draws on an older sense of that word—the muse as conduit to inspiration, the guide to logos, knowledge, and the one who helps understand and unlock the creative spirit. A muse helps link the artist to the deepest sources of meaning, the unconscious currents that Steinbeck yearned to express. "From the phalanx," writes Steinbeck, unit man "takes a fluid necessary to his life."

Edward F. Ricketts, marine biologist and Steinbeck's closest male friend in the 1930s and 1940s, was also part of Steinbeck's visionary drive and a muse in this expanded sense. So were loyal friends. As Steinbeck admitted, he was a "shameless magpie" who picked up and stitched into his fictive vision fragments of local history, scraps of dialogue, amusing tales, eccentric behaviors. "I spread out over landscape and people like an enormous jelly fish, having neither personality nor boundaries," he wrote in 1934. "That is as I wish it, complete destruction of any thing which can be called a me. The work is necessary since from it springs all the other things." That was Steinbeck's concept of himself in relation to his work—the creation was greater than the creator. That exalted notion of creativity, the power of art to alter and clarify human understanding, swept up those who floated by. The writer was simply the one in whom the ideas came closest to consciousness.

This story is about a delicately constructed team, the essential units John and Carol and the company they kept. To see one is to see both. To see both in shifting circles of friends is to recognize the vital importance of others to John's creativity—as muse, as audience, as participants. The Great Depression was the necessary crucible for this gritty pair, the decade when banding together meant survival. "A man's history," insisted Steinbeck when pressed for biographical details, "should be the history of his people." In 1936, he wrote this to a would-be biographer, essentially a cultural and ecological expression of his phalanx theory: "It seems to me that if you could write the biography of Captain [John Paul] Jones not only as an individual but also as a part of this movement, you would be doing a unique and useful thing. It is constantly strange to me that the ecology of humans is so completely ignored." That is good advice for any biographer—to consider the notion of human ecology, the connective layers of family and friends, histories and places, politics and philosophies, spirituality and religion and psychological depths that make up a life. This book considers the ecology of Carol Henning and John Steinbeck: their shared roots, cultural moment, friends, travels—and art.

The story of a fragile unit coalescing into something magical, something with a shared purpose and destiny, also reveals the thread of its inevitable unraveling, as Steinbeck suggests in *Tortilla Flat,* a novel structured around the Arthurian myth of the Round Table. And yet Carol and John's phalanx, held together by the keystone of art, brought forth one of the most compassionate, urgent, and enduring novels of the twentieth century. *The Grapes of Wrath,* "Carol's book," is the apogee of their tale of bright visions and ragged disappointments and the fulcrum on which their lives tipped.

CHAPTER ONE

Renegades

THEIR CHILDHOODS WERE HAPPY ENOUGH, yet neither Carol Janella
Henning nor John Ernst Steinbeck was a particularly settled child. Both
felt like outsiders. John told his younger sister Mary that he "was never at
home in Salinas," where he was born in 1902. "I was a stranger there from
birth." And Carol, born sixty miles north in San Jose, was the black sheep
in the Henning family's Christian fold. Nellie Henning lavished attention on
Carol, her firstborn, planning excursions to Carmel-by-the-Sea, reading to
her, carefully pasting tiny paper bunnies around toddler photos in a lovingly
assembled scrapbook. But Nellie was also a rigid, exacting, and self-righteous
mother. Carol grew up tilting swords with this woman who expected lockstep
devotion to family and God, expectations met by her younger daughter, Idell,
but not the older. Carol grew up with a lopsided vision of love and fairness
and maternal devotion. Well before age ten, she was known as the naughty
child, whereas tractable Idell was sociable and gracious, maturing into a "God
fearing woman" who was easily "intimidated, faint of heart, and demure."
Those female roles of angel and vixen stamped the two Henning sisters for
life: Idell's path was smooth, Carol's rutted and twisted. Whereas Idell was
like her father, "quiet and more receptive," the kind of child that parents
wanted to coddle, Carol was combative, saucy, and unconventional, more
like her mother, in fact, but also bucking Mrs. Henning's religious beliefs,
Victorian rigor, and conventional expectations. And yet Carol yearned for
the unconditional love that was given readily to Idell. In Carol, Idell quipped,
the lamb and the wolf wrestled for ascendancy. Negotiating that gap between
a vigorous resistance to the Hennings's middle-class values and a deep need
for love, connection, and domestic harmony is the central dynamic of Carol's
life story.

John Steinbeck's psychological inheritance and artistic terrain evolved
from a similar landscape, although he sparred with community, not family. His adolescent fury at the bourgeois pretensions of Salinas growers and

shippers matured into a lifelong disdain for the selfishness, greed, and complacency of the powerful, coupled with a great sensitivity to human despair, often his own. In a 1962 interview after the Nobel Prize ceremony, he clarified that conviction:

> The thing that arouses me to fury more than anything else is the imposition of force by a stronger on a weaker for reasons of self-interest or greed. . . . It's the one unforgivable thing I can think of. . . . And I suppose that's the fury that comes on me when someone is mistreated. There's a waste there somehow, a waste among people because it seems to me people want more than anything else to associate. I think we're such a lonely species and always crying out for companionship of some kind and when we destroy it willfully it gives me great fury.

Marriage to Carol helped him transform that cultural disequilibrium as well as his own inner demons into art that explored uncertainties of edges and borders, the pathos of the marginalized and disinherited, the psychic depths of despair and loneliness, and the passionate dream of meaningful participation with another human.

These two unsettled souls, John and Carol, were raised in equally idyllic slices of the American West, and their families and environments were, in many ways, similar. Second-generation Californians, the Steinbecks and Hennings aspired to turn-of-the-century Progressive ideals; they were high-minded people, mindful of civic obligations. Both families gravitated to enterprising communities located on some of the most productive agricultural land in the state. Salinas was "the richest community per capita, we were told, in the entire world," recalled Steinbeck, writing in the mid-1950s about his hometown. "Certainly we Salinians never questioned it, even when we were broke." First wheat, then sugar beets, and, early in the twentieth century, lettuce made fortunes for Salinas Valley farmers. Visiting Salinas in 1879, Robert Louis Stevenson characterized it as thoroughly Protestant—in contrast to Spanish/Mexican (and Catholic) Monterey—and it so remained during Steinbeck's youth—conservative, insular, and prosperous. An hour north, the Santa Clara Valley was similarly Edenic. A half century before Carol was born, John Muir effused about "bloom time" in the Santa Clara Valley, when the land was "quivering with the songs of meadowlarks, and the hills were so covered with flowers that they seemed to be painted." By the turn of the century, it was touted in brochures as the "Valley of Heart's Delight." San Jose

was "the Garden City," a lush agricultural community that, like Salinas, proclaimed the West's fecundity and inhabitants' energy.

Situated at the southern tip of the San Francisco Bay, San Jose, population twenty-five thousand in 1906 when Carol was born, may have lacked
San Francisco's polish, but it boasted a sunny climate, rich soil, and urban
prosperity. A "little farm town," said one of Carol's high school friends, "where
everybody knew everyone, a nice place to grow up." Since the mid-nineteenth
century, the Santa Clara Valley had been orchard country planted with apricots, plums, prunes, peaches, and pears, mostly from cuttings brought to
California by enterprising migrants—Italians, Spaniards, and Slavs. They
made fortunes on fruit that was shipped first to San Francisco and to the
Sierra Nevada mines, and by the 1870s by railroad to Chicago and New York.
To avoid transporting easily bruised apricots and pears from California to
eastern consumers, drying and canning techniques were developed, and by
1900 prune and apricot orchards covered the valley, which stretched north to
Palo Alto and south to Gilroy, sixty miles of fertile soil that provided a third
of the world's prunes. Carol and her sister, like other San Jose teens, worked
summers in one of the region's many canneries.

Carol's parents settled in San Jose at the end of the nineteenth century,
sending down deep taproots. Wilbur Fisk Henning, born in Stockton, and
Nellie Gould Bowen, a Sierra Nevada girl, moved to San Jose as young adults
and later met at the First Congregational Church of San Jose, where both
were active in youth group activities. "Each one was considered quite a catch,"
noted their daughter Idell. Each was college educated, he the son of a Unitar-
ian minister, she the daughter of a man who owned the profitable Stanford
Mine in Michigan Bluff, where she had been raised. After graduation from
Heald's Business College, Wilbur Henning had spent his early career as a
secretary to a Southern Pacific Railroad executive, traveling throughout the
West, representing the railroad that was bringing prosperity to California,
building a nest egg for a future family. By the time of his marriage, "He really
felt like he'd seen everything he wanted to see and had his fill," reported Idell.
The traveling salesman was ready to settle down.

Young Nellie's devotion to music brought her out of the mountains to San
Jose when she was about sixteen. Her own brilliant parents, both well educated, certainly weren't going to have their only daughter's musical abilities
shrivel in bleak mountain winters. "She wanted to become a better pianist,"
said Idell. "Also, it was one of the more acceptable ways for a young woman
to further her education and to achieve more 'graces.' People pursued such

things for their own entertainment and to entertain others." Nellie and her mother left Michigan Bluff and boarded with friends to be near both the San Jose State Normal School and the King Conservatory of Music where Nellie studied piano and voice from 1899 to 1900, giving recitals, developing her keyboard techniques. In February 1894 she graduated from the Normal school, a three-year program with instruction in language, math, science, as well as drawing, history, and government. About the time that Nellie enrolled, the curriculum was revamped to include "physical exercise and current events as well as new courses in geography and history: observation lessons upon plants, insects, birds, domestic and wild animals, people, rain, wind, sunshine, minerals." Nellie had a far better training in music and liberal arts than many women of her time. A neighbor who enjoyed her company late in life said that she was "smart as hell," always "a fairly good scholar and knew what was going on." Nellie modeled the literate and gracious ideals of the turn of the century.

Wilbur and Nellie married in an evening ceremony at the First Congregational Church when Wilbur was thirty-five and Nellie thirty-two. Eleven months after their April 10, 1905, wedding, on the ides of March, Carol Janella was born, and a month after her birth, on April 18, 1906, at 5:12 A.M., an earthquake rocked San Francisco, sending tremors down the coast to San Jose, Salinas, and beyond. John Steinbeck, age four, would remember being taken to see a crumbling downtown Salinas, "brick buildings, spilled outward." Only a month old, Carol could hardly have remembered anything—except through the oft-told story of her mother's response to the quake. The shaking so startled Nellie that she leapt out of bed, dashed out of the house, and left baby Carol inside. That episode may be symbolic—or it may indeed have left psychic scars. Fear of abandonment would be one of Carol's deepest fears. Hers was, in truth, a shaky beginning.

In many ways her childhood wasn't shaky but ordinary, like John's. In 1908, the year that Idell was born, Wilbur Henning took a position as a real estate agent, joining the firm of Johnson and Temple and eventually becoming vice president of the Nucleus Building and Loan Association (until he was ninety!) and president of the San Jose Realty Board. Throughout his long career, gentle, kind, and honest Wilbur was beloved by many in San Jose. Initially the family lived in downtown San Jose; then, when Carol was four, they moved to 40 Lincoln Avenue in Willow Glen, a snug San Jose community about five miles from downtown. When Carol was nine, entering fourth grade, the Hennings moved back to downtown San Jose, near where

Nellie had lived with her mother before marrying. The family's new home at 235 South Sixteenth Street was in the city's first housing development, where codes dictated that homes had to cost at least twenty-five hundred dollars. Designed for ambitious professionals, the Naglee Park subdivision, built between 1909 and the 1920s, boasted wide-paved streets designed to accommodate the new automobile. In this progressive development, livery stables and wood yards, harkening to a bygone era, were prohibited. The Hennings lived in close proximity to successful and enterprising westerners: Paul Masson, the winemaker, and auto industrial pioneers Clarence Letcher and Arthur Holmes, the latter the builder of the Sunset automobile, whose body was constructed of wood. Although their home was not in the most fashionable section of the tract, the Henning neighborhood was solidly middle class, "quiet, with nothing outlandish and no signs of great wealth," noted a neighbor.

Nellie and Wilbur Henning "fitted into the community," said Idell. "They were very much like John Steinbeck's mother and father," middle-class exemplars, civic minded, church going, active. Growing up in solid, outwardly peaceful families gave both Carol and John much that was good—belief in hard work, a love of books, and freedom to explore. And for both families, two-story clapboard homes signified those exemplary values and their own evident success, very much like John Whiteside's white house in Steinbeck's early novel *The Pastures of Heaven*. In a draft of this story, written in 1931, Steinbeck writes that Whiteside gave up mining in the Sierras to build a home in the Salinas valley, a symbol of his stature: "John Whiteside's house was to his body what his body was to his mind. The identification was exact; the house was John Whiteside, his personality solidified. . . . A mental picture of him was incomplete unless it included his house." The house where John grew up on Salinas's Central Avenue was the stateliest address in town; Olive wanted precisely what John Whiteside wanted, a firm foothold in the community. "To the Progressive point of view," writes Kevin Starr, historian of California, "the entire Far West—California especially—offered a tabula rasa upon which might be projected and achieved a society based upon values of education, taste, beauty, and restraint." Both John and Carol, however, would grow up to resist those values, that notion of the West.

Carol was a precocious child, with what her mother called a "jolly, alert smile." She and Idell attended Willow Glen Elementary and, in fourth grade, rode roller skates to Horace Mann, or "Horse Man" school, as Carol dubbed it—she was a wit early on. At home, both played endless games of cards and read and reread *The Wizard of Oz* and other childhood favorites, going to the library "about twice a week," Idell recalled. "We spent far more time reading than doing our assigned homework. . . . Carol was even more wrapped up in reading that I was." But Carol never quite fit into the family groove. Aunts and uncles thought her too saucy: "That girl needs a surprise," Idell remembers them saying as they shook their heads at family gatherings. "She was cocky and outspoken . . . a perverse thing," added Idell, with a "wild and dippy slant" that her mother corralled, or tried to. As an adolescent, Carol was the "maverick in the group . . . bumptious," said her sister.

Nor could Mr. and Mrs. Steinbeck convince John to take the easy path. He was always "straining at the leash," said his older sister Beth. Apparently Mr. Steinbeck daily asked his nine-year-old if he had been whipped at school. John meandered in Salinas fields, trudged up the surrounding hills—golden, dotted with oaks. Or he rode to the Salinas River on the red pony that his father had given him when he was four. Teenage John snuck away like Cal Trask, "night wandering," which gave him "the first sense of being one's self and of being free," and heading toward Salinas's lively Chinatown—the east side of town where there were "so many saloons . . . that women rarely walked on that side." But John did. Firm-minded Olive Steinbeck tried to rein in restless and sometimes indolent John. As a young woman, she taught school in Palo Colorado Canyon in Big Sur, a wild and remote spot in the late nineteenth century, and she expected each of her four children to meet exacting standards. Mrs. Steinbeck, said daughter Beth, was "a woman who had a code of beliefs and ethics . . . a sense of what you should do and what you shouldn't." Too often, John did what he shouldn't. As the only boy in the family, however, he generally got away with it; his three sisters—Beth, Esther, and Mary (who was his favorite, she as imaginative, funny, and creative as he)—adored him, and he them.

Salinas residents, however, did not. Childhood buddies found him moody, a storyteller who sometimes hoodwinked them into thinking his fictions true. Schoolmates didn't think he mixed too well with the crowd. And their parents thought young John was lazy, the Steinbeck family a bit uppity.

For the restive John and Carol, grandparents cast the heroic shadows that their Progressive Era genteel parents did not. A great bond of Carol and John's marriage was their shared fascination with the "westering" sagas of their grandparents, an inherited wanderlust, and a deep love of the West. The dreams that drove their ancestors from Missouri and Florida and Massachusetts to the California frontier became the stuff of Steinbeck's fiction—most vividly in *East of Eden,* John's saga of his own childhood. Stories of his paternal grandfather, Johann Großsteinbeck, most likely gave texture to *East of Eden's* Adam Trask. (In about 1946, two years before he began the novel, Steinbeck was given his grandparents' diaries and papers.) In 1849, Johann and his brother, Friedrich, as well as his sister and brother-in-law, left Germany for the Holy Land to teach farming to Jewish settlers. Both brothers married sisters of another missionary family, the Dicksons from Massachusetts, and the tribe settled into their work. Their admirable purpose was foiled, however, in January 1858 when Bedouin tribesmen attacked the family compound in Haifa, murdering Friedrich. Retreating to the United States, Johann (now John) and Almira Steinbeck (they simplified the German name) settled first in New England, then in Florida, where the apolitical former missionary eventually deserted the Confederate army that demanded his loyalty. Like Adam Trask—also a deserter—John Adolph found his way back to his Dickson in-laws in New England, managed to have his wife and four sons brought North, and after the war headed west, followed by Almira (and by now five sons). In 1873 the family settled in Hollister, about an hour's ride from Salinas. Steinbeck's father, John Ernst, born in Florida in 1862, grew up in Hollister, where the Steinbeck family, adventures over, owned an orchard and where the indomitable Almira canned fruit into her nineties. Indeed, the iron will and visionary wanderlust in all of Steinbeck's westering males— the grandfather in *The Red Pony,* monomaniacal Joseph Wayne in *To a God Unknown,* Adam Trask in *East of Eden,* as well as the Joads in *The Grapes of Wrath* and the upstanding Whitesides in *The Pastures of Heaven*—have roots in the author's paternal line.

The Henning family often recounted the story of Carol's great uncle and aunt Henning. John Pennell Henning had been a cabinetmaker with his brother Alpha Wood Henning (Carol's great-grandfather, father to George William, her grandfather) in Lexington, Missouri, for ten years when gold fever struck him hard. In 1849 he left for California, returning in 1854 for his family. With a herd of cattle and a bag containing eight thousand dollars of gold coins, John Pennell drove teams west with his redoubtable wife, Mary Catherine Van Meter Henning, and their three young sons, twelve-year-old Irving, ten-year-old Addison, and seven-year-old Abraham. With *Horn's Overland Guide to California* to chart their passage across the plains, the pioneers had little trouble finding water and places to camp during the five-month, two-thousand-mile journey. Fording rivers and dodging giant hailstones in the Black Hills, Mrs. Henning handled her own team with

cool precision, while her young sons drove cattle and watched for maraud-
ing Indian bands. At one point Irving was asked to join in the "fun" of chas-
ing Indian parties, with the possibility of earning a new "buckskin suit." He
declined. The family landed in San Jose, farmed for three years, and then
John Pennell purchased land and a sawmill above Los Gatos (not far from
John and Carol's second Los Gatos home) and eventually laid out the community of Lexington on December 2, 1858—naming his community after his
former Missouri home. He sold that township in 1861 and moved to Eden-
vale, then to a Lompoc temperance colony, then to Cuyucas, and then to
Nevada to mine in the 1880s. Typical of a certain pioneering breed, Carol's
much-admired great uncle and aunt lusted after fresh adventures. At some
point in this history, George William, Carol's grandfather, joined his uncle in
the west.

Nellie Henning's father, Augustus Caesar Bowen, was yet another intrepid
forty-niner. As a child he had been adopted by a kindly, unmarried Ohio
doctor and Latin scholar, Ebenezer Bowen, and his unmarried sister, both of
whom "wanted to raise a bright boy from a large family and make him his
heir." After his adopted family died, Gus, aged nineteen, left Ohio and came
to California via Panama, keeping a diary of his trip (that Carol's mother
treasured all her life). Quick witted, well educated, and enterprising, he went
into the Sierra Nevada in the mid-1850s, purchasing with his inheritance a
mine and a cabin from Leland Stanford in Placer County's Michigan Bluff, a
prosperous center of hydraulic gold mining and the last station on the Wells
Fargo route. For twenty years or so, Augustus Caesar helped blast hillsides
with water to extract ore, until the practice was banned in 1883. Bowen's
Stanford Mine, the first hydraulic operation, extracted a fortune. According
to his granddaughter Idell, Augustus was a "brilliant and successful man. "In
addition to his mining he was interested in a productive home garden. He
used to correspond with the university to get advice about improvements. He
was also a woodcarver and painter, and his oil paintings hung in the Michigan Bluff home as well as in Carol's childhood home. One showed Indians
killing buffalo and another a scene from the Isthmus of Panama. The carved
frames extended the action of the pictures: monkeys in Panama, Indian
arrows on the other. This man had power, money, creativity, grit—what was
not to admire? Carol's grandmother, Jeannie Bogue Bowen, was also intrepid
and well educated, a schoolteacher in Michigan Bluff. Tiny, assertive Jeannie
"lay down the law" in her one-room schoolhouse.

Together Carol and John mimed the scrappy self-determination that their pioneering relatives modeled. One friend of John's later described Carol as "looking like your grandmother might have looked while crossing the plains." It's a dismissive but also apt observation. In Carol there was a bit of Mary Catherine Henning, driving a team west. A bit of Jeannie Bowen, laying down the law. And a bit of Nellie Henning, lover of nature, conservationist. In Carol were deep wells of resilience. "Too much pioneer spunk or New England grit in us to want to lie around helpless," Idell would remind Carol in 1935.

Nellie, proud daughter of a forty-niner, often told her daughters rollicking accounts of her childhood in Michigan Bluff, stories of young Nellie trudging to school through snowdrifts, stories about miners and grizzlies, blizzards and mountain rescues, or her father's brush with Indians in 1870. "The stories went on forever about every phase of life in Michigan Bluff," reported Idell. A favorite yarn recounted Nellie's perilous journey at age three and a half when she tagged along behind her older brothers, who were headed for a swim in a reservoir filled for hydraulic prospecting. Not surprisingly, the two boys had refused to take their baby sister with them—"too far, couldn't be done"—so resolute little Nellie and her dog went searching for her beloved brothers. Seeing wild flowers near a ditch, she and her dog fell into a "washed out place in the field." That summer night, all the miners in Michigan Bluff as well as their wives searched for toddler Nellie, thinking she'd drowned in the reservoir.

Such tales of endurance must have sparked Carol's love of stories—she read voraciously all her life—and strengthened her ties to the western landscape. Much later in life she regularly contributed to "Save the Redwoods" and bought a Lake Tahoe cabin, returning to her grandparents' and her mother's beloved Sierra Nevada.

But if Nellie's pioneer sagas delighted Carol, much else about Mrs. Henning irritated her daughter. Throughout most of Carol's childhood, the mother-daughter bond was stretched and frayed, and the residue of this tension would mark Carol's marriage to John and her life after: "There was always tension around her mother," Carol's stepdaughter, Sharon Brown Bacon, recalled. For both John and Carol, in fact, a dominating maternal presence was a shoal to be navigated cautiously. Forceful and independent mothers leave their mark. Admirable in their values, ethics, energy, generosity, and wide-ranging interests, adamantine Olive Steinbeck and Nellie Henning were too controlling and, for the sensitive and offbeat John and Carol, too rigid. Carol alternately wanted to please and to resist her mother; to imitate

Nellie's accomplishments—cook, gardener, manager—and to reject her Christian faith; to shun maternal comfort and to yearn for it.

Nellie's religious fervor never became Carol's. For years before and after Carol's birth, Nellie was a proud member of the First Congregational Church of San Jose, downtown on San Antonio Street between Second and Third. (In 1952 she was honored for fifty years of service in the church choir.) Religion was Mrs. Henning's mainstay. Unfailingly, she said grace daily at lunch and read the Bible nightly. She played hymns on the piano that sat in the darkened parlor, covered with doilies; "Rock of Ages" was her favorite. Every Sunday, Nellie went to church and insisted that her family accompany her, at least while the girls were young enough to comply. She always sat in the front row of the congregation, unleashing her trained voice and singing with "full vocalization," embarrassing for both daughters. She organized refreshments for after the service, and church socials were a chief source of family entertainment. As teens, however, Carol and her sister would sneak off from church to gawk at boys or smoke cigarettes. And Mr. Henning "finally escaped church to the golf course," added Idell, "and that was not easy to do in our house." When Nellie read her nightly scriptures, Carol—joined by the more compliant young Idell—would mock her: "Begetting of begetting," the girls would sing out. "Girls!" Nellie would respond—and then finally laugh. She was not without a sense of humor.

Mrs. Henning's wanderlust was also a mixed blessing for her daughter. A lover of "mother nature," Nellie seized opportunities newly available to an educated, curious woman in the first two decades of the century. Before her marriage Nellie went on numerous trips with the church group to the Sierras, usually to Yosemite by horse-drawn coach. Nellie took four-month-old Carol on a junket to the Carmel beach; three years later she took her young children and her mother-in-law back there; and when the girls were old enough, Nellie planned yearly summer camping trips, often to Big Basin in the Santa Cruz Mountains "among the semper virens redwood groves." (Thirty years later Nellie reminisced about lying on her Musso Auto Home Camp bed and looking through the tent flaps, "up and up nearly 300 ft— at stately, proud redwoods—then on *and on* into God's star lit *outer space.*" Underlining throughout the letter conveys Nellie's breathless religious fervor.) Or the family camped in Yosemite in their huge, cumbersome tents with wooden supports—"with full head room for standing, room for dressing and an entire bed," recalled Idell. Nellie was undaunted by the primitive conditions at campsites in the first decades of the century. Escape from home was possible because first her parents and then Wilbur's mother, Caroline, lived with the family and could stay and "see after" Wilbur when she went off. Since Wilbur disliked camping and "just wasn't interested" in Nellie's outings, Carol's mother found friends to accompany her on her western adventures when her girls could not go.

Increasingly, Nellie's vistas widened and the girls were left home. The automobile gave women freedom and the chance to see the West that *Sunset* magazine, first printed in 1898, so gloriously promoted. When Carol was about fifteen, plucky Nellie and "a group of San Joseans" motored to Northern California and beyond, a junket over the "picturesque Redwood highway" that was described in the local paper: "The ladies are motoring north in a leisurely fashion, visiting places of interest on the way. They have no fixed destination or time for return, but intend to continue the trip as long as fancy dictates." Such leisurely travel throughout the West was encouraged by *Sunset,* which published lavish descriptions of Yosemite and the California missions, the redwoods and Monterey's Hotel Del Monte—as well as of the far West, Hawaii, and Alaska. In 1923, when Carol was a senior in high school, Nellie and Mrs. George G. Davis, a neighbor, took a three-week car trip to Salt Lake City and Denver, south to Colorado Springs and Manitou Springs, and then back through Denver to head in a zigzag path to Yellowstone National Park, Spokane, Seattle, Victoria, BC, and Portland, an ambitious excursion for two women in that era. Two years after that trek, Nellie, Mrs. Davis, and Idell sailed on the *Matsonia* from San Francisco to Hawaii. The six-week trip was Nellie's graduation present to Idell—and undoubtedly satisfied some of her own wanderlust. The three women stayed at the YMCA women's facility, Hotel Fernhurst in Honolulu, where everyone swam and surfed. Intrepid Nellie stood up on a surfboard at age fifty. Imagine how Carol would have received stories of the remarkable journey, particularly when funds had not been available two years before to send her to college. Nellie and Idell's expedition made Carol even more resentful of her mother's diverted gaze, as well as the cash that flowed to her sister, not to herself.

Carol felt neglected and deprived, emotionally and financially. Nellie could be miserly, keeping little stashes of money hidden around the house, and stinginess would, in time, become one of Carol's most unattractive traits (even as her mother's frugality became one of her best). Because Nellie had inherited money from her father the gold miner, everyone in the family on both sides came to her for funds. "She was the pigeon for all people's problems," said Idell, and as a result she became very thrifty. "Save and make do," she would chirp to her daughters. Her generosity was reserved for family funeral funds (one Christmas she presented John and Carol with money for a burial plot), a quality that did not endear her to relatives. Carol resented her mother's thrift. Again and again she told the story of Nellie funding Idell's trip to Hawaii and not her own college expenses. She told how Idell went to the University of the Pacific, while she, Carol, worked as a secretary in San Francisco. That became a lifelong bruise. Daughters who grow up without mothers nurturing their quest for intellectual and economic independence have a much tougher time. Denied some of the gifts bestowed on her more compliant sister, Carol grew up feeling, to some extent, unloved, unacceptable, the ugly duckling. Behind her mother's back, Carol called her mother "Nellie," obviously with some disdain, and jeered at religion and her mother's devotion. Nellie, in turn, complained frequently about Carol: "I don't know where that girl came from. She's not a part of our family at all." That can't have been pleasant to hear. Carol's deep self-doubt would, in time, shake her to the core, baffling John and others who loved her.

And yet Nellie's "strong personality" was also Carol's. Both women were creative, captivating. They shared a love of the outdoors. Nellie was a "beautiful cook," and canned plums from her trees, put up applesauce, made all the food for parties and church gatherings. Nellie was "very friendly, an extrovert like her daughter Carol." And like Carol after her marriage to John, Nellie could "do anything" and "fix anything" and "grow anything." Wilbur Henning once bought a book called Mr. Fixit for his wife, but scratched out the "Mr." and put "Mrs." on the front. Nellie tackled leaking faucets in the house. She rigged up a watering system for her garden, "with short lengths of hose attached to faucets outside." Gardening ran a close third to music and religion as Nellie's abiding passions. "She knew a great deal about transplanting and grafting and kept a compost pile." Indeed, the only thing that frugal Nellie would spend money for was gardening tools and "nice harvest bulbs." It was always Mrs. Henning who brought bouquets of flowers to parties. In her garden, she always fed birds; they would "flock to her." That green thumb would, in time, become Carol's own.

One clipping in Nellie's scrapbook encapsulates her flinty will: "Grabbing a prowler on the steps of a neighboring home, Mrs. W. F. Henning marched the man—nearly twice her size—through a drenching rain toward the county jail. A passing motorist gave her and her prisoner a lift to the county jail, where she bounced the burly prowler out of the car and turned him over to the jailer. She then reported the case to Sheriff Langford."

Nellie Henning was, in short, "a person you would not overlook." Certainly Carol could not. Her indomitable mother was the single most important figure in Carol's childhood, the outgoing woman with pioneering roots, adventurous spirit, and eyes fixed on Judgment Day. To her daughter Idell, who shared a close relationship with her mother throughout her life, Nellie's best side was always uppermost—the woman who was "sparkling and full of energy," the "salt of the earth type, not a high tea sort." But for Carol, the critical, opinionated, and unflinching side of Nellie was foremost, and Carol responded in kind. Carol spent much of her life grappling with her mother's ferocious shadow—and probably casting John in Nellie's combatant role all too often, criticizing him as her mother had her. Although Carol and her mother were "very much alike" in tastes, talents, and energies, maybe the two were "too close," mused Idell, too much alike for them to swim in sync. They argued "about everything, absolutely everything! They fought all the time. There wasn't a moment's peace. I think Carol was resentful of Nellie's authority. This was before the days when Carol's language became as 'wild' as it finally became." Nellie's earnestness grated on young Carol: Nellie was a staunch Republican, Carol a liberal. Nellie was frugal; in high school, Carol loved the latest fashions that would "shock" others. Nellie liked to cook, whereas Carol "didn't go into the kitchen" during high school.

John married a woman who was, in fact, very much like his own mother, a woman whom he admired and resisted, loved and fled. John balked at Olive's assertive nature and developed a complex, uneasy relationship with her. "John never liked his mother from what he told me," claimed Dean Storey, a college friend. Perhaps John and Olive's relationship is best captured in a series of letters that John wrote home weekly while in Lake Tahoe during the winter of 1926–27. While he wanted his mother to send a weekly allotment of eggs on the train from Salinas to Truckee (in that era, shipped in metal egg cases), which she did and for which he dutifully thanked her, he resented even the occasional gift of wool socks or sweaters, and returned these unwanted presents, which, no doubt, Mrs. Steinbeck had spent some time knitting for her only son. Prickly and independent, he simply did not want his mother to go beyond certain maternal limits. But she was perpetually extending her domain. John felt more comfortable with his sisters, and his younger sister Mary, in particular, was his comrade, she as imaginative and intrepid as he. Together they waded in the Salinas River, plucked radishes before they were ripe, and read the "gauzy beauty" of King Arthur; on one occasion, John memorized a late installment of the 1914 twenty-three-chapter film serial *Million Dollar Mystery* and told hospitalized Mary "everything" she had missed.

That family dynamic—sisters as comrades, mother as commander in chief—would color his fiction. While housewives come off badly in his work, guardians of righteousness, the mother image becomes a complex site of meaning, in part citadel of society's idealism, in part archetypal "'Great Mother,' a force for change in the individual and society," as Lorelei Cederstrom notes of Ma Joad. Mothers guide Steinbeck's fictional males to deeper understanding: fierce, unpredictable Rama in *To a God Unknown* or Liza Hamilton in *East of Eden* or Juana in *The Pearl*. In other books, brothel madams are surrogate mothers who shelter and nurture "girls"—Dora Flood in *Cannery Row* or "Fartin' Jenny" and Faye in *East of Eden*. These vigorous women destabilize essentialist notions of motherhood. Closer to natural processes, Steinbeck's fictional mothers value familial, communal and spiritual bonds, thus modeling an integrative dynamic that is ecological, not hierarchical. In his own life as well, Steinbeck admired or married strong women like Olive, like Carol. And as he did with his sisters, he formed tight bonds with women who became friends, confidants, advisors—and fishing companions.

From his mother John imbibed a love of stories and relished the lilt of speech, books read aloud, a Steinbeck family tradition. However much he resisted Olive's certitudes, he also learned to expect firm opinions and actions from women in his life, and he wanted witty, highly verbal Carol to fill the same role, to read and listen to his prose, to make him laugh, to argue with him and inspire him, to nurture him and connect with his spiritual yearnings. She was the muse, the keystone of his artistic endeavors. Her significance was replicated by many other intelligent and learned women in his life who played temporary, if vital roles—Edith Mirrielees, his creative writing teacher at Stanford, to whom he sent his stories years after he left the university; Katherine Beswick, a Stanford girlfriend, poet, and career woman, to whom he wrote deeply confessional letters well into the early 1930s; his literary agents, all women: Elizabeth Otis, Mavis McIntosh, Annie Laurie Williams, each of whom became an intimate confidant at one point in his life; and throughout his life, his sisters, Esther, "the steady one," Beth, the "outgoing" sister who loved having people around her, and Mary, to whom he wrote frequent letters, urging this more reclusive sister throughout the

1940s to complete a play she had begun about Salinas women. With Mary he had an especially strong bond, almost mystical, since both believed they had inherited Olive's sixth sense, and both were restless, imaginative, "content within themselves." Much later in life he described the moral imperative of the Steinbeck sibling bond:

> We were four and we remained four. No one ever understood us because we seemed so remote and cool toward each other, but my god, how we rallied when there was need. No one very understood that either. Because we were not lovey dovey it always surprised people that we were so close. And we were strong. Damn it, we were strong. Dad once said, and I used it in a book, that he had little to leave us but good and clean blood. And he did and we have it. . . . We have never had the almost universal tragedies of dishonesty, or cowardice, of meanness, of drunkenness or vice or cruelty and we have never brought shame to our parents.

Firm-minded and imaginative women march through Steinbeck's fiction as they marched through his working life—protecting, nurturing, guiding, knowing—and creating as did John. Like Carol, they played essential roles in the phalanx of John's art. He valued their wisdom and heeded their counsel.

Indeed, his first extant poem is about the power of women's language to shape opinion. One can imagine impish John lurking behind a doorway, listening to his mother's bridge parties, to women's speech. When he was eight or nine years old, he made a gift of his poem to Olive, writing a card to her: "Mother: This is called, The Salinas Saga":

I.
Mrs. Abbott, Mrs. Striening,
Mrs. Murphy, Mrs. Graves,
Give my life a deeper meaning;
Raise my head above the waves.

II.
"Are you positive they're married?"—
"No, I said I lead a trump—"
—"Couldn't walk home. She was carried—"
—"Had to use a stomach-pump."

III.
Mrs. Hebert, Mrs. Theile,
Mrs. Krough and Mrs. Hughes.

"Yes, she had the baby while he,
So they say, was selling booze."

IV.
Mrs. Hargis, Mrs. Porter,
Mrs. Lacey, Mrs. Day,
"If she wore her dresses shorter—"
Mother's girl friends at their play.

Steinbeck appreciated the "play" of female company. He found women's voices compelling and yet too often silenced, like Curley's wife in *Of Mice and Men*, by the social norms that constrained or silenced them. Carol's unedited quips delighted him.

Like his mother, John's father set the moral bar high. Unlike Olive, however, Mr. Steinbeck was "a pessimist at times," said his daughter Beth, "moody, gloomy sensitive—suffering for others in trouble—sometimes stern." And a disappointed man. When the Sperry Flour Mill in Salinas closed in 1911, Mr. Steinbeck felt washed up, an old man at forty-eight. He rallied to open a feed and grain store in downtown Salinas—an enterprise that brought him closer to his own life's dream, "a good farm and a sure crop every year." But the store failed, and he struggled for years to regain a financial foothold and a respectable job. Only in 1920 would John write home from Stanford that his family's rocky times seemed finally to have ended with Mr. Steinbeck's employment at Spreckels Sugar. But Steinbeck grew up knowing that his father was a profoundly disappointed man who "had never done anything he wanted to do," as Mr. Steinbeck told his son; "worst of all," said John, "he hadn't done the work he wanted to do." John's admittedly "selfish," even monomaniacal, commitment to his art was his response to his father's capitulation. When Carol and John were living in Pacific Grove in the early 1930s, for example, Mr. Steinbeck would sneak meat to the impoverished couple, fully aware that Olive would not have approved. Neither he nor Mr. Henning, in fact, was born with the combativeness to resist their wives' firm ways. They were ethical and quietly efficient men who often preferred the company of other men—Mr. Steinbeck in his Masonic Lodge and Mr. Henning at the office or on the putting green at San Jose Country Club or fishing.

And while John was only briefly a Mason—undoubtedly at his father's urging—and eschewed memberships in general, he found in nonhierarchical male camaraderie an ecological ideal. In *Of Mice and Men* as well as the three Monterey novels—*Tortilla Flat, Cannery Row,* and *Sweet*

Thursday—"Steinbeck's ecological community liberates male relationships from the market place and from conventional heterosexual relationships, which encourage competitive jealousy," Leland S. Person notes. Saddened by his father's failures and by his silences in the family home, Steinbeck envisions solace in male companionship. Male friendship, not marriage, was Steinbeck's great and recurring theme.

Quiet, forgiving, and introspective, Mr. Henning and Mr. Steinbeck were far less vivid personalities than their wives, and each was overwhelmed by his more forceful mate—so much so that Idell Budd said of her father that "He didn't have a personality." Wilbur Henning had to hide his whiskey behind their house or in his closet because Nellie did not allow him to drink. (Consider Steinbeck's short story "The Harness," where trussed Peter Randall, whose wife "didn't seem to boss me, but she always made me do things," must squirrel away his bottle of whiskey in the barn. Steinbeck's fictional marriages mirror the dynamic that he and Carol grew up with.) Wilbur was a "tolerant," a "sweet gentlemanly man" who "always wore a dark suit and bow tie. A very proper man." His daughters called him "Wilbur," undoubtedly with true affection. One of Carol's friends remembers him as "a doll," a man who went fishing all the time. He would take the girls to nearby New Almaden and the Almaden River, where they would picnic and where he could sit all day long, showing the girls how to fish as well. Carol adored her father and was proud of him, the father who sent her postcards when she was young, comparing her to a fair rose. "What she did, she did to please him," said Carol's stepdaughter

But Wilbur could hardly have felt that life rewarded him richly. He put his heart into a single creative venture, focusing his "out reaching" mind on the creation of a deepwater port in San Jose at Alviso—an idea that had floated around San Jose since the late nineteenth century, when lumber and hay schooners came down San Francisco Bay with cargo. Wilbur seized on the notion in the 1920s; he had relatives in Stockton and knew how profitable shipping was to that town. Somewhat like Adam Trask's lettuce venture in *East of Eden*, Wilbur's plan was brilliant but ill-timed and costly. He proposed to dredge the Alviso mudflats so that San Jose's fruit could be shipped to San Francisco and then around the world, saving railroad fees. To that end, the San Jose Deep Water Port Association was formed in 1929, and it remained active from its inception until the start of World War II. Although Wilbur had the backing of the city council and the county supervisors from the start, the chamber of commerce scoffed. For years the persistent "Skipper," as friends called him, made speeches on the plan's behalf, and his vision was amply covered in the local newspapers. The US Congress even appropriated $810,000 for the project, while the rest, $990,000, was to be raised by a bond issue. In 1939, however, the plan went down in defeat, a "betrayal," said Wilbur, by "selfish interests." Local papers reported that "its defeat can in part be attributed to powerful interests, including a major canning corporation which owned a port in Encinal, and a powerful railroad." In addition, the threat of possible labor unrest was noted, linking the project with the San Francisco dockworkers' strikes of the 1930s. Some feared a reprise of the protests staged by Harry Bridges's waterfront unions: "conservative San Jose easily responded to the argument that a port would be a costly adventure, if shut down for long periods in labor disputes." The Skipper was a visionary, dogged in his beliefs, quixotic and stubborn—and deeply disappointed at his failure to bring his dream to fruition.

Nor could Wilbur Henning be considered a successful businessman—at least as the world measures success. Had he been a more ruthless real estate agent, he could have made thousands on land deals in San Jose. But as one childhood friend of Carol's put it, he was "too nice a person in the business world." He lacked the "push to make himself rich," said his daughter Idell, and was "the only honest real estate broker I knew." Mr. Henning remained a gentleman, honest and kind and well meaning well into his eighties, where he could still be found working occasionally as vice president of the Nucleus Building and Loan Association at 66 West Santa Clara Street, "putting in 8 of the 40 hours he works each week at his desk," reported the local paper. While Nellie inherited her own money, Mr. Henning made money for other people. "He could have made a fortune," insisted Idell, but he was incurably honest and "wanted to sell orchards to the right people—he liked country property." Furthermore, Mr. Henning apparently made a bad business decision involving Nellie's family money from the Stanford mines. Nellie never forgave him, and the family was never permitted to forget it.

Like John Steinbeck Sr., Wilbur Henning felt no deep satisfaction with his life's choices or achievements. With an astonishing degree of empathy, he told John after his 1941 separation from Carol that he, Wilbur, had stayed in an unhappy marriage. If he'd had the money, Wilbur sighed, he would have walked out when Carol was a child. Sad fathers leave scars. Families tipped to one side leave irregular imprints, and some of the paternal disappointment of Steinbeck's father is limned in Steinbeck's fiction, full of yearning men, punctuated with absent or beleaguered fathers—the stern Carl Tifflin in *The Red*

Pony, supplanted by Billy Buck in Jody's eyes; the elder Tom Joad—displaced by Ma in *The Grapes of Wrath;* the dishonest Cyrus Trask and the ineffective Adam Trask in *East of Eden;* disappointed Ethan Allen Hawley in *The Winter of Our Discontent.* In *To a God Unknown,* Joseph Wayne abandons his son, and Joe Saul of *Burning Bright* resists fatherhood. Even admirable Sam Hamilton in *East of Eden* is troubled by his role as father. Fatherhood is an uneasy state in Steinbeck's fiction. Fathers rarely speak with an authoritative, reliable voice. Steinbeck sides with those who puncture and subvert paternalistic rhetoric: the outsiders and misfits, the impoverished and the scorned.

Perhaps some of Carol's unshakable loyalty to John's writing was her way of healing a similar familial imbalance, her own psychic discomfort. Her husband would—must—realize his dream as her own father had not. She would provide the healing power as her mother had not.

As he was composing *The Winter of Our Discontent* in 1960, giving a great deal of thought to the raising of children and the ethical responsibilities of parenting, John wrote this passage on adolescence, lines from a chapter cut from the published novel:

> Puberty is such a shocking experience that we seem to build a wall of forgetfulness against it . . . [a] cold and lonely time. . . . Can't it be argued at last that if the first monocellular blob of life had found continuing security, no other form of life would have evolved? For we are the versatile and complicated products, not of love and of security but of pain and danger and fear. It was not comfort that made us, but unease and endless insecurity. And it is in that time of change when the body receives the order to survive and to procreate, that the impulses cease to be the tropisms of babies and become confused and painful feeling and sometimes thought.

This is a compelling response to Carol and John's turbulent adolescent lives, his seared by his father's job losses, Carol's by her mother's rigidity. Without fierce agonies, neither would have become, in John's eyes, sentient beings. A month before his marriage, he wrote to college friend A. Grove Day that Carol's mind was "as sharp and penetrating as your own" and added two weeks later: "I'd like you to know Carol. She doesn't write or dance or play the piano and she has very little of any soul at all. But horses like her and dogs and little boys and bootblacks and laborers. But people with souls don't like her very much." Soulful people were Nellie's people. Carol was John's sort, a woman with empathy and grit.

Carol stumbled through high school, the years when the soulful shine and the less polished suffer. Carol and Idell attended San Jose High School on Seventh and San Fernando, built in 1908. San Jose's only downtown high school was about ten blocks from their home, and Carol and Idell would bike to high school or else Mr. Henning would drive them in the morning and pick them up for lunch—since he often went home at noon. "Nellie was always 'potting about the garden,'" recalled Idell, and "lunch was never ready. We had to go dig up something to eat ourselves. It was pretty miserable." Pretty miserable might describe the whole of Carol's high school experience, and missed lunches at home were the least of it. She was not a particularly engaged student—"she settled for average grades in high school. There was no particular pressure or status connected with getting good grades," recalled Idell. A friend, Harriet Eels, said that Carol did not much like school and was only "a pretty good student," perhaps because she was bored at San Jose High. Bored or rebellious or both. She kept separate from the usual round of social activities, refusing to join clubs (the yearbook lists her in none) or enroll in the school's active sports program or attend social events. She had few friends and no dates and skipped the weekly noon dances, saying "she didn't like boys." With her loud voice, prickly ways, and flashy, often shocking clothes, Carol was a little too precocious, too sharp for her contemporaries. "She was all show off," said Harriet, who could hardly comprehend what all that bluster masked.

Carol pushed boundaries of high school propriety whenever she could, making enemies of those holding the strings. She was the type who would always be late to school, putting on mascara in the car on the way to morning classes. More troublesome to authorities, she swore—vividly and often. She talked back to teachers, even to the principal, who once told her not to talk again in the library; for her flippant response she nearly got herself kicked out of school. "The principal, named Major, called 'Maj,' was a figure whom all students loved to poke fun at," recalled Harriet. "He'd say, 'Those in the back pass out first.' He meant leave, but we'd all laugh." Probably Carol laughed the loudest and longest. Harriet also remembered being warned by the gym teacher, Cecilia O'Neill, that "If you don't stop going with Carol Henning, I'll tell your mother." Carol was the bad girl, like Cal Trask. When Harriet worked for the secretary of the high school, office workers were "really catty about her. . . . They called Nellie and told her different things Carol did in school." Harriet didn't remember any of them defending Carol. Clearly much of Carol's behavior reflects the actions of an unhappy young woman, someone craving attention. She didn't confide her unhappiness to her close friend, however, but rather complained often about her mother, and how she was misunderstood.

Carol the outsider spent hours in her room reading. She reread the Oz stories of her childhood, picked up one of her favorite writers, Willa Cather. When she made a friend, she would as quickly lose her through some small meanness—a quality there from birth according to her sister. One boy who went to high school with her remembers her as a "wild Indian" or 'a young colt" who was outspoken, an outsider, "ornery, nasty and very independent." But Harriet remembered her with great affection. They went through high school as special friends, perhaps Carol's only one, the two sharing a love of clothes.

Like many others throughout Carol's life, Harriet cherished what was best in Carol—her buoyant spirit and intelligence and full-sail approach to life. As a leader to one of a more compliant nature, Carol was a life force. Since Harriet had no father and a prissy mother, she "needed cheering up all the time," and Carol was very good as a nurturer. "Carol was a typical example of the Charleston gay '20s," declared Harriet. "She had the courage, as an individual, to start new styles. She didn't date much as the 'sheep men' of high-school found her too different." Not that Carol "didn't like [boys] but she never talked about them." Harriet admired Carol intensely. We had "a lot of jokes together . . . little codes. She loved intensely . . . was sincere, devoted, loyal. . . . I can't rave enough over her sincerity and courage." They went to films together—*Birth of a Nation* for one—and read naughty books together and took the San Jose trolley—Carol dubbed it the "Tooterville Trolley" after a popular comic strip—to Los Gatos or Alum Rock Park for picnics.

One summer, Carol wrote Harriet one of the only extant letters from her youth, a missive that suggests Carol's restlessness, spunk, reading tastes, and love of words. The greeting reads: Professor Reedem N. Weepe

> Tutoring to kill time—have taught little Kathryn next door the rudiments of profanity—her 'hell' is very realistic but her 'goddames' lack the force of her teacher's . . .
>
> Well my beloved Pader Pants—haven't any news so will fill up space with my usual line of bull and bluntness.
>
> Am reading Black Oxen and Children of Shame—Just finished The Breaking Point. All good. By the way you still have one of my library cards, old thing.
>
> Went to town and gave the [] the treat of a view of me. Went all alone to 'The Spoilers." Went for the first show. Took my lunch and made a day of it . . .

Idell said she saw you at Coffee Dan's necking . . . Sat nite. She said you were coming thru the Rye at a pace equal to Ogden's.

Wish to lodge a complaint about short letters. If you don't write more than that I'm going to blow myself up and come back to haunt you like Marg's friend—

Well frisky little rabbit, a week from to-day we'll be . . .

Last evening played cards for a couple of hours with some friends and Idell and Mama. Got up early this A.M. and went down town—saw my cannery friends by the millions yesterday P.M. when I went down. They all spoke real correct—So charitable of em.

Clearly, lonely Carol felt out of everyone's orbit, even her closest friend's. Harriet spent summers in Los Gatos, and only occasionally came to town, so Carol wrote her letters: "Why didn't you phone me Tues? I'm gonna tell the Royal N.W. MP on you—oh hell I feel asinine—sound it too—huh?—well be charitable to me, I'm only a poor half-wit. Seeyasoon—Cheezir Thekops." The words are both playful and plaintive—at the time, Idell and her best friend Margie had taken off for a weekend away, and Carol sulked in her room.

In her senior year, things got a little better. Not only was Harriet a good friend, but Idell and Margie finally included Carol in their activities, allowing her to "tag along." Idell came to realize, even then, that Carol "probably hurt like hell" much of her adolescence.

On June 26, 1924, Carol graduated from San Jose High School. The class motto was "Honor before Honors," a virtuous sentiment for the majority, no doubt. In the yearbook, Carol was dubbed "Husky" and the motto beneath her senior photo was "Ambition." Hers was the ambition to carve a remarkable stance and she wasted no time preparing herself to greet the world. After graduation, she went to what Harriet called the "new and refined secretarial school," on Market Street in downtown San Jose. Harriet went there too, as did a daughter from the well-regarded Hart family. (The same family whose son, Brooke, was kidnapped and killed in 1933. When the two culprits were caught, they were lynched in St. James Park, San Jose's last lynching and the source for Steinbeck's short story "The Vigilante.") Mrs. Henning paid that bill and, when Carol graduated, took her picture and noted beneath: "Carol our snappy business girl."

That girl tested her mettle in San Francisco—undoubtedly wishing to put some distance between herself and her less than satisfying youth. San Francisco was the "Paris of the Pacific," a city of about five hundred thousand residents where there were more bars per capita than in any other American city, for Prohibition in 1920 had been met with hostility. Harriet was in the City as well (it was always "the City" to Northern Californians)—often the two went to movies or about the town. Carol easily found a job in the Publicity Department at Schilling Spice, a company known for selling pure spices and flavors (some of them with a high alcohol content that was wildly popular during Prohibition). For two years, competent Carol was the personal secretary to the owner of the company, August Schilling. Schilling was the first to give his employees a lunch hour, and he posted a sign in the workplace: "A time for work; A time to rest; A time to eat your meal with zest. This office is closed between 12:00 Noon and 1 PM."

Carol seems to have taken the rest and zest to heart, for she spent the summer of 1927 in Yosemite Valley, one of the most popular tourist destinations in California and a national park since 1890. Familiar with the valley after numerous camping trips with Nellie, she, Idell, and Margie planned a getaway. Margie and Carol picked Idell up at College of Pacific in Stockton and in a few hours they found themselves at housekeeping cabins in Yosemite Valley's commodious Camp Curry with its four hundred tents and dozens of housekeeping cabins, where they were charged seven dollars a month. The cabins came with pots and pans and a stone fireplace for cooking. It was a glorious two and a half months for Carol. Each girl had a boyfriend who worked in the valley—Carol's was Billy Goodman, MC for the George Burns and Gracie Allen show. During the day, none of them worked at all, but swam in the Camp Curry pool, hiked, and did everything for free. (In the 1920s, Camp Curry had a bowling alley, a pool hall, a film-developing studio, a movie theater, and a soda fountain.) In the evenings, after the popular Firefall from Yosemite Falls, dances were held in the Pavilion and the three young women "danced every single night I think," Idell recalled. "We were so popular that our dance cards for 12 dances were filled before the music started. It was Carol's first fling at popularity." The Henning parents were forgotten: "Our parents were very lenient—and trusted us—or they wanted to get rid of us or whatever." At age twenty-one, Carol Henning was coming into her own.

After that summer, Idell joined Carol in San Francisco and the good times continued. Carol bought the latest clothing—the career girl loved new clothes. She and Idell went to films, read, trolled Golden Gate Park and the de Young Museum on weekends, and on special occasions went to Nob Hill for drinks at the Mark Hopkins Peacock Court, where they danced to Tommy

Dorsey and Benny Goodman. Idell recalled: "Once in a while we'd go to Sausalito, but it was a very long drive. There wasn't any Golden Gate Bridge yet, so it was a long drive down around the South Bay and then up through the East Bay and over." Carol saved her salary and bought a Buick roadster. "The three of us, Margie, Carol, and I fit perfectly in its front seat! What fun we had. It opened a whole new world to us—being able to go anywhere at anytime. Margie and I were still dominant over Carol at this point. We'd say, 'I'm driving!' and make her sit in the back seat! I remember Carol complaining bitterly to Nellie, 'They won't even let me drive my own car!'" This must have been only a slight irritant, however, since Carol had her independence in San Francisco. And she had her sister, new friends, and popularity with men.

This is the Carol that John Steinbeck would soon meet, an increasingly self-confident career girl with abundant good cheer.

After writing *The Grapes of Wrath*, depressed and weary, John wrote to college friend Webster "Toby" Street about another Stanford friend he'd recently run into. She told John that in college "she had been very much afraid of [him] because—she said, 'I was afraid if I stopped listening to you for a moment, you'd flare into rage and knock me down.'" As several other Stanford classmates noted, there was in young John a barely suppressed anger and intensity that daunted classmates. Not Carol, who met him three years after he had left Stanford. With a year of San Francisco polish on her, snappy Carol was poised to never stop listening to the man whose words shone and whose wit danced with her own.

CHAPTER TWO

Make It New
Lake Tahoe, San Francisco, and Eagle Rock

YOUNG CAROL HENNING AND JOHN STEINBECK struck iconic poses in post–World War I California. In San Francisco, Carol reinvented herself, undergoing a metamorphosis from gawky high school wallflower to career girl. Secretarial school was the path of a 1920s "New Woman," a modern option that led to a socially useful career in business. Meaningful work helped women achieve economic freedom—and with that came intellectual and sexual freedom. New Women were ambitious, sassy, and sexually liberated. That was Carol, who opted for a well-paid job, urban excitement, and an apartment shared first with her friend Harriet, then with her sister. By nature a hell-raiser, Carol was, in fact, a poster child for the decade: she smoked freely, swore energetically, and set her own rules. She bought a car. Like John, she could toss down her liquor, and she must have endorsed one of his favorite sentiments at the time, "Heaven is a place where you're always drinking your thirteenth glass of cognac."

John was equally determined to "make it new," with experiments in clean sentences and bold visions—reacting to T. S. Eliot's *The Waste Land,* as Louis Owens notes, with his own mythic constructs, parched landscapes, and ecological sensibilities. "The only advantage I can see about writing at all is to try to overturn precedent," he wrote to a college friend in 1931. "All of my work has been built on plans more or less unused. It is the only way I can take any pleasure in the work." No less than was true for Hemingway, honing sentences in Paris cafés, work was his antidote to the profligate spending and easy living of the "roaring" decade. During Steinbeck's 1925 stint in New York City, there was no roar for him in a city that seemed "cold and heartless"; he scratched by as a laborer and cub journalist, succeeding at neither, and dated a dancer who wanted a wealthier man. When work and love fizzled—the city having "beaten the pants off me"—he returned to California and retreated to the Sierra Nevada, where he lived in Spartan simplicity and wrote and rewrote his first novel, *Cup of Gold*. He was doing precisely what he wanted, wrestling with sentences and the Grail myth in the wilderness.

By the time Carol appeared on the scene, John had spent nearly two years as caretaker at the Brigham family estate on the south shore of Lake Tahoe. (Dr. Brigham had been a prominent San Francisco surgeon, whose widow hired Steinbeck in 1926.) The lake was one of the loveliest, most pristine of the accessible spots in the high Sierra, popular in the summer months with tourists and with those who could afford estates on the shore or cabins in the hills—and in the winter months it was home to a couple of hundred stalwart souls. In *Roughing It*, Mark Twain describes his first view of the lake, "a noble sheet of blue water lifted six thousand three hundred feet above the level of the sea, and walled in by a rim of snow-clad mountain peaks that towered aloft full three thousand feet higher still! . . . As it lay there with the shadows of the mountains brilliantly photographed upon its still surface I thought it must surely be the fairest picture the whole earth affords." Some sixty years later, Steinbeck was similarly dazzled, especially after spending most of 1925 grubbing for jobs in New York City: "You cannot imagine the coloring of the lake and the hills at this time of year," he gushed to his parents as soon as he was installed there in the summer of 1926. "If it were not 'nature' it would be frightfully bad taste." Winter hardly dampened that exuberance, even when winds tore about his tiny cabin near the Brighams' home, and snow piled relentlessly outside his door. Drifts up to his waist made it a tough trek to the post office when the mail boat, the *Nevada*, arrived in nearby Camp Richardson on Tuesdays and Saturdays, the social oases of his week. For relaxation and sustenance he fished for trout, trapped, and hunted rabbit, mallard ducks, goose, quail: "I knocked over two quail for supper," writes hunter/gatherer Steinbeck, who later in life would come to resist hunting expeditions of any kind. Enjoying his pioneer life, he cooked a "bread pudding of my own invention," and created a recipe for "the heavenliest sweet buns. I guess I invented them. You take equal parts of rolled oats, white flour, farina or finely cracked wheat and corn meal. I use four tablespoons of dried milk, it makes them very rich, add baking powder, sugar, lots of it, and a number of raisins, put in a hot, greased pan and sprinkle with cinnamon. Then let them become quite crisply done on a slow fire. They are fine . . . do not add shortening." John was proudly self-sufficient in the mountains, as he reported to his parents in weekly Sunday letters: "I found a piece of wool felt about three quarters of an inch thick in the basement yesterday and made a new kind of muffler. It comes clear up around my ears and then buttons down over my chest as far as my stomach. I am becoming expert with a needle. I even made quite good button holes." This inventive, burly, physically fit man of pioneering sensibilities would be the man Carol fell in love with.

Or perhaps she fell for the inner man, the maker of sentences and juggler of words. Through two years of blizzards and wet springs, he had hunkered down in his mountain lair and written and rewritten *Cup of Gold* (1929), which would become his first published novel. He told some friends he started over six times, others that it went through nine revisions. Although he had not been totally alone during his Sierra sojourn, he had been solidly focused on writing. His dogs were diversions: Omar, an Airedale, was with him, and for a while he had two dogs, the second, Jerry, enjoying "glorious fights" with Omar. A few friends scheduled visits—but the one who cut through midwinter isolation the longest, Stanford classmate Carl Wilhelmson, also sat in the cabin and wrote daily on a novel, the two writing men sometimes clawing at each other's nerves. John's father came up for a week, and ended up scrubbing the cabin. Occasionally Steinbeck dropped in at nearby Fallen Leaf Lodge, open during the winters, where he was served up hearty meals and companionship with Stanford cronies, who had cabins lining Fallen Leaf Lake. The mail boat brought newspapers for the Brighams—both the *San Francisco Examiner* and *Chronicle,* although he barely glanced at news, preferring headlines and comics. But the outside world intruded very little, in fact. For most of his Tahoe sojourn, he crafted sentences that, he wrote his parents with conviction, "will grow increasingly good as I go on." When he wrote, he sometimes listened to Dvořák's *New World Symphony,* fitting strains for what was about to break into his Tahoe retreat and self-imposed isolation, someone to hear his sentences when read aloud.

In late June 1928, the riotous summer beauty drew Carol and Idell Henning to McKinney's, a Tahoe retreat since 1863, advertised in the 1920s as "an old-fashioned mountain inn, but not a dressy place." Twenty-two-year-old Carol was recovering from the mumps, and her doting employer, old Adolph Schilling of Schilling Spice, was worried about his young assistant's health: "You need to get away and have a good rest, young lady. Here's some money. Take a trip." Mr. Schilling rewarded his talented assistant with a three-week vacation for a job well done. When he found out that Carol and her younger sister planned to visit Lake Tahoe, he gave each an additional twenty dollars for hiking boots. Off they went, planning to stop first thing to see one of Idell's boyfriends, Lloyd Shebley, at the Tahoe Fish Hatchery. Although

Idell and Carol weren't sure they could duplicate the rollicking good times of their previous summer in Yosemite, they were both determined to wedge as much fun as possible into their three weeks, and Shebley was a cornerstone of their plans. That summer, John Steinbeck was Shebley's roommate. He had resigned his caretaker position with the Brigham family and taken a job with the Tahoe Hatchery, in part to avoid "another summer of children. They are nice children but they take up too much time and they get on my nerves"—a comment that foretells his need to keep babies in the background of his writing life. Since early June he had been working as a temporary assistant with Shebley at a salary of $115 a month. John's job was to feed the fish eight times a day, clean troughs, maintain hatchery grounds, and guide tourists through the hatchery, "pleasant and highly interesting work," he recalled years later in *America and Americans* (1966).

The two sisters went straightaway to the hatchery near Tahoe City. Who should greet them but tour guide John, alone that day feeding fish. He told the visitors that he was a writer, and Idell piped up, "Oh, what have you published?" That query started the two of them on the wrong foot. But Carol was intrigued. She must have chuckled at the sign that hung above John's desk, "Piscatorial Obstetrician." When Shebley returned later that afternoon, John's eyes were shining with excitement, eager for the evening's dinner with the two young women. John and Lloyd barely made it to their first date, however; on the way to McKinney's, Lloyd's old Dodge had three flat tires. The flustered pair didn't arrive to pick up Carol and Idell until 9:00, and both young women were sure they'd been stood up. But the evening was salvaged when the foursome went to dinner and then dancing at lakeside resorts, many with a clubhouse or dance pavilion over the water.

That night of dancing sealed it. John and Carol fell in love immediately, "*instantly.*" Idell knew her sister had met a man who appreciated her earthiness, honesty, and sharp sensibilities: "John fell upon Carol like a bear coming out of hibernation would fall on a fresh beef steak!" said Idell. "He was mad about her. He called her Miss Wonderful. The two of them were inseparable and very 'lovey-dovey.'" Carol had never been a "player," or a flirtatious woman, but "then she met John and wham." The sexual freedom demanded by the New Woman brushed aside barriers to "petting" or sex. (In Louis Paul's *Hallelujah, I'm a Bum,* when self-employed Nina Gumbottle, modeled on Carol, first meets Resin, modeled on John, she says: "It is time that we ceased to think of the sex mechanisms in bated breath; to most thoroughly explore the things that we like within us. . . . If we could but convince humanity of the kinship of sex with poetry.") John became so lovesick and satiated that he could barely get out of bed, and his fish feeding became more and more irregular. Apparently, he had prepared for a willing woman's appearance at the hatchery by making condoms out of fish skins—one in a long line of quirky inventions during his life—and if Carol tolerated that, she was certainly his match. His height and bulk, toned by winters of chopping wood and carving out winter ice for the Brighams, must have enticed her, his intensity tallying with her own. "In general, his expression was serious and dignified," said his college roommate, "but when he laughed, as he often did, one suddenly noticed how blue his eyes were and what an intense sparkle they had. They seemed to dance with merriment and delight when something pleased him." Carol pleased him. That first week together, they were inseparable. John set up a warning signal for his roommate, Shebley: when the hall light was on, stay away.

Carol was handsome, forthright, lively. She was also very, very funny and irreverent, a wicked woman with a bon mot—perhaps not quite Hemingway's version of the New Woman, Brett Ashley, but close enough for John. Her voice was husky, and with gestures and wry asides she could amuse a roomful of people. For a man who would later admit that the loneliness of his Sierra Nevada sojourn "thickened" his reactions, Carol must have seemed manna to both his heart and his mind: "As the time went on" at Tahoe, he wrote some thirty years later in *Travels with Charley*, "I stopped conversing with my dogs, and I believe that subtleties of feeling began to disappear. . . . Then it occurred to me that the delicate shades of feeling, of reaction, are the result of communication, and without such communication they tend to disappear. A man with nothing to say has no words." The first shoot of his phalanx theory emerged from the Tahoe snows: an artist needs others, or another. With Carol, a woman of quips and asides, curiosity and intelligence, he most certainly found words—they talked nonstop. Carol was a catalyst for John, essential to his creativity. That was true from their first meeting on.

During the long summer days they were together, Carol wore her new hiking boots on trails around the lake, and she and John, hand in hand, trekked day and night. John loved to prowl the darkness, when stars were thrown across mountain skies and silhouettes of black pines were etched against the horizon. He would have taken her to the Brighams' house and up a steep road to Fallen Leaf Lodge, a lively resort during the summer months. Perhaps they sailed the lake's perimeter on the two-hundred-seat *Tahoe* steamship that made circuits daily during the summer. Every night John and Carol, Idell and

Lloyd, had dinner together, either at one of the resorts with dance pavilions—McKinney's or Tahoma or perhaps the elegant Tahoe Tavern—or at Shebley's small cottage. One evening they all drove twenty miles west to Truckee, the raucous town where the Southern Pacific Railroad stopped on its way to Nevada. The "juvenile delinquent" of Sierra mining towns, Truckee satisfied anyone looking for a wild night. Only a couple of decades earlier gunfights were common and drunken loggers and ice cutters and railroad workers more so. By 1928 the place was glazed with respectability, but it remained a bar-hopping mecca during Prohibition, every "soda fountain" retaining someone who was willing to go to jail for the owner if there were a raid. Fine bootleg whiskey sold for a dollar a shot at the Silver Mirror (also a speakeasy with blackjack, poker, and slot machines). To enter, patrons passed through a door into a cage, where they were scrutinized, and then were allowed through a second door and into a saloon—the back door led to brothels. At the Roma Club, a blind piano player took any "drinks and dope available" for his tips. Slot machines on wheels could be rolled out of sight when the law knocked. John and Carol undoubtedly went to John's favorite bar, the Capital Saloon—also a hangout, beginning in about 1914, for movie stars and other luminaries such as John Wayne, Douglas Fairbanks, Buster Keaton, and Clark Gable. Truckee was a Sierra "film mecca," with three westerns filmed there in 1928 alone: *The Red Dance, The Michigan Kid,* and *The Wrecking Boss.* Another stop was the Bucket of Blood, a bar so rough that the bartender gave John a pistol to protect the ladies.

One day John and Carol went to the Truckee Rodeo, held in early July. When they pair returned to Tahoe, John's college roommate, Carlton Shef-field, was waiting for them. He thought John's new girlfriend looked about sixteen years old: "They had been attending a rodeo and parade in Truckee. She wore a light summer dress with a bandana at the neck and had a smudge of dirt on her nose." Smitten John wrote home to his parents: "This summer is a good deal more festive than last and I am enjoying it tremendously." He'd found his mate.

What might the lovers have talked about during those first days together? If John chortled at Carol's wisecracks and puns, she would have been equally amused by his masterful stories—well-worn tales he told to all his friends. Both of them were very funny people, though in different ways. Carol daz-zled and slashed with quick retorts, undercutting pretension and balder-dash and tedium. John relished conversational patterns: "dead pan logic which demanded neither sense nor continuity" or ludicrous tales to explain commonplace events or his masterful stories. "A fellow suspected a mouse in the woodpile . . . ," John would drawl, and then tell how the man restacked two piles to find the errant mouse. That was a favorite. So was the saga of Jimmy the Indian, a local resident who cured his stomach disorder by taking a trout to Half Moon Lake and feeding it to the resident mermaid. So was his drawn-out account of Omar and the garbage bear ignoring each other. Perhaps he withheld another chestnut—the stretcher about his first sexual exploit with a one-legged babysitter (a story that found its way into *The Grapes of Wrath*, told by Tom Joad). John had a knack for spinning what one college friend dubbed "Jackie Gleason stories," which would have appealed to Carol. "He would begin very slowly and as he reached the end, he got faster and faster and faster and then . . . his face would turn red and he would get up and walk around and scratch his ass and kind of come back and sit down like a little kid. It was very funny. He hadn't a very good speaking voice, a very low voice—low register, but he would tell these things. He also would make a grimace quite a bit when he got kind of perplexed or disliked something, he would make a face. He would throw his head up and act as though he was thinking about it and I know damn well he was just doing it for effect. He was a ham."

Carol must have howled at his yarns and listened attentively to his occult fare: he intoned reverently about ghosts. A gentleman ghost named Herbert inhabited his Salinas house, a spirit roomer who came and went in the spare attic rooms and was particularly fond of Mary, John thought. When Steinbeck lived in a Brooklyn boarding house, a female ghost pulled out nonexistent dresser drawers in John's room, and he asked her, one night, what she was doing. Wintering at the Brigham estate, he had seen "an elderly man . . . with grey hair, clothes of a different era, a gold watch and chain. John queried the intruder, 'What do you want?' The man smiled and disappeared. It was the ghost of Mr. Brigham," John told friends. The spirit world intrigued young Steinbeck—he had checked out the *Hermetica* of Hermes Trismegistus three times from the Stanford library to learn about alchemy and spells, as well as the tradition's philosophical grounding in Egyptian and Greek history. Any young man who wanted to impress an eager, intelligent, and wacky young woman would certainly pull out all his cards, including the Tarot stack.

Undoubtedly John's writing was discussed. He had just completed the final draft of *Cup of Gold,* a novel about Henry Morgan, pirate, and would surely have read parts aloud to Carol. That was his practice, listening to the rhythm of sentences as one friend or another served as audience. When reading aloud, he struggled "between self-consciousness and emotion," recalled one friend. "His voice went higher than was normal for him and he read rapidly, with words quickly pronounced by tending to blur at the ends as if he were embarrassed at uttering them . . . one eyebrow . . . arched high as he reached something that he liked. . . . When he finished, he never looked at his auditor but grimaced deprecatingly, the single eyebrow as high as it would go and his hands fumbling . . . at arranging the sheets or putting them away while he made some off-hand comment about the piece he had been reading." Who would not be drawn in by such an act?

But perhaps most important was the couple's psychological and intellectual bond. In the three weeks they were together at Lake Tahoe, Carol wove herself into his artistic endeavors and boosted his ego, willingly typing his new manuscript, "The Green Lady," based on a play written by Stanford classmate Toby Street, whose mother-in-law ran the Fallen Leaf Lodge. Young Carol Henning fell unerringly in step with Steinbeck the young visionary, a man with an intriguing mix of self-effacement and self-assurance. Confident men are alluring, and burly John Steinbeck was propelled by a single-minded quest. "He was absolutely convinced that he was going to be a great novelist. He just took it for granted, I mean it bled from him," recalled one college friend. That would have enthralled Carol, who was nudging toward confidence in her own abilities. Steinbeck also exuded a childlike innocence and what might be called fragility or shyness—and that would have appealed to the resolute side of Carol. With John, she found a mentor, partner, and purpose in life. Together both were stronger. If John fell into troughs of self-doubt about his manuscript—as he often did—Carol's ebullience revived him. Only four months before her appearance in the mountains, a crestfallen and discouraged Steinbeck had written "Dook" Sheffield, his Stanford roommate and confidant, that his latest draft of "Cup of Gold" was no good and compared himself to his defeated characters. Furthermore, he moaned, he had no visionary woman, no woman at all. But one materialized, a woman as verbal, passionate, and cockeyed as he. A funny woman. "What this country needs is a belly laugh," Steinbeck had told friends while at Stanford. Carol provoked belly laughs, an antidote to his own self-absorption and intensity. Her love of the English language—the gravity and bounce and richness of words—tallied with his own. In many, many ways, the two were soul mates.

The Henning sisters stayed three weeks in the mountains, After the Fourth of July, Carol returned to San Francisco and her work for Mr. Schilling. Although John suggested that she come back and spend a winter in

Tahoe with him, that plan was nixed, since Carol loved her job and didn't want to abandon lightly a promising secretarial career for the isolation of Tahoe. Love-struck John lurched around in the Sierras for another couple of months, having dalliances with others—so his devotion to Carol had not completely jelled. Perhaps Truckee's feckless ways inspired an outlaw pose— he packed a revolver, drank heavily, and lusted after vacationing women. But by the fall, love triumphed, and he moved to San Francisco, near Carol.

After two wilderness years, he came down from the mountains with tablets etched with the germ of the phalanx theory: he needed "one or two things, a patron or a guardian," he wrote home. "Really I haven't the slightest conception of taking care of myself." Actually he could and did take very good care of his physical self—eating well, working well. But the mentor he needed was an intellectual sparring partner and something more—secretary, audience, editor, typist. And even more essential to his psychic balance was the group dynamic of the phalanx: Carol's presence.

Many years later, in a 1955 essay entitled "Some Thoughts on Juvenile Delinquency," John considered the phalanx in terms that eluded the self-conscious young writer, not yet seared by loneliness and loss: "I believe that man is a double thing, a group animal and at the same time an individual. And it occurs to me that he cannot successfully be the second until he has fulfilled the first." With Carol he fulfilled the first, becoming a group animal. The unit Carol-and-John became the keystone of his art, although she was not the first phalanx participant who served as a creative bulwark, nor did the notion of a collective identity become first apparent in her company. At some level, Steinbeck was aware of his deep need for others to complete him—as audience, as muse, as buffers to his personality. At Stanford University he had "developed a theory that one had no personality in essence, that one was a reflection of a mood plus the moods of other persons present." Although he claimed to have "no more poses" once he left the mountains, his need for an audience remained. During those two years, he had been writing long letters to Katherine Beswick, a Stanford friend who had left California for New York City in a quest to become a poet. To Kate he had sent versions of "Cup of Gold," and she had dutifully read, commented, encouraged, edited. He told her of plans to write biographies of five saints and a book called *The Vagrant*. None were written, but Kate was his sounding board. Carol, however, was nearer at hand and stepped into Kate's shoes, listening and encouraging, nurturing and supporting his drive. An audience in thrall was indispensable to this artist.

Although writing is a solitary endeavor, authorship is a public art, and Steinbeck was keenly aware of the difference: "I've never looked upon myself as an author," he insisted in a 1962 interview. "The word author has always horrified me, the quality of phoniness, fakeness about it you know. . . . I've considered myself a writer because that's what I do. I don't know what an author does. An author collects the things, a writer does the work." For this writer, Carol would become the public presence, his conduit to the world, his ballast. She nudged him toward authorship—not in any artificial or forced manner, as he feared, but living in a world beyond his own mind. Years later Burl Ives would comment on the equilibrium essential to Steinbeck's working life: "He was the kind of man that needed to go out and get drunk with the boys and come home and have mama say it's alright. He had to have that in order to be able to write." If that need seems selfish, it is certainly not unusual for an artist, male or female. And if John needed to be nurtured and petted and protected, to exchange ideas with another, Carol in turn needed to stand firm for another. The two meshed.

Their year of courtship, from the fall of 1928 through the fall of 1929, was a charmed time, spent largely in what John called a "magic" place. For Northern Californians like Carol and John, San Francisco was simply "The City," a glorious, legendary, gilded metropolis. As a child, John was "blooded with culture" here. While Carol's mother took her daughters to the woods, John's, "a lady with a high church attitude toward culture," took her children to the Clift, Olive Steinbeck's favorite hotel on Geary Street, and then to the opera to hear "Caruso, Melba, Tetrazzini, Scotti and the rest of that fantastic band of Archangels." Even as he prepared for his last overseas trip, to Vietnam in 1966, John recalled the keen anticipation he felt as a child before a San Francisco junket. And even before that, Steinbeck's Uncle Joe, who worked for the *San Francisco Wasp*, told young John story after bejeweled story about "The City":

> I figure that Julius Caesar was stabbed near the arched entrance of the old Ferry Building, that Market Street led under the Arch of Titus, past the Forum which was of course the Palace Hotel, and went thence up the Capitoline or Nob Hill. It was obvious that Joan of Arc was burned in Union Square with her eyes fixed on the Fairmont, that Moses went up Twin Peaks to receive the Tables of the Law. You may understand that through my uncle's star-dusted eyes, I knew The City quite well before I ever went there.

For both, San Francisco fulfilled its fabled reputation, and their relationship jelled during their vagabond year roaming the city's streets.

In the late 1920s, the Paris of the West offered fresh crab on Fisherman's Wharf, Chinese noodles on Geary, and cheap spaghetti at "a cave in North Beach" that John and Carol haunted. They took "a streetcar ride to the Beach" and lay "breathless and dry-mouthed in the shelter of a rock while the fog dancing dawn came up." Nearby was the Cliff House on the Great Highway— once a watering place for the likes of Mark Twain and Frank Norris—probably too expensive for John and Carol, who lived on "sardines and buns and doughnuts and coffee in the best tradition." Also on the Great Highway was Chutes-at-the-Beach, by the late 1920s called "Whitney's Playland," where visitors were promised "More than 1000 Laughs and Thrills." John and Carol might well have let the maniacal laugh of six-foot-tall "Laffin Sal" draw them into Playland's Fun House (Carol loved them) where a couple could pass through the Mirror Maze to the Barrels of Fun and then down the "longest indoor slide in the world." Or they might have ridden on the Big Dipper rollercoaster or Shoot the Chutes and then munched on a new regional favorite, an It's-It ice cream sandwich, sold only at Playland. Or they might have eaten and danced at Topsy's Roost nearby.

On weekends they certainly would have strolled through Golden Gate Park, passing the Dahlia Dell or listening to the California Ramblers (with Jimmy and Tommy Dorsey) play jazz at the band pavilion. They cavorted in Italian North Beach when it awakened "with lights in a misty evening," John later recalled in a nostalgic essay on San Francisco, and "long tables clad in white oilcloth, the heaped baskets of our bread, the pots de chamber of beautiful soup du jour, then fish and meat, fruit, cheese, coffee, 40 cents. With wine, and that means lots of wine, 50 cents." Carol often ordered trout almandine, her favorite San Francisco meal. Bootleg liquor was readily purchased and John was adept at finding it—having undoubtedly sipped his share of absinthe at Madame Torelli's, a Stanford hangout, when he was an undergraduate.

The two were inseparable. College friend Amasa Miller remembers a scene where John and Carol were pinching out each other's blackheads on a San Francisco street corner—not the kind of intimacy most relish. One day waiting for bus, Carol irritated John beyond measure, as she could with her strong opinions and salty tongue. John groused at her: "I can't hit a woman in a public place." Carol quipped back, "I have no public place."

During those happy months in San Francisco in the fall of 1928, off and on in 1929, Steinbeck lived in apartments near Carol or with her—often displacing Idell as a roommate. His first home was a tiny room at 1901 Vallejo Street in a "nice neighborhood," as he told his friend Kate Beswick, who was scraping by in New York City, and with whom he still kept up a steady correspondence. In those early months, John and Carol accepted one another's foibles and friendships. Carol's response to Kate was warm curiosity; she later urged John to invite her west for a visit: "Carol has read the letters you have written to me and she has conceived a very curious affection for you for, she says, 'She lives so gracefully and so exactly as she wishes.' She is nearly as anxious to meet you as I am to see you." Carol's acceptance suggests the solidity of her bond with John as well as their shared determination to create a relationship on fresh guidelines. In Kate, Carol saw an admirably resolute New Woman of the 1920s—self-reliant, creative, bold, and graceful, the contemporary icon that was her own model. Carol may or may not have known of Kate's earlier offer to John—that he father her children and that Kate give up her own writing career for his. John's monomaniacal commitment to writing was, it seems, magnetic to independent women.

John and Carol allowed one another breathing space—that was part of being modern and scorning the lockstep patterns of their parents' generation. The career girl changed jobs, moving from Schilling Spice to the *San Francisco Chronicle* to train in advertising: she wanted an intellectually challenging career, and John was proud of his wage-earning, ambitious girlfriend. He quit the grueling work he'd taken on with Bemis Bag, a business owned by the family of sister Mary's fiancé, where he had loaded trucks with bales of jute. Like Nathaniel Hawthorne, he learned that being utterly exhausted by the day's end didn't nurture the imagination. So he moved back to his family's Pacific Grove house in early 1929 to save money and maximize his writing hours. Although he felt that he was "growing rapidly" in his abilities, perhaps an admission of how much Carol's support meant to him, he had written fewer pages per day since meeting her—a mere hundred over several months—and he retreated to Pacific Grove in order to hone his sentences. Carol dubbed the stylistic flourishes of *Cup of Gold* "Irish blarney," and he appreciated her sharp critiques. She was one of the few people who could offer suggestions and criticize his work without being snapped at. Others who offered advice might be told they really didn't understand his point. Since John had avoided all courses in grammar and composition, Carol, with secretarial skills under her belt, also helped him edit his fiction.

And she recommended books—by Ernest Hemingway, Willa Cather.

Hemingway's spare sentences stunned John in late 1929: Hemingway is "the finest writer alive," he told Carol. Cather was one of Carol's favorite writers, and her lucid sentences, paucity of modifiers, and reliance on place also influenced Steinbeck's own prose. (In 1935 he wrote Lewis Gannett that "Willa Cather writes the best prose in America.") Shifting reading tastes marked Steinbeck's post–*Cup of Gold* writing, Carol's imprint being clearly evident. By his own admission, he paid more attention to sentences, avoiding the flabby prose of George Branch Cabell, a former model. All during the wet winter months of 1929–30 he worked steadily on "The Green Lady," the first draft of *To a God Unknown*. In February he went to Mendocino with Toby Street to look over the locales (the mossy rock of the published version is in Laytonville). "The Green Lady" had been Toby's conception (originally a play) and was set in his country. Off and on for the next three years, Steinbeck wrestled with this borrowed conception and unknown turf; only gradually did Carol help guide him to Anglo-Saxon words, spare sentences, and the Salinas Valley.

He and Carol brought out the best in each other in those early months and years together—talking, working, playing, surviving. If Carol had often been "obnoxious" as a teen, she was "warm, kindly, and fun" with John, said her sister. Her gregariousness muted his shyness; her inquisitive mind, rooted in the world, countered his introspectiveness; her fervid belief in his prose complemented his own obsession with writing. Theirs was what one friend called a "symbiotic relationship," deeply satisfying for both. It's hardly surprising that "The Green Lady" manuscript, so long in gestation—1929 through 1932—is such an ambitious, teeming, raw, and inventive novel. In it Steinbeck crammed his love for Carol—his hero Joseph Wayne's love for Elizabeth and Rama—as well as vertiginous intellectual pursuits. The novel digs vertically into a layered sense of history and place, then horizontally to consideration of mythic structures and spiritual moorings. The published text is a monument to holistic connectivity—to nature and history, individual and culture, God and gods. It is his hymn to what would become deep ecology, a concept that Steinbeck himself used in 1932 to describe his manuscript: "Each figure is a population and the stones—the trees the muscled mountains are the world—but not the world apart from man—the world and man—the one inseparable unit man and his environment. Why they should ever have been understood as being separate I do not know." Carol and John's own relationship was similarly ecologically based—grounded not in a hierarchical control, but in mutual respect, shared pursuits, and attachment to place, with Carol playing multiple roles for John: partner, mentor, muse, secretary, and lover. Without the grounding that she provided, John might not have persevered through rewrites and rejections.

And in Joseph Wayne's ferocious ambition there is some of their own transgressive sensibilities. Only by crossing boundaries could a genuine relationship be established. Carol was unpredictable, which was satisfying to John. At parties she was naughty. Later in the marriage, radical politics marked her; Carol joined the Communist Party in 1938, primarily, she said, to irritate John's relatives. Neither she nor John wished to accommodate a world where, as he writes in *Cannery Row*, "All of our so-called successful men are sick men, with bad stomachs, and bad souls." The young couple prefigured fictional Mack and the boys, who are "healthy and curiously clean. They can do what they want. They can satisfy their appetites without calling them something else." As partners, Carol and John stepped into a world of their own making, and John wrote fiction about outsiders like themselves. For ten years, his prose vision and their life values meshed. And in their relationship, the two played out alternating roles of neediness and strength, he tolerating her transgressions, she his writerly detachment. "John was not a nurturer," one friend noted. Carol accepted that.

In Steinbeck's work of the next decade, his most sensitive female portraits act with some of Carol's decisiveness and vulnerability. Some are trapped in roles traditional society has created for them and tentatively cross social boundaries: Rama in *To a God Unknown*, for example, takes Joseph to her bed because her need for sexual fulfillment is as strong as his. Frustrated Elisa Allen in "The Chrysanthemums," Steinbeck's most anthologized short story, written in 1933, longs for the freedom to roam as a tinker. Although Danny eyes her lustfully, Sweets Ramirez in *Tortilla Flat* is hardly a sexual object, as critics have read her. She eyes him back, her sexual drive equal to his. Unhappily linked to a husband who was her ticket out of an unhappy home, Curley's wife in *Of Mice and Men* envisions a career in Hollywood film, a plaintive dream that lends her character shape and purpose and wins the reader's sympathy. Ma Joad wields an ax handle, and Rose of Sharon pulls out a dry breast in spite of her shame. His are nuanced female portraits, where the societal and psychological restraint that characterizes women is coupled with singularity of thought, portraits drawn with some of Carol's complex mix of neediness and courage.

Before he met Carol, he wrote to Kate Beswick from Tahoe about his female characters: "I play safe. I use only the outward manifestations of some

I have known. I make no attempt to enter their minds except where their thoughts have been obvious to me in some given experience." Understanding Carol helped round Steinbeck's women.

Later in that spring of 1929 Steinbeck moved back to San Francisco and rented for $1.90 a week an attic room in the house where Carol lived at 2853 Jackson Street. By this point, John and Carol "went steady" with an established daily rhythm. While she worked, he wrote in the mornings, walked in the afternoons, and ate nightly with Carol and Idell, reading "The Green Lady" to them late into the evening. Although Idell and John tolerated each other, the two were never a particularly good mix. Idell lacked Carol's joie de vivre and was far more respectable by nature. Nor was she very happy about her new rooming arrangement, particularly since Carol and John got the bedroom and she the couch. When the opportunity arose to return to Hawaii, she was off. Earlier, on her 1925 cruise to Honolulu with her mother, Idell had met the wealthy pineapple heiress May Dole, who had then just eloped; May invited Idell for a visit—an opportunity not to be missed.

Thoreauvian simplicity suited John and Carol, a fact clear from John's oft-repeated monetary calculations in letters. He liked paring his living expenses to the bone, noting amounts spent—and Carol appreciated his thrift. "I'm really very fond of her," he wrote to Kate. "I intend to live with her, and the trouble is that she makes three times as much money as I can hope to. . . . Anyways she's a nice girl and doesn't mind my poverty in the least." John's acute awareness of money would be a constant during their marriage, and Carol's equally compelling need to monitor pennies would come to define her role in their partnership. When pennies were few, her thrift was essential; when money flowed, the two floundered. But in 1928 and well into the 1930s poverty was concomitant with artistic commitment.

For several weeks in the late summer of 1929 the two camped in a redwood grove near La Honda in the Santa Cruz Mountains on the coast, where they had a one-room tent cabin where they slept on cots and relied on an outdoor fireplace to keep them toasty on chilly nights when the fog rolled in. On hot days they bathed in the nude in Pescadero Creek, which ran through their campsite. Carol read countless books, as was her want, and John "with a distant look" took off every morning to write under a favorite redwood, his desk a redwood stump. The young comrades frolicked with John's dog, Omar, and munched on ambrosia: "bread, bacon squares (then selling at 10 cents a pound), bacon gravy, beans, corn meal in various combinations, and hamburger." Crayfish crawled from rock to rock in the little stream, and with a bit of hamburger on a string, they were easily caught. When Carlton Sheffield, John's college roommate, and his wife came one weekend to camp with them, the foursome had a great feast of crayfish and miner's lettuce plucked from the slopes and corn bought from a local farmer. For these two latter-day pioneers, domestic economy was a delightful challenge.

And that fall, 1929, John spent a few more hand-to-mouth weeks in the city, moving into his third residence, 2441 Fillmore Street, with Carl Wilhelmson —the college friend who had shared his Tahoe cabin for months at a time. Both wrote novels. Carl "had one side in a spider webby corner and I a nice place looking out on a roof where cats fought." Most nights were spent at Carol's. One evening when Carol and Idell (returned from Hawaii) were away, Carl and John put sardines on each spoke of the fence around the women's apartment, an emblem of true love, no doubt, and characteristic of John's playfulness. Although neither he nor Carol was particularly interested in tapping down the levity—or legalizing their status—commitment hung in the air. John declared that he wouldn't make a good husband, since work was his singular passion. John's college friend Toby Street had warned Carol never to marry John because, he told her, "You're not as important as his work." The comment hardly came as a surprise, and she was troubled that Toby thought she didn't already know that about John. Carol probably never was as important as John's books, but for a long time it hardly mattered, since she considered his books hers as well. They were a team, married or not.

And Carol herself was wary of marriage, because it would, of course, compromise her status as a self-sufficient New Woman. If she left San Francisco, as John wished, then she would abandon her promising career in advertising; if they married, both might be succumbing to bourgeois expectations. Carol wobbled. During their months together, she had expanded in this relationship built on an ecological model of connection and mutual purpose. She embraced his notions of creativity rather than the New Woman's of success—essentially another kind of hierarchical relationship—and she opted out of consumerism (no more new clothes) rather than viewing buying power as part of her freedom. To marry or not was a choice that confronted many, many women in the 1920s, who were reluctant to abandon newfound independence. Carol's solution was a companionate marriage—John's partner, not his subordinate. Together they "made their own rules," insisted Idell, and "challenged all they'd been taught." Carol could hardly become a pliant wife. Nor could such a woman embrace a patriarchal model for a union, even if, in fact, her needs were always at the service of John's career.

Proximity to both sets of parents probably nudged them out of San Francisco; neither Olive nor Nellie, had they known about it, would have condoned John and Carol's living arrangements. Every two or three weeks the elder Steinbecks came to the city for a "family get together," and masking their physical intimacy must have grown wearisome for the young couple. Carol's mother, whom John would soon call a "devil," sometimes visited for several days. In the end, the urge to "get out from under" parental attention drove the young lovers forward into an engagement and southward to Los Angeles. They packed their possessions into Carol's Buick, but the car broke down about an hour out of San Francisco. They bought a new car, a Marmon, and finally arrived in Los Angeles in late fall. They planned to stay in Eagle Rock with Carlton Sheffield, who was teaching literature at Occidental College, and his second wife, Maryon. Their visit seems remarkably ill timed, since Carlton and Maryon had been married only about eight months, and Sheffield had a fairly demanding job as a new teacher. But John and Carol, as well as their friends, Richie and Tal Lovejoy and Tal's sister, would crowd into the Sheffields' tiny home in order to launch a business, "The Faster Master Plaster Casters." The endeavor could have been a fine pilot for *I Love Lucy.*

The key players didn't have Lucy's red hair—although Carol dyed John's flaming orange briefly—but all had oversize personalities. Steinbeck's closest friend in the group was Sheffield, a college roommate and a "warm, relaxed person," recalled one friend. "We are not alike," John wrote to Sheffield's first wife, Ruth Carpenter Sheffield, explaining their friendship, "rather we are opposites, but also we are equals. . . . He was the cathode and I the anode. We laughed, quarreled, drank, were sad, considered life, ethics, philosophies. We did not always agree. More often we openly disagreed. But always in the back of the mind of each there was the thought that the one was not complete without the other and never could be." This sounds surprisingly close to a description of John's marriage to Carol; John liked and needed creative and combative relationships based on strong mutual interests. Only thus was he whole.

Carlton's marriage to lovely, dark-haired Maryon in February 1929 was his second. Ruth, to his horror, had gone mad and "tried to kill her mother with a butcher knife and nearly brained Duke with a rock," as Steinbeck had written his parents from Tahoe. Sheffield adored Maryon, although she, sadly, was less committed to marriage and domesticity than he, and others found her a bit creepy, ghostly: "I could bring myself to believe that she sits in front of a mouse hole all night," John admitted. Their house was stark, with few feminine touches; the twelve Sheffield cats used the fireplace ashes as a litter box. While with Sheffield Maryon had two abortions. At that time and place, many women knew a doctor willing to perform an abortion, and she freely discussed both with houseguests. Indeed, she kept "our Oscar," the fetus, in a jar on the mantle. Although few were shocked by the abortions, the fetus was discomforting. And Sheffield himself was not particularly pleased by her abortion stories.

The other couple that moved to Los Angeles was a Pacific Grove pair, Ritchie and Tal (Natalya) Lovejoy, lifelong friends of John and Carol. Ritchie, a journalist and illustrator, was a bashful, gentle, sometimes inept, and always-creative young man originally from Mountain View, who shared Carol and John's askew sensibilities—a "sensitive, suffering poetic type," said one friend. He had moved to Carmel in 1926 at the urging of a former high school teacher, Jack Calvin. His wife, née Kashevaroff, was an arresting, exotic beauty with "Tartar eyes" and the stature of an elegant ballerina. She was the daughter of a Russian Orthodox priest and his Alaskan Tlingit/Aleut wife, one of a "wild bunch of girls," five sisters, all of whom grew up in Sitka, Alaska. The Kashevaroffs were uninhibited, joyous, hard-drinking women. Winsome and creative Tal was "witty and intellectual," also a woman who never learned to drive. Tal was the model for Mary Talbot in *Cannery Row*, a pixie who gives tea parties for her cats. "I once knew a girl," Steinbeck recalled in 1962, "an Alaskan Russian girl, very pretty, very nice, who put over the fireplace a milk bottle with a sign and it said, please contribute to a very worthy cause, and we did and we put nickels and dimes and quarters in because she was a nice girl. We discovered that the worthy cause was to buy beer for her but because she was a nice girl she shared the beer with us if we continued to contribute to a very worthy cause."

When not drinking the beer that Sheffield brewed illegally every week in greater and greater quantities, the three couples envisioned making a fortune, or at the very least eking out a living, by casting the faces of Hollywood stars in plastic to create realistic busts. It was Ritchie Lovejoy, living near Steinbeck in Pacific Grove, who had introduced Steinbeck to the amazing properties of the Swiss plastic Negocol, which sold for an affordable eight dollars for a two-pound package. When Negocol was heated to 120–130 degrees, it could be poured into a mold; it set rapidly and dried to what Carlton Sheffield called "a glossy, elastic surface." The material reproduced with "remarkable fidelity," Sheffield recalled in his memoir, the source of a merry account of this venture. The product could, if necessary, be reused and had magical properties, so it seemed, fascinating those drawn to the occult and novel potions and such.

But "The Faster Master Plaster Casters" was an ill-fated venture if ever there was one. Sheffield's prose bristles with the improbability of it all. The few Hollywood starlets they enticed to the project were unhappy that their casts revealed every flaw. Even though John "bubbled" with ideas for the Negocol casts—mannequins in department stores or models of insects and marine specimens that schools might use—his interest fizzled soon enough. It is hard to imagine hardheaded John and businesswoman Carol embracing such a scheme beyond the idea stage.

More serious was their decision to marry on January 12, 1930, a reluctant affair that took place in a Los Angeles courthouse with only Sheffield and Maryon in attendance. (Although the announcement in the Salinas paper said that the Dekkers, John's sister Mary and her husband, were in attendance and that all enjoyed a "delightful dinner . . . following the simple but impressive ceremony." The announcement also praised the bridegroom for having achieved "considerable fame" with *Cup of Gold*, "one of the most discussed books of the past year." One suspects that Olive Steinbeck composed the whitewashed version of John's nuptials and achievements.) John and Carol had to be dragged into the building because neither wanted to be married in a "God-damned church," as Carol moaned, and at the final moment, neither wanted to sign any official document at all. But they did (in one last eruption of independence, John listed "retired" as his occupation—signing forms always brought out the rebel in him). After the courthouse ordeal, the Sheffields hosted a marriage feast at White Spot, ordering deluxe hamburgers all around, the special fifteen-cent kind. Carol and John each ate two, appetites healthy, vigor intact. When they got back to the Sheffields' they got in a loud and joyous fight. Their marriage was, in effect, consummated. John wrote home: "Concerning the announcements that mother suggests, they are absolutely out. I wouldn't have them at all. I don't like announcements anyway nor Christmas cards nor birthday cards. Carol doesn't either so there you are." Nor did he want presents. Nor did he want an announcement in the newspaper. "I consider it evil advertising." Theirs was a marriage eschewing, from inception, any imprint of middle-class expectations.

More and more John and Carol dressed alike in slacks and work shirts, even though a woman in pants was considered risqué at the time. Traditional gender lines blurred as John and Carol launched their egalitarian marriage. Several friends noted that there was a masculine quality about Carol. She was tough, or at least projected toughness, and thought a great deal like a man in many ways. And John's rugged exterior shielded a very sensitive, vulnerable man. That fluidity of roles sustained both. "Everything is run on a fifty-fifty basis," John proudly wrote Kate.

Living in an era of shifting values sparked creativity well beyond the capacities of the Faster Master Plaster Casters. Possibilities at boundaries often seem endless. Shortly after arriving in Los Angeles, John started a new book, "Dissonant Symphony," which, appropriate for their new situation, explored the very basis of human personality. As Sheffield notes, John became "fascinated with the idea that personalities are not actual, objective qualities but interpretations formulated in the minds and eyes of observers, almost like two chemicals interacting on each other, changing the original character of each. He was thinking about the many factors that enter into the pictures people have of other people: prejudices, associations, social and economic relationships, mental states, and the like." This seems another version of ideas about a collective "mood" he had considered while a Stanford student. Aggregate identities long fascinated this writer. And like other modernists, subjectivity intrigued him, as did the realization that objectivity was a chimera.

Newly wed Carol blossomed as well, having more time for her satirical pen and ink drawings. No period of John and Carol's lives together is better tracked from Carol's perspective than their few wild weeks with the Sheffields. Freed from her job, newly married, relaxed and happy, at last fully a part of a group, Carol wandered about with her sketchpad capturing moments of haphazard bliss. "Carol spends much of her time playing in the hills behind the house," Steinbeck wrote to Kate Beswick. "It is very good for her." He was right. Her drawings from this period have a delicacy and precision missing from any later extant work. John Held cartoons from the *New Yorker* were her favorite ("Girls with long legs, short skirts, spread knees . . . so you could see their underwear," recalled Sheffield), but there were other influences as well. "We greeted *The New Yorker* with joy," recalled a student who came to the Sheffields' parties, Margaret Ringnalda. "Someone started collecting immediately. We were very much interested in caricature and prints and we looked forward to the Peter Arno's cartoons in particular. We had discussions at the Sheffields' of Grant Wood . . . of Emil Kosa. . . . Then there was the revival of interest in Aubrey Beardsley. I made copies of Salome with John the Baptist's Head and of Salome dancing for Murco's [her husband's] studio and Murco and I made a Salome puppet with a stomach that moved—to the delight of both the house on the hill and the house in Eagle Rock. We were in awe of Diego Rivera and Orosco." It was a time of ferment in Los Angeles, and John and Carol soaked it all up.

Carlton Sheffield's memoir tallies with Carol's drawings, fulsome accounts of revelry in prose and cartoon. Carol depicts one scene of Sheffield running after his wife with a raised chair. Seeing it fifty-eight years later, he only sighed in dismay at what once had been, the turmoil and churning energy. Another of Carol's drawings depicts a Temple of St. Anthony, the patron saint of lost items, and a man with a beard. Ah, recalled Sheffield: "A little girl that somebody brought in . . . wanted to see me. I was asleep. She came to see me on the sleeping porch. She astonished I was naked. I did throw something at her. I guess a water bottle I had by the bed." Sorting through Carol's drawings, Sheffield lamented: "Can you imagine people living like that?" "Once we almost got arrested," Sheffield chortled. "We went roller-skating at night around 10:00 P.M. to Glendale." Sometimes they skated a pound of calf's liver home. And lots and lots of beer was consumed, alcohol consumption being part of the bohemian stance. Sheffield increased his beer-making operation to eighteen gallons every five days, "and at that could barely keep up with consumption." John wrote that his beer drinking induced "a state of lassitude intershot with moments of unreal romance." Years later he concluded: "As starved and happy a group as ever robbed an orange grove. I can still remember the dinners of hamburger and stolen avocados."

Carol learned to play Sheffield's accordion—haltingly, practicing a quarter of a mile up a hill ("a place from which by some atmospheric or acoustic peculiarity every sound . . . was carried undiminished and undistorted throughout our house," moaned Sheffield). And she frolicked with the three young women who formed the Eagle Rock Self Expression Society. They sunbathed in the nude—there was "some, shall we say, informality at the house," Sheffield admitted, and added that he was a little worried when his students dropped by. Not surprising. Behind the house and up a hill, the sun bath was secluded and surrounded by mattresses, a place so popular that sometimes six or eight people lounged about, all nude, including Agnes de Mille on one occasion. One afternoon, Carol and Maryon spent long hours bleaching their pubic hair, then turned to experiment on John's hair, turning it "flaming pink with strong overtones of salmon—a color that none of us had ever seen in hair before," writes Sheffield.

The Eagle Rock Self Expression Society "initiated" a new couch by leaping on it. They planned cross-country scavenger hunts. Maryon Sheffield and Carol wrestled together and concocted games. The former career girl embraced the freewheeling life with women whose tastes and intellect and sense of humor harmonized with her own. Carol too discovered the magic of the phalanx, group creativity.

Others joined the revelry, students and faculty from Occidental and UCLA. One, Carlyle MacIntyre, was a celebrated classicist, poet, translator of Rilke and Baudelaire, and charismatic figure. It was he who taught Sheffield to make beer. (MacIntyre set a room on fire with his conversation and would spark what bookseller Jake Zeitlin called "a small renaissance" in Southern California. He would mentor and inspire generations of students at UCLA, where he went to teach after leaving Occidental. MacIntyre had even more parties than the Sheffields.) On New Year's Eve 1929, Sheffield invited MacIntyre and other friends to a publication party for *Cup of Gold* where one young student clearly remembered Carol's arrival: "Carol came back from Hollywood where she'd been, dressed in dark blue men's pants with a front zipper. She tried to shock everyone and unzipped." She had been to a lesbian bar and wanted to startle everyone with that bit of lore as well. (But unsettling people wasn't confined to Carol. Sheffield and Maryon were visited once by a very dull man; Sheffield simply disrobed, hoping he'd leave. Then he started unbuttoning his wife's blouse, and finally the young man dashed out.) During parties with Occidental students, the Sheffield record player turned nonstop, Margaret Ringnalda recalled, playing "blues and labor songs to classics and some jazz—I remember Bix Beiderbecke who died young, and Billie Holiday, and Bessie Smith and Louis Armstrong. The labor song I remember because of Steinbeck was 'Joe Hill.' John took the last verses of that and made Tom Joad's speech as Tom left after the murder of his preacher-friend's killer. . . . And we listened to the black singer Leadbelly," no doubt after his first recording in 1935. Parties at either the Sheffields' or MacIntyres' were, she insisted, "alive as I have not known parties since." "Carol didn't drink as much as others," and Margaret Ringnalda's impression of her, like so many others, was that Carol seemed most interested in "her own and John's work." And for his part, John never paid "attention to anyone else"—any other women that is.

For a brief time, Carol and John were nibbling at the edge of a yeasty intellectual circle at UCLA, "full of striving and creation and zaniness." And in spite of his scorn for Los Angeles artificiality, John never lost his interest in the film industry that drew so many creative spirits, and Carol loved the jazz she heard at Sheffield's parties. Margaret Ringnalda mused, "All of us believed we would be great one day—or at least noticed."

But the newlyweds needed space, a home, and respite from notched-up and nonstop revelry. Even before they were married they found a shack to rent for fifteen dollars a month at 2741 El Roble Drive, only a few hundred yards from the Sheffields'. In a few weeks John and Carol made the "tumbled down house" a home. Carol, "busy as a bird dog," stripped ancient wallpaper, helped dismantle a wall. John shoveled out debris, replaced floorboards and windowpanes. Carol insisted they add light to the dank interior, and helped install a large front window salvaged from a wrecking company. In every home they built, a place for parties was an important feature of the design, a warm communal center with a fireplace.

Their industrious homemaking prefigures Mack and the transformation of the Palace Flophouse in *Cannery Row,* where a fishmeal storage shed becomes a showplace, a communal retreat, a home—complete with Darling the puppy, the fictional equivalent of the Steinbecks' first dog, Bruga, a Belgian shepherd puppy. Imagining or finding or personalizing domestic space is a central motif in nearly all of Steinbeck's fiction. His characters yearn for home, for interiors that shield reconstructed families from an unaccommodating world. Consider George and Lennie's plans for acres with clear division of masculine labor; or the paisanos' home in *Tortilla Flat,* which centers and contains heretofore random lives. Danny's house and Danny are one, Steinbeck insists. That urge to imprint space with one's identity and purpose was also the author's. He personalized his childhood room by painting it black at one point, and then other colors. At Stanford, he slapped wallpaper on the white walls of his sophomore dorm room and set up an altar to the "Goddess of Chastity," a kewpie doll lit by a Sterno flame. He also kept a menagerie of pets in his freshman room. At Tahoe, he insisted on curtains for the cabin, "the home symbol" he told his folks. John Steinbeck knew the meaning and purpose of home.

And in this endeavor, as others, Carol was fully in step. She craved a home with all the poignancy of Ma Joad, whose visionary white cottage keeps her moving west.

With evident pride and fulsome description, John wrote his parents about their elegant new space. Undoubtedly he wanted to convince them that he was happily married, thriving. But the detail also conveys the importance of domesticity to him.

> There is a thirty-foot living room with a big stone fireplace in it. The walls and floors were rough and badly painted. The paint we took off with lye and then stained and polished the floors so that the grains of the pine boards show through and look very nice. ["We all polished the floor by skating around in sandboxes," Sheffield recalled.] On the walls I made a wainscoting of dark brown and then painted the upper part of the walls a dull red. The ceiling is high and supported with beams and it too is stained so that the grains of the wood show. One whole end of the room is window from floor to ceiling. This is curtained in dull red. With the furniture we have, a Navajo rug over the fireplace and our pictures it is the most comfortable room I have seen in a long time. The kitchen we painted a light yellow and I put up green gingham curtains like those in the grove house. The bathroom I wall boarded and painted a cream yellow and it also has a green gingham curtain. . . . The house was an eyesore and now it is entrancing.

Such a fulsome account drew his gentle father south. Mr. Steinbeck wanted to see their garden and make sure that the newlyweds had planted the "proper flowers."

Carol was a "good influence" on his work, John reported. He completed a draft of "To an Unknown God" and started another book. Bruga grew "like a weed." The newlyweds called theirs "bluebird love," and John became "Dog-face," Carol's pet name for her new husband. One room of their house was the "Royal Tomato Chamber," in their bedroom was the "Bed Room Bean," a plant, and Bruga became "Bruga the North West Mounting Police Dog." They had fun. But Dogface and Carol did not remain long in LA, since the owner of the house reclaimed it after its facelift, moving his own relatives into the restored abode. And John and Carol could barely afford to rent any other house, even with the twenty-five dollars a month Mr. Steinbeck provided them. After John took an August trip to the Sierras, hiking Bishop Pass with Sheffield, John and Carol drove with the North West Mounting Police Dog in their touring car, "The Bathtub," back north, back to under parents' watchful eyes. Although they would make visits south, in 1931, '32, and '33, they never stayed in Southern California more than a few months.

Monterey County, not Los Angeles, was to be "Steinbeck Country," the region stamped with his own memories, a "remembered symphony" of associations, as he said of his hometown, even though he couldn't yet begin his "novel of Salinas." I "hate too many people there. I would do them and their characters injustice." The next home for Carol and John would be the beloved family cottage in Pacific Grove, not Salinas.

Three anecdotes from later Los Angeles visits reveal Carol at her liveliest, her best. The first is Carol as cowgirl: "Never will I forget you and my cousin Martin Biddle shooting fruit off the tree burgeoning just outside the living room window in North Hollywood. You shared elaborate disregard for some bossies in bosky dell, directly opposite; they scampering off and away from fusillade, milk bags a swingin'."

The other memories belong to Margaret Ringnalda, student of Carlyle MacIntyre and part of the circle that met at his house in the early 1930s, a circle that included John and Carol whenever they were in Los Angeles: "I remembered in every meeting where they were present that John sat quietly and there was a real stillness about him, but Carol, even when still, was like a taut wire," she recalled. But Carol was kind to Margaret. Once Margaret made an unannounced visit to the Sheffields in the fall of 1931 after attending a wedding reception in Eagle Rock:

> Since the Sheffields were close by, I suggested stopping there. I did not know them well, but wanted the friend with me to think that I did. As it happened, the Steinbecks were visiting, and since both of them could give such entertaining reports of people they'd met, I set out to entertain them with imitations of the wedding guests, and as I finished, Maryon Sheffield, a gorgeous woman with coal-black hair and milk-white skin, said coolly, "Margaret is rather like [some name I've forgotten]; she takes the center of the stage the same way." As I absorbed and saluted inwardly the wit, I still wanted to slink out the door, but I saw Carol's face. Her look was so quizzical, her eyes laughing as she waited to see what I would do, that I burst out laughing and so did she and everyone else, and I bowed and made my exit laughing too.

A 1933 Christmas party also shows Carol's warmth. Margaret's frail, artistic brother was enticed by Carol's spicy talk and masculine pose. She was dressed in a turtleneck sweater and slacks. He flirted and chirped at her, "fantasizing a life for himself and her," recalled his sister, embarrassed beyond measure at the time. But Carol, who could have brushed aside such a pesky young aesthete, didn't. After exchanging quips with Carol throughout dinner preparation, Margaret's brother "sat down beside Carol on the bench that served for seating at Mac's table and confided to her: 'I am going to build a house for you, and we'll have a little baby.' Carol put up her hand, 'No baby,' she said. 'I'd like the house though.' When she was ready to leave with John on Mac's shaky outside steps, I thought my brother would get at least a push into the night, for he leaned out, announcing that he must kiss her. She shrugged her shoulders and sighed, but she turned her cheek for the kiss and he was at too perilous a slant in the doorway to pursue further."

Carol liked to be noticed.

CHAPTER THREE

Home in Pacific Grove

FOR THE NEXT FIVE YEARS IN PACIFIC GROVE, John and Carol lived a pared-down life. Mr. Steinbeck had the tiny board-and-batten retreat constructed in 1903, and young John had spent many foggy summers there, poking in tide pools along the rocky coast two blocks from the cottage and riding in the community donkey cart. That little house was his home base—true in 1930 and equally true a quarter century later: "I long for it with almost a pain sometimes," he wrote to his sister Mary in 1955: "it has a pull almost irresistible. I have never slept in my life as I can sleep there."

But Carol may not have slept quite so well. To shift from communal antics in Eagle Rock to solitude in staid Pacific Grove must have been unsettling for her. Even John admitted that sometimes both felt marooned on the Monterey Peninsula's foggy tip, where "nothing happens" and they found "no companionship of any kind" for the first year or so. In the 1930s Pacific Grove was insular, far more conservative than the other Peninsula towns—"lackadaisical" Monterey, capital of Spanish/Mexican California, and "bohemian" Carmel, mecca for artists. The local paper bragged about Pacific Grove's singularity, a "City of Homes" in the "Old American Strain . . . a New England village, a Rochester, Indiana, a Clinton, Iowa, rolled together . . . with all the architecture and traditions that are purely and exclusively American," a town buffered from Depression woes—hardly the spot for a New Woman. Founded in August 1875 as a Methodist seaside retreat, incorporated as the city of Pacific Grove fourteen years later, the community had long been earnest, pragmatic, and stiff lipped. Until the 1890s a fence surrounded the town with gates locked ceremoniously at 9:00 P.M. each night. Denizens were proud of their conservatism. No "objectionable attractions" like poolrooms or saloons were permitted. Nor was alcohol. "The driest little town on earth" repeatedly "vanquished" any attempts by wets to bring bars to "saloonless streets" well into the 1960s. "People in Pacific Grove kind of stayed away from New Monterey. All foreigners," mused gas station owner Red Williams, a man featured in

Cannery Row. "There was a division between here and there." "There" Italians covertly bottled homemade wine during Prohibition. "Here" in Pacific Grove, announced promotional brochures of the 1920s, a "high moral tone" was cultivated among the Methodists, along with spiritual uplift and "innocent amusement," perhaps sea bathing or a stroll along the beach or a spot of roque at local courts. Both physical and mental refinement were encouraged. Summer meetings of the Chautauqua Literary and Scientific Circle, beginning in the 1880s, featured lectures on everything from opera to marine invertebrates. The natural history museum housed a vast collection of stuffed local birds and mammals as well as a world-class library on the South Seas.

Summer festivities and the promise of cool weather brought visitors from California's hot Central Valley to the foggy Monterey coast. Beginning in 1905, July's Feast of Lanterns was patterned after lantern parades held in Lake Chautauqua, New York. All over town Japanese lanterns hung from the Victorian cottages and festive boats sailed on the bay at night, decorated with more lanterns. In 1914, as a twelve-year-old, John might have relished two hours of "military stunts" at the celebration, including the engineering corps dynamiting a pontoon bridge and a mounted cavalry equipment race (the cavalry from the nearby Presidio of Monterey). In 1935, the Feast of Lanterns queen was crowned by full-suited deep-sea diver Eddie Bushnell (one of the men responsible for maintaining the underwater pipes that carried sardines from fish hoppers—floating boxes located five hundred to a thousand feet out in the bay where boats unloaded sardines from the late 1920s on—to canneries along the shore). Crown in hand, Eddie emerged from the bay in a hundred pounds of armor, nearly collapsing on the queen. A Butterfly Pageant was begun in 1939 to honor the thousands of Monarch butterflies that landed on Pacific Grove pines each November: "Any Person caught molesting the butterflies will be prosecuted to the full extent of the law," proclaimed a sign at the entrance to the grove. The fine was a stiff five hundred dollars. (Fictional butterflies in Steinbeck's 1954 novel *Sweet Thursday* get "cockeyed" on pine nectar—a late-life jab at Pacific Grove's earnest dryness.)

In an aborted 1920s story he set in Pacific Grove, Steinbeck writes about a boy named Mizpah who collects pinecones from the forest—as did young John—and loves the travels of Marco Polo above all other books. Like Mizpah, John himself must have enjoyed as a child the "camp meetings, the watermelon festivals, the strawberry parties, the pie bazaars. . . . In the early evening the people gathered at the public parlor to discuss their emotions over the day's sermons. . . . There would be speeches and singing; the just arrived children would play furiously in the dusk. Summer was movement and color and clear shouting voices."

Connected to the area by innumerable nostalgic threads, John thought Pacific Grove a "grand place," as it certainly was. But Carol must have gritted her teeth on occasion, capped her restlessness, and shouldered through days with laughter and love.

Certainly Pacific Grove's earnestness amused both of them. John had long thumbed his nose at local proprieties. While staying in the Eleventh Street house and taking classes at nearby Hopkins Marine Station during the summer of 1923—general zoology as well as classics and exposition from Stanford University's Margery Bailey—John and his sister Mary went to dances held twice a week at the pavilion, where brother, sister, and visiting friends ignored local blue laws that forbade "corrupt" dances like "the tango, turkey trot, bunny hug, or shimmie." Chaperones scolded Carlton Sheffield and Mary for dancing "Stanford style" and practicing their "collegiate glide," which involved, for matronly watchdogs, objectionable "twinning legs." John complained to Sheffield's sister about the "stern and rockbound row of old ladies who have constituted themselves chaperones. Eager they are to pounce out upon those young vile minded moderns. They are living lessons in purity. It is strange that one looks with disapproval on tag when one is too old to play tag."

He and Carol spoofed the town's quixotic politics. In 1929, there was indeed a showdown over whether the Ancient and Honorable Roque and Horseshoe Club of Pacific Grove should remain located across from the Pacific Grove Museum, and when the roque court was relocated, wickets were nipped by one faction. Steinbeck puffed up that scuffle in *Sweet Thursday* (a novel where the Pacific Grove mayor is caught in a King City brothel and a Pacific Grove child comes home with crayons wrapped in the dust cover of the Kinsey report).

He and Carol probably relished the 1932 swimsuit ordinance, which never made it into John's novels:

> It shall be unlawful for any person wearing a bathing suit or portion thereof, except children under ten years of age, to appear in or upon any beach or in any place open to the public . . . unless attired in a bathing suit or other clothing or opaque material, which shall be worn in such a manner as to preclude form, from above the nipples of the breast to below the crotch formed by the legs of the body. . . . All such bathing suits shall be provided with double crotches or with skirts of ample size to cover the buttocks.

Picture a town council debating double crotches. Twice. In 1933, a more for-giving wind blew into town, and the swimsuit law was repealed. All fodder for guffaws.

But adaptable Carol found much to interest her on the Monterey Penin-sula, undoubtedly including the formidable Pacific Grove mayor, Dr. Julia Platt, who proposed the swimsuit ordinance. When she was elected to office in 1931 at age seventy-four, one of her first actions was to insist that sea-bathing men cover their torsos because, declared Mayor Platt: "I don't like just trunks. It isn't a question of whether it's proper or not, it's just ugly." Julia was a woman of strong opinions, "hell on wheels," complained some resi-dents, and also brilliant and energetic—a woman who must have fascinated and amused Carol. (A decade after Julia's death, Toni Jackson, Ed Ricketts's common-law wife in the 1940s, wrote a tribute to this great woman who "knew she had more intelligence, honesty and aggressiveness that most of the other citizens and never hesitated to admit it.")

In the 1890s young Julia Platt had done graduate work in zoology at Harvard and by 1898 had earned a PhD in neuroscience at the University of Freiburg in Germany, publishing a dozen important scientific papers on embryology and neurobiology. ("I am told," wrote Toni Jackson, "that some forty years later, there were still ladies in PG who never forgave her that embryology.") Denied a teaching post in the United States because she was a woman and because she was also an outspoken critic of sloppy research conducted by male colleagues, she retired to Pacific Grove in about 1900 and turned her considerable energies to local affairs—horticultural, ecological, and civic. As president of the Civic Improvement Club, she planned flower beds and selected plants for the town, often pushing her own wheelbarrow to her projects. One hundred yards from the Steinbecks' Eleventh Street cot-tage runs a parkway between upper and lower Lighthouse Avenue because Julia Platt decreed that there should be green space in the wide central street through town. Decades before her mayoral campaign, Julia showed up for every town council meeting and "pounced on every irregularity, evasion, sen-timentality in civic affairs, mincing no words at all," taking action frequently. Dissatisfied with the town's charter, she wrote her own version in 1927, circu-lated a petition, and got it passed.

In 1930 Julia stood her ground on civic matters with characteristic flam-boyance: a stubborn resident, Mrs. Mattie McDougall, owned the bathhouse near Lovers Point (where John and his sisters often swam as children), and the Pacific Grove council condemned her dilapidated property. In retaliation, she built a gate to her land, thus blocking public access to the beach. Julia not only demanded the gate be opened but also marched to the property and filed off the lock—twice. When Mrs. McDougall nailed the gate shut, Julia chopped it down, leaving this sign behind: "Opened by Julia B. Platt. This entrance to the beach must be left open at all hours when the public might reasonably wish to pass through. I act in the matter because the Council and Police Department of Pacific Grove are men and possibly somewhat timid."

Her subsequent mayoral campaign made the national news: "It will take a good man to beat me, and if a good man is elected that will be all the better." No good man prevailed.

Julia's feminism was more civic minded than Carol's, to be sure, but her flamboyance must have been inspirational. And her environmental aware- ness made a much more lasting impact on the town than did her stance on the male physique. Julia was responsible for the Pacific Grove Marine Gardens. In June 1932, the city council unanimously passed City Ordinance 284, which gave the town control of two miles of waterfront along the bay "together with certain submerged lands in the Bay of Monterey contiguous thereto." Pacific Grove was the first community in California to control its own beaches, a legally unique situation where local law trumped state regulations. Along that stretch, no one could collect intertidal specimens (curtailing the harvest- ing of sea urchins and abalone by the Chinese, who some complained were stripping the intertidal) or fish for commercial purposes. Violators were pun- ished by a fine of up to three hundred dollars and a month in jail.

Julia's approach to governing was certainly unorthodox and, in her final stance, unpopular. She lost public support with her objections to a children's playground in the park behind the post office, because it would cease to be restful spot for adults; she wanted the playground farther from downtown. "Cruelty to children," local mothers cried. Even in death she made her iron hand felt, decreeing in her will that her ashes be taken twelve miles out to sea by the town council. No councilmen, apparently, dared to defy that command.

Carol had some of Julia's starch. And like Julia, she gave up her profession to live in a lovely, but subdued, locale. Like Julia, she made do.

In the late summer of 1930, she and John set about refurbishing his beloved family cottage. John constructed bookcases and a fireplace hood of his own design, "the cone of which is a large part of its charm." (He loved watching the fire, especially when a day of writing left him gloomy.) They transformed the large garden. With his father's assistance, John built a stone barbecue pit and a rock-lined lily pond "under the acacias. I am enjoying the building very much." (When completed, the two scratched into the cement: "Johanni, Pater et Filius, Fecerunt ad Gloria Stomachorium, 1930"—Johns, father and son, made this for the glory of the stomach.) As the men worked, Carol planted red geraniums and nasturtiums and iris, strawberries and vegetables. John was also a "beautiful gardener," one friend recalled, and John himself tended to agree, especially after building a pond as well: "My garden is so lovely that I shall hate ever to leave it," he would report in a few months. "I have turtles in the pond now and water grasses. You would love the yard. We put a six-foot fence along the front and are growing a hedge over it. We have a vine house in back with ferns and tuberous begonias. We have a large cineraria bed in bloom and the whole yard is alive with nasturtiums." The fence and the mattress vine blocked both prying eyes and sea winds that rustled his writing papers. John liked privacy.

The interior of the Eleventh Street house was compact: it became the setting for his first attempt at a play, "The Wizzard," written in 1930 or early 1931. According to Carol, this is an accurate description of the "shack" where they lived:

SCENE: A tiny living room of a compact little house. Rather run down. . . .
On each side hand made bookcases with uneven books, pamphlets, stacked
magazines—very messy. . . . There are Japanese prints . . . on the walls—none of
them very good nor very well hung. A kerosene heating stove is in the middle
of the room and, since only a student lamp is burning, when the scene opens,
it throws a porous pattern on the ceiling. . . . A low cheap table just off center
stage, a typewriter and a great many of those thick dark green and blue books
associated with college—designed apparently to give students a foretaste of the
importance and dullness of an education. Some of them are open and piled on
another which, since they are library books, is practically vandalism. During the
whole play there are pleasant traffic noises outside—not Gershwin noises but
the hum of an occasional motor and quite rarely a sounded horn. The house is
on a mildly trafficked street (phonograph records are very cheap . . .).

In John's postmarriage letters and prose, there is a physicality and expansiveness that suggests his satisfaction with marriage and homebuilding. Undoubtedly Carol relished this flurry of activity too. But she had moved into her mother-in-law's house and, as Olive decreed, slept with her new husband on the sunporch. Since interior decorating was curtailed, she rose to other domestic challenges—editorial, financial, and culinary. Putting food on the table called for all of Carol's resources. In January 1931, for example,

the couple lived nine days on $2.05, after Christmas "broke us." Carol pre-
pared creative rice dishes on the waning days and stirred up hamburger
gravy. "Only a fool would throw the juice away," John wrote years later in an
essay on the 1930s. "Browned flour added to it and we had delicious gravy."
The times demanded strategic adaptation. There was a report of John and
Carol mournfully sitting on the beach, having only enough money for a cup
of coffee, eagerly sharing strangers' picnic lunch when offered: they really
did struggle, said the friend. Before going to bed, the two often prepared a
"delicacy that they called 'depth bombs' which consisted of toast with lemon
juice and sliced garlic. They said it enabled them to sleep very well." Both
Carol and John were wizards with a can of beans. Her favorite was "Geb-
hart's chili beans mixed with lots of melted cheddar cheese and served on
toast," and John's was a "Starvation Special": cans of chili and beans mixed
together. The two ate a lot of beans—John joking that Carol's Mexican cooking would "make a normal woman pregnant, so potent is it." And the pair
gathered mushrooms from Jacks Peak (porcini, *Boletus edulis,* no doubt) and
bought cheap hamburger (twenty-five cents for three pounds on the weekends). Mid-decade Carol and a friend started to compile a cookbook, "101
Ways to Cook Hamburger."

And Carol learned to cook the fish she and John caught from their little
skiff, *Yancy* (although Carol called it the "Goon," since it looked like a comic
strip character that was half bird, half outlandish creature). The *Yancy* had
been purchased for thirty dollars and was stored—for free—at Hopkins
Marine Station. John snagged sardines and salmon, blue rockfish and squid,
sea trout and yellowtail near Point Pinos at the tip of the Bay. Sometimes the
couple feasted on abalone that friends dove for and pried off the rocks. Sometimes Italian fishermen took the two farther out into the Pacific. Sometimes
John and Carol hauled the skiff to the no parking area at Hopkins, set nets,
and came back the next morning to pull out nets crawling with fish. Sometimes they caught crabs off Pier #2 in Monterey. When John and Carol were
surprised by Fish and Game as they illegally dug for clams, Carol stuffed the
clams down her bra.

Buying bootleg liquor was a lark. On a small beach at Hopkins Marine
Station, clandestine booty might be safely landed, and one evening there was
"wholesome neighborly interest" as liquor was unloaded in thick fog. "Very
exciting," John reported. Most often the couple bought wine, twenty cents a
gallon, from one of Monterey's barrel houses (which also offered free sam-
ples). "It didn't kill us," John quipped later. Indeed, one visitor to the Pacific

Grove cottage said that the couple seemed to subsist on only French bread, wine, and fish.

Innovation and thrift and simplicity were prized.

These values helped make the Pacific Grove years John and Carol's happiest. Little routines cemented the newlyweds' bond—as they sought out whatever cheap entertainment the Peninsula afforded. Since Carol quickly landed a job as "secretary to the Secretary of the Chamber of Commerce of Monterey," one of their first outings was to the Monterey County Fair in August 1930, "with steeple chases and flat races which we patronized heavily on account Carol got a pass for the whole thing," he wrote to George Albee. (Albee, a young man he had met in Los Angeles, replaced Kate Beswick as his most intimate epistolary contact. John's letters to Albee had "a tendency to become essays.")

Five blocks away was Holman's Department Store, whose ads announced that it had "the most varied lines of any store between San Francisco and Los Angeles." John and Carol often trolled Holman's aisles, and the store was a favorite place to take guests. Undoubtedly the two watched the flagpole skater take residence at Holman's roof in 1932—the skater makes a cameo appearance in *Cannery Row*. And Carol and John loved to mock the likes of Zena Holman, wealthy and aloof, who represented the privileged life. John and Carol dubbed their own empty piggy bank "Zena."

During their first winter in Pacific Grove they "indulged" a few pennies in the luxury of a chessboard to "eat up the winter evenings." Both rolled their own cigarettes, John keeping a bowl of Bull Durham by his side. And John vowed to save money by giving up liquor and drinking only jasmine tea—a short-lived effort. Carol made Christmas gifts, stitching handkerchiefs. And listening to the radio cost nothing. Carol and John, as well as the Sheffields, were "addicted" to a fifteen-minute comedy that debuted in 1930, *Frank Watanabe and The Honorable Archie*, about a Japanese houseboy who referred to his boss, Archibald Chiselberry, as "The Honorable Archie."

Another favorite comedy, broadcast beginning in 1932, was Paul Rhymer's *Vic and Sade*, radio's "home folks" who lived with their son Rush in a "small house half-way up in the next block" in Cooper, Illinois. Vic was a bookkeeper for Consolidated Kitchenware Company, his lodge the Drowsy Venus Chapter of the Sacred Stars of the Milky Way. One of the wittiest shows on radio, voted the best soap in 1943, the comedy focused on the idiosyncrasies of small-town domestic life, undercutting those with power and status—like the town mayor. Ideal fare for John and Carol, who, like so many in the 1930s, turned to radio series for entertainment, laughter, and a brief respite from daily troubles. The show's humor was broad, dependent on odd juxtapositions and absurdities—"tall talk," notes historian Daniel Boorstin, speech in the American grain. Sade's gossiping friend was Ruthie Stembottom. Vic and Sade Gook knew a Rishigan Fishigan from Sishigan, Michigan, who married Jane Bane of Pane, Maine. On another episode, Vic defined love: "You can wear it on your head like a gauntlet glove, you may throw it to the four winds like canned salmon; or you may rub it in your hair like potato peelings. In the end it always narrows down to the same thing—vanilla." A lovely and absurd reflection. One can imagine John and Carol hunkered over Mr. Steinbeck's radio, laughing merrily. John may have drawn from radio's participatory techniques in his own prose. The domestic dramas on radio seemed to address audiences directly with witty back-and-forth dialogue. That's precisely what Steinbeck was most conscious of in his own prose, sharp and simple sentences, participation of readers, and an audience that, beginning in the early 1930s, he addressed directly, selecting a friend or relative as his intended audience. (Throughout his career, John appreciated popular entertainers and artists who connected viscerally with fans. He later wrote essays on Woody Guthrie, Gypsy Rose Lee, Al Capp, jazz musician Eddie Condon, and Bob Hope.) There was also a strong oral tradition in the Steinbeck family that made a deep imprint on his prose. Just as his mother had read Greek myths to him, John read to others. He wanted readers to feel, connect, experience.

John also loved Milton Caniff's *Terry and the Pirates* (the first strip in 1934), particularly Dragon Lady, "a powerful but prickly woman," not unlike Carol herself.

"For entertainment we had the public library, endless talk, long walks, any number of games," John wrote thirty years later. "We played music, sang and made love. Enormous invention went into our pleasures."

On Sunday afternoons, the couple, carless by mid-1931, drove Mr. and Mrs. Steinbeck in their new Buick "into the hills"—undoubtedly to Jacks Peak near the bay, to Point Lobos on the Pacific coast, or along the Salinas River Road to Soledad Mission. That tradition was not too onerous since Carol enjoyed Mr. Steinbeck. But Olive could be ornery. She and Carol were cut from the same cross-grained cloth, with sharp and forceful personalities. Both were highly opinionated, both loved to argue. Undoubtedly John and Carol wrangled with as much pleasure as John, Mary, and Olive had around the dinner table when he was young. Occasionally John and Carol had time to themselves with gentle Mr. Steinbeck, who helped around the Eleventh

Street house, brought meat from Salinas, and, on one occasion at least, in the spring of 1931, took John and Carol to Lake Tahoe on one of his twice yearly trips in an armored car to deliver money in person to the state treasury: "The meadows will be flaming with flowers," wrote an excited John. Mr. Steinbeck was as proud of his son as Carol was, painstakingly binding in leather John's first novel, *Cup of Gold,* and buying up the plates when the publisher, McBride, went belly up. Although distance from Salinas was welcome, John was close to his parents and sisters, and Carol did her best to fit in. Every month they went to Salinas to use Mrs. Steinbeck's Maytag washer and dry and iron clothes while visiting with the family. All three of John's sisters liked Carol, particularly warm and personable Beth, eight years older than John.

Dogs were a necessity, not a luxury, in the impoverished Steinbeck household, then and throughout the marriage. After Bruga was poisoned in Los Angeles, John and Carol bought a "darling little Airedale," named "Tylie Eulenspiegel," after Till Eulenspiegel, the German trickster figure who, in picaresque stories, exposed the world's follies. Carol was crazy about dogs, not soupy but affectionate and kind; they took the place of children. In scrapbooks she kept during the 1930s people are rarely identified beneath their photos, but dogs always are. John, on the other hand, tended to enforce dog behavior firmly and a bit erratically. His friend Ed Ricketts described him as "very strict and Prussian . . . but affectionate with dogs," and another friend said, more darkly, that John needed a dog to dominate. John was certainly attentive to dog personality, nearly as much so as to human foibles. Tillie, he wrote to Albee, is "stalking a moth on the floor and she will eat it and it will make her sick because moths always make her sick. No other kind of bug does, only moths." He taught Tillie—a dog that hated waves—to dive into the ocean. A few months later, he pulled out all of Tillie's whiskers to "strengthen their growth," as he wrote to Albee. "She looks like hell now. We are ashamed to be seen with her." John reported all of Tillie's accomplishments, drawing humor from each. When she ate a quart of bacon grease, he noted that a "stomach ache and a bad conscience are ruffling her ordinarily volatile disposition." Spoiled dogs and smelly dogs, family dogs and dignified dogs flop down in Steinbeck's books, in his letters, in his jokes: "That dog doesn't look so good," remarked Stanford friend Bob Cathcart when he came for a visit one weekend. "Fact is," said John "the dog's got a hell of a hangover." John planned to write stories about Tillie as soon as she had puppies for him to watch.

Beloved Tillie only tolerated interlopers. In 1931 John and Carol spent their "amusement quota for this month" on two mallard ducks for the garden, Aqua and Vita. Carol "hated to go to work this morning," he wrote Albee, because the ducks were "so interesting. They do not ever step on the plants— just edge between on their big clumsy feet. . . . You never saw anything so beautiful in all the greenness of our garden as these luxurious ducks." The ducks lasted only a few weeks, alas. Although lovely, they unearthed lobelias and muddied the pond.

But the fact that John and Carol wanted ducks points to the fun-loving sensibilities that bound the couple and helped push them through the slough of the Depression. John's laughter ran deep. He wrote to Albee in 1930, for example, about a character in a new novel he was writing, an old man who "breaks wind almost constantly. I have precedent for the fart in literature in many data besides Mark Twain's attempt. . . . I might say that you can judge a man by the way he breaks wind as surely as you can by his English or the timbre of his voice. You have heard vulgar raucous farts, just as you have heard little mincing affected ones, the sinister whisper, the underhand or gum shoe fart, the Pegasus or whistling fart, the brutal or detonating fart, the flaccid blubbering variety, the mean crabbed pinched fart which indi- cates the miser even of wind." That madcap sensibility is an important vein in Steinbeck's prose—in books, letters, journals. He was a teller of jokes, a concoctor of pranks, a whimsical gift-giver and a ham. His humor was often a little bawdy, especially if he thought he could shock people. "That scar on my shoulder, got that when copulating with a Mexican woman."

And Carol's jaunty humor charmed John. With obvious pleasure, he would observe her in a room of people, taking center stage with her "amazing," if also caustic wit. Often the two were "witty together. Both loved to come up with schemes. Both loved to poke fun at friends." Carol clipped John Held car- toons from the New Yorker and continued her sketching, pinning both New Yorker covers and her own drawings on the bathroom walls. In Pacific Grove she began a hilarious series on pink nude sportswomen—one beefy woman per sheet. Women leapt from diving boards ("The Swan), hurled the discus, ran footraces ("The Fugitive"). These were extravagant women of action, hardly a cultural ideal. Her art celebrated the oversize female body and over- sized Carol wit. One Christmas she sent friends cards from her series—a lady Santa dumping out a galvanized iron garbage can, decorated with tinsel and holly: "Bringing Christmas to the piggies," she wrote beneath. (Charlie Chap- lin framed a few of her drawings, and Pascal Covici, John's editor from the mid-1930s on, considered publishing a book of her sketches, probably with

Chaplin's promise of financial backing for the text.) Much later Carol would describe her artistic output as "all caricatures. . . . I see things that way."

Dogs and ducks and fart jokes and pink athletes surrounded the toilet. The scrappy couple was poor and happy. She improvised and was resolute and supportive and cheerful. John worked doggedly on his fiction, discarding "Dissonant Symphony," rewriting, "To an Unknown God," and composing pulp fiction with a "burlesque tone" that he hoped might sell. Over and over he said in letters that characters "are my own children," Carol's children too, they felt. John appreciated Carol's sacrifices and devotion, writing to a friend: "She grows visibly in understanding, in culture, in kindness and in erudition. She understands many things more quickly and more thoroughly than I do. And the old defiance, which came from young wounds and disappointments, is wearing off. She is grand. I would have great difficulty in living without her now." And to Carl Wilhelmson, who was contemplating marriage, he wrote this about his own union:

> When I married Carol my friends, excluding you who knew her, were hostile. I think you will agree that I was as restless, as filled with wanderlust as you are although mine was probably more vocal than otherwise. My reputation for a bad and touchy disposition out shown yours. In spite of those things, I have been happier than I ever was before and I have done four times as much work as I ever did before. The first is probably dependent upon the second. . . . There are hard times in being married but nothing that compares with the abysmal feeling of loneliness and lostness.

As he himself recognized, as many, many friends recognized, Carol was his ideal partner in the 1930s.

Bare-bones living was unavoidable in a household where Carol worked sporadically and John earned nothing, but it was essential to their companionate marriage. Their bond was cemented by shared sacrifices and equality of effort. Every month, twenty-five dollars of Carol's wages went to the couple's shared expenses; "of course" Carol supports herself, John wrote to Amasa Miller in June 1931. (Mr. Steinbeck covered John's share, another twenty-five dollars a month, because he had promised that if his son published a book, funds would continue.) Shared poverty, androgynous dress, incisive humor, and a joint mission—John's art—brought out the best in both, cemented their bond.

"These years of leanness are probably the best things on earth for me," John wrote to Carl Wilhelmson in August 1931. "I am as convinced as ever that eventually I shall do very fine work." If financially their life was a mess, spiritually, "we ride the clouds."

Carol was eager to find jobs. The eight-hundred-square-foot house was cramped—and John filled it, writing daily at the kitchen table or on a portable table in the living room. When her secretarial job ended, she found another position interviewing Mexican laborers for the Monterey Chamber of Commerce. And sometimes, whenever she was restless in tiny Pacific Grove, she went to San Francisco and worked as a nude model for a group of artists. But in December of 1930, she landed her most fulfilling job, her own advertising agency, an endeavor that drew on many of her best traits—skills entrepreneurial, secretarial, artistic. A month into the venture, John, the nominal head of the agency to thwart any "anti-feminist propaganda," wrote Albee that the agency "made a good profit. . . . She is enjoying it so much. It is the thing she has always wanted to do." Once again, Carol reenvisioned herself, now as entrepreneur. One measure of her marital happiness was, in fact, how sharply defined and satisfying was her work.

Her partner was Beth Ingels, whom Carol had met when both worked for the *San Francisco Chronicle*. Both had "extensive experience in advertising and publicity." Carol and Beth understood one another, admired each other's talent, and shared an offbeat humor—a characteristic of most of Carol and John's friends. Beth loved books and words and scorned proprieties, as did Carol and John. She read "two or three books a night," said her brother, and "hated to go to funerals and hated to go to church." She took to hanging her Christmas tree upside down from the ceiling of her home. Beth was a character, a woman known by many on the Peninsula, someone who played a mean hand of bridge and who had a "kookie, dry" wit. Beth's "remarks were always interesting—if sometimes caustic," said another. She had a "sharp tongue," noted her editor. To Francis Whitaker, the Carmel blacksmith, Beth was a "strange character in a way—very independent . . . but a lot of fun. She was outgoing, gregarious, a good conversationalist." It's hardly surprising that she and Carol hit it off. They were foils, bickering and challenging and stimulating one another. The woman who drank "like a fish," who had one long-standing relationship with sculptor Peg Carroll, who was fully accepted as a lesbian by the group of artists and writers who hung out with John and Carol, who longed to publish her own fiction but never did, and who made others laugh gleefully would have a marked impact both on Carol Steinbeck's contentment and on John Steinbeck's writing.

Like John, Beth had deep roots in Monterey County. She spent her earliest years in Monterey and then moved to the Salinas Valley—a Corral de Tierra ranch east of Monterey, not far where Steinbeck's Aunt Molly had lived. John had run cattle in the valley when he was young and had played knights and squire with Mary under towering Castle Rock, and had, no doubt, searched for the reputed hillside hideout of nineteenth-century Californio bandit Tiburcio Vasquez (mentioned in *The Pastures of Heaven*, his book of stories about the locale). Beth attended Monterey High School, where she took courses from Spanish teacher Sue Gregory—one of the women who told Steinbeck countless tales about Monterey's paisanos—and she was editor in chief of the school paper, graduating in 1923, a year before Carol. After high school, Beth went to the University of California at Berkeley, worked briefly in advertising, and then returned to the Monterey Peninsula to become the first advertising director for Holman's department store. Keenly interested in world events as well as local history and culture, she then became a journalist, writing for various local papers—*All Arts Gossip, Pacific Grove Tide, Carmel Pine Cone, Monterey Herald,* and *Pacific Grove Tribune*—and at one point she edited her own paper in Carmel Valley, *The Paisano.* Everyone on the Peninsula knew Beth.

She mined local history and wrote stories for area newspapers recounting tales of Monterey's past—Vasquez as bandit, or how William Tecumseh Sherman, stationed in Monterey in 1846, wooed a local woman, Senorita María Ygnacia Bonifacio. Beth's sense of history was layered—with tales of priests and lovers, Indians and soldiers. But if she supported herself as a journalist, she also longed to write fiction. Her notebooks include plotlines for tales that eerily parallel Steinbeck's interests. Dogs: "Anecdotes and Ideas, A parody of serious dog books, with photos of dogs doing things they shouldn't. First chapter on Heide, outlining her points, methods of training with no results, pictures . . . Picture of Heide rolling garbage can . . . with sweater on for morning workout. . . . Fox-hunting—at the kill—with toy animal." And she planned to tell the story of Honey, a dog who "retrieves rocks" and sits in flowers. And Apples and the Nazi. And the "dog conference every morning at the mouth of [the Carmel] river." Beth loved wonky dogs, John's métier as well.

She also sketched a "Series of tales about C.D.T. [Corral de Tierra] and country childhood: 1. War and a Country School 2. Bobbed Hair 3. They Talk in their sleep 4. Spinach and Joe Mathias 5. School election." Beth's outline is not, of course, John's book *The Pastures of Heaven,* but there is no doubt that his inspiration came from Beth's projected series about the valley where she grew up.

Much has been written about John "using" others' material—"stealing" is sometimes the charge. To some it seems an apt accusation. Over the years, friends and associates would accuse Steinbeck of filching: a story told to him by a childhood friend's mother, Edith Wagner, became "How Edith McGillicuddy met R.L.S." (Robert Louis Stevenson); his sister Mary wrote a story about their mother Olive's World War I airplane ride, which she sent to *Reader's Digest* years before John included the family tale in *East of Eden*. Indeed, Mary threatened, with mock seriousness, to sue her older brother.

Reviewing his writing during the decade he was married to Carol gives a similar impression of indebtedness. John imported story lines. Unlike William Faulkner, he did not have a mind that teemed with overlapping narratives and histories. He relied on inspiration, and that inspiration was dependent on the group dynamics of the phalanx. Consider: His first novel, *Cup of Gold* (1929), was historical, drawing from accounts of the pirate Henry Morgan as well as the Grail myth. His second, *To a God Unknown* (1933), began life as a friend's play, "The Green Lady," which he and Toby Street, a college friend, discussed at length. His third, *The Pastures of Heaven* (1932), leaned on Beth's narratives. Many of the short stories collected in *The Long Valley* (1938) were based on Salinas gossip; the Williams sisters, for example, told him local tales, including their family scandal that would become "Johnny Bear." His fourth novel, *Tortilla Flat* (1935), relied in part on stories told by Beth Ingels's Spanish teacher Susan Gregory, who lived next door to the prototype for Danny, and by Hattie Gragg, an elderly woman who lived in downtown Monterey and frequently entertained John with local lore. Hattie also told him "the best story in the world" in 1938, "the tripes of Josh Billings. I must write this some time," he wrote in his journal. He eventually did, as a chapter of *Cannery Row*. His fifth book, *In Dubious Battle* (1936), grew out of interviews with strike organizers—others' firsthand experiences. His sixth, *Of Mice and Men* (1937), was reportorial, if John tells it true, and is based on a scene he had witnessed years earlier, a troubled man killing a straw boss. And the final book of the decade, *The Grapes of Wrath* (1939), was launched shortly after John read camp manager Tom Collins's reports of migrant labor in California. Although John had been working as a journalist covering migrant housing in California, the key stimulus to creation of both the "Harvest Gypsies" newspaper articles (October 1936) and *Grapes* came first from Tom's reports, conversations, and tours. (And there was a nasty and suppressed accusation that the germ of Casy's story came from an unpublished manuscript, "Daonda," that was sent in 1936 or '37 to Covici-Friede by Taylor

Gordon. Covici had published Gordon's memoir about the Harlem Renaissance, *Born to Be* (1929). In 1940, Taylor tried to sue Covici after *Grapes* was published, claiming that Steinbeck plagiarized from "Daonda," which begins with a preacher on the road.) Finally *Sea of Cortez*, published in 1941, was collaborative, based largely on Edward F. Ricketts's log and field notes of their 1940 trip to the Gulf of California.

To recognize that Steinbeck mined sources need not compromise his achievements or undercut his talent—but it does help clarify the participatory impetus that was crucial to his imagination. Although Beth Ingels seemed as eager as John to write local stories, her voice was not his, her command of language not his, her mythic and ecological vision not his, and the urgency of conveying "felt" experience was his, not hers. As one friend noted, Beth lacked discipline, was a little lazy. Other ideas she had were never fully realized, one about Monterey's Mexican neighborhood (known as Tortilla Flat/s in many California towns). In 1932 Beth sent "Romance on Tortilla Flat" to *Woman's Home Companion*. In manuscript, the story begins:

> High up on a hill behind the town, behind the pretentious mansions of the rich, lies Tortilla Flat. Downtown the businessmen struggle to 'put the town on the map' by tearing down those adobes that interfere with their ideas for growth and progress. But Tortilla Flat is not disturbed by this hustle and activity. A dirty road still winds in and out through the pines and manzanita. Fat Spanish women still sit and doze on the front porches of their tiny white-washed shacks each afternoon, while their black-eyed children play in the dirt with shabby dogs.

Beth sketched plans for more paisano stories—"Palomino Pete, The Pirate, Dog Gone"—but never wrote them. That raw material would soon become John's: the locale on a hill above Monterey (which, in fact, was where Tortilla Flat was located), the loafing Spanish workers who embraced a different time-sense than Anglo Monterey, and the well-known local tramp named "Old Shakey," who lived in a one-room shack with twenty dogs and bragged that those dogs could sing better than Bing Crosby. (After Old Shakey tried to shoot someone who threatened his dog, he went to trial and was placed in an asylum.) If setting, gentle class fission, and at least one character in Beth's outline are identical to Steinbeck's, it's also true that Beth did not finish the series of stories she planned. Steinbeck did.

She also wrote a novella called "Cannery Row." Beth's "Cannery Row," written in the late 1930s, is a fifteen-thousand-word, first-person novella about efforts to organize cannery workers. Unlike Steinbeck's twilight world of Cannery Row denizens, Beth's manuscript treats a daylight world of harsh managers, disputes between fishermen and cannery owners "about the price of fish for the season," and simmering labor tensions, "our own little war" that made Hitler's movement toward Poland seem "far away." As the story opens, her female narrator, working as a sardine packer, is making do: "When you are learning the work you cut your hands a lot on the cans as they come by, and the woman in charge of the girls bandages your cuts. Sometimes you don't take your hands away quickly enough, and then the blood drops on the sardines. When this happens everyone laughs and says it will never show when the tomato sauce is added. You learn, though, and when you are as experienced as I am you can make around two and a half a day."

The story taps into the ethnic diversity of cannery workers: Nuni, the boss, is an Italian who "swaggers up and down the floor like a miniature Mussolini. He has the job of manager because his uncle owns most of the stock in the cannery." The narrator and Jack, her boyfriend, are white workers; their friends, Ramon and Maria, are Mexican; Ito is a Japanese fisherman, befriended only by Jack and the narrator. Beth's story blends ethnic and class tensions with a fine sensitivity to the workers' powerlessness, be they white, Mexican, or Japanese. Hers is a sociological study of Monterey's 1930s cannery workers. John's *Cannery Row* is about a twilight ecosystem revealed only when business was done, when the tide went out revealing the specimens: Mack and the bums, Dora Flood and her girls, Doc and Frankie and the Malloys—fringe dwellers all. Only in title and locale, in fact, are the two works similar.

The resonance between Beth's material and John's, however, suggests the intimacy of three creative and liberal souls who shared a fascination with regional issues and people, histories and legends. Their experiences overlapped. Carol brought Beth to the house knowing that John would enjoy her stories—and also thought that her friend knew what she was getting into when talking freely to a novelist. John was a "lint picker," Carol declared. He admitted to being a "shameless magpie" who mimicked sounds, stories, events. He "sponged up" knowledge, facts, humors, "what have you, from every place and from everybody," said a friend later, and those stories heard and reportorial scraps were woven into all his writing. While the catalogue of Beth's and John's overlapping titles is fodder for those who would call him a "cagey cribber," as did F. Scott Fitzgerald (complaining that *Of Mice and Men* was lifted from Frank Norris's *McTeague*), he was no cribber. Yes, he relied on Beth's material for *The Pastures of Heaven*. In particular, his Malloy family is modeled on a real family, the McCoys, who were surrounded by "a kind of cloud of unintentional evil," as Steinbeck wrote a friend. "Everything they touched went rotten, every institution they joined broke up in hatred." Beth had told him about the McCoys, but admitted that "I could never write them like John did." John had the raw talent and the fierce sense of purpose that Beth lacked, and she accepted that—at least in the 1930s and 1940s. (Even after John divorced Carol, Beth remained his friend.) Ed Ricketts's sister, Frances Strong, had another perspective on John's fascination with others' stories: "If John got events and personal affairs that belonged to other people mixed up with his own it was not exactly lying—but it was because he was so interested in it . . . certainly anything that was very important to another person interested John very intensely."

"Participation" was one of the most significant terms Steinbeck and his friend Ed Ricketts discussed. Although writing was a lonely act, as he reiterated throughout his career, inspiration was mutual, based on a group dynamic, participation with another—his mother reading aloud, friends telling stories, Carol nudging and critiquing and discussing ideas, Ricketts sparking philosophical debate. Through discussion and epistolary exchanges, Steinbeck honed ideas. What theoretical biologist Stuart Kauffman notes as essential to the "creative matrix of life"—mutualism and group selection —were key to Steinbeck's creativity. Indeed, the deepest source of Steinbeck's art was ecological, based not on a Darwinian model of competition, but on connectivity.

As Carol's business partner in the ad agency, Beth helped with a project that Carol hoped would fare better than the "Faster Master Plaster Casters"— a directory of Carmel businesses. In January 1931, Steinbeck reported proudly that the two had "no competitors on the peninsula" and were "raising hell with business proceedings. . . . A pair of cutthroats they are. . . . They are having a lot of fun." The purpose of their Carmel directory was to "answer the most important questions that are asked of the village." In many ways, it was a superb plan. A rather sleepy town in the 1930s with "a quality of being on a dead end, like a cul de sac," Carmel, home to artists and writers, had no directory. Before the Holman Highway linking Pacific Grove and Carmel was constructed in the mid-1930s, the only way to reach Carmel was to take Highway 1 from Monterey—and the hill out of Monterey was much steeper than today. (Mack and the boys' car couldn't make it up the hill in *Cannery Row* for good reason.) The little community of Carmel felt isolated, the last town on Highway 1 before the road curved along the coast to Big Sur. As outpost and artistic mecca, the village had an undeniable charm. Streets were dirt, electric streetlights nonexistent, and houses built of board and batten, all without street numbers, and sidewalks were boardwalks. Ocean Avenue, the town's broad central street, ran straight from Highway 1 to the pristine white beach that had drawn artists and writers to this spot early in the century— including Jack London and Mary Austin and poet George Sterling. Artists liked that dead-end, secluded quality of Carmel, and there was "lots of talent" in town, said local blacksmith Francis Whitaker, and a good measure of "tolerance, live and let live," as well as a certain "freedom of ideas and expression. Anyone could talk . . . a wonderful free time. Beth Ingels in a dirty T-shirt could rub elbows with anyone in an evening gown." It was, as California historian Kevin Starr notes, "an early example of the leisure community."

After trudging through the streets, knocking on doors, begging for ads, contacting artists for ink drawings, alphabetizing and typing, Beth and Carol published their idiosyncratic directory in June 1931. For one, the residential listing is by cottage name, not resident, perhaps working on the assumption that the cottages were more permanent that the residents, or perhaps thus avoiding knocking on all doors to create a directory. Only unnamed cottages—those sad little places—were identified by owner's name. A directory of businesses is also a prominent feature, thus combining, in effect, the yellow and white pages. The editors' personalities are apparent in their introductory column: "Carmel by the Sea is a surprising place," which "surprised" Spanish priest Junipero Serra as well as David Starr Jordan (Stanford University's first president, who made a land survey of the area) and developers J. F. Devendorf and Frank Powers, the men who developed the town as an artist colony in 1903, luring "Teachers and Brain Workers at Indoor Employment." Carmel's early "milk shrines," placed every one to two blocks for delivery of milk, also "surprised" visitors, as did the town bulletin board. "All in all," the introductory list of surprises concludes wryly, "Carmel has used more energy in its attempt to remain unpretentious than most small towns use in striving to become business centers."

In other columns the tone is warm and personal: "Carmel is governed wisely and well by a Board of Trustees, headed by Herbert Heron, poet, playwright, producer and business man, as mayor." The police force is described as "the most careful and conscientious police force in the country." Gentle advice is administered: "if a person just wants to know the time or the date or where to find Mrs. So and So, they are asked please not to phone Carmel 100"—the police department hotline—"because this number both sounds the alarm and rings the phones in the houses of fire and police officials." And the centerfold features a foldout map as well as "A personally conducted tour of Carmel-by-the-Sea," where it is clear that shops have been inspected by the writers. A clear favorite is The Sign of the Papoose on San Carlos, deserving of a separate mention, probably because the store paid heavily for back-cover advertising. So did the Sierra Quarry, office on San Carlos; it garnered special mention for supplying "chalk rock" to "the Carmel Building Stone Company": "Mr. Rogers has some interesting specimens of plant and animal life in the fossils which have been found in the quarry. Antelope bones were discovered there in a fossil formation at one time." The eclectic publication notes art gallery openings, the bus schedules, and "Who's Who" in the town. There are columns on "Education" and the "Library" and "Edward Weston," a photographer famous for having been mentioned in the "January 17 number of the *Saturday Review of Literature*." Indeed, Carol and Beth's illustrated publication, charmingly incomplete (the two authors admit at the end that it would take "several volumes" to cover Carmel), is populist in intention—its audience both residents and visitors and its scope a useful overview. It was Carol's first published text.

A few years later, Carol wrote a poem about the town of cottages, several of the most unusual of which were inspired by fairy tales:

To Carmel
Cunningly you moulded
The soulless wood and stone,
In each brick enfolded
The soul that was your own.

Gay turrets rose, and spires,
Fancies from Mother Goose,
All of childhood's desires,
Blithely running loose.

A charcoal burner's clearing
Found in a magic wood,
Each faggot house endearing
A fairy wish made good.

John claimed never to like Carmel, scoffing that the town was full of artistic poseurs concerned only with sales, and Carol more or less agreed. "My own mood is not too good," John wrote in June 1931, as Carol was completing her project. "I see the people in Carmel deluding themselves that they can write. Perhaps I am deluding myself. Maybe these things I am working on are as worthless as the work of the Carmelites. One can't tell. They are just as earnest as I am. I don't think they work so hard, but maybe they do." The village represented a kind of foil to him: artificiality flourished there, while he cultivated authenticity in his prose and in his stance as a serious writer.

Nonetheless, John was happy working long hours while Carol was tramping around Carmel with Beth. Carol "gets prettier all the time," he wrote to Albee. "I'm more in love with her than I ever was. Sometimes I waken in the night with the horrible feeling that she is gone. I shouldn't want to live if she were." He was living, he admitted, "almost the perfect life."

So was Carol, no doubt, although without extant letters or a diary, she must be seen through John's prism and others' recollections. It cannot have been easy to be married to John Steinbeck, a man obsessed with words. "Carol and I were married tentatively and we like the state," he writes. "Of course it is habit but it removes a lot of troubles and leaves more time for work." Work absorbed him utterly, as countless letters and journal entries attest to. Surely he must have worked harder at his writing than any Carmelite, save poet Robinson Jeffers. The word itself—"work"—strikes a drumbeat in his letters. Both waking and dreaming moments, he admitted, were taken up with his work: "The troubles of hypothetical people overshadow my own." Composing a novel, he admitted, didn't cease when he put down the pen: "You'll be having dreams about it that wake you in the night, and maybe you'll be kissing some girl the way she expects it, and all the time your mind will be saying, 'I'll do the thing this way, and I'll transpose these scenes.'" That peek into the bedroom suggests a mind detached, writing, in effect, 24-7. Once seized with an idea, John retreated to his own mind, the shadowy regions that excluded all others.

Years later, when he was counseling his sister Mary about how to complete a play she was writing, he explained his own writing, the fullest account extant:

> You have your basic story—that's what it is going to be about. Then set aside a certain time of day—say two hours in the morning. I take more but it isn't necessary. You think about the people until you can see them—all of them— how they dress, the tone of their voices, what their hands are like, where they come from. You go way back in their lives to little episodes you won't use in the story at all. Then—gradually you let them begin to talk in your mind until you

know how they speak and why they say what they do. Now you start thinking about them in bed before you go to sleep. You let things happen to them and see how they will react. And then you begin fitting them to the episodes of your story and then you are ready to start writing. Then you hold yourself down to a certain time or a certain word rate per day. I use the latter. If you don't do that you will get excited and anxious to finish. In a long novel it goes on for months or years. And then pretty soon it is done and you feel terrible. But that's one way to write them. . . . Try that two hours of thinking about your play. You'll see how quickly the people become real people. You've got to see every bit of them or you can't make a reader see them. And, oddly enough, the reader will too, even the things you don't put down.

After earning money all day at one of her jobs, Carol returned home often enough to dejected John, still writing, his mood black because his characters wouldn't come to life. John brooded over the "pictures" in his mind and the little dramas that played out there (many of his fictional characters mention actors and internal dramas, like Mary Teller in "The White Quail" or Lennie seeing a Big Rabbit). In a private journal, Stanford classmate Toby Street complained about John's dark solipsism, asserting that his friend needed to get out more: "I envy JS his poverty. He has always been poor and he always will be. What he needs now is a change of environment and a new desire to keep his eyes open. He is steeping too much in his own thoughts—imagining incongruous little incidents and writing them down. They have no relation to life, or at least too little." In 1930 and 1931 John received rejection after rejection for those little pieces: "The editors of this magazine cannot take time to encourage unknown writers," one letter read. John pinned that one on his wall. Throughout his life Steinbeck had moody spells. He was depressive, a "perfect Pisces" said his third wife. The power of blackness sometimes overwhelmed him—evident in journals he kept throughout his writing life where he confessed to looming despair. Most Americans, he believed, hid from the deeper places of the mind and thus would never be drawn to his kind of fiction, stories that challenged a reader's compassion and understanding. Yet in the slow months of 1931 he forced himself day after day to continue with short stories—putting off completion of the longer fiction, the "Unknown God" manuscript, because he might sell a story, and thus earn money and self-confidence. In the early 1930s, John was, so to speak, playing a nickel slot machine, waiting for the payoff to get him to the big table. A disciplined work life would get him there, he wagered. Each morning he sat down to write until four o'clock. As he worked in the central room of the tiny cottage, staring at the little garden, he admitted to Albee that he didn't "like to write [stories]. They don't let me stretch. Writing them is like sleeping on an army cot." Much of 1931 was spent in that procrustean bed, wrestling with tales that kept getting "in each other's way." By December 1931, however, a manuscript he was "quite pleased with" was ready to send to his New York agents, *The Pastures of Heaven*.

Carol helped him untangle those stories that tripped over one another; she suggested the unifying device of the Monroe family for *Pastures*. She was an indispensable editor, filling a role similar to that performed by Una Jeffers for her poet husband, Robinson Jeffers, living on the Carmel coast, writing about Big Sur: "She never saw any of my poems until they were finished and typed," Jeffers wrote, "yet by her presence and conversation she has co-authored every one of them. Sometimes I think there must be some value in them, if only for that reason." Carol's presence and conversation were equally as essential to John's creativity. He needed a sanctuary, which she provided, and a creative foil, her role as well. Her gaiety muted his dark moods. And he needed an editor and a sounding board. That she was too. Carol willingly accepted all roles necessary to the creative process. In letters to friends, John always wrote that "we" worked on manuscripts. Carol brought home jokes and stories that became a part of *Tortilla Flat*. She came up with the unifying theme of the Round Table for that little book. She gave *Of Mice and Men* its title. She "willed" *The Grapes of Wrath* into being. Sometimes in those first months in Pacific Grove when he received rejection after rejection, she'd call him a "stupid Irish bastard" for not realizing how good he was. "Stubborn Kraut," she'd add, don't you see your talent? She nudged and bullied him to carry on writing.

Creativity was circular for Steinbeck, a process of engaging and disengaging, from participatory inspiration to the isolation of work. When writing, he surfaced to read manuscripts aloud to Carol, to friends. Carol was always his first reader, first participant, first listener who savored each work. "Our minds are somewhat drawn together," Steinbeck would admit a couple of years later, "so that we see with the same eyes and feel with the same emotions." Completion of the circle was his anticipation of a wider audience who would "participate" in his work. Steinbeck wrote to George Albee that he wanted the stories in *The Pastures of Heaven* "to put a kind of charm on the reader. He may forget what they are about, but I'd like him to remember how he felt as he read them. I'd like that feeling to be one of warmth and almost deific tolerance." That "charm" is the keying mechanism of his art, the emotional resonance that reaches deep streams in readers' psyches.

For Christmas 1931, John acknowledged gender equity and bought Carol a gift that was his highest compliment to her capabilities and camaraderie, "a 22 rifle, a little beauty." Perhaps the gun was a tribute to her pluck or a necessary firearm for hunting trips the two planned—John had grown up shooting rabbits and gophers. But the present is emblematic as well: Carol drew a bead on life, racing into the world with rifle in hand, so to speak, vigorous, energetic, engaged, loving the world "so much" said John. And he loved that quality in her—Carol "was unabashed by anything."

CHAPTER FOUR

At Ed Ricketts's Lab

THE STORY OF CAROL AND JOHN STEINBECK is enmeshed with that of marine biologist Edward F. Ricketts, a remarkable man whose scientific curiosity was as deep as his philosophical ruminations; whose love of Walt Whitman's poetry and Gregorian chants was as palpable as his tolerance for nearly everyone who entered his orbit. From 1930 to 1948, the year Ricketts was hit by a train rumbling through New Monterey, he was Steinbeck's most intimate male companion. When Ed died, Steinbeck buried part of his own soul. While Ed lived, he was the third element in a creative triad, a tight and vibrant phalanx—Carol, John, Ed—whose emergent voices would resonate in all the books that John Steinbeck wrote during the 1930s. Scores of friends from that era insist that without Carol and Ed, John Steinbeck would never have developed into the writer he did. That duo of comrade and wife steadied and stimulated, absorbed and provoked him.

When he met John and Carol Steinbeck in 1930, Ed Ricketts owned a biological supply laboratory that was wedged between sardine canneries on Ocean View Avenue in New Monterey, more commonly known as Cannery Row—an enclave of canneries and reduction plants, little Chinese stores and brothels and cafes and houses for cannery workers and superintendents alike. Ed started the business in 1923, when he and his wife Anna first came to the Monterey Peninsula from Chicago. With his partner, Albert Galigher, Ed opened a laboratory and collected marine specimens, mainly from the California coast, sending animals to high school and college science classes for study and dissection. Although Ed's first lab was in Pacific Grove, he moved his lab to Cannery Row in July 1928, and the clapboard structure at 800 Ocean View Avenue eventually became his home and lab as well as a local salon, a hub for parties, a place of wild enthusiasms, and a retreat for anyone interested in serious conversation or a cold beer.

As Steinbeck described Ed through the character Doc in *Cannery Row*, he looked "half Christ and half satyr," which was true in art and in life. Ed was a lonely and "set apart man" who sometimes plummeted to the same inner blackness that Steinbeck did, who had a phobia about rats, and who insisted that "people who are concerned with 'the eternal verities' would do well to remember that fun is one of them." Ed was a paradox, as Steinbeck described him, a "very complicated man." He had "a genius for human relationships," said Toni Jackson, his common-law wife of the 1940s, a man sought out by legions, an innovative scientist, a vivid presence, an enigma.

Like Danny and his house in *Tortilla Flat,* complex Ed and his hybrid lab were one entity, real and mythic. His lab was a homeplace, "a haven," insisted one friend, that, like Steinbeck's description of Cannery Row, held the gathered and the scattered, Carol and John included. The centripetal pull of compassionate, kindly Ed held disparate parts together, a mix of people, a network of ideas, a tapestry of music and philosophical speculation and antic maneuvers. In Steinbeck's art, Ed's presence is centrifugal, projecting outward into myth, the Doc of "The Snake" and *Cannery Row* and *Sweet Thursday* and the musical *Pipe Dream.*

Five years older than John, slight of build, gauntly handsome and ever curious, Ed Ricketts drew people to him magnetically—not only Carol and John, but also artists, writers, and friends both wise and ridiculous. And women, many women. (He took most to bed—including Carol in 1940, one friend insisted.) Local and visiting scientists from nearby Hopkins Marine Station went to Ed's to talk about invertebrates, and bums who squatted in abandoned pipes across from his Cannery Row lab or lived under wharfs put the touch on Ed for money, dropping by the front door to ask if Ed needed frogs—like Mack from *Cannery Row* and *Sweet Thursday.* He "took under his wing" a friendless little boy, ill-fed, ravaged by eczema, slow to understand, who became Frankie in *Cannery Row,* the forlorn boy who loves Doc. He befriended Won Yee, who owned a Cannery Row grocery with a gambling room in back, and engaged the Chinese man in philosophical discussions. All found refuge in Ed's attentiveness and sweet temperament. Rolf Bolin, a professor at Stanford University's Hopkins Marine Station, put it best—Bolin "went over there for the purpose of feeling better."

Ed demonstrated an evenhanded acceptance of folly and eccentricity, wit and pedantry, extravagance and neediness. Typically he would greet visitors to his laboratory cordially, hand them a glass of wine, and want to know what everyone had seen and done and heard lately. Gatherings were lively, often just "fun and games, with music," said Toni Jackson. Conversation drifted to Ed's recent thoughts and projects, a kaleidoscopic mix: "Nietzsche,

Schopenhauer, and Kantian philosophy, what's right and what's wrong, and all the other kinds of things people talk about when they're young," as one friend described conversational shards. Ed might pull a book from his shelf to clarify a point or discuss the gravitational effect of the moon on "man's bloodstream and his body," one of Ed's "fetishes." His daughter Nancy described his mind in another way: her father conveyed a "sense of wonder after explaining this or that to me—a sense of wonder at the expansion of thought within his own mind, an acceptance of further truth than he had known before, a feeling that in trying to explain something to someone else his own horizons had advanced." And his sister Frances Strong thought that it was Ed's deep compassion that made the troubled and the vain, the wise and the foolish, the needy and the steadfast love him equally: "It seemed to me that as well as being so knowledgeable and full of understanding Ed poured out to people what must be called love—it had to be that—although I doubt that many people thought of it that way." In many ways, Ricketts lived the ideal of his favorite poet since childhood, Walt Whitman, embracing as comrades all whom he encountered—as well as the entire living world. His was a holistic appreciation of human experience and natural history. ("Oh by the way I use the term holistic in the sense that Jan Smuts considers it in his essay 'Holism' in XIV Encyclopedia Brit," Ricketts wrote to Joseph Campbell in 1940s, "a light; the integration of the parts being other [and more than] the sum of the parts; an emergent.")

Invertebrates were Ed's "first love," the most enduring, the reason that he had crossed half a continent to open his biological supply laboratory, one of the first on the West Coast. Before he came to the Monterey Peninsula, Ricketts had studied biology at the University of Chicago with ecologist Warner Clyde Allee, who was interested in the interdependence of organisms and their physical environment. Allee's work on the cooperation among species was the foundation for Ricketts's studies of the interactions among intertidal species and his developing a "toto-picture" of animal communities on the Pacific coast. But he left Allee's orbit and the University of Chicago without taking a degree, continuing his studies on his own and accumulating an intimate knowledge of marine invertebrates. Around Monterey Bay and on the Pacific coast, he observed how different habitats supported certain species: mussels and gooseneck barnacles occupied high intertidal rocks exposed to ferocious waves, whereas keyhole limpets and chitins clung to fissures where water surged somewhat less menacingly. Starfish and octopus tended toward a deeper and hence more protected distribution.

As noted in one of the several essays he wrote and revised during the 1930s and 1940s, "Wave Shock," the animals he watched so closely occupied separate "zones" of the intertidal. Distribution of animals fascinated him, and this complex subject included aspects of the physical environment and interactions within and between species. Communities of organisms were his chief interest, how they assembled, survived, and functioned. He thought far too much attention had been paid to Darwinian competition rather than to the equally compelling study of interdependence among intertidal animals.

Group behavior of humans became John's chief interest in the 1930s, and similarities between intertidal and human societies engaged both. Ed wrote John in 1946: "I am interested now more than ever in comparing the action of human society as is—and how it got there—with the presence of societies in the tide pools, and their controlling environmental factors."

Ed was a marine ecologist when the term was used sparingly, if at all, in mainstream scientific circles. His book published in 1939 as a result of his long, though technically informal study of the intertidal, *Between Pacific Tides*, treats different intertidal environments—the exposed rocky coast or sandy beaches or wharf pilings—showing what species inhabit and interact in each locale. In an era when biologists were trained to group animals taxonomically according to established scientific classifications—the methodology of the standard intertidal texts of the 1930s and 1940s (Johnson and Snook's 1935 *Seashore Animals of the Pacific Coast*, the 1941 *Light's Manual*, and George and Nettie MacGinitie's 1949 *Natural History of Marine Animals*)—Ricketts's vision of intertidal communities was arguably revolutionary. His text was, and remains, a unique contribution to marine ecology, a handbook in holistic thinking, which sees assemblages of animals as an integral part of their environment.

Scientists from around the globe corresponded with Ricketts, responding to his ideas, sending him scholarly offprints. He in turn sent them copies of his repeatedly revised scientific essays or discussed his current interests. His mind was kaleidoscopic. In 1936, for example, he was experimenting with the liver oil of great basking sharks, mailing a vial to John and Carol's close friend in Los Gatos, Charles Erskine Scott Wood. "I heard of shark liver oil first through G. E. MacGinitie, the associate professor at the Hopkins Marine Station (of Stanford University) here at Pacific Grove," Ed wrote. "I had in my files, now burned, letters from several hospitals, clinics, and individuals who commented on the successful use of this oil in conditions of post-operative shock following removal of ovaries, etc. There is abundant evidence of its efficacy in arthritis and asthma." Wood and his wife found it successfully treated their arthritis. Ricketts's mind turned in all directions. As early as 1938 he bemoaned overfishing of the Monterey Bay sardine—"the signs of depletion are serious"—and he considered several possible causes of the decline, including cycles of climate change, in brief essays written for the *Monterey Herald* in the 1940s. In 1946 he wrote to Steinbeck, then living in New York City, that there "ought to be more work on cycles. Lemmings, natural production of wheat, economics, purchases of furs from trappers. But it's proven so far a thankless and frustrating task even tho fascinating. Sudden plankton imbalances. Couple more lifetimes needed. Good long ones too." His curiosity seemed boundless. For Steinbeck, as for Carol and countless others who came into Ed's orbit, his "mind had no horizons." It was "the best mind I have ever known," Steinbeck wrote sadly, a month after Ed's death. "It was a mind that knew itself and yet was apart from itself. Ed's mind had no reticence's from itself. . . . It was . . . the most complicated affair."

Along with science, braided into the fabric of Ed's life were literature and philosophy, medieval music and Bach's *Art of the Fugue* (a nearly perfect piece of music, he thought), Jungian psychology, Chinese poetry and the verse of Walt Whitman, Robinson Jeffers, and William Blake. Ed relished the cultural sweep of music and art, philosophy and history, and he was ever the cataloguer, whether the object of attention was holothurians, Brahms and Beethoven, poetry or paintings. He cherished a theory that cultural "flow of genius" reached plateaus after great struggle ("There are spurts, everyone stimulates everyone else, then the thing dies out, there's a period of sterility, and a new thing pops up")—a version of the emergent function that intrigued him. To demonstrate that theory he created great charts that hung on his laboratory walls with lines in different colors comparing Chinese, European, Greek, Roman, and Egyptian art and music. Those charts fascinated Carol, who years later wondered "who ever got Ed's long chart on his Plateau theory of great jumps in all phases of culture, and then long plateaus. It was all over his wall, yards of it, on graph paper." In such ideas Ed was again prescient and holistic; the modern evolutionary theory of "punctuated equilibrium" may have developed from the work of Ernst Mayr during Ed's lifetime, but it didn't reach mainstream scientific thinking until long after his death.

Also lining the lab walls were art prints that Ed ordered from the Chicago Art Institute or from museums in Boston, London, and New York City. After a 1936 fire that destroyed the lab, he sent away for specific reproductions to replace ones lost: an El Greco, a print of a fifteenth-century German wood

carving, William Blake's *Flight into Egypt,* several Vermeers, as well as copies of paintings by Durer, Hans Holbein the Younger, Cezanne and Degas,
Picasso and Renoir. His reading was equally broad and eclectic, his conclusions firm. Goethe, he wrote a friend, was "to me the peak of an age" and
Faust "a refutation of reason and of its possibilities"—Ed was something of a
mystic. He was also a dedicated keeper of notebooks. During one two-month
period in 1939, he mentions Ernest Hemingway, Willa Cather, and the Bible;
he takes notes on two books on modern Mexican art, one on anthropology,
and one on nihilism; and he copies several passages from English Romantic
poets and "Black Marigolds" into his journal. That erudition, worn ever so
lightly, inspired Steinbeck, Carol, and others for twenty-five years, perhaps
because Ed never imposed his ideas on anyone. Instead, as a friend recalled,
he could say "that is good" with the most nuanced and positive connotations:
dogs were good, an El Greco painting was good, Beethoven's symphonies
were good.

After invertebrates and women, music was Ricketts's chief passion, and he
had an especially fine ear for medieval, Baroque, and classical pieces. Both
Carol and John were educated by Ed's musical tastes, although John preferred
classical recordings and Carol came to love jazz even more than John did (an
interest she shared with Ricketts's son, Ed Jr., who lived with his father at the
lab beginning in 1938; Ed Jr. claimed that it was Carol, not John, who had a
"real feeling for music"). Ed played records endlessly on the turntable located
next to his cot. He would pull out Mozart's Piano Concerto no. 20, a favorite,
or Palestrina or Byrd's Mass for Four Voices: "About all that gets done is listening to music," he wrote to one friend. To another he reported happily that
on Sunday mornings, patrons coming out of Flora Woods's brothel across
the street "would have their car doors open so as to hear better Beethoven's
music." For Ed, Beethoven's *Emperor* piano concerto evoked brotherhood and
joy, and the music was a conduit to what he called "THE GREAT CONTINU-
ITY." He also wrote essays about pitch and interval in the chromatic scale and
then compiled data on tones: "I know now that part of the charm of that litur-
gical music lies in it's [sic] frank departure, maybe into modal music, from
the highly artificial (as I'm increasingly convinced) present piano scale. Wish
I could have a set of 9 tuning forks, 6 in the usual tones, 3 new according to
the mathematics of harmonics. I bet the new tones would come out not far
from some of those stuck in old sung music." Ricketts's notations undoubtedly informed Steinbeck's own ideas about the "mathematics of music" that,
Steinbeck claimed on more than one occasion, provided the structural basis

for his fiction. "From the beginning," he wrote to a friend in 1939, "I have tried to use the forms and mathematics of music rather than those of prose. . . . It accounts for the so called 'different' technique of each one of my books." (Steinbeck structured *Cup of Gold*, for example, on Dvořák's *New World Symphony*—"all movements represented, sounds, movements, background," he told Sheffield.)

The startling overlap between the writer and the scientist is apparent here and in nearly everything they wrote and said and created for the rest of their lives. The two men discussed group behavior, emergent functions, Carl Jung, "participation," "levels" of ecological understanding, "survivability" of the most resilient species, and Li Po's poetry. "Inter-relation seems actually to be pretty much the keynote of modern holistic concepts," Ricketts writes in 1940, "wherein the whole consists of the animal or the community in its environment, the notion of relation being significant." That statement is the key to Ricketts's worldview and to Steinbeck's ecological vision—in *The Grapes of Wrath*, for example. Their collaboration was intimate, intense, and prolonged.

Perhaps *both* Carol and John fell in love, just a bit, with winsome Ed. They all met in 1930 through a friend, Jack Calvin, who lived in Carmel and who was collaborating with Ed on *Between Pacific Tides*. (Steinbeck wrote in "About Ed Ricketts" that the two met in a dentist office, but this was possibly an insider's joke as John once lent Ed a hundred dollars for a tooth extraction.) Calvin was a Stanford graduate and a writer of boys' adventure books who cultivated a "literary circle" in his Carmel home. Stanford classmates— A. Grove Day, Webster Street, Harry Wilcox—as well as Calvin's former students from a brief stint teaching high school in Mountain View—Ritchie Lovejoy and Fred Strong (who became the husband of Ricketts's sister)— dropped in to discuss books and writing. Carol vividly recalled her pleasure in being at Calvin's: "We met in this very friendly house," she recalled years later, "where a simple jug of wine made a party. You would gather in a ring, sitting on the floor and drink a jug of wine . . . this during Prohibition." In time, John would scoff at the pretensions of Calvin's circle—artistic pretenders of Carmel who "depress me pretty much. . . . They talk of nothing but sales. They think of nothing but selling." Nonetheless, individually he liked many whom he met at Calvin's home—particularly Ed. Carol remembers seeing Ricketts "dancing around the fire at Jack Calvin's; he had a neatly trimmed brown-red-golden beard which seemed to deceive a lot of people into thinking of him as a Christ-like father confessor."

Eventually, the circle shifted to Pacific Grove, where Ricketts rented a house with his wife, Anna, and three small children, Ed Jr., Nancy, and Cornelia. A group of friends first gathered in homes, and then more and more often, as the years went by, at Ed's Cannery Row lab in New Monterey. The lab became Ed's workplace and home after his wife, fed up with his many amorous adventures, left him for good in 1936. (The two never should have married, insisted both daughter Nancy and son Ed.) In the early 1930s, the core group was Tal and Ritchie Lovejoy, who moved back to the Peninsula after their brief sojourn in Southern California; Peg and Jim Fitzgerald, a watercolorist of some renown who ended up in Monterey in 1929 and introduced Ricketts to Buddhism, Taoism, and the poetry of Li Po; Barbara and Ellwood Graham, both artists, he a committed modernist painter, "the Painter Laureate of Cannery Row," said John and Ed; Toby Street, John's Stanford classmate and a Monterey lawyer, who had given John his undergraduate play, "The Green Lady," to transform as he pleased and which became *To a God Unknown;* and on occasion Marjory and fisherman Frank Lloyd or Carmelites Lucille and Gustaf Lannestock, the American translator of Vilhelm Moberg's Emigrant saga (*The Emigrants, Unto a Good Land, The Settlers,* and *The Last Letter Home*).

Artists and writers and creative spirits, they formed a rough kind of salon seared with a California brand. John and Carol were key players, but Ricketts was the magnet, the keying mechanism of the lab group. At Ed's people sought something outside boundaries to match their own edge-of-the-continent locale. Unlike salons of the East Coast and Europe, nurtured in urban environments with proximity to museums and galleries, liberal newspapers, and avant-garde writers and artists, western creative enclaves, such as Charles Lummis's turn-of-the-century Pasadena "noises" held in a stone house of his own construction or Mabel Dodge Luhan's artist colony near the Taos Indian pueblo, seemed to grow from the land itself—with an easy harmony between place and residents and artists. A modernist westerly wind blew from late-nineteenth-century Europe to New York and Chicago and beyond: "In its American version," notes Robert Crunden, modernism "distrusted authority, scorned politics, and feared boredom more than hell." That describes the lab group. There was little political talk, "although everyone was interested in the Russian experiment," said Marjory Lloyd. But "Ed was totally unpolitical and totally just not oriented to current social problems in any way," insisted Toni Jackson, his partner in the 1940s. Philosophical inquiry of any kind intrigued him, and conversation was his elixir and the

core of Ed's magnetism in the 1930s and '40s: "He always said the most stimulating things," said actor Burgess Meredith. "He was one of those men that
would . . . try to get at the kernel of truth at anything that was brought up."
With Monteverdi playing in the background, conversations dwelt on tonal-
ity of medieval music, the authenticity of modern art, or the possibility of a
"truly unified field hypothesis" that would consider both the objective and the
"non-objective situation, the abstract, the divine geometry."

But more than providing intellectual inspiration, Ricketts provided an
accepting atmosphere in which the ideas of others, as well as his, could
expand. Gustaf Lannestock describes an evening with Ricketts and John Cage
at a party in Carmel:

> John [Cage] arrived early, because he said he wanted to fix the piano. He
> brought along a collection of musical objects: two large knives, pieces of wood,
> empty tin cans in various shapes and sizes. . . . He placed these "instruments" in
> strategic positions among the strings inside the piano.
>
> No one in the audience had heard John Cage's music before. Most of them
> were exponents of classical music; they did not understand what these sounds
> meant. . . . The reaction was intense and instantaneous. Older people looked
> bewildered, almost as if in agony. Younger people more familiar with jazz, how-
> ever, seemed elated and on the verge of applauding.
>
> Ed Ricketts was sitting on the hearth, his head in his hands. His face took
> on a very sad appearance, but he didn't move a muscle. . . . A volatile argument
> broke out the moment the playing stopped. Ed listened but did not enter into
> the discussion. His only comment was: "What a future that boy must have to
> get a reaction of such intensity and magnitude."

That kind of acceptance, along with Ed's conversations, were manna for
John and Carol. Often after a day of writing, John would walk down to the
lab, about a mile from the Steinbecks' Pacific Grove cottage. Sometimes Carol
came with him, sometimes not. Often Ed and John would read to each other.
Ed had a "beautiful speaking voice—very soft, melodious, sympathetic," and
he had "a great calming influence on John." And he was one of the only people, Carol being the other, who could freely criticize John's writing. Ed would
listen to John read with eyes half closed, beer or rum in hand (he rarely drank
wine, since it made him ill), and comment honestly.

Together, Ed, John, and Carol had fun, as did everyone else who came to
the lab for parties and conversation. Ricketts was a bit of a pixie. He might
have friends follow his car on serpentine trips around Monterey streets. Or

nudge them into mental traps. His son Ed recalled that "when we were lit-tle he convinced us that squirrels flew from tree to tree to get rid of fleas." He told his three children, all "Mugwumps," stories of twin animals who got into all sorts of trouble. Wit bubbled from Ed, and he and John together were "constantly witty," Ed bursting out with "little pieces of spontaneous wit" so that both would get the "old fashioned giggles." Where John might defer to Carol's wordplay and clever retorts, he engaged Ed's. Toni Jackson tried to put her finger on Ed's charm: he had "great humor and a sort of wit . . . and you wouldn't call it fantasy and whimsy is a bad word. There really isn't a word for it."

Ed once sent this "headline," in caps, to his daughter Nancy: "'INJECT RICKETTS,' FURIOUS CATS DEMAND."

He enjoyed life as much as possible, and in his presence others did too. In a story that Toni Jackson wrote from Ricketts's perspective, based on true anecdotes, the lab group went through a brief craze for wearing false noses. One day, John and Tal went to Holman's department store and bought all the noses in stock so that everyone at the lab had one and "we'd all howl with laughter," even more gaily after a very dignified person dropped by that eve-ning. Once during Prohibition, Carol and Ed got drunk on laboratory alco-hol flavored with elixir of terpin hydrate, a recipe that Ed obtained from an English zoologist. On another occasion, Toni writes, the group tried to make plaster of Paris face masks (an extension of the Faster Master Plaster Casters scheme). The model was to lie down on the floor with a straw for breath-ing, as the face was covered with plaster. John volunteered. But the plaster of Paris got stuck, and Tal kept saying, "Suppose we can't get it off at all, and John has to go around this way the rest of his life—won't that be wonderful!" And everyone howled at the idea of John unable to speak. John, of course, was furious.

Ritchie Lovejoy told hilarious stories when he got drunk, taking off his shoes and socks, curling his toes, and crying and laughing as he told about his boyhood in Mountain View, when he chased a chicken into the outhouse and fell in. He once gave a "fine monologue on the death of some sow bugs," reported Ricketts. Generally Ritchie's wife Tal took life as it came; nothing fazed her. She "really loved parties," young Ed remembers, "and exploded in company." She would sit and blow "the most beautiful smoke rings, each a little smaller and following a larger one," or play the accordion, doing a little chant "Pe dad a," and drink vodka until she fell over. Once Tal organized an eviction party, she doing a pantomime of a forlorn mother, clutching a baby (doll) at the doorstep of the Steinbecks' Eleventh Street home. Dramatic photos captured her desolation. To one costume party she wore an upside-down lampshade and managed to look more exotic than anyone else in the room. Another night, Ritchie, Tal, Ed, and others created a percussion ensemble: Ed reported that he "was beating time with my removed shoe, pots and pans, boxes, a drum, spoons, and fireplace implements were going. So we had a pretty good time." For Ed, fun was foremost. One clear day he took Tal up Chews Ridge off Tassajara Road, a good hour and a half drive from his New Monterey laboratory; she and Ed stripped and ran naked "for hours," probably making love as well. For Ed, as for Whitman, body and soul were honored in equal measure.

Without a doubt, Ed's bond with John was deeper and more extraordinary than was Ed's fondness and respect for Carol. Carol's zest and drama, her tendency to take center stage in a group, sometimes exasperated Ed. But often Carol and Ed talked at great length, once working out "the effect of man on his physical environment," agreeing that while animals make little attempt to change their environment, "their racial stress toward adaptation (but not conscious)," humans are "constantly changing the face of the earth, draining swamps, building dams for power and irrigation, cutting down forests in one place, and growing them in another, consciously attempting to make the world a better place to live in, rather than adapting himself to live in a place." Both were ecologically minded and endorsed the "super-civilized minority" that was "building homes with a minimum of scars or changes" and making an "inner adjustment which is regarded enjoyably as rest and quiet." That conversation took place in the mid-1930s, before Carol designed the Los Gatos houses, but the houses she helped create made small footprints on the terrain. Carol, John, and Ed shared ecological values.

For John, Ed was a soul mate—John's first philosophical friend, claimed his sister Beth—and Ed, in turn, appreciated John's wonderful curiosity and his great strength of purpose, that driving will to write. Indeed, Ed marked the "immediate background" of his own psychological growth from the moment of "Jon's regard." The two complemented one another in complex and shifting ways, a commensal bond that was intellectual and deeply personal. While Steinbeck was practical and grounded, Ed was a visionary, a bit of a mystic. But Ed himself saw their connection the other way around: "Jons . . . interest prim[arily] in beauty thru form and arrangement in art forms. Mine as a stickler for factual truth. My prim[ary] interest in truth." Concern for form and for truth cross-pollinated. In Ed's mind, as in John's, friendship was a "third entity," treasured and nurtured.

That notion of a "third entity" came in part from reading Carl Jung, who "postulate[s] what he calls, a third person," John wrote, "which is exactly what I have called the keying mechanism of the individual with which he plugs into the phalanx. It is curious to note what happens to the individual when that mechanism is allowed to atrophy. I noticed it in the mountains. When the possibility of joining and becoming part of a phalanx is taken away, the mind becomes dull and those individual qualities which have raised the human race become lacking." This idea was compelling to Steinbeck throughout the 1930s and beyond: in isolation his mind had shriveled. For John, as well as for Ed and Carol, relational living was essential to creative thought. To be part of a group, large or small, was not to lose one's identity but to allow its discovery. Coming out of the Sierra Nevada, first to Carol's love, then to Ed's regard, John developed artistic urgency and experimented with decentralized narratives. Ed's scientific and psychological inquiries lent substance to Steinbeck's experimental prose. For his part, Ricketts ruminated endlessly on "emergent" functions, the "new thing" growing synergistically out of component parts. In the 1920s, English philosophers were debating emergent behavior, decentralized rather than centralized control, a focus on the whole versus the parts. Ed's ideas followed the same grooves, adding a spiritual depth to notions of emergence. To read his journals is to sense a mind that ceaselessly connected divergent points of view:

All this is tied up with the religious ideas of the trinity, with the old sturdy ideas of Hegel and with the new ideas of holism and of the ecologists and the Jungians and the 'mathematical physicists': the issue of the union of two struggling opposites, each honest in its own right but in scope limited, as a 'new thing' which completely transcends the old which is part of it in a rooty sense only; which uses the old forms of duality—form and function, matter and energy, material and spiritual—only as emergence vehicles towards an integrated growth.

For John, marriage and friendship were emergence vehicles. As was art. Ed's ideas are woven into John's writing, which eschewed a strong narrative line for decentralized structures. The notion of the phalanx and emergence are thus key to understanding Steinbeck and Ricketts's friendship as well as their joint work and thought in the 1930s—culminating in the 1941 collaborative text *Sea of Cortez,* the book that illuminates more than any other the quality of their conversations throughout the decade.

The heartfelt male friendship between John and Ed bled into a love that became, in Steinbeck's fiction, the stuff of myth. Ed became John's ideal other, the writer's projection of all that he admired and valued in men, the projection of a love that, if expressed physically, would have been forbidden. Through sublimating his regard into fiction, he found a way to honor Ed's great soul and complex mind. In book after book, one exceptional character is modeled very much on Ed, his keen perceptions and his ability to push through to a larger, more accepting vision. There is some of Ed in humane Doc Burton, critic of the steely Mac in *In Dubious Battle;* some of Ed in regal Slim, the jerkline skinner in *Of Mice and Men,* who figuratively takes George's hand at the end of the novel. Ed is the restless visionary Casy in *The Grapes of Wrath,* the model for Tom Joad's ecstatic commitment to mankind's suffering. And Ed is essentially himself in *Cannery Row* and *Sweet Thursday.* In each of these cases, another man or a group of men deeply admires this person of insight, wishes to emulate him, befriend him, give a party for him. But it's also true that Steinbeck's men of insight and fine perceptions are also lonely men, without the deep, meaningful love that Ed himself yearned for.

John may have found friendship a more accessible, more psychologically flexible relationship to plumb artistically than marriage. While he loved Ed and Carol in equal measure—a phalanx unit knows no gender—a marriage bond is complicated by legal ties, sexuality, and the possibility of children and family obligations in ways that friendship is not. The clarity of friendship gave Steinbeck the means to explore what he called his great thesis of the 1930s, how the phalanx or mutualism can determine not only the "emergence vehicles" of art but political movements and historical currents as well, from striking workers to mobs to migrants on the road. As Ricketts suggests and as Steinbeck's art demonstrates, a group forms a personality separate from that of each unit member; groups "are of all sizes," John insists, from the creative phalanx to the lab group to "the camp meeting where the units pool their souls to make one yearning cry, to the whole world which fought the war." To paraphrase a famous line from *Sea of Cortez:* John looked from Ricketts's lab to the stars and back again.

The intensity of this interaction no doubt sidelined Carol at times. But John needed Carol's roiling immersion in life as much as he needed Ed's calm acceptance, philosophical curiosity, and scientific acumen. The two intense personalities that flanked Steinbeck throughout the 1930s were indispensable to his art.

In February 1932, after John, Ed, and Carol had become fast friends, Carol went to work half days as a bookkeeper and secretary for Ed—a "crash" secretary she called herself. Ed had employed both his father, Abbott Ricketts, who helped prepare shipments, and his sister Frances, who was his secretary, but by early 1932 it was obvious that the business could not support Frances's $100-a-month salary. Carol offered to work half-time for fifty dollars a month, and Ed secured her services. Delighted to have work again, she took her new responsibilities very seriously: "I can see myself now as I went to work, dressed in hat, gloves, stockings; to walk down the railroad tracks to the lab I was a San Francisco business girl and no one was going to forget it. It was like dressing for dinner in the jungle I guess." There's a dollop of whimsy in Carol's memories—her only recorded reminiscence made forty-five years after her employment. But she took her new position as seriously as she had the task of compiling a Carmel directory. Trained as a secretary, apprenticed in advertising, she was a highly skilled woman and wanted to use those skills.

By all reasonable estimates, Ricketts needed her help. He was, on the one hand, the most meticulous of men, keeping precise records of collecting data: numbers of specimens collected at a site, vertical distribution levels, features of the local environment. He recorded all this information, as well as class, order, family, and position and surrounding vegetation, on green, blue-, yellow-, buff-, red-, and salmon-colored cards, each color representing a region. He also read an amazing number of scientific articles and seemed to digest what he read and file them accordingly. He wrote several scholarly and philosophical essays during the 1930s and '40s and compiled material for a four-hundred-page text, *Between Pacific Tides*. All this while he was also preparing numerous specimens and sending them to high schools and colleges. In every room of the lab he set up work areas: in the back room were snakes (two rattlesnakes) and, according to John, "about 200 white rats"; outside were frogs and turtles in redwood tanks (the real-life counterparts of Mack and the boys collected twelve hundred of these in Carmel Valley on one 1937 trip) and other specimens in large concrete tanks, as well as shark oil in a big round barrel; in the basement he prepared animals for shipment. It was a complex operation, housed in a building with no hot water. Ed needed a secretary/bookkeeper/receptionist, and Carol functioned as all three, being as adept in these roles as she was as John's editor/muse. At Ed's lab, she perched at a desk just inside the door of the Lab, greeting callers and keeping track of Ed's finances from her small office, six feet by ten feet, next to a safe that Ed never locked. Carol remembered it as a

> pretty businesslike operation, but ever so slightly offbeat. He had a father, very loveable old man, who helped in packing, a little pixie who came bubbling up out of the basement with Alka Seltzer foaming out of his mouth; I think Alka Seltzer was the death of the man. Over my desk—I was in the front reception room at top of stairs—there was a very weak plywood shelf on which balanced one gallon jug of pure cyanide, and every time a train went by, it teetered and rocked so precariously that I didn't know whether to head for the hills. I asked Ed once, if that jar does go off, do I have any chance making it to door. And he said "nope."

Carol had fun at the lab, some of it generated by her pride in the job, some by Ed's constant presence, some by the location. Across the street was Flora Woods's brothel, the Lone Star Café (in *Cannery Row* it becomes Dora Flood's Bear Flag Restaurant), owned by a woman every bit as generous, kind, and spirited as her fictional counterpart, a woman beloved by many in Monterey, and not only her patrons. She operated gracefully on the boundaries of illegality. Prostitution was tolerated in Monterey, a "necessary evil," as newspapers occasionally reported, because soldiers were billeted nearby. But the local paper had an unwritten rule never to write an article about her, never bring her unwanted publicity. Flora operated as a free agent and survived as a "great giver . . . to the poor and everyone else." She bought tickets to anything having charity connected to it. She gave anonymously to Wednesday night prize fights at the Presidio, and when an officer would send ringside tickets in appreciation, Flora sat her "girls" there for "advertising purposes." At Christmas she purchased "carloads of food" for destitute families, telling the owner of a grocery store on Monterey's Alvarado Street: "Mr. Ferranti, if anyone finds out where this came from I'll cut your throat." And she probably meant it. Flora was tough and kind in equal measure, running an egalitarian and "really high class joint" catering to fishermen, policemen, local dignitaries, guests of the Del Monte Hotel, and soldiers.

Flora had started her career in Monterey with a "Tamale Parlor," which may have been Steinbeck's model for Maria and Rosa Lopez's establishment in *The Pastures of Heaven*, which is first a house serving "Spanish Cookings." Like Maria and Rosa, Flora realized that she would never get rich on tamales. A savvy businesswoman, she owned other brothels around Monterey, although the Lone Star Restaurant was the jewel in the crown, with a large foyer and bar in front and maybe ten rooms. (There were sometimes shows, occasionally jazz, late into the night; Flora always invited Ed, also John if he were around.) The bar itself was Philippine mahogany, a gift from an army officer who had offered to send Flora anything she wished from overseas. Flora asked for wood for a bar.

Secretary Carol relished the show at Flora's: "God knows I was a teetering voyeur," she admitted. And "Ed seemed just as interested." From her desk by the front door she could see "prominent businessmen in town parked in back near railroad tracks" so they would not be seen from Ocean View Avenue. Like John, she loved to catch the guilty in their tracks: "We would toddle over and see who was there. During the day girls would go on their little errands—never minked up floozies as in Hollywood version, very disappointing to see them come out in worn out tweed or flannel coats, very inconspicuous, and they were told never under any circumstances to speak to clients on the street."

Under Flora's roof, all were nurtured: patrons, visitors at the bar (even high school boys could come to the bar for a Coca-Cola), pregnant "girls" and troubled ones. Hers was a matriarchal home, one depicted in Cannery Row as in opposition to the "twisted and lascivious sisterhood of married spinsters whose husbands respect the home but don't like it very much." Marriage is an unhappy institution in that novel, where both women and men conduct protracted skirmishes. Mack is not happy at home; Gay's wife is unhappy; the Captain's wife is a domestic shrew. Married pairs eschew cooperation for dominance and elect to misunderstand rather than appreciate each other. For both genders, imaginative spaces of cooperation are separate from traditional domiciles and competitive patterns. Cooperation defines the phalanx: Mack and the boys gathering frogs on the Carmel River, parties at Doc's, or women-to-women relationships at Dora Flood's. Although these relationships are fictional, they cast light on the transformative power of the phalanx.

If outside Ed's lab was Vanity Fair, inside was Scientific American. Patiently, Carol typed out the binomial scientific names for the multitude of species used to prepare zoological and botanical preserved specimens. The first Pacific Biological Laboratory catalogue in 1925 listed zoological material from two hundred species, many locally collected marine invertebrates. One day Ed spread living starfish out on the sidewalk in front of the lab, carefully timing five-minute intervals as they lay their eggs (and blocking sidewalk traffic, noted Carol). But she loved her new job, and, despite the scientific rigor, Carol found ways to infuse the scene with gaiety. On one occasion, she and John hefted Ricketts's Gila monster out of its cage, strapped it on a roller skate, and pulled it around Cannery Row on a leash—or so he said. On another occasion, when Ed was out of town,

> a large barrel of turtles was dropped down in the office. Ed's father and I opened it, released a dozen or so turtles, and I turned to my typewriter and typed up that little jingle by Ogden Nash "Turtle lives twixt plated decks / Which practically conceal its sex / I think it clever of the turtle / In such a fix to be so fertile." Well I typed 24 of those little slips, glued them on the back of every turtle that was running free through the office, and Pops Ricketts and I slammed the door and fled for home. I don't know when Ed got in. He never acknowledged our prank, and I don't know if he was furious or whether the turtles are still floating around.

That kind of good cheer seeped from the laboratory walls, especially at night, party time. In the unlocked safe next to Carol's desk were kept rare cheeses for parties. If strangers dropped by, especially wealthy women, Ed's humor turned bawdy: he teased them about the "big thing up over the door." If they asked what it was, he would say, "That's the foreskin of a whale." Carol chuckled at another recollection: "We were idling around in front of Ed's lab window one day. Up drove a car, and out stepped some people we thought strangers. One was an extremely well endowed woman, and one man looked up and said, 'a balloon smuggler.'" Such was the tone.

In 1939, John fulfilled a decade-long promise to Carol: if he made money, he told her when he proposed in 1929, he would swathe her in furs, build her a swimming pool, and put her name up in lights. Ten years later, he did all three and more, but the lights first went up in front of Ed's lab: "CAROL'S PLACE" flashed the red neon sign. For that night, it seemed as if Carol were giving Flora Woods or Wide Ida down the street, another popular brothel owner, a run for the money. Of course the sign had to be taken down. Ed didn't really want to run a brothel and Carol didn't want to be a madam, but everyone got a belly laugh out of it for the few hours it beamed down on Cannery Row.

It is much more apparent how Ricketts helped shape Steinbeck's thinking than what his impact on Carol might have been. The only way to reconstruct their relationship may be to consider Ed's attitudes toward women. Those ideas were shaped by his incompatible marriage to Anna, a conventional

Yugoslav woman (the model for Jelka in "The Murder"), by liaisons with countless other beauties, and by reading Carl Jung's ideas on sexual difference. Throughout the mid- to late 1930s, Ricketts consulted Jungian therapist Evelyn Ott, who lived in Carmel, and from her he gained a deep appreciation for self-actualization, his own and others. For the most part, he found women less fully actualized: he once jotted down in a notebook that he wondered if his close friend Tal Lovejoy could write. Of course she can, he quickly corrected himself. On another occasion, he wrote about another artist's self-awareness:

> Barbara [Graham] dropped by . . . and we talked, about music, about Marian
> Anderson, about personalities and relations, Bruce [Ariss], Peggy [Street], Jean
> [Ariss]. Listened to liturgy, and some of the Beethoven mass. Barbara is coming
> along alright, she constantly improves, she's working on a good honest relation
> within herself and with Ellwood; she's discovered and is treading a pathless
> way of her own—the only difficulty is chiefly in her getting the idea across due
> to inarticulateness, plus maybe still some remnant of "screwiness" and lack
> of mature discipline. However she's just simply forging ahead even if no one
> person understands what she's doing—I didn't even fully at first, a year or so
> ago—and she's getting that discipline and even getting to the point where she's
> slightly articulate, now I at least can understand practically everything she says
> of that sort.

Ricketts's work with Evelyn gradually deepened his perceptions of women. Her Jungian training was exemplary—she had lived in Vienna and studied directly with Jung—and her ideas had a profound impact on both Ed and John. Evelyn was brilliant, cultured "in the deepest sense," philosophical and personable, a "superior type," recalled one friend, piling on superlatives. She was also elegant and beautiful. There is no record that Carol or John went to consult Evelyn, however, although Ed's sister Frances may have and Bruce and Jean Ariss did see her. As did Ed. Evelyn was "devoted" to Ed and Ed to her. Both found in Jung the "spirit of the depths," and in the late 1930s, under her guidance, Ricketts recorded his dreams in notebooks; he repeatedly acknowledged Evelyn's influence as both a good friend and an insightful therapist: "her specialized training in the classifying and analyzing of human situations, especially the unconscious ones understandable thru the technical interpretation of dream life, is very helpful to anyone trying to understand himself and friends, and the world." He spent a great deal of time in the late 1930s trying to deepen his appreciation of all three, admitting that in earlier years, people had said that to openly discuss "little known" subjects like "love, companionship, human relations" was to destroy those emotions. He clearly thought differently, and conversations at the lab often focused on human psychology. Ricketts gave as much attention to his inner landscape as he did to the outer, a rapt attentiveness that noted each contour of his psychological state, and he was as detached and honest as he could be—as he was in describing Barbara Graham.

Another female therapist, also a Jungian, was a woman named Lucille Elliot from Berkeley who found it "a relief" to be at the lab, as Ricketts recounted in his journal, "to be able to discuss interestingly, friendly, and profitably, the things that are the subject matter of her work" and were treated in Berkeley "either pathologically or more or less secretly." At the lab, no intensely personal subject was taboo, and behavior outside norms was not considered aberrant. Ed accepted transgressive behavior as he accepted human folly and need. He was, quite simply, intensely curious about the human condition: psychological, social, philosophical, and ecological—and sexual.

Using Ott's work based on Jung's 1921 text, *Psychological Types*, Ricketts, once again the cataloguer, set up a chart of personality types "illustrating individuation" that he included in an essay, "Ideas on Psychological Types." Herein is found the best gauge of Ricketts's response to Carol and John's marriage, a bond he thought less than ideal. Only those free of projections could move fully into self, he believed, and John Steinbeck "is almost pathologically projected unconsciously onto his work," leaving little enough emotional energy for his wife. He was certainly right on that score. For Ed, John and Carol's marriage was thus not true—true in the sense of the deepest, most actualized love, the kind of love he sought for himself after his own marriage to Anna crumbled, an ideal close to the filmy romanticism of Byron or Shelly, absolute physical and psychic harmony with a soul mate. Ed's notion of actualized love was akin to "breaking thru" to spiritual union, a state he reached only with Jean Ariss—a young woman who came to Monterey in July 1934 to marry artist Bruce Ariss. A year or so later she had an affair with Ed. Over and over in his journals, well into the 1940s and long after Jean had broken off their relationship on June 5, 1939—the date was etched in Ed's mind—he talks about the "deep thing" he had with Jean. Most couples probably fell short of Ed's definition of actualized love, including John and Carol. (Years later Jean discussed her 1930s affair with Ed openly, with acceptance of its complexities, a stance that must have been Ed's as well. And Bruce's: he was always around and knew of his wife's indiscretion, even accepted it to some extent. The triangular relationship simply "was" and, in effect, Jean didn't care who knew it.)

According to Ed's catalogue of personality types, John was not like "most men" who fell into the category of "sensation-thinking (concerned with ana- lyses, evaluations and logical conclusions with reference to the objective and factual physical realities of measurements)." John was instead an "Intuitive- feeling" type in Ed's schema, which made him an introvert: "The unconscious psyche (the female compensatory spirit, the anima) is in western males intuition-feeling introvert, concerned archaically with subjective evaluations spiritually apperceived in dreams, in the symbolism of fantasy, or at times of affect." What Ed called John's "inner insecurity" caused John to wall himself off, "dancing on nothing" but his own "terrible and intense drive," and making him a poor candidate for intimacy. But Carol went into her marriage under- standing that drive—as long as it included her on some level of intimacy. She found it when she could. Although introspection and monomaniacal devo- tion to the visions in one's mind are tough on a marriage, John's darkness and moody dreams were the key to his art, and Carol and Ed accepted John and his art as one entity. Furthermore, Ed and Carol understood "dancing on nothing" as well, since darkness sometimes swamped both.

On Ed's chart, Carol fell into the practical category. He grouped her with Evelyn Ott and Xenia Cage (John Cage's wife and Tal's sister) as a "sensation- thinking" type, again not the typical female of the "Intuition-feeling" type. To be a "sensation-thinking" woman was to have "common sense" and an "appreciation of methods of construction"—certainly positive characteristics for intellectual women. But in Ed's taxonomy, practical, sharp-tongued Carol had little truck with the unconscious, which he found bothersome, while John had little practicality or "intellectual cognition," also an anomaly in his schema. Little wonder the two clashed at times. Little wonder that two oppo- sites, despite an obvious attraction, seemed mismatched to Ed.

And yet it was that very difference he charted that made the marriage work for so many years: pragmatic Carol tended to worldly necessities while brooding, introverted John wrote. And neither was as polarized as Ed's chart suggests, since Carol could be darkly introspective, and John had a good measure of common sense. From the syncopated rhythm of opposition, their frequent squabbles, they improvised their lives, navigating eddies and shoals of poverty and self-sufficiency. The times demanded adaptability, and both were adept at what Catherine Bateson calls "composing a life." Carol's fierce

practicality was leavened by her own shifting creativity in several mediums—
poetry, drawing, sculpture, editing. And John's "terrible and intense drive"
found relief in Carol's grounded tolerance and keen participation in the world
as she found it. If that did not meet Ricketts's ideal of great passion, neither
Carol nor John defined marriage thus.

And yet, Carol was fleetingly derailed by a captivating new friend in their
midst, Joseph Campbell.

In 1932 Joseph Campbell, an unemployed twenty-eight-year-old classics scholar, drove west across the country and knocked on Idell Henning's
door on Sixteenth Street in San Jose. Idell had met the handsome Campbell
in 1925, when both were sailing to San Francisco from Hawaii on the *Matsonia*. During the intervening years they'd written each other occasionally,
and Joseph had sent her books on Indian teachings, undoubtedly including
those of Krishnamurti, whom he'd met on another ocean crossing. It was an
awkward reunion for the recently engaged Idell—she and Paul Budd were
to be married the following May—so she took Campbell to Carol and John's
house in Pacific Grove and then helped him find a place to live in Carmel, the
"Pumpkin Shell" on Lincoln Avenue. That first evening with John and Carol
was an extraordinary success, on all sides: Joe found Carol to be a "dandy....
She has a way of twinkling when she smiles, and there is a frank straightforwardness about her," he wrote. After dinner the four talked about religion
and "art, fireplaces, and Los Angeles." John and Campbell sat up late reading
parts of his new manuscript, "To an Unknown God," and Campbell suggested
that John revise the manuscript and help readers see images more clearly:
"You say someone's opened the door and comes in and I don't hear the door
squeak." Campbell wrote about that evening: "I had the curious feeling ... as I
met Steinbeck and he walked towards me. I thought I was seeing myself." The
two men even looked alike, both "serious and sturdy chaps," in Campbell's
mind, and were once mistaken for brothers in the local butcher shop.

Campbell adapted nicely to his new environment in Carmel, but moved
in March to a little house close to Ed Ricketts, Canary Cottage on Fourth
Street in Pacific Grove, where the fifty cents a week rent was far less expensive. There he was closer to the lab group that he bonded with immediately,
a group that kept him from his "deep swamps at the time". He had not found
a job in five years, even after sending out eighty-five resumes before heading west. For people who had never graduated from college—Ed, John, and
Carol as well as Ritchie and Tal Lovejoy—Campbell's resume and his worldly

assurance must have dazzled. He brought erudition and European sophistication and added zest to their little group.

In contrast to John and Ed's own incomplete undergraduate educations, Campbell's had been rich and varied. After a year at Dartmouth, where he pursued a biology major, he shifted to Columbia University and English, eventually earning both a BA and an MA in literature, his thesis, "A Study of the Dolorous Stroke," focusing on the wasteland imagery in the Arthurian tales. The midtwenties found him in Paris, immersed in modern art, reading James Joyce, and studying languages at the Sorbonne. Along the way, often on numerous family junkets abroad, he'd debated the dynamics of spiritual freedom with Jiddu Krishnamurti, discovered Carl Jung's works in Germany, and practiced the saxophone and writing short fiction—determined to compose in the American vein. He liked Walt Whitman and jazz and open spaces. He was drawn to communist ideas. While in Monterey he considered using "the darker races of America for my materials. I have often thought of treating America from the point of view of its victims: Indians, Negroes, Polynesians. . . . As I sat before the fireplace . . . I felt the whole thing in my mind." His mind was constantly turning over new material, which he filed away—his filing system and systematic program of improvement perhaps not so different from Ricketts's passion for charts and classification.

Campbell joined the tight-knit group of John, Ed, and Carol, Ritchie and Tal Lovejoy. The six bubbled with conversation and adventure. Exploits were varied: target shooting at the beach or perhaps a picnic at Point Lobos, collecting trips to Santa Cruz, hikes up to Mount Toro above Monterey Bay. Dinners were turkey meatloaf and oyster stew and abalones. Conversations were ambrosial. John told Campbell that "a great artist does not attempt to arouse pity. He is above pity," an idea that intrigued the scholar who was moving toward understanding the power of symbols and mythic narratives. He and John shared a fascination with King Arthur, and the two talked endlessly of the knightly tales. In the late 1920s and early 1930s John often spoke about "racial memories," another topic that intrigued Campbell. The group would have "let's get together and read a book parties," according to Campbell, focusing on Eddington's book on new physics and Goethe's conversations with Eckermann. Politics or sociology was never discussed.

One day Carol urged them all to do something new. So the Lovejoys, Steinbecks, and Campbell started experimenting with the Ouija board at Canary Cottage, sending messages to the nether world. The table shook. "Is it for me?" squeaked Carol. "No," said the voice. "For me?" said Tal. "No," said the voice. "For me?" Ritchie asked. "Yes." When Ritchie connected with his stern grandfather, Ricketts walked in and accidentally knocked over the table, causing frightened Ritchie to fall into the fireplace. "Well your grandpa certainly knows how to bust up a party," they laughed. Another day they had a party to get Campbell very, very drunk—that was an initiation they thought he'd missed. And on yet another day the group went to Mount Toro, lay down on the grass to look up at the clouds, and Ritchie Lovejoy said, "You know, I'll tell you, we're all dead and we're in heaven and that's why we're so happy." Years later when he was interviewed, Campbell concurred, his face "lighting up" when he talked about Carol: "It was a happy, happy time."

"Our year of crazy beginnings," Campbell would call it. For all involved, the synergy led to new levels of awareness—the phalanx sending up new shoots. As both he and Carol insisted, Campbell gleaned as much from Carol, John, and Ed as they learned from him about the relevance of myth. All three men, in particular, were on an intellectual cusp, working to unite the physical and metaphysical, the immediate and the visionary in their prose. Long before Campbell's arrival, Ed and John (and Carol to a much less extent) had been drawn to the occult, the mystical, the transcendent—what Ed called at various times the "other side," the "Great Continuity," or the "deep thing." Indeed, at least one close acquaintance, Toni Jackson, thought that the "big bond" between John and Ed "was the mystical." Ed's sister, Frances, agreed, adding that it was artist Jim Fitzgerald who sparked both John and Ed's interest in Eastern religions, in Krishnamurti. In 1931, before Campbell arrived, Steinbeck told Albee that he planned to cut the manuscript of "To an Unknown God" into eight pieces, tear it "down like a Duzenbuerg having its valves ground" so that he could incorporate his ecological and pantheistic ideas. He was starting to piece it back together just as Campbell arrived on the scene. Conversations with Campbell, Ricketts, and Carol considered human bonds with nature as well as nature as generator of myth. (After the novel was published, Steinbeck wrote to a book critic that he was trying to touch "the great submerged part of man, the unconscious.") Ricketts was composing his seminal essay "The Philosophy of 'Breaking Through.'" And Campbell was wrestling with a "synthesis of Spengler and Jung" as well as the germ of *The Hero with a Thousand Faces*. What was found in the hero's journey was relief from tensions—a place of repose, a center. Myths connect humans to the spiritual, something all three men yearned to articulate. All were reading Oswald Spengler's *Decline of the West* (a book that Jeffers read as well, according to

Sara Bard Field) and James George Frazer's *The Golden Bough* ("Jon's *vade mecum*," wrote Ed to psychiatrist Lucille Elliot in 1937).

Robinson Jeffers's poetry inspired the group; he was the formidable absent presence in the mix. He lived nearby on the Carmel coast, although the reclusive poet, fifteen years Steinbeck's senior, was rarely seen on Carmel's Ocean Avenue, and it's doubtful that any of them had met Jeffers. (When John and Carol finally stood face to face with him in 1938, a meeting arranged by Bennett Cerf, John was struck by Jeffers's "unreal quality.") Perhaps Carol had talked to his wife, Una, when she and Beth worked on the Carmel directory, but Jeffers himself avoided people as much as he could. "No Visitors Until After 4 O'clock" read a sign on their gate. Certainly the couples were aware of one another, however. (By late 1933, Una had been given and read with appreciation both *The Pastures of Heaven* and *To a God Unknown*.)

Jeffers was a celebrated American poet, whose hewn face graced the April 4, 1932, cover of *Time* magazine. The 1925 publication of *Roan Stallion, Tamar, and Other Poems* had created a stir. The *New York Times Book Review* compared Jeffers to Thomas Hardy in its January 3, 1926, edition, noting that both poets fixed their gaze on nature. The Big Sur coast "is the world's end," Jeffers wrote in "The Torch-Bearer's Race," and "This huge, inhuman, remote, unruled, this ocean will show us / The inhuman road, the unruled attempt, the remote lode-star." The wild coast was Jeffers's terrain, where he set violent dramas like "The Roan Stallion" and "Tamar" and wrote about the permanence of stone and sea and hawk. For too long, Jeffers insisted, humanistic accomplishments had trumped man's consideration of his relation to nature. Like Spengler, whom Steinbeck and Ricketts and Campbell read, Jeffers recognized the decadence of contemporary society, and his response was to "uncenter the human mind from itself," to move readers from self-absorption to awareness of non-human, and things more permanent than man, the natural sublime. In sexually explicit, often violent narrative poems of incest and brutality in the Big Sur wilderness, he shocked complacent readers into awareness of deeper psychic needs.

Carol was actually the catalyst for the lab group's appreciation of Jeffers's transcendent voice. Campbell remembered Carol "coming in one day and saying, 'Really, I've got the message of "Roan Stallion"'—and she recited":

Humanity is the start of the race; I say
Humanity is the mould to break away from, the crust to break
through, the coal to break into fire,

The atom to be split.
Tragedy that breaks man's face and a white
fire flies out of it; vision that fools him
Out of his limits, desire that fools him out of his limits, unnatural
crime, inhuman science.

In focusing on the choral interlude, Carol put her finger on the central thrust of Jeffers's poem. Here, as always, her intellect sharpened ideas—and the men around her grabbed hold of the gifts she brought. She later pasted the Jeffers passage into her scrapbook, a fragment preserved and cherished. For her it was a scrap, but for Steinbeck, Ricketts, and Campbell, nearly divine inspiration. The notion of a "mold to break through"—from reality to transcendence—riveted all four. Reading Jeffers's poetry moved Carol and John, Ricketts and Campbell beyond the tragic tensions of life to a vision of unity with nature. The phalanx had burst into full bloom.

Ricketts responded to Jeffers's call for transcendence with two essays. "Breaking Through," its title from "Roan Stallion," was revised throughout the 1930s, and was a seminal work for Ricketts that outlined his ideas about emergence and metaphysical awareness. The modern "trend" of moving beyond struggle and conflict, Ricketts argues, is "reflected philosophically in holism—that the whole is more than the sum of its parts; that the integration or relation of the parts is other than the separate sum of the parts. Recently, I have been inclining toward the belief that the conscious recognition of this "breaking through" quality may be an essential part of modern soul movements . . . dirt and grief wholly accepted if necessary as struggle vehicles of an emergent joy—achieving things which are not transient by means of things which are." In "magnificent tragedy" humans are carried to "appercep-tion of the whole."

In a second essay, "A Spiritual Morphology of Poetry," Ricketts further clarifies what he means by "emergent joy," classifying his favorite poets according to how well they express the "'beyond' quality" he admired in Jeffers. Like Blake and Whitman, Jeffers is an "all-vehicle-mellow poet" in the schema Ricketts sets up—this his fourth and highest category, consisting of those poets who glimpsed "the heaven-beyond-the-world-beyond-the-garden." Consider "most of all Jeffers's 'Signpost,'" Ricketts writes, "the most conscious statement I know of yet from this emergent country: '. . . At length / you will look back along the stars' rays and see that even / The poor doll humanity has a place under heaven. / . . . but now you are free, even to become human, / But born of the rock and the air, not of a woman.'" Ricketts's emergent country is, of course, Steinbeck's keying mechanism of the phalanx.

Campbell too was drawn to "the other side" evident in Jeffers's poetic vision; he memorized and recited lines obsessively while in Pacific Grove—and well after. Throughout that magical year, Spengler, Jung, and Jeffers, he insisted, were his chief sources of inspiration. Steinbeck's as well. In "To an Unknown God" the hero, Joseph Wayne, is moved beyond his self-absorption to pantheistic wholeness—finding his father's spirit in an enormous oak tree, sensing racial memories in a rock circle sacred to native peoples, and acknowledging the power of sacrifice when he visits a seer who lives on Big Sur coast and sacrifices an animal each sunset. In 1935, Steinbeck told a reporter that Jeffers poetry "is perfect to me," and he would write Lawrence Clark Powell in 1937 that Jeffers "should have the Nobel." In the late 1930s he claimed that his favorite Jeffers poems were "The Roan Stallion," "The Loving Shepherdess," and "The Tower Beyond Tragedy." And years later Ed would tell a friend that in *Sea of Cortez* the key to holistic appreciation is grounded in Jeffers's thought: "Jon said it well . . . the words are his rather than ours or mine . . . 'man is related to the whole thing, related inextricably to all reality, known and unknowable. . . . Each of them in his own tempo and with his own voice discovered and reaffirmed with astonishment the knowledge that all things are one thing and that one thing is all things.'" This was the emergent country that all three men and one woman sought.

Perhaps it was discussion of Jeffers's poetry that drew Joe and Carol closer. Or perhaps talk about male and female artists. About that time Campbell wrote that the feminine had little place in art because women imitate men rather than discover inspiration in their own souls. Women, he thought, were "essentially cosmic" and as such in touch with "soils deeper" than a specific culture's roots. It was up to women, therefore, to recover "cosmic world feeling." Carol would have understood that. And she was, by nature, a woman who fit Campbell's definition of a creative, spontaneous female. Each relished the other's "free thinking," one of the keys, Campbell thought, to a "civilized primitiveness." He would write in his journal that it was essential to break "whenever possible the rule of the Golden Mean." Carol was not a woman given to equipoise.

With her, there was no golden mean. She slid down banisters at the Ricketts home, "just for fun," Ed Jr. recalled. And "she was a tree climber. She just loved to climb pine trees," at least once clad in nothing but black gloves. She and Tal "were always inventing and making some crazy things," recalled Anna Ricketts, such as making party favors with feathers, gluing feathers to nuts and by the end of the afternoon there was no place for anyone to sit because "glue and feathers were all over the place!" Carol and Tal just sat on the floor in the midst of the mess, having fun.

Carol and Joe Campbell also had fun. She would say then and later that their flirtation was never sexual, that the two were attracted to each other but broke it off before it became "too thick." But good-looking, sociable, and intellectually rigorous Campbell briefly won a good part of her heart—and much of her mind. Quite simply, Carol relished his sympathetic ear: "The Word I Never Hear is Darling," she pasted into her scrapbook. Perhaps "darling" is just what Joe whispered. The two became "very fond of one another," Idell admitted. "Joe was single, unattached, knew no one," and Carol was a sympathetic and perhaps vulnerable female presence. Carol and Joe talked for "hours on any subject," a meeting of the minds.

But one late spring night at Ed's Pacific Grove home, their bodies tentatively reached to each other, at least according to Campbell's account of the two side by side in oak trees. In his journal, Campbell recorded every pulse of their passionate exchange. Carol is perched in one tree singing and cooing at Joe, while Joe, also soused, sits in his tree and tells Carol that she is the woman meant for him. Both of them wallow in that fantasy, that they met each other "too late." In Joe's mind, the separate trees symbolize their impossible situation. Although John is witness to this interlude, he returns to the house in disgust.

> "Carol," I said, "there's a bastard who sits around outside me, and I've got to get drunk like this to make him melt away."
>
> "I know!" she said. "I know! I'm that way too." . . .
>
> Carol reached again and took my foot.
>
> "You beautiful thing!" I said.
>
> "Oh, Joe! Only to touch you!"
>
> Her glass fell from her hand and thumped the ground.
>
> "I'm going to get down, Carol. I'm going to get out of this tree now."
>
> I twisted and struggled, and got down to the stoop. Then I walked around to Carol's tree, and I kissed her ankle. I kissed her ankle twice, and then I got down on my knees to find her glass. "Where is the blasted thing? Oh, here it is!" And

I picked it up. I scrambled up the stoop and set the glass upon the parapet. Then the door opened and John appeared with a thunderous look in his eye.

"Shut up," he snapped. "Quit shouting. You're making too much noise. —I could hear every word you said in the house."

That sent a chill through me, but I soberly straightened up.

"Getting a lady down out of a tree," I explained.

Carol began to stir, and I tried to help her out of the oak tree. She slipped and barked her shins; groaned; and I helped her to the ground. Then she staggered into the house and flung herself into a chair beside the table, took her face in her arms and wept—I knew she wasn't weeping about the barked shins.

Reading the account brings relief—that one's own drunken lapses and giddy lines are not recorded with such precision. Later that same evening, after talking some with John, Campbell found Carol in a bedroom at Ed's, curled into the fetal position. He kissed her once, then "again and again," declaring, "Do you realize that in all our lives, this is probably the only hour we'll ever have together?"

"Kiss me just once, Joe. Crucify me with a kiss."

I kissed her a long time. "Jesus Christ!" she moaned. "Jesus Christ, Jesus Christ."

"Before we only felt it," I said. "Now it is explicit."

We were both feeling pretty awful.

"I hope that this is hurting you as much as it's hurting me," she said.

"It is. It is, by God," I said.

In Campbell's scrupulously precise notebook (he later wrote a novel based on this material, and one almost suspects he's writing the dialogue for the fiction as he's living the event), the next day Carol and Joe accompanied Ed and Ritchie and Tal Lovejoy to Santa Cruz on a collecting trip, where Carol and Joe spent the day in their "mutual admiration society," as Carol quipped. She had struck a deep chord in romantic, lonely Joe, and he soothed a similar place in her soul. Feeling neglected, no doubt, and flattered, no doubt, by Joe's attentions, she did not resist his overtures. Nonetheless, it's also possible to stand back and see this flirtation as part of a more generalized love, the emergent country experienced by all in those few weeks together. In his journal Campbell confesses that at Ed's house that evening everyone in the group, including John at this point, were more or less in love with each other, I guess. It was almost like a little fugue of loves—or a rich chord of mixed feelings, all mingled to a harmonious single entity. But the dominant, so far as I was concerned, was this deep mysterious love that has suddenly welded Carol and myself into something like a team.

Before, when I had visited John and Carol, I had felt myself to be the visitor to a splendid little home. Now it is John who seems the outsider. He is like someone who simply captured the girl that I was meant to have married.

The intense little drama continued. Ever honest, Carol admitted to John that she felt attracted to Campbell, and John paid a visit to his rival, acting, according to Campbell's account, chivalric throughout: "How much are you in love with Carol?" he asked Campbell. Since John admired Campbell, he felt him a worthy rival: "If Carol had fallen for someone less than himself, he wouldn't have been afraid to kill—to shoot," John admitted. "I don't need anyone's pity," John said, "A thing like this can't touch me. This is outside me." If Campbell records John's lines accurately, it seems that John wants to detach himself from a plot not of his own making. At this stage, Campbell suggests that the wronged husband seems determined to act with dignity and allow his wife and Joe to discover whether or not their attraction is more than a passing fancy. Trying to explain his emotions to John, Campbell admits that not lust but something more drew him to Carol: "It isn't so much the physical beauty that I'm in love with," he told John.

But that flash of attraction withered quickly enough in the chilly light of Campbell's logic. Campbell considers everyone's perspective, and in a few days convinces himself that Carol, so thoroughly a California girl, would not be happy with him on the East Coast. "The major question, therefore, is how best to help Carol slip out of her present painful infatuation. . . . I am sorry for the discord that my presence has created. I shall do anything in my power to resolve it back to the harmony that I found here."

There's something a little self-absorbed about the entire account from Campbell's perspective—as perhaps journals and reworked fictional accounts have a right to be. But at this point in her marriage, as at so many other times, one longs to hear Carol's side of the story. Certainly she was attracted to him (as well she might be to someone who so passionately declared his love), and certainly John was hardly a doting husband. But according to Idell, Carol never intended to leave John, no matter how gratifying the brief inter-lude with Joe. And Campbell's record of her own comment on the cooled attraction testifies to her resolve: "Isn't it swell!" she said. "And it worked out just as we hoped it would—in a perfectly marvelous friendship."

But that wasn't quite the last word, after all. Carol and Joe dallied about in June 1932, and John simmered, eventually ordering Campbell to "disappear"—a decision that Carol and Joe had also agreed upon. The group split on June 25, after John had, in the end, ordered Campbell out of town at the point of a gun—literally. John headed south to Los Angeles, Carol fled to Sausalito to stay with a friend, and Campbell and Ricketts went on a collecting trip to Alaska, meeting up with Ricketts's coauthor, Jack Calvin, his wife Sasha (Tal's sister), and Xenia Kashevaroff, another sister.

On the boat, Campbell reassessed the whole Pacific Grove episode, once again, and came to the conclusion that in fact it was not he, the interloper, who was most at fault, but rather John, the selfish husband. Joe absolved himself in what seems a spectacular display of self-absorption, convincing himself that John's dramatics were the central problem, that John blew up the episode to "tragic proportions."

> What might have been a sweet, gentle attachment or affection he compressed to dramatic form. Right off the bat he discovered himself in a traditional role, and with all the overemphasis of a ham actor he began to play it in orthodox fashion. At first he was the big, strong, silent, self-sufficient genius, whose wife was merely one of the life incidents to his incidental body. And he was too magnificent to be profoundly touched by the accidents of the flesh. That role, however, soon became a lot too painful, and he [became] the enthralled husband, fighting manfully for the love of a wife who was supremely vital to him. . . . Finally he was the great, strong, virtuous husband, cruelly betrayed—pressed to the point where nothing remained but the hope of a final desperate chance. Nothing daunted, the great, strong, virtuous husband would not hesitate before the inevitable. He issued his ultimatum. He suffered like a god. He triumphed. And in triumph he was magnanimous and wise.

Rivals are not judicious critics. Campbell cast John as well as Carol's marriage to John in the worst possible light—in part, one suspects, to achieve his own detachment. Distance from John and Carol made husband John monstrous and wife Carol a victim. John, Campbell felt, "had a touch of the sadist in his character. He took it out a little bit on the dog, I think he took out a little bit on Carol and he started taking a little bit on me." Carol, on the other hand, was "courageous and very loyal to John," a woman he later described as "a lovely woman . . . resilient and alive, intelligent, bright, sparkling and full of fun." She and John, he thought, were "about as different as two people could be." But Campbell remained resolute that he and Carol could never get together on a permanent basis, although clearly marriage had been discussed. Joe ponders Carol's situation in his journal, and concludes that two mistakes—that is, marriage to John and then to him—would not make "one right." He believes that John would insist on an honorable solution, that he and Carol marry, but he wants Carol to resist that solution, "stand on her own two feet"—as even "girls" can, he concludes. What Campbell found most distasteful in the John/Carol marriage was their childlessness; for him the central purpose of marriage was to have children. In his mind, self-absorbed John refused Carol an "old fashioned honor virtue marriage with children," as well as denied her a modern marriage with mutual freedom: "he has split the thing—giving her an honor-virtue, 50-50 responsibility, childless, husband-dominating monster of a marriage which looks very cozy at first glance, but pretty sad on a little inspection. Carol has been jipped."

Soon Ed received a frantic letter from Carol. Apparently John had disappeared, fleeing to the high Sierra. She was worried. Campbell was even more disgusted with John's theatrics:

> The laws of high tragedy would demand a flight to the Sierras. . . . He has focused the amazed attention of all society upon the hole that has been left behind him. He has no doubt excited the profound pity of his most immediate family. He has demonstrated to Carol how violently unhappy his sensitive soul's reactions will be to her most little peccadillo. She will understand in the future what tragedies may result from her departures from the rules set down by John—and by all right thinking people.

Campbell's narrative line includes no understanding of John's feelings and only limited appreciation of Carol's devotion.

A man who has known a woman for a few weeks is probably not the best judge of a marriage, particularly a romantically inclined young man who headed west to seek release from his own immersion in intellectual pursuits. The episode provides a window on Carol and John's marriage, to be sure. But John had never pretended to be anything but monomaniacal about writing. Carol knew that, and yet was tempted, as who would not be, by Joe's full-throttle attention. With her curious mix of neediness and strength, Carol was just the woman to be resolute and then waver, to be susceptible to the attractions of a twenty-eight-year-old, highly intelligent, merry and footloose young man who told her she was wonderful. What the affair reveals, in the end, is both Carol's vitality—how appealing that was to the many people who knew her—and her terrible vulnerability, not in finding Campbell attractive, but apparently in not having the tools to cope after Campbell left, as evidenced by what Campbell terms her frantic letters. It was not so much the marriage that was tested as it was Carol herself—the woman who never had the security to know she was valued. Carol relished the temptation, the passionate moments, and the chase itself, and then had to deal with the fallout of a deeply wounded husband. Here are the elements of Greek tragedy in the ecology of the phalanx.

While Carol and John suffered, Campbell spent his summer in company with Ricketts, collecting marine specimens, hiking to glaciers, enjoying late-night parties and songs until 1:00 A.M. At stops in Sitka and Juneau Campbell received messages from Carol, and he wrote her back, but he was increasingly distracted by lovely Xenia Kashevaroff, Tal Lovejoy's sister. Early on, he told Xenia of the "John and Carol adventure," and the complexity of the story may have sparked mutual interest, certainly Xenia's sympathy (she knew John and Carol from spending some time in LA at the Sheffields'). Some collecting certainly was accomplished—two hundred sea cucumbers one day, five hundred pink jellyfish another. At odd moments, Campbell proofed the manuscript that Calvin and Ricketts had completed (*Between Pacific Tides*)—chiefly correcting the grammar, which didn't improve Calvin's temperament. Evening discussions were characteristically intense: Ricketts would later write a sheet entitled "Worth remembering concepts arrived at or considered during the 1932 BC Alaska trip—differences in intellect, intuition, and instinct; the physics of light; and Spengler's chief classifications." And there was the usual talk of "Spengler vs. Sociologist" and "Chinese Theatre" and "Art vs. Science."

Probably Ricketts was more affected by the trip to Alaska than anyone else on board. Observing waves pounding on the Pacific coast and the contrasting long swells in the inside passage, he developed his ideas about wave shock and how it affects evolution and distribution of intertidal invertebrates exposed to surf. The emerging notion of "survivability" would be one he shared with John.

For all four, the intensity of the Campbell-Ricketts-Steinbeck-Carol interlude would linger. Years later, Campbell wrote Ricketts that "you and your life-way stand close to the source of [my] enlightenment." Ed was "not quite a guru," said Campbell, but almost. What must have inspired Campbell—as it did Carol, in her way, and John, in his—was not just Ed's presence and the circle of friends and the biological curiosity and the spirituality, but, with Joe himself as catalyst, the rarified group dynamics. Add Joe to the Ricketts mix, and all the individual units gleamed more intensely, discovering parts of themselves heretofore masked. As the phalanx expanded in Ed's presence, there were more opportunities for inspirational fire, catalyzed by Carol. And Campbell also exposed the human foibles behind the magical entity. After all, these seekers and yearning spirits were only human.

Even after John left the Monterey Peninsula, even after Ed's death in 1948, there is little doubt that Ed's ideas continued to influence John, in particular. Throughout the 1940s John and Ed wrote at least two letters a week to each other—letters Steinbeck burned after Ed's death in 1948. Even when separate, the two remained one, sometimes eerily so. After Pearl Harbor, for example, Ricketts wrote about Hitler and war, and his perspective is, in part, John's when he wrote *The Moon Is Down*. Ricketts wrote: 'In war, thoughts are acts.'" He followed that observation with an essay, "On Man's Approach to the Problems of International Understanding," and sent the manuscript to *Harpers, Atlantic Monthly, Cosmopolitan,* and *Reader's Digest.* It was rejected by all. In it he urges Americans to go to local libraries and try to understand the Japanese mind and the German mind by assuming the enemy's perspective: "according to enemy psychology and coordinated to our own, and then applied and supplemented by geopolitical intelligence, to the military problems and to the subsequent international problems facing us." John wrote *The Moon Is Down* from a similar awareness, giving an imaginative context both to the notion that "in war, thoughts are acts" and to Ricketts's suggestion that Americans try to think from the perspective of their enemies. In his play-novelette, Steinbeck imagines what it might be like to live in a Northern European village, occupied by German soldiers, some of whom are sympathetic. His play-novelette was written for a wide audience, a reading, theatrical, and cinematic audience (book, play, and film followed in short order in 1942), and Steinbeck wanted the theatrical audience, in particular, to "participate in the production. The perfectly effective drama is consummated rather than produced—a kind of mystic trinity of play players and audience become one unit." Another iteration of the phalanx, the transformative power of art. For Ricketts as well, participation was "the most deeply interesting thing in the world." Their friendship and love was fully participatory for both; they were a unit.

For several years, Carol was a participant as well. She sensed that Ed's 1948 death was a suicide, and there are a few hints that might be so. At least one friend thought Ed had an incurable medical condition. And Ed wrote a letter to his beloved Jean Ariss before he died, suggesting that he had a sense of the end. Ed was very spiritual and, according to Jean, communicated with people psychically. The day he was hit by a train was also Jean's birthday. Steinbeck also was uneasy about Ed in the days before the accident. In a journal entry written in the days before Ed's death, separated by a continent, unhappy in New York City, John senses that something is terribly wrong with Ed.

And Ed himself left a note in his lab, found after his death:

Sunday night
Now from my grave I wake this place.
Since I no longer walk on hill nor lea.
And am forever from the sight of man.
Forget my grave—and just remember me.

Ed. R.

Most friends, however, as well as his family, insisted that Ricketts's death was accidental, that he stalled his car when crossing the railroad tracks in New Monterey. Probably that's the real story. A month later after the funeral, Steinbeck wrote friends Ritchie and Tal Lovejoy: "Wouldn't it be interesting if Ed *was* us and that now there wasn't any such thing—or that he created out of his own mind something that went away with him. I've wondered a lot about that. How much was Ed and how much was me and which was which." Readers and scholars and fans have wondered the same ever since. John kept Ed close to his heart, telling the Stanford University Press editor a month after Ed's death that he would finish the book Ed started, edit Ed's journals for the last twelve years, "a valuable thing." In 1950 he wrote a portrait of his friend, "About Ed Ricketts." In the mid-1950s he wrote *Sweet Thursday*, a novel that was the source for the musical *Pipe Dream*, featuring Ricketts—Doc—in love. And as he was drafting his final novel in 1960, *The Winter of Our Discontent*, he discussed survivability and endurance of the battered human, essentially echoing Ricketts's notions of wave shock. And in that novel, Ethan Allen Hawley's friendship with Danny preserves many of the fine sensibilities of John and Ed's bond.

Maybe Carol just couldn't get a firm foot in that lab door, and perhaps that mystic and intimate friendship was one of many, many reasons why she remained, throughout most of her marriage, vulnerable. Perhaps deep trust of the kind Ricketts and Steinbeck shared eluded the Steinbecks. At least one friend, Jean Ariss, said that John didn't want anything to come into his inner sanctum—except Ed—and that Carol sometimes complained about that. Undoubtedly Carol was vital to John's work—and treasured as well. But the scrap of "The Roan Stallion" pasted in her scrapbook may be emblematic: being the preserver of fragments, not the creator, may have been excruciatingly lonely.

Carol in front of her childhood home in San Jose, 235 South Sixteenth Street. This is probably her eighth grade graduation; she would then enter San Jose High School, graduating in 1924. Carol's parents lived in this house until the early 1960s.

John and his red pony, Jill, in the front yard of his Salinas home on Central Avenue, circa 1907. John was given the pony when he was four years old. (Photo from Carol's scrapbooks.)

"John and Carol gathering cephalopods." Carol is playing the accordion, an instrument that she purchased from Carlton Sheffield, Steinbeck's college roommate, for one cent. Her playing drove Sheffield to distraction. (Drawing from Carol's scrapbooks.)

Carol, John, and Ritchie Lovejoy, mid-1930s. Ritchie and his wife, Tal, were close friends of John and Carol's throughout the 1930s. Ritchie was an artist, designer, journalist, and writer. In 1940, Steinbeck gave him the one thousand dollars from his Pulitzer Prize for *The Grapes of Wrath*.

John and Carol with duck in photo booth, mid-1930s. His friend Bo Beskow felt that John was fun loving, but he also recognized the profound sadness in the man. Carol, he insisted, understood him completely. (Photo from Carol's scrapbooks.)

Woodcut of John by Ritchie Lovejoy, mid-1930s, from Carol's scrapbooks.

Carol on the deck of the SS *Drottningholm* in 1937, bound for Denmark. John insisted that he was restless all his life. The trip to Europe in 1937 was the first time overseas for both of them.

FACING PAGE:
Top: Carol in Mexico City, 1935, with the maids Candelaria and Appolonia, whose nicknames were "Candy" and "Apple." John and Carol rented an apartment in Mexico City for several weeks from folklorist Frances Toor.
Bottom: Carol, mid-1930s. "Carol was a plain dresser," insisted the butcher in Los Gatos. It was about this time that she registered as a Communist in Santa Clara County (November 8, 1938), but she changed her affiliation to Democrat in 1939.

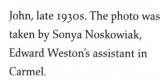

Carol at the Dickey Wells Club,
New York City, 1938. Wells was
a jazz trombonist. Carol loved
jazz and went to clubs in the city
in January 1938, when she took
a train east to see the Broadway
play *Of Mice and Men*. John
stayed in California.

John, late 1930s. The photo was
taken by Sonya Noskowiak,
Edward Weston's assistant in
Carmel.

Brush Road ranch, Los Gatos. As John was writing *The Grapes of Wrath* in the summer of 1938, Carol found a lovely piece of land to buy in the Santa Cruz Mountains, forty-seven acres that overlooked the Santa Clara Valley. They built a home and moved there in late 1938. For a couple of years, John and Carol were happy on the ranch, where visitors included Charlie Chaplin, Burgess Meredith, and, of course, Ed Ricketts.

Carol and Elsie Ray with rattle-snakes, Brush Road ranch, circa 1939. Carol had gone to high school in San Jose with Elsie Ray. According to Elsie's husband, Martin, Elsie repeatedly insisted that Carol hire help for housecleaning. She was, he said, trying to do it all on the ranch—wash clothes and bedding as well as entertain.

Edward F. Ricketts, 1930s. In Ed's copy of *Cannery Row*, John wrote: "With all the respect and affection this book implies, John Steinbeck." From 1930 to 1948, marine biolo-gist Ricketts was Steinbeck's closest friend. (Courtesy of the National Steinbeck Center.)

Humanity is the start of the race; I say
Humanity is the mold to break away from, the crust to break through, the coal to break into fire,
The atom to be split.
Tragedy that breaks man's face and a white fire flies out of it; vision that fools him

Out of his limits, desire that fools him out of his limits, unnatural crime, inhuman science,
Slit eyes in the mask; wild loves that leap over the walls of nature, the wild fence-vaulter science,
Useless intelligence of far stars, dim knowledge of the spinning demons that make an atom,
These break, these pierce, these deify, praising their God shrilly with fierce voices.

Joggi

old Moonlight

Page from one of Carol's scrapbooks: photo of Carlton Sheffield, Steinbeck's Stanford roommate; a photo of Moonlight, John's father's horse in Salinas; a few lines from Robinson Jeffers's "Roan Stallion"; and a photo of one of the Steinbecks' dogs, Joggi.

Carol's drawing from the sportswomen series "The Diver." Another friend called the series her "Rosey Nymphs." Carol also made small and whimsical clay sculptures, "cartoons in clay," she said, when voted into the Carmel Art Association in 1942.

Gwen Conger, publicity photo, circa 1938. Gwen was born in Wisconsin in 1917
and died at age fifty-eight in Boulder, Colorado. John's cousin Stanford Steinbeck thought that Gwyn, like Carol, was "mercurial"—and also witty, lively,
funny, and unreliable. (Photo by Maurice Seymour, a Chicago photographer.
Courtesy of Ron Seymour.)

Carol volunteering for the Red Cross during World War II. Beneath this photo in her scrapbook is a clipping from a local paper: "Carol Steinbeck Takes on Three Jobs This Week," a "triple load in the Carmel Red Cross office on Dolores Street." Next to that clipping is a typed note: "Carol is a delightful nut with character . . . a fine female of rare vintage."

Carol's marriage to Loren Howard at the East Garrison Chapel, Camp Roberts, Sunday, July 4, 1943. She wore a "silk suit of periwinkle blue patterned in burgundy and white with a frou-frou jabot," her wedding announcement noted.

Carol's passport photo, 1948. The year of
her divorce from Loren Howard, she went
on trips to Hong Kong, India, and the
Philippines.

CHAPTER FIVE

Wave Shock, 1932–35

IN THE SUMMER OF 1932, with the equilibrium between John and Carol precariously tipped, the two stood in separate corners, chastened. The wronged husband had borrowed a scene from a pulp western in ordering Joseph Campbell out of Pacific Grove and then stalking off into the hills. Eventually he made his way to Carlton Sheffield's house in Los Angeles and there received solace from Maryon Sheffield: "I never knew anyone who had more kindness," he later wrote to Sheffield. "She and you pulled me through a very bitter time and I can still feel how very bitter it was." For John, Carol's full attention had long seemed a given. With that devotion compromised, he must have suffered greatly. Although the disequilibrium in their marriage would be corrected soon enough, the imbalance tested loyalties.

And yet the fallout from the Campbell dalliance seems, in the main, more positive than not. The entire episode—the spark of rivalry, the charge of attractions (both physical and intellectual), and the eventual change of scene to Southern California—released energies in both John and Carol. "Surviv-ability" was a notion that Steinbeck embraced throughout his writing life, insisting that the "survival quotient" (Ricketts's term) of any species was largely based on the ability to withstand or surmount extreme conditions. When conditions were too favorable, when a species was overfed, overly safe, surfeited with "plenty" (like Steinbeck's gopher in *Cannery Row*, for example), individuals grew "soft." At the same time that John and Carol were renego-tiating their marriage, Ed Ricketts was sailing along the Alaskan coast, con-sidering the effects of wave shock on the Pacific littoral and concluding that wave shock was the most significant factor determining the distribution of intertidal organisms on the Pacific coast.

Wave shock is an apt trope for the next three years of the Steinbecks' lives. During these stressful years, however, Steinbeck's writing drive was renewed and increasingly intense, and Carol felt needed. She could show her best self when confronting adversity with an undaunted spirit. Challenges clarified

and intensified her role as staunch companion, made the "we" of their partnership more evident, and produced a phalanx ever more resilient and tough.
Steinbeck admitted in 1936 that he needed "opposition to work against," and
Carol, pushing and pulling and nudging, served as his foil and "literary conscience." She "didn't spare him any criticism of his person or his prose," said
one friend, and John recognized that her toughness was good for him. Theirs
was a restless relationship, with both accepting the inevitability of fights
and tensions and perpetual, rugged little arguments. What Steinbeck said of
Granma and Granpa Joad in *The Grapes of Wrath* was, in fact, probably a
description of his own marriage: "They fought and they loved and needed
the fighting." Resistance sparked new ideas as passivity or complacency
would not have. Undoubtedly Carol scraped John's ego, but she also gave him
certainty in the torn places. Theirs was a tenacious little unit, with conflict
bringing forth their fiercest and most creative selves.

"Nearly everyone can write the first four chapters of a book," John would
write sixteen years later. "It is writing the third book when no one would look
at the first two that makes a writer." In the summer of 1932, that's what John
did, write that difficult third book. Having burned seventy old stories in late
spring of 1932 and abandoned much of the original "Unknown God" manuscript, which he had been wrestling with since he met Carol, he began the
final revision of *To a God Unknown*, weaving into the narrative Campbell's
ideas, Jeffers's poetry, and Carol's betrayal. As it took shape, for the first time
he addressed his prose to an imagined audience, Carlton Sheffield, his friend
of a decade and the man who helped pull him through his recent pain. This
handwritten manuscript with notes to Sheffield—as well as the published
book itself—sheds some light on his feelings during that time.

At some point in 1932, in the same ledger book where he'd written the
stories of *The Pastures of Heaven*, he "begins a narrative built from the ruins
of the Unknown God" and pens an invocation to the story itself, to male
virility—his own so recently tested—to his hero Joseph Wayne's power, and
to his own creativity. All three fuse in a kind of Whitmanesque declaration of
creative ardor: "Now the new work starts—a good plan, a good story; strong,
sturdy, standing with fine legs set wide, and contemplating the wreckage of
the earth-body. His chin is down and his bewildered eyes look at the ground.
And then his active love arises, a force as mighty as the thrust in the thighs
of a bull when he drives the invincible phallus into the quivering yoni. And
the love grows like a black rain until he drains the good blood from his throat
upon the dying earth." Pent-up sexual energies, those of the book's hero as

well as Steinbeck's own, one suspects, explode onto the page. Fictional trans-
ference vitalized his own artistic and personal powers.

It's tempting to read elements of Joseph Wayne's courting story biographically. Early in the book, Elizabeth, Joseph's intended, looks down from
her second-story window on a drunken Benjy, Joseph's brother, and barely
resists the urge to descend the stairs into his arms. This brief and rather odd
episode—an aborted fictional betrayal—may owe something to Carol's attraction to Joe. And John rewrote this scene; in the original manuscript not Benjy
but strangers sing under Elizabeth's window, surely a less charged encounter
than the yearning for a brother's arms. Subsequently in the novel, Benjy is
murdered during a stolen tryst with another man's intended. His punishment
for philandering is, in effect, a fictional erasure of Campbell. (Much later in
his career, Steinbeck would parody Campbell's earnestness in *Sweet Thursday*
when he created Joe Elegant, who explains to Fauna the "myth and symbol"
in his novel: "'You see,' he said, 'the grandmother stands for guilt.' 'Ain't she
dead and buried?'[says Fauna] 'Yes.' 'That's kind of messy guilt.' 'It's the reality below reality,' said Joe Elegant. 'Balls!' said Fauna. 'Listen, Joe, whyn't you
write a story about something real?'")

On the other hand, virile, creative, empire-building Joseph—whose creative drive, curiosity, and spiritual yearning were the author's own—attracts
both his own wife, Elizabeth, and his brother's wife, Rama. He's a stud, a lover
as intense and passionate as John was purported to be—in his own estima-
tion at least. Joseph's punishment for abundant passion is to suffer—his wife's
death, Rama's departure, and the earth's sterility. Although Steinbeck and his
hero are hardly one, nonetheless some of the book's strange betrayals, sexual
energies, and uneasy familial bonds owe something to the Carol/Joe tryst.
While Steinbeck's impulse is largely symbolic and mythic in this ambitious,
uneven novel set in a valley near Mission San Antonio, the autobiographical
imprint cannot be dismissed.

There is one more important consideration about these uneasy months
in mid-1932. Carol, a woman who once gaily rode in a wheelbarrow to Monterey's Hermann's café, had a highly developed sense of the absurd, the
unpredictable, the unwarranted. She loved to shock people, to tip balances.
The Campbell episode had certainly accomplished that—and perhaps unconsciously that is what she intended, to shake things up a bit. Recent studies
show that such absurdities are palliative, sending observers like John, who
so often relished Carol's antics, back to highly patterned activities. Carol's passions and outbursts and eccentricities were precisely what anxious,

depressive John needed in those apprentice years. Her unpredictability charged his disciplined writing life, his search for patterns.

One way to consider many of the short stories he wrote after the two got back together is as a dialectical exploration of order and disorder, rooted in his own marriage dynamic: In "The Chrysanthemums," Elisa Allen is tempted to abandon her clean swept house and careful husband to follow the ramshackle but sweet-talking tinker; in "The White Quail," Mary Teller obsessively guards her sculpted garden from the disorderliness of slugs and dogs and weeds—and from a passionate husband who can't "understand" her neat patterns; in "The Harness," Peter Randall wears physical and emotional harnesses—shedding both during his yearly pilgrimage to San Francisco brothels, breaking away from his shackled Salinas life; in "The Snake," Doctor Phillips's careful routines are disrupted by the mysterious dark woman's intense desire to possess and feed a rattlesnake. Over and over Steinbeck's stories balance order and stasis with disorder and unpredictability. Wild impulses and random incidents disrupt characters' settled ways and opinions. John's plots key into some of Carol's transgressive behavior. He had a deep attraction to the unpredictable.

While John worked through his pain in fiction, Carol blocked her own. Throughout her life she confided her deepest feelings to few and left no record of her inner demons. She was, on the one hand, extremely loyal to people, and on the other hand, "hard to know . . . had a shell" around her, as one friend described her character. She had a "way of deriding everyone," and yet if something happened to a friend, "she would show sympathy, empathy." Perhaps only her carefully assembled scrapbooks offer some clues to paradoxical Carol. A delightful unpredictability characterizes the scrapbooks that she compiled during her years with John, each one foregrounding John's experiences: if the arranging hand is Carol's, the narrative is largely John's. The scrapbooks mirror the plot of their lives together, a dynamic that, at this point in their marriage, worked for both: "Jn could never tell what he was going to do, probably didn't even know, without having a cue from Carol," said Ricketts a few years later. But it's also true that her creative output relied as much on his presence in her life.

The urge to clip and save, arrange and paste is autobiographical, of course. Carol's "visual autobiography" is a testament to enmeshed lives. About half the pages in her first scrapbook, contained in a ledger book similar to the ones John wrote in, include photos, reviews, and clippings about John. But if his steady accomplishments are the book's spine, their shared world is its flesh, pages filled with photographs, friends' wit, whimsical clippings, her poetry, others' drawings, and here and there a letter or a telegram or a postcard. The chronology is loose. Very few captions appear. Photos of friends are unidentified. Undoubtedly a large part of her autobiographical urge was to document his fame and her marriage, but another, equally compelling need was to assemble her own idiosyncratic record of random moments, a composition as disorderly as Carol's own spirit (as disorderly as John's later fictive autobiography of the 1930s, *Cannery Row*, a book that captures, as do Carol's scrapbooks, life as lived—plotless and formless). Her ledger scrapbook celebrates the carnivalesque in their lives. The authentic and the offbeat are placed side by side, snippets that amused and delighted, flotsam and jetsam that inform and record.

That whimsical organization—a not uncommon feature of scrapbook compilers, who arrange artifacts according to their own fancy—is also artfully and carefully arranged on each page, clippings and photos neatly blocked. Hers is trimmed spontaneity.

The first scrapbook begins on page 31 of a ledger book, with a news clipping about John's reaction to a January 1933 Laguna Beach earthquake. (Some twenty pages on—chronology be damned—is a clipping from the San Jose paper that quotes Carol's response to the quake—"Quake Terrors Told by Local Girl at Beach Home"—on the same page as a 1907 photo of John, his sister Mary, and the Red Pony.) Also on page 31 are two small photos of the couple's dog, "Joggi 14 months" and "Joggi 2/18/34," as well as a letter addressed to an unknown Mrs. West, which ends "J. Steinbeck . . . He is demon." Humor erupts in these pages. Five pages on is pasted a November 9, 1925, postcard to John from artist Mahlon Blaine (who created the cover art for *Cup of Gold* and *To a God Unknown*), then living on Green Place in Brooklyn, while beneath is a photo of Ed and Anna Ricketts taken in the 1920s and next to their photo a calling card that must have made Carol chuckle: "Maury Maverick, Texas, Member of Congress.") On page 44 is a photo of "Tillie's intended," a dog named "Western Boy" from Flashlight Kennels. Since Tillie died in 1932, it's difficult to fathom why material from 1933 and 1934 is placed a dozen pages earlier. Or why "Tilly after a bath" is pasted on page 72 (or why the dog's name is spelled two different ways). Or why the American Kennel Club registration for their first dog is folded on page 68. Or why a 1925 or 1926 note from Mahlon Blaine about where John might submit the *Cup of Gold* manuscript is pasted on page 87, followed by a 1933 postcard on the next page, noting that Una Jeffers was *"thrilled* at the *great* power and beauty" of *To a God Unknown* and wants also to read *Pastures of Heaven*. Chronology is simply abandoned.

The scrapbook is Carol's eye on the world. And that eye is not telling a linear story. Childhood photos of John and Jill the "Red Pony," as Carol notes, appear several times. John's sister Esther is here, age fifteen. Mr. Steinbeck stands before the Eleventh Street cottage. Carol smiles beneath a bonnet as a little girl. One suspects she pulled out childhood photos from a drawer or a box and pasted them in to fill random spaces—ever resourceful, ever practical, ever guarded.

But strands of this eclectic book reveal much about this marriage. Dogs are clearly beloved. Included are photos of Bruga (bought in 1930) and Tillie (bought in Pacific Grove, 1930, to replace Bruga, who died too soon) and Joggie (1934) and Toby (1936, the puppy that ate Steinbeck's manuscript of *Of Mice and Men*), and Airedales Omar I and Omar II. All dogs are identified; people rarely are. Dogs assumed an elevated status in Carol's book. Emblematic is a caption beneath a 1927 photo taken at Lake Tahoe (and pasted twenty pages from the opening): "'Jerry' (and John)," parenthetical John. On the next page John's childhood dog appears: "Teddy [line one] John + Mary on Jill [line two]." Dogs trump people in such captions. Excepting dogs, very little else is identified in these pages—no sources given, no dates noted. Indeed, Carol seldom writes in her scrapbooks, eschewing any explanation of what things mean, never contextualizing.

Many pages honor John's work. A letter from the mother of a childhood friend, Mrs. Edith Wagner, dated November 17, 1933, acknowledges his gift of *To a God Unknown*: "I love every word you use about California. You bring home to me the smells, the sights, the sounds the feeling of California. John Muir does that for the Sierras. But he, of course, could not create, out of words, a live man. That is your privilege. . . . Your fond and admiring friend, Edith Wagner." Two pages later, upper right corner, appears a 1929 review of *Cup of Gold* from the *Stanford Daily*, praising the novel written by a former English major: "It is the vivid, complete, and truly introspective picture of Henry Morgan's life and character that make the book a thing to be remembered," writes A.M. A 1931 letter from John's Aunt Carrie Danks praising *Cup of Gold* (page 60, next to a photo of "Ballou's Dalmation" on page 61) must have both pleased and amused John and Carol in equal measure: "I hope that the talent of writing which God gave you may be used to point the way that Christian civilization has progressed from the bloody days of the buccaneers to the present age when the selfish passions of the human heart are just as strong and deadly, although more refined in their methods of operation." And on page 90 appears a telegram from George Albee (clearly referring to *Tortilla Flat*): "Covici says greatest discovery ever will print anything hurray. Congratulations." Carol preserved and celebrated John's accomplishments, his writing through others' eyes.

The compiler also stamps her book with a fine sense of life's absurdities: "Beach Property: Hermosa: $450 Full price. 2 shacks, gar. Full lot. Awful condition, poor location 5 blks. To ocean. Hermosa Realty, 140 Pier." Or this one on page 73: "Tall Stories but True: For Your Salvation Army Scrapbook," a yellowed, illustrated clipping: "Five Buckets of Hot Soda Water used by slum lassies to determine whether woman is white or black . . . she had not been washed for six years (London)." John adored Carol's fine-tuned sense of the ridiculous. The two "laughed about the same things," recalled photographer Peter Stockpole, "the human scene, human frailities."

Friends' wit punctuates the scrapbooks. Their whimsy was far more important to Carol, it seems, than the fact that 1932 was the worst year of the Depression; or that in March of that year, Charles Lindbergh's twenty-month-old son was kidnapped from his New Jersey home. Or that FDR was elected president that fall. Or, in 1934, that Upton Sinclair's "Campaign of the Century" for governor of California captivated everyone in the state. Carol read the *New Yorker* but assembled the "Pacific Grover," her world with John. The outside world enters in only as it applies to John's work, dogs, their friends, or her own sense of the absurd. After John was turned down for both a Guggenheim and a Phelan award in 1935, a friend sent a hand-lettered "certificate" from the "Refused Awards Club (R.A.C.)." The proclamation states: "Your application for membership in the club has been carefully considered by the jury of selection. We regret to inform you that the judgement [sic] has been that other applicants had a more worthy claim on the few memberships we were able to extend." Drollery was preserved.

Included is a birth announcement from John's Stanford friend, lawyer Toby Street, "Announcement of Street Improvement":

Announcement is hereby made to those concerned that the area bounded by Webster and Frances Street and intersected by Margery and Nancy Street has been improved by the addition of a small new avenue to be known as Mary de Laguna Street: Total length, nineteen inches: Excellent grade throughout. Work completed April 28, 1931.

This little Street is not yet completely curbed, but is equipped with beautiful ornamental lamps. (water and gas mains now being tested) No stop signs: horizontal parking until further notice.

Frequent inclusions are Ritchie Lovejoy's deft missives, clippings, and drawings from Alaska, where he and Tal moved in 1932: "This place is like the veldt. You cant stand it but there you are. Everybody is as terrible as they are likabele [sic]. I crap on them. You sit around in your long underclothes getting chirhoosis of the liver and rectal fistuals. . . . If you go into the hills you have to pack a hundred pound rifle and tickle bears with it, and they get mad and eat pieces off your spinal cord." John wrote a tongue-in-cheek letter in response, addressed to the editor of *The Arrowhead*, Ritchie's new Alaskan publication: "Shrdlu Etoin From California: . . . When are you going to have a limerick contest because we do them so good. Frankly, Mr. Lovely, and all joking to one side, we think you got something there. Signed, Jon." Minds mesh in this scrapbook. In the 1930s, the written word cemented relationships, particularly valued if jocular, extravagant, and clever. Wordplay countered Depression despondency.

A splendid artifact is a 1936 poem sent to Ed Ricketts from Alice and John Cohee. Alice was the one who urged John to send the oft-rejected "Tortilla Flat" manuscript to one more publisher, who accepted it for publication (and Alice was presented with the manuscript):

We introduce two nubile newts,
Or efts, or some such lowly brutes,
Suitable packed, as you'll discover
Proceeding under separate cover

We found them wandering in thickets
And thought at once of Edward Ricketts.
We'd like to know—please don't revile us—
Some facts about Diemeictylus.

Does nutsis come from the newt?
And do newts mew or are newts mute?
If not mute, is the newt disputant?
Why are newts' noodles often mutant?

. . . .

Can newts knit parachutes of jute?
Do newts take notes on King Canute?
We want to know—we really do
Please answer, meanwhile, newts to you.

Who wouldn't hang on to that? Carol must have spent hours assembling the shimmering fragments, creating a kaleidoscopic memoir of her life with John. But one longs for keys to the most tantalizing items, some bits in the self-revelatory mode. They surface rarely: one is a yellowed 1934 *Chronicle* clipping on page 84: "I saw you" by wolo. Columnist wolo sketched random San Franciscans and recorded their conversations. If you recognized yourself in one of his columns, you went to the *Chronicle* office and were given the drawing. Perhaps this is Carol—it certainly sounds like one of her terrible dreams, told to Marge: "SAY-MARGE!—what I was gonna tell ya!—I HAD A AWWWFUL DREAM LAST NITE—just DREADFUL!!!—can't remember just HOW it STARTED, but I do remember that I had to walk over a lot of HORRIBLE SNAKES!!!—and one GREAT BIG ONE—AT LEAST THAT BIG AROUND—was CRAWLING UP MY LEG!! BBBRR!!! And of course I was AFRAID TO TOUCH IT and I COULDN'T RUN AWAY OR CALL FOR HELP OR ANYTHING!!! I am TELLIN' YA MARGE—I COULDA DIED— but I DIDN'T—" Carol had repeated and chilling nightmares; this may have been the closest she came to confessing their hold on her.

In short, Carol and John emerged from the Campbell cul-de-sac as creative, energized individuals, "wrapped up in each other, happy," said Sheffield, who saw their partnership as renewed, energized. They were soon enough ensconced in his Southern California home—a magnet for the two. LA was a magnet for the two, or else they liked taking a road trip with a friendly face at the end of it. Once at the Sheffields', Carol, true to form, gleefully sawed away at Sheffield's accordion. That fall, Sheffield and Carol sealed a pact concerning her determined assault on the instrument, Sheffield selling it for one cent to Carol with the understanding that she limit her playing to one thousand feet from the house and one half hour per day. The long contract, issued to "Carol Steinbeck, her heirs or assigns, forever and forever, amen," is another fragment of Carol's tomfoolery.

Living in Montrose and then in Laguna Beach, John wrote steadily, finishing the manuscript of *To a God Unknown* in February 1933. Although they wanted another dog—Tillie had died—they were "very happy" and very, very poor, "heading for the rocks," John wrote, since the power was soon to be turned off in their Montrose home. "My wife says she would much rather go out and meet disaster, than to have it sneak up on her," he wrote a friend. "The attacking force has the advantage. I feel the same way. We'll get in the car and drive until we can't buy gasoline any more." Being on the precipice of financial ruin, homelessness, and hunger galvanized John and Carol. Taking off down the road gave the restless pair a sense that they were, as always, moving ahead, even if only to the south end of LA, Laguna Beach, where they found a shack to rent for a couple of dollars a month. The rundown house had only a tiny bathtub, where John would sit with his knees drawn up. Carol would "laugh like a banshee" at him and charge visitors five cents to see John's "enormous back." John would give a "royal wave of the hand" when a visitor entered. One friend swore that you "got your money's worth to see John doubled up in that tub."

Another crisis hit. On March 10, 1933, a 6.4-magnitude earthquake struck Long Beach, killing over a hundred people in the area from Compton south, toppling buildings, pushing others off foundations. In Long Beach, the front of a hotel peeled away, leaving bedrooms exposed. Living in Laguna Beach, John and Carol had been near the epicenter of what proved to be a major earthquake, which demonstrated to Californians how fragile were the state's reinforced masonry buildings. Describing the destruction to their own house, Carol told a reporter: "the south wall seemed to snap into the room. The windows shivered violently. Another shock followed, hurling me out the door as the windows beside it crashed on me. I caught sight of a cascade of falling dishes as I landed on my hands and knees. The lights went out. Neighboring chimneys started to topple." After the quake, she and John "went to town immediately to see the damage." Quoting Carol's account, the article continues: "All the street chandeliers were shattered and still falling. Brick walls were literally pealed [sic] off. The stock in stores was in a really funny mess. . . . All night the house shuddered and made grinding noises. We spent all Saturday on the lawn. We are still having quakes. The whole earth shakes constantly, but it isn't at all dangerous—just makes one a trifle seasick."

John was also interviewed: "The earthquake is a movement that kills stagnation. Only static things are heartbreaking."

But he quickly realized that change is heartbreaking too: a few days later Mrs. Steinbeck fell ill, went to the Salinas hospital, and, in April, suffered a major stroke. Although John had long resisted his mother's overbearing ways, he was, of course, devastated by her illness. Strong, resolute, and fearless mothers are not supposed to lie helpless before their offspring, one day doing a little better, the next slipping back. Since John and Carol were the only family members without small children to care for, they took on home care in Salinas, moving north almost immediately after hearing the news. Weeks turned into months of caregiving, grueling for both. Carol took charge: she "is working like a dog," John wrote to Albee shortly after the couple arrived in Salinas. "She stays cheerful and makes things easier for all of us. . . . There are terrible washings every day. 9–12 sheets. I wash them and Carol irons them." Imagine ironing sheets, nurturing a stunned Mr. Steinbeck, and typing John's stories when she had time. Carol became a lifeline for both Steinbeck men. John, emotionally drained, wrote stories next to the bed where once larger-than-life Olive, who had spent her life with a steady hand on everyone around her, lay helpless, nearly lifeless. It's a common enough scene, but it awakens in any child a new maturity, somber thoughts of mortality, nostalgia, and depression.

The shock brought John to his best work to date, his sharpest thinking. Just as the crisis in his marriage gave him the discipline to complete *To a God Unknown*, the crisis of his mother's immobilized frame fired the "good discipline" to compose *The Red Pony*. For Steinbeck, life's blows were intense and also palliative; he wanted to "prove to myself that I can write in any circumstance," he wrote to George Albee. As he sat near his mother, he keyed into his own past and wrote "the whole thing . . . as simply told as though it came out of the boy's mind." Not only *The Red Pony* stories, but also "The Chrysanthemums," and then *Tortilla Flat*, arguably some of the finest prose of his career, were written near Olive's deathbed.

Out of that grief also emerged his great "theme"—group man, "whirling like sparks out of a bonfire." That theme, he believed, was "much huger" than *To a God Unknown*, just as that book was "larger" than *Pastures*. That theme changed his vision, he declared, gave him "ferocious pleasure" and made his mother's illness, source of his idea, "worth it." (That last comment was evidence of how his writing life engulfed him at times.) To John it seemed that the cells in his mother's body had rebelled, leaving her another person altogether. As John wrote to George Albee, the phalanx theory "has caught Carol and engulfed her" as well, so he must have explained group man to her as carefully as he did in letters to Albee and to Carlton Sheffield. To these old friends he lay out the full range of the phalanx. The greatest group unit, he wrote to Sheffield, is "the whole race," which "remembers a time when the moon was close, when the tides were terrific. It remembers a time when the weight of the individual doubled itself every twenty eight days. . . . The human unit has none of these memories." He elaborated on racial memories to Albee, and then turned to other examples of the phalanx—religion, mobs: "And the phalanx has emotions of which the unit man is incapable. The emotion of destruction, of war, of migration, of hatred, of fear. Man unit acting as a part of the phalanx loses his own nature in the nature of the phalanx. . . . Religion is a phalanx emotion and this was so clearly understood by the church fathers that they said the holy ghost would come when *two or three were gathered together.*" Of course, John and Ed discussed the phalanx, Ed observing that part of his attraction to the Middle Ages was the anonymity of the art: the great cathedrals, he said, were constructed by hundreds of anonymous artisans, not an individual architect. That idea appealed greatly to Ed, and to John, who used the metaphor in his own discussion of group behavior.

And the phalanx operated in microcosm as well, a notion that crystalized as he sat by his mother's bedside. It was at this time that he could fully articulate the Jungian idea of the "third person" that girded his need for both Carol and Ricketts, "the plug which when inserted into the cap of the phalanx, makes man lose his unit identity in the phalanx." And it was the artist, he insisted, who was that plug, that keying mechanism, because in the artist "the phalanx comes closest to the conscious. Art then is the property of the phalanx, not of the individual. Art is the phalanx knowledge of the nature of matter and of life." In his notebook he elaborated, rejecting the notion of an autonomous "I": "What is this I?" and mused that "My body is not I—my mind is not I. The mind that [looks] around the house is not I but the combination of these things produce an emotion which is I." To one degree or another, he would incorporate this "discovery" of how unit man was distinct from group man in all the stories he wrote in the next few months, and arguably for the rest of his career.

During the "very long siege" of Olive's illness and his own furious need to write and reconsider his new theme, Carol remained John's sounding board, critic, editor, and typist. As critic, her love of Willa Cather may have helped him hone the lucid precision of these stories, the style much sparer than the textured, symbolic prose of *To a God Unknown,* completed only two months before he began the first Red Pony tale, "The Gift." Returning to Salinas, looking out at Fremont Peak and the Salinas Valley fields, brought Steinbeck vividly back to a sense of place, which Carol had always nurtured in him. Certainly the restraint of the short story helped him tap this remarkable creativity. By May 1934 he had composed five narratives in the Red Pony cycle, all "about Jody or in which Jody was the eyes."

Beginning with "The Gift," the first tale about a boy and his horse, Gabilan, who sickens and dies, he tapped into his own and his character's sense of wonder at the natural, animal, and human world. "The child's sense of wonder, displayed as surprise and joy," writes Edith Cobb in *The Ecology of Imagination*, "is aroused as a response to the mystery of some external stimulus that promises 'more to come' or better still 'more to do'—the power of perceptual participation in the known and unknown." In each of the four stories of the Red Pony cycle, the young boy is aroused to such mystery: of life and death, age, birth. Jody is thrust into the full range of human emotions and, concurrently, the child's eye is sharply focused on the natural world—"dumpling summer clouds," grasses and flowers, horny toads and grass lizards. In the second story, "The Promise," Gitano helps him comprehend the mystery of nature beyond the ranch. Jody dreams of the Great Mountains where he senses "something very wonderful because it wasn't known, something secret and mysterious." His yearning, stifled by his father, is an attempt to unlock a box that contains "racial memories" and to connect to things unknown. (A fifth story, abandoned and never published, is about a ghostly white house in the field, seen by only Jody and his mother as they walk home after Christmas school celebrations—both John and Campbell tell of a similarly spectral white house seen on a hike taken months earlier. Carl Tifflin rejects ghosts because "everything is fixed and real for him." The story is "very simple," Steinbeck writes in his journal, "and a very difficult one to get over. At the same time it might be good to give some little explanation of how people take their ghosts.") The fourth story, "The Promise," shows Jody conforming to his father's expectations, taking care of the horse that bears his new pony. And in "The Leader of the People," the fourth and final tale, his grandfather's narratives help Jody understand migrations, a group unit moving to a larger purpose. In the four stories, Jody moves from "unit Jody" to a boy who fleetingly grasps a mystic whole, "westering" across the continent, as his grandfather describes it.

Longing for a deep connection informs "The Chrysanthemums" as well. It was "written in the attic in Salinas while his mother was downstairs dying, and he was drained," Carol recalled. In this story—Carol thought it his best— he tapped into the "eternal feminine," writing from an acute awareness of Carol's own capped spirit. She spent her days dutifully working: typing John's manuscripts and ironing Olive's sheets and cheering up Mr. Steinbeck— homebound, like Elisa Allen, yearning as does Elisa for a wilder horizon, no doubt. Carol certainly thought the story described her, both physically and mentally. Like Elisa, she "liked to grow things" to express herself. Like Elisa, Carol cultivated a tough shell—she was caustic, "on guard." And like Elisa, only once in a while did she let down and open up, connect deeply. Elisa Allen's aching need to expand beyond the role of housewife, to engage in a bright world beyond her Salinas ranch, captures much of Carol's restless spirit, as Carol herself recognized. (One is tempted to read rootless Joseph Campbell as the tinker who energizes housebound Elisa.)

In the fall of 1933, John began writing the stories that would become *Tortilla Flat*, droll tales inspired by two women Carol and John knew well, Hattie Gragg and Sue Gregory, the latter of whom "was Tortilla Flat," according to Carol. Sue taught Spanish at Monterey High School for years, ran the Spanish club, and lived in a Mexican enclave of Monterey called "Tortilla Flat," in a house so full of termites that later residents had "duck the termites" parties in the spring. The model for Danny was Sue's neighbor. Since Sue was ill and knew she would never write the stories she had heard over the years, she encouraged John's "borrowing" of her tales. A few stories were Hattie Gragg's, an elderly woman who was also connected to the paisanos and lived in one of Monterey's oldest Spanish adobes, near the little drainage ditch where the French doctor dumps Josh Billings's tripas in *Cannery Row*, which was another tale that Hattie told Steinbeck. And Carol brought John a story or two: "Montey Shortridge . . . was transposed into one of the leading characters in *Tortilla Flat*," she recalled, "and is a story in himself—the complete picaresque remittance man."

During these wrenching months of grief and creativity, two things about John's fiction seem particularly clear. He turned to the women around him to shore him up, provide him stories, offer emotional release, and that connection makes its way into the stories themselves. The spirit of Olive is in Jody's firm-minded mother; of Carol in "The Chrysanthemums"; and of Sue and Hattie and Carol herself in *Tortilla Flat*. Critics see the women characters in the paisano stories, in particular, as stereotypical. But another way to consider *Tortilla Flat's* Sweets Ramirez or Mrs. Morales is as independent, feisty, sexy, and assertive paisanas, each as determined to satisfy sexual desires as the paisanos themselves.

Equally important in these stories is John's newly articulated thesis, the phalanx in different iterations. In the months when Steinbeck himself suffered, he imagined a gallery of emergent characters—a child, a woman, and paisanos—who, however buffeted by loss, momentarily "break through," to use Ricketts's term, to something vital and true in relational moments. The child, Jody, vibrates with the mystery and empathy he feels when talking to old Gitano and to his grandfather; Elisa Allen voices her deeply felt connection to the earth when she speaks to the tinker; and the paisanos, merging into a unit, flame to life together in Danny's house. One senses Steinbeck's phalanx thesis rippling beneath his depictions of youth, gender, ethnicity, and class.

Carol had her own gift for her husband. The grief that brought Steinbeck to the cusp of success released creative chords in Carol as well. By December 1933, she had compiled her third text. The Carmel directory was her first, an edited text; the scrapbooks her second, compiled volumes; and a book of poems was her third, bound together as John's Christmas gift, 1933. This Christmas before Olive died was, John later recalled, "the most terrible wrenching scene" of misery he had ever witnessed, with his father trying to "make the Christmas jokes" while Mrs. Steinbeck, "eyes—cold as marbles," lay in her room dying. To cut against this gloom, Carol knitted John a little testicle-warmer of pink baby-wool (she often called him her "cow with the crumpled horn") and presented him with "A Slim Volume to End Slim Volumes," a mimeographed book of her poems, illustrated with a few wry drawings. On the first page she wrote, "This is #1 of a Limited Edition by Carol Steinbeck. To John—my *Inspiration*!" In fact, her inspiration was Dorothy Parker's sophisticated, cynical, and witty view of love. There are no serious love poems in Carol's chapbook. Her poetic stance is like Parker's "ironic self representation," with a keen nose for pretense. "Foundational to the ideology of Modern Love," which Parker espouses, "was the assumption that gender relations were permanently and intrinsically flawed," notes Nina Miller.

What Carol offers John is droll love, in verse that is playful, sometimes acerbic, always humorous. Like Parker, Carol "breaks up the loving dyad of male and female through the implied intervention of her audience, for whom the joke is staged."

The first cheerful little poem suggests that her intended audience is broad, the verses not for John's ears alone. The speaker longs for significant gestures, balm to the needy:

My Mission
May my wee piping cheer the way
For all on beds of pain.
    If I can bring them poesy,
    I shall not sing in vain.

And may my message reach the hearts
Of toilers in the gloom.
I'd carry them one single rose
Or sprig of sage in bloom.

I fain would enter every slum
And mine-shaft with my trill.
I fain would carry words of joy,
Those songless lives to fill.

To mothers bowed with grief and toil,
Soothing their starving broods,
I long to bring one scarlet leaf
Gathered in autumn woods.

Her stance was often winsome, the poet skipping through a disapproving world as muse, minstrel, or "a gypsy dreamer." Here, as in other poems, a twist, or a barb in a final couplet undercuts sentiment:

A Wandering Minstrel, I
I'm just a whimsy madcap scamp.
I rove with the vagrant breeze,
On the highways and byways a singing tramp,
Akin to the birds and the bees.
Life with its stern reality
I spurn with a regal scorn.
It shall never make a slave of me,
I am a monarch born.
Good-bye, good people, I regret
The envy you feel for me.

Drop those feathers and that tar,
I'm going, can't you see.

Although the speaker addresses the envious "good people," ready to tar and feather a carefree "wandering minstrel," Carol's audience is a sophisticated reader who appreciates a playful and disruptive voice. That would be John, certainly. And other unorthodox souls.

Carol's muse was Parker, whose contributions to the *New Yorker* she read avidly, saving each issue. She probably picked up copies of Parker's verse, *Enough Rope* (1926), *Sunset Gun* (1928), and *Death and Taxes* (1931). Like

Parker, Carol skewers the elite or achieves in her verse a detached and aslant perspective—drawing in other savvy readers as her audience. "Grandeur" echoes Steinbeck's fine scorn in *Tortilla Flat* for women who drink gin fizzes all afternoon; "America" mocks patriotism; and "The Unfinished" punctures sentimentality.

Grandeur

Miss Kunkle sits upon the sand,
Curling her shrimp-pink toes.
A silver ribbon in her hair,
A purple hat, a lap dog and
A real watch that goes!

America

America, my land so rich
In ore and lakes and wheat.
I love each ocean and each bitch,
And oranges and meat.
Everything's in order there,
With rabbits nesting in her hair.
Though cynical you all may be,
You cannot pass a redwood tree
Without a doffed, respectful hat,
And bated breath, and things like that.
I love your oceans on each side,
Kept far apart by prairies wide,
Else there would be no inside,
But only oceans wet and blue,
And no U.S. for me and you.

The Unfinished

Whene'er I raise my hand in wrath
I shatter all upon my path.
Last night I tore in two a fish
That lay in parsley on the dish.
And on another, brighter day,
A little baby came my way.
His eyes I plucked, and little toes.

I spilled his blood upon my clothes.
I sometimes wonder,
But who knows?

One poem is, in fact, inscribed to Dorothy Parker—and another to Gertrude Stein. The poem to Parker gently satirizes the sexual tensions of the Western romantic tradition, as in these Parker lines: "Woman wants monogamy; / Men delights in novelty. / Love is woman's moon and sun; / Man has other forms of fun." Carol also writes against romantic clichés, and while freely drawing from female stereotypes in her poems—usually gentle and vulnerable lasses—as does Parker, she shows how stereotypes mask more troublesome issues facing women. In "To Dorothy Parker," the woman is twice rejected—but humor deflects abandonment:

To Dorothy Parker
A shepherd lad came piping
Adown from over the hill.
For him I tore my cap off
And tossed it over the mill.
Gaily I followed his piping
Through meadows far and near.
But when at last he left he took
My watch for souvenir.

And next I loved a madcap boy.
Reckless and proud his sway.
With ice and fire he scored my heart
And then he rode away.
But he has not forgot me,
I know he holds me dear,
For on his wall is hanging
My little pink brassiere.

A women might be spurned in love, as was Parker herself, but certainly not defeated.

To Gertrude Stein
Wee winsome woman—thing,
More butterfly than girl.
What rude hand

Has dast to crush thee
In thy flight?
>   . . . old subscriber

So what does this flight of poems reveal about the author? Perhaps things already clear: Carol's wit punctures complacency; a sense of joie de vivre makes these verses dance. Final couplets, like her own retorts, upend expectations: plucking a baby's eyes and toes? The verses speak resilience and lightly brushed sadness. In the middle of the book is a drawing of a woman with a clock for an abdomen: the biological clock, ticking? Carol's yearning pictured amid the carefree lines? This odd blend of joy, wordplay, and the merest suggestion of her own needs was Carol Steinbeck at twenty-seven years old.

Invictus—(or Ophelia)
Though angry Fate may bow my pride,
My song is glowing safe inside.
Though broken on the torture wheel,
I still give thanks for the power to feel.

Life has shorn me of friends and goods,
But there's welcome for me in the winter woods.
The snow is my friend, and the stormy sky,
No king can be more gay than I.

Rain cannot quench my god-sent fire.
Hunger can bring me no desire.
Brother wolf will his warm cave share.
And I've pretty straw to weave in my hair.

Perhaps the last line tempers this somber verse, but the couplets (her favored form) also convey the poet's heart: unbowed, sweeping the world before her (unlike Ophelia), and using humor as a torch to light the path.

Carol received some recognition for her little booklet: John thought the poems were "swell," as did many friends, who "swamped" her with requests. She sent a copy to Steinbeck's publisher, Robert Ballou, who had asked to see them, but then received no response from him. Ballou's finances were spongy, so it's hardly surprising that frothy poems did not appeal. A few years later, when they visited New York City, John reported that Carol was seeing her publisher about a forthcoming book of her poems and drawings—clearly it was important for her to produce a book. But it never happened.

And after Carol and John separated, she told a reporter in 1941 that "they'll" buy her work "if I sign it Mrs. John Steinbeck. I'll be damned if I do that. I want to be plain Milly Glutz. I want the work to sell because it's good." But in January and February of 1934, a few of her poems were published under the pen name Amnesia Glasscock in a local arts magazine, the *Monterey Beacon*. Each title puffs sentiment, only to dismantle it in lines following. The first stanza of "Baubles" publicly declares Carol's poetic stance:

Baubles
There's pity in me for the prosey folks,
Their stupid doings and pointless jokes.
In their goings and comings it's hard to see
The touch of the fey that I find in me.

Would they, on seeing an acorn cup
Ever think to pick it up
And dream of a Brownie's golden chalice
Stole from a feast in a fairy palace?

Likely as not their clumsy feet
Would crush it into the dirty street,
And so I cherish each tiny cup,
Doing my best to make it up.

A broken shell, a tiny nest
Where birdie babies used to rest—
If only the whole wide world could see

The beauty in things so dear to me!
If others found them precious too,
And all this lovely treasure knew,
Then would I other beauties find,
AND LEAVE THIS PILE OF JUNK BEHIND.

During the same months that Carol's poems were introduced to the Monterey populace, January and February 1934, Olive's life slowly ebbed. She died in February. As always, Carol leavened the sadness, slipping an ornately decorated poem, like a bouquet, into a note John was writing to friend Hugh Miller about his mother's death: "Carol is writing a personal poem for you. Her eye brows act as though they were pumping out the words":

I.
My tiny throat is bursting
With melodies of Spring.
My eager soul is thirsting
This ecstasy to sing.
Chorus:—shrdlu shrdlu shrdlu
'Tis Spring, Spring, Spring

II.
The daisies dot the field,
Their perfume fills the air,
My winter wounds are healed
It's time to wash my hair!
Chorus:

Carol shot light into souls.

Carol's unflagging energy kept everyone upright even though, as John admitted, she had shouldered a lot—and agreed to more, staying in Salinas to care for his ailing father. Mr. Steinbeck was fond of her and wanted to lean on her efficiency and good cheer, so much like Olive's own, while John hunkered down in Pacific Grove, writing five, six, and seven hours a day, feeling he had to produce a story a week, "never com[ing] up to the surface." The whole of 1934 would be a year of intense writing, mostly the short stories that would later be collected in *The Long Valley* (1938). John overextended himself, working "like a dog," straining for success with ever greater urgency: "The time must be put in," he wrote in his journal of 1934. "If Carol can work over in that gloomy house for me, I must work enormously for her. There are certain new things I want to try but they must be done at night or not at all. The daily work time must be devoted to the end of a little security." He hoped a few stories would be published and earn him cash. Ninety dollars had come from the fall 1933 publication of *The Red Pony* stories in the *North American Review*, and now he aimed for the "more expensive market." The 1920s and '30s were, perhaps, the "golden age" of the short story—that is, golden for writers who could break into the market. Some, like F. Scott Fitzgerald, made a living writing about 1920s flappers; others made fortunes on detectives and gunslingers. Steinbeck sought not a fortune but a working wage for his stories about the "color of realities."

Apart much of the time in the months after Olive's death, he and Carol were lonely: "There's a haunted quality in her eyes," he admitted in his journal. "I'm not good company to her. I can't help her loneliness and she can't help mine. Perhaps this is a good thing. It may prove some kind of integrity. Maybe it is exactly that kind of hunger that keeps us struggling on." Again and again in letters and ledgers he reiterates his conviction that adversity cemented their bond. A few days later, having written six stories in five weeks, he wonders whether any will succeed: "I wonder in the long run, how many disappointments we can weather. An infinite number I guess. There doesn't seem to be any limit to our endurance."

His choice of words is important. Always "our" and "us." Always "endurance" and commitment. Always hard work, day after day, for each. The two years from his mother's illness through mid-1935 would be a period of outward misery but inner drive and a renewed sense of purpose for John—and for Carol, of course—and an equally compelling sense of themselves as a committed pair: "I wish I knew Carol wasn't hating it too," he wrote of those tense, sad months of 1934. "If I were able to do as much for her as she is doing for me, I should be very happy. I work hard enough but nothing happens. Carol works something happens." In letters and in his journals, John repeatedly acknowledges his reliance on grounded, practical Carol. By this point in their marriage, he said, their minds were "somewhat grown together" so that the two saw with "the same eyes" and felt with "the same emotions": "I love Carol but she is far more real to me than I am to myself. If I think of myself I often find it is Carol I am thinking of. If I think what I want I often have to ask her what it is. . . . If one should want to think of me as a person, I am under the belief that he would have to think of Carol."

During this time of emotional upheaval, the Great Depression continued in full force, and politics and the plight of workers began to swirl into the mix of their lives. Carol's more muscular social conscience spurred John toward political engagement. To a large extent, her political savvy became the catalyst for three books that are, for many readers, the signature works of Steinbeck's career: In Dubious Battle (1936), Of Mice and Men (1937), and The Grapes of Wrath (1939).

One labor organizer who knew John and Carol, Caroline Decker, later said that "you had to be a hunk of protoplasm" not to be drawn to the workers' cause in the mid-1930s. In 1934 California, as elsewhere across the nation, the division between the powerful and the powerless was stark, and a combination of factors made that reality more pressing, honed John and Carol's political edge. One friend said that Carol became a partisan after working in Holman's department store, where she became more acutely aware of the people's woes, was reawakened to the equality of humanity. While caring for Mr. Steinbeck, treasurer of Monterey County, Carol worked in the Salinas courthouse and undoubtedly had daily contact with the "Salinas fatcats" that John despised. In 1934 many of these wealthy California farmers and ranchers organized into the Associated Farmers, joining hands around the state with other like-minded men—growers and shippers, representatives of banks and businesses and transportation and power companies, the California Chamber of Commerce and the California Farm Bureau, local city councils and chambers of commerce. The Associated Farmers was a statewide organization bent on protecting the status quo at any cost. That meant suppressing any efforts to organize workers. Never again, they vowed, would striking farm workers cripple California agricultural interests as had occurred in the fall of 1933, when more than thirty-seven agricultural strikes broke out, one of the most violent in Pixley in the Central Valley. On October 10, 1933, two strikers were killed during a labor stoppage organized by Communist organizers. The Associated Farmers was dedicated to snuffing out all subsequent attempts to organize the state's agricultural workers. With chapters in forty-two out of fifty-eight counties throughout California, the Associated Farmers "engaged in a reign of terror and intimidation against the efforts of farmworkers to unite and organize, becoming," as one historian asserts, "the most virulent and notorious right-wing American group, with the possible exception of the Ku Klux Klan."

In addition, Carol and John's political sensibilities were stirred by the 1934 race for California's governor, with socialist Upton Sinclair promoting his EPIC campaign—End Poverty in California. "God what an election this is," Steinbeck wrote to Albee in May 1934. "I look for some riots in LA." Capitalism was shriveling from the effects of "overproduction," Sinclair told state voters, and the solution was to encourage "productive labor." Workers must move into factories and fields and create goods for barter: "We plan a new cooperative system for the unemployed," he reiterated in pamphlets and speeches. The final version of his EPIC plan was printed in a fifteen-cent pamphlet published that fall:

> In the little book, "I, Governor of California" I have drawn a picture of land colonies, in which great tracts of land are worked by modern machinery under the direction of agricultural experts, and in which the workers are comfortably housed in modern dwellings, with the use of social halls, community kitchens and dining-rooms, theaters, schools, churches, etc. I have imagined

great factories placed near the sources of raw material, and with model villages erected for the housing of the workers. All that is within the scope of the Plan, and all that will be done; but it cannot he done at once, and we are discussing here the emergency steps to get production going; the method whereby the people of California, who have not forgotten how to work and are still willing to work, are to get the opportunity to work.

Small wonder that many of the state's residents found this kind of talk incendiary, socialist propaganda coming from one who would be governor of the state. (Sinclair did, however, exclude Communists from an EPIC convention.) Giving workers jobs was fair enough, but "social halls" and "community kitchens" in Fresno? "Model villages" in Orange County?

For John and Carol, however, Sinclair's words must have reached sympathetic ears. His radical solutions for Depression-era California were not unlike the chords Steinbeck struck in *Tortilla Flat*. Danny and friends are not unlike Sinclair's model group, living in a kind of "social hall"—Danny's house—and relying on cooperation and barter, not money, for their needs: "For two generations or more," Sinclair wrote, "the American people have been victimized by a propaganda which identifies Americanism with capitalism. For my part, I assert that these self-help and barter groups represent Americanism more truly than any other phenomenon of our time. They embody all our true pioneer virtues—self-reliance, initiative, frugality, equality, neighborliness. They are the most precious products of the depression." Oddly enough, *Tortilla Flat* adumbrates Sinclair's vision. It may be that this picaresque tale and not *In Dubious Battle* was Steinbeck's first work to reveal a layer of nascent political and social awareness.

In 1934, it was impossible to ignore the state's woes. Work stoppages on San Francisco's wharves fanned California's smoldering politics. The International Longshoremen's Association, led by Harry Bridges, demanded wage increases, fewer working hours, and control of the hiring hall. In the summer of 1934, a longshoreman's strike that began in May left container ships at the docks of San Francisco, Oakland, San Pedro, Seattle, and Portland with cargo rotting in the holds. The impasse over a unionized closed shop for maritime workers (bosses wanted open-shop organization), lighter loads, and larger crews resulted in bloody action on the wharves by the summer. Teamsters and other workers around the state were roused to support. On June 29, farm laborers in Hayward walked out of an orchard in support of the longshoremen. An alleged interview with CAWIU organizers Pat Chambers and Caroline Decker resulted in this headline: "Communist Chiefs Declare Open War Against California: Valley Farms to Be Battlefields in Platform to Overthrow Government." California newspaper publishers had banded together in a Publishers Council to ensure that newspapers depicted strikers as radicals. Small wonder that tempers flared, each side hunkering down for battle. "Bloody Thursday" was July 5, 1934. Two picketers in San Francisco were killed, and a general strike in the city was organized. Sympathy ran high for the workers.

Carol composed verses that, according to Carlton Sheffield, who retained the only copy, were sung by the strikers, "The Man in the Shiny Silk Hat":

A girl of the laboring classes am I,
I've seen my dear playfellows sicken and die.
Betrayed by a serpent who should be boiled in lye,
The man in the shiny silk hat.

He grinds up their bones to make concrete,
And mixes his mortar with blood.
The dear golden curls of the tiniest girls,
He makes into bricks mixed with mud.

Carol also urged John to attend meetings of Carmel's tiny but fierce John Reed Club, founded in mid-1932, a "near-Communist organization for near-writers and near-artists," wrote the muckraking journalist Lincoln Steffens (*The Shame of the Cities*, 1904), a resident of Carmel since 1927. His wife, Ella Winter, was "founder and boss." The John Reed Club, about twenty strong, met weekly on Sunday nights in a converted barn. The group included acquaintances of the Steinbecks: Francis Whitaker, blacksmith; Dan James, writer and Charlie Chaplin's driver; as well as Steffens and Winter. They studied Communism, with lectures by Winter, who had visited the Soviet Union in 1930 and 1931 and had published an account about postrevolutionary Russia, *Red Virtue*, in 1933. Steffens, although not a registered Communist, believed that "the next order of society will be socialist and that the Communists will bring it in and lead it," a conviction formed largely in 1917, when he witnessed the Russian Revolution, and solidified in the years since. In 1934 the tiny band of would-be Communists marched along Carmel's Ocean Avenue to lend support to striking workers, both on the docks and in the fields. The aging muckraker Steffens and his fiery wife also started a small socialist paper in Carmel, the *Carmelite*, and later took over the *Pacific*

Weekly, a newspaper dedicated to showing how worldwide groups are "riding the same storm"—a depression and revolutions—and can work "to a common solution." Among local solutions were fair wages for California fieldworkers, long left out of unions and fair labor practices.

Carol was hardly a passive witness at these meetings. Injustice against farmworkers was objectionable, to be sure, but for Carol the club's membership was also objectionable, as Dan James recalled: "She would rail against 'the rich commies.' . . . On one occasion, we were all drinking. And she took off on the whole group as 'Carmel phonies.' She said I was a 'rich kid talking big about revolution' and 'spouting like a typical punk.'" If neither John nor Carol were joiners—apparently John listened quietly in the back of the room to the club's vitriolic chatter—they were both sympathetic. And both found a kindred spirit in Steffens, frequently visiting his cottage, "The Getaway," on San Antonia Street in Carmel. Steinbeck respected his work, his honesty and compassion and commitment. "Care like hell!" Steffens told journalists who worked with him in New York City early in the century. "Sit around the bars and drink, and pose, and pretend, all you want to, but in reality, deep down underneath, care like hell." He probably said something similar to Steinbeck as well as to journalists and writers and activists who frequently gathered at his home after the 1931 publication of his autobiography: "As a liberal bourgeois I have come to see not only that the Communist Party is the only organization in existence that really wants to deal with our situation in all its phases, but I see also, as few liberals do, that the workers and peasants, the dispossessed who have no privileges to lose, the proletariat and their very own leaders, must lead, control, and carry through this program. . . . The liberals, all privileged persons, and all the associates of the privileged, belong in the second line—when their eyes are opened."

It was he who helped open John's eyes, probably suggesting that John interview strike organizers hiding out in Seaside and, by recording the workers' words, compose an autobiography of a strike organizer. Carol may have contacted her friend, activist Sis Reamer, to take Steinbeck to Seaside to meet the two fugitives, and she undoubtedly later assisted him with interviews and research, cooking dinners when organizers came to visit their cramped space. Steinbeck "got everything he could" out of the strike organizer he spoke to, giving them a real "third degree" recalled one activist. The book he would write from those interviews of 1934 was *In Dubious Battle.* What began as an autobiography became a novel after Mavis McIntosh, his agent, suggested fiction rather than journalism. The book mimes upheaval, psychological and social: "I wanted to get over unrest and irritation and slow sullen movement breaking out now and then in fierce eruptions. And so I have used a jerky method. I ended the book in the middle of a sentence. There is a cycle in the life of a man but there is no ending in the life of Man. I tried to indicate this by stopping on a high point, leaving out any conclusion." The book was an honest attempt to survey the situation, as Steffens, for one, recognized: "It is a stunning, straight, correct narrative about things as they happen," he told Sam Darcy, the West Coast head of the Communist Party. "I think it is the best report of a labor struggle that has come out of this valley. It is as we saw last summer. It may not be sympathetic with labor, but it is realistic about the vigilantes."

John and Carol began attracting a wide circle of equally energized people. "John and Carol would hold an open house at 4:00," said Idell. "People liked to go over and talk. Most often tea was offered. Both John and Carol rolled their own cigarettes—John had a shower of tobacco all over the floor. John loved to talk. He demanded floor and got it. Then he would say to Carol, 'that's your story; you tell that.' And she would."

When he completed *In Dubious Battle* in January 1935, Steinbeck wrote a friend that he had not gone "partisan" in this novel, an anatomy of a strike. His was a detached perspective, he insisted, examining labor conditions with the cool rationality that Ricketts brought to the study of intertidal animals. But his great strike novel is hardly as dispassionate as he may have wished. The novel is a shaggy beast, about faceless and vicious owners; about ornery, scrappy organizers; and about befuddled, earnest workers. Steinbeck's great heart beats below the surface. His phalanx thesis, group action, is fully fleshed out. Mobs have a personality separate from individuals, as do striking workers, as do the Associated Farmers. Where the phalanx is most poignantly evoked, however, is in the connection between two organizers, Mac and Jim. Their tough friendship is complex, part mentor and pupil, part sage and novice, part father and son, and the friendship surges and ebbs. That emergent bond is at the heart of this book about the potential for social change.

Perhaps the decision not to have children was mutual—John insisted that the books were his children, and Carol joked that she would "rather have rabies than babies." And perhaps consciously shared goals gave them little choice. But in 1934, Carol told at least one friend that she wanted children but that John didn't, that he insisted that books are children. At some point that year or after, Carol almost certainly had an abortion, perhaps more than one. There are varying reports of dates and results. One version, that of her third husband, Bill Brown, has it that in 1934 Carol had a "botched abortion" in Mexico and a hysterectomy after. Jean Ariss thought that Ed drove Carol to Mexico before 1935. Carol's sister Idell told another version: "Paul and I were living in Pacific Grove at the time [they returned to the Peninsula from Hawaii in 1935]. Carol and John went to Mexico. They drove in John's beat-up Ford sedan named 'Nancy.' When they returned they told us about it—an abortion, I believe." And yet another friend said Carol had two abortions, one before she was married—when they had no money—and then another because John didn't want children. But, she added, "She didn't seem to regret it, didn't need children." She and John "liked dogs and had two minds that never stopped."

But if she couldn't have children from a botched abortion and hysterectomy in 1934 or 1935, then why would she have been examined by a doctor in 1941 to see why she could not conceive, as Pare Lorentz said occurred when he and Steinbeck were working on the medical film *A Fight for Life*? According to Lorentz, a doctor in Chicago told her she could indeed have children. And if she needed an abortion in the mid-1930s, why Mexico? One friend insisted that "abortion was pretty much taken for granted among the young people that we knew who had professional ambition or poverty to battle. Everyone, it seemed, knew someone who knew a doctor. Sexual emancipation for women after WWI did not include much knowledge of contraception, even for otherwise knowledgeable women."

The subject is murky, to be sure. Carol's own maternal instincts seem to have been diverted into her many projects: scrapbooks, poetry, drawing, gardening, socializing, working—and of course editing and typing and encouraging John's work. She was a busy woman in the mid-1930s. Some friends say that she didn't like—or want—children. Certainly John didn't, asserting again and again that his books were his children. But Anna Merkel, Ed Ricketts's wife, said that "Carol played with children beautifully. I remarked upon that and she replied, 'I play with them because I'm scared of them.'" Years later, she would tell her sister-in-law that she had a miscarriage, yet another explanation for Carol and John's childless state. But her sister-in-law also said something very revealing about Carol: She would brag, and you couldn't know "when something was really true or wishful thinking." Throughout her life, Carol's deepest sensibilities and pains were masked by a salty tongue. As she must have recognized, John was her child, the man she nurtured through the pain of losing his parents, the man she believed would soar to the top of his class, the man who embroiled her in the passionate political debates of California in the late 1930s, the partner whose own achievements lent testimony to her devotion—the other half of the creative phalanx that gave meaning and purpose to her life. "Carol had strength. He had talent, she had the strength to make him use that talent . . . she made him sure. Quit talking. Do it."

Helping him do it put children on a back burner.

CHAPTER SIX

"Viva Mexico!"

TO JOHN, Mexico had always been "the golden something," a place he longed to visit with college friends—a remote destination for Stanford undergraduates, "for all our talk." Since childhood, he'd listened to the mother of his friend Max Wagner describe her years as a journalist during the Mexican Revolution, exploits that fired a young boy's imagination. In high school and college, he worked side by side with Mexicans at the Spreckels sugar beet plant near Salinas, listening to their stories and sharing jokes. Add to those reasons Mexico's proximity to California and the imprint throughout Monterey County of Spanish/Mexican occupation of Alta California: residents who were Californios, paisanos, and Mexican Americans and spoke Spanish in fields and cafes; adobes melting back into the earth; Mission San Antonio and Soledad and Carmel, crumbling and in need of repairs; ranchos carved from Spanish and Mexican land grants. Furthermore, Steinbeck sought in life and art a kind of authenticity that he associated with Mexico. As early as 1930 he had written to George Albee that "the whole civilizing process might be defined as a deadening of enthusiasms," enthusiasms that paisanos and other marginalized Americans managed to preserve. In Mexico he sought life lived close to the bone.

By the fall of 1932 a restless Steinbeck, briefly separated from Carol, again considered a Mexican sojourn, this one without Stanford buddies and without Carol. His intention was to gather material for a loosely connected story cycle, something like *The Pastures of Heaven*. He told Elizabeth Otis that he was going to Mazatlan, "and from there I shall go on horseback in the general direction of Guadalajara. . . . [I want] entrée into a number of tiny villages. . . . I plan to do a series of little stories on the road—local sagas. . . . Such things might well be done with simplicity, with color and with some charm, if one were able to present the incident against its background and at the same time permeate it with the state of mind of its community." That quest for the marrow of a place is pure Steinbeck—seeing the "incident" and context as one was

a holistic perspective. The plan also conveys the appeal of postrevolutionary Mexico for many artists, anthropologists, and intellectuals in the 1920s,
'30s, and '40s. In Mexico one could study indigenous cultures and folkways
close at hand, this the material for the "local sagas" Steinbeck sought. This
proposed Mexican venture remained a template for the many trips he took
throughout his long career—through which he hoped to link peoples' stories
and histories and states of mind, be it in Mexico, in Russia in 1947, or on the
road with Charley in 1960. But in 1932, age thirty, John tabled what would
have been a quest of many months. Renewed harmony in the marriage, post-
Campbell, made any solo trek unwise.

A year later the young couple tossed around the notion of a joint Mexican venture, the motivation largely financial. They were broke and Mexico
was cheap. They considered drifting south to Santa Rosalia halfway down the
long Baja California peninsula. But Olive's stroke and Mr. Steinbeck's failing
health cemented them to Monterey County—although after Olive died John
longed for La Paz, "forgotten by all world planners." But instead of setting up
a Mexican household, Carol became "assistant treasurer" to kindly but stern
Mr. Steinbeck, who, with his wife's illness and death in February 1934, could
barely keep up with his county duties at the Salinas courthouse. He died a
year after his wife, in the spring of 1935. *Tortilla Flat* was published a few
days later. John and Carol planned the long-anticipated Mexico sojourn for
the fall.

For many Depression-era Americans, Mexico seemed exotic, inaccessible
to tourists, dusty and dangerous. Californians knew that Ambrose Bierce,
the dyspeptic journalist, had mysteriously disappeared on a Mexican sojourn
in 1913, and that seemed a representative destiny for those who dared venture south. One legacy of the Mexican Revolution (1910–17) was to stamp
the land below Texas with an image of "banditry and backwardness," where
tourists might be waylaid or jailed. In the 1920s only hardy Americans, like
Bierce, or "political pilgrims" disenchanted with US capitalism, or a few artists and journalists ventured across the border into Baja California, Sonora,
Chihuahua, or Tamaulipas, or settled in Mexico City. Indeed, it took until
1928, a decade after the revolution, for the Mexican government to organize
a tourist commission to begin burnishing the country's image and encourage
tourism. Yet in the first months of that effort, in 1930, a mere twenty-four
thousand foreigners visited the country. For American tourists, the notion of
north/south travel cut against American identity. "Westering" to California
from the East Coast was the country's Manifest Destiny.

But in the 1930s, more and more "cultural pilgrims" traveled to Mexico. John and Carol were among those who appreciated the "enormous vogue of things Mexican," as the *New York Times* put it in 1933, when improved diplomatic relations made the country seem safer, more alluring. John and Carol knew the work of folklorist Frances Toor, who in 1934 had published the popular guide *Frances Toor's Guide to Mexico: Compact and Up-to-Date*. They went to Mexico with a letter of introduction to Toor, a letter undoubtedly generated by Carmel photographer Edward Weston, who had also lived in Mexico City in the 1920s and knew the folklorist well.

The 1920s Mexico City of Weston and Toor, and that of artists Diego Rivera and Jose Clemente Orozco, was a vibrant place, the seat of efforts to nurture a postrevolutionary national identity that included indigenous cultures. Diego Rivera's murals depicted the people's Mexico, a national identity separate from European influences. "As always with a Rivera painting," observed *San Francisco Chronicle* book critic and author Joseph Henry Jackson, also in Mexico in 1935, on first seeing Rivera's Cuernavaca murals, "when you look at it you can make no mistake about what the painter is driving at. The patient, suffering faces of the Indians under their loads of cane (in a fine, bright green that dazzles you) and the cruel, vicious countenances of the Spanish overseers tell their story. You can entertain no doubts about the moral"—a Mexico blighted by European conquest. With a similar intent, starting in 1925, Toor edited and published a bilingual magazine directed largely at an American audience, *Mexican Folkways*, which "described customs, [and] . . . touched upon art, music, archaeology, and the Indian himself as part of the new social trends, thus presenting him as a complete human being." What Carol and John sought in Mexico was what Toor researched and Rivera painted—the folk of Mexico, accorded dignity, freed from the vision of Spanish colonialism. (Consider the corpulent, selfish Doctor in *The Pearl*, a synecdoche for European imperialism in prerevolutionary Mexico.) All of Steinbeck's subsequent work on Mexico—*Sea of Cortez, The Forgotten Village, The Pearl, Viva Zapata!*—would seek to reveal that same Mexico, the lives and cultures of indigenous peoples as they confronted a rapidly changing world.

In 1935, a trip south of the border was made more tantalizing by the opening of the Pan-American Highway, an ambitious project first envisioned in the 1920s by US businessmen and politicians, all of whom saw clear financial benefits to linking North America to Mexico and Central and South America. In the grand plan, the road was to extend south to Buenos Aires and loop across the Andes to Santiago, Chile, bringing the intrepid back north along the Pacific, through Peru. By the 1930s, this vision of Pan-American solidarity had contracted to a 3300-mile road from Nuevo Laredo, Mexico, to Panama City. Mexico funded their 1700 miles, and the United States coordinated the project to Panama. The Texas to Mexico City stretch of the new highway opened just as John and Carol got underway, 730 miles of what was touted as "the most spectacular highway in the world," an engineering triumph as it snaked over the Sierra Madre. As well as carrying tourists south—drivers crossed the border easily enough, since no passport was needed (another 1935 innovation) and a tourist visa cost one dollar, good for six months—the road, many hoped, would also transport good will between America and its neighbors to the south.

Carol and John were brimming with good will when they bumped into Nuevo Laredo that September in a Model A Ford sedan that Carol dubbed the "Antsi tansi van." Freed from family responsibilities and debt—John's advance for *Tortilla Flat* seemed a princely sum, and while in Mexico the film rights were sold for four thousand dollars—they must have been giddy as they crossed the border and officials slapped a large red and green sticker, "Tourista," on Antsi tansi's windshield. Certainly Carol's copious notes from the trip suggest release of pent-up frustrations and a heady embrace of the sights and colors and foods of Mexico. She is at her most effusive in this, her only extant journal, a logbook of their course along the new highway and a text that reveals her penetrating gaze. Their time in Mexico is also amply documented by observations made by new friends, Joseph Henry Jackson and his wife, Charlotte, who would follow the same route a month later and join the Steinbecks in Mexico City. Jackson published an account of that trip, *Mexican Interlude* (1936), and just as the Steinbecks play a role in his story, he would play a role in theirs. His is the more dispassionate account of the trip, while Carol's fairly erupts with joy.

The new road to Mexico City was broken up by cities and towns. From Nuevo Laredo to Monterrey, where they spent their first night, the "empty" road sliced through 146 miles of high desert, with only a couple of inspection stations slowing the travelers' pace. From there it was 150 miles to Ciudad Victoria and another night; another 150 from Victoria to Tamazunchale, their third night; about 50 from Tamazunchale to Jacala; and a final jump to Mexico City, 200 miles.

Carol was hooked as soon as she and John crossed into the Mexican desert—and she didn't want to forget one detail. Her logbook sparkles with

immediacy. While her prose is impressionistic, Jackson's measured sentences
are evaluative, his responses tempered. Read side by side, these twin accounts
of a Mexican journey reveal her sharp and discerning eye. As John and Carol
drove between Monterrey and Victoria on Friday, September 20, for example,
Carol writes about the region that, Jackson notes, "hasn't yet bothered much
about Americans." Corn grew in small roadside fields; sugar cane and orange
groves flourished in semitropical climes; oxen carts or donkeys carried loads
of grain and sugarcane. No detail was lost on Carol:

> 9:00–10:30 2 racing oxen—red & yellow cart 2
> drivers laughing at runaway.
> 2 wheels on cart
> naked black baby sucking 6 foot sugar cane
> pig in front door pulquence
> fields of orange cosmos—wild—lantana
> jungle country—desert all left behind.
> . . .
> oleander, cypress, orange, mango,
> avocado trees. *white* lantana.
> higher mountains all day—tops covered
> with clouds—baby in muddy ditch
> *howling.*
>
> 10:30—12 66 m. from Monterrey
>
> No people for miles now.
> . . .
> Road all signed "Pomado Muevo Seon
> Quito Collos"—means "Corn Remedy".
> Swell Road
> Many pulls on brandy bottle. All sunny interior.
> . . .
> Another perambulating haystack! Sucking
> limes. Men ride—women walk! Gentry wear
> stockings & shoes—Village of Linares—
> a riot of vehicles. Bumpy streets & how!
> steamy hot. Tired "fannies" are unimportant
> suburbs thanx to brandy. Ache still
> but no importa.

. . .

Worker carrying olla full of pulque
10 yr old boy waved bottle of wine
as we passed. Cigs cheap—matches
higher—but fancy. Govt. concession
I guess. Festoons of morning glories—

. . .

3:00 Yokes for oxen are merely sticks tied to
Their horns—not across necks.
Entering Victoria—hibiscus—Stayed at Hotel
Victoria. Lovely cement floored room—tile floors
Red & white chicks in bath. 15 ft. ceilings room
3 shades of blue & red stripes. Patio outside door
ferns, tables—drank beer—read—siesta—beer—
picked up 2 Americans—dined together talked till
midnight. Hotel servants sang harmony practicing all night.

A few threads here are markedly Carol's own: her love of flowers and all
plant life as well as her ebullience, stoked by nips from a brandy flask. Carol
sought what was authentic along the route, relishing Mexican life as witnessed. In her log, she notes the hues of men's shirts, the butchering of animals, scraps of conversation. While the Jacksons, driving through a month
later, found the semitropical region "creepy," full of sluggish rivers, the area
"overwhelming" and "unknown . . . full of sounds and odors we could not
interpret and strange insects," Carol's log never expresses alarm, only wonder and curiosity. Even when warned about the difficult road from Victoria
to Tamazunchale, where "fogs and mists obscure the road," she and John kept
driving:

Victoria to Tamzunchale Saturday Sept 21
Left Victoria about 9:30. Reports on mt.
road most apprehensive. "They say "it is
only with greatest difficulty one can get thru."
Rainy day again. If impossible, can
lay up at foot of grade and wait a few days

. . .

Gorgeous road used only by cows, goats—horses.
festoons of thick red berries & *intense* blue flowers.
Flowering acacia—cream colored with pale green

globes for buds. Pink, blue & magenta
morning glories, very heavy bloom.

. . .

View of mesas & cone shped mts.
below us. Pale orange creepers like Cup of
Gold—more orange cosmos. Road crew
with tent on side of road. Families go
along & just camp where repairs go on.
donkeys, kids & all. About 6 cactus now.
Bananas, hibiscus. Band of cowboys ahead
of us now on bridge. Pink, blue, green Am.
shirts. Indian women carrying head jars
of water. 2 men skinning calf on road.
Going thru canyon—huge blank mts
ahead. Very low clouds—hand painted pink &
red truck. Every manure clump has a toadstool
elephant-ears along road.

. . .

—Crew just butchered ox in ditch.
Palms—groves of 'em. Very swampy. Crossed
very swift, milky green river. Big cheer
from Jon. Li

. . .

Perfectly sq. mountain
ahead—above in plain—looks like jello
naked kids & donkeys swimming in canal.
Passed thru village in carnival. Everyone pulling
chairs, fowl, sodapop. Growth thinning out
steamy air still. Baby donkey looked like
grey rabbit almost got run over. Flowers & flowers.

. . .

Dangerous
spots in road marked by piles of brush
which finish blocking road entirely.
Tractor with palm leaf canopy.

Fording rivers was far more unsettling to the Jacksons than for John and Carol. Tourists were faced with what Carol calls "rogue" ferries "to cross wide river—pulley & cable" to carry them across, "2 car cap[acity]. everyone in village cheering." Jackson writes that "flat barges that hold two cars in a squeeze and float you across by the force of the current dragging on an overhead pully that strains against a cable running from bank to bank." In the fall of 1935, the bridges to replace the ancient ferries were not yet complete. It was a harrowing journey:

And now we are in a thunder & lightening [sic]
Storm waiting for another ferry. The roadbed
Is like a stream—just gushing down.
Parrots in doorways. Ferry looks downright
Dangerous. OK. . . . Still alive. Another
Village—another grade and the final ferry.
Rivers up already. We wait. Bring a
Huge Pickwick bus over on that rickety ferry.
We wait. They bail. Workmen swimming in
river. Hair raising rescue. Me & truck are on ferry.
Truck gets in river at end of trip. So do we. Cobble streets
running streams. Hotel Vega full—hotel Cabera
full. DZ auto court full. We are offered cots
in unfinished part. Accept. American engineers

As bad as the river crossings were in 1935, an even worse part of the road was ahead—climbing the Sierra Madre. "Narrow roadway; precipitous drop!" warned maps. Boulders regularly crashed into cars. Slopes collapsed. Curves had names like "The Neck of Death." Driving to Mexico City in 1935 was not for the faint of heart. Although Carol and John escaped slides, the Jacksons encountered a closed road near the Neck of Death, and only made it along the remaining slice of road after a dozen or so workmen pushed cars over the fallen rocks. Other friends of the Steinbecks, the Kitteridges, encountered even worse conditions later in the month. When John learned of their adventures, he decided to ship Antsi Tansi partway back, writing to a friend in October: "Once over the road is enough. It is a devil. Constant land slides and it is getting worse. The Kitteridges were nearly killed on it last week. Their car was four hours in a slide with the big rocks rolling down."

But once in Mexico City, on the other side of that rocky divide, the drive seemed worth the white knuckles, at least in Carol's eyes: "I feel like a Pilgrim approaching Mecca," she writes in her logbook. "Traffic is startling after 2,800 miles of deserted roads. Lost! We find a gas station and the attendant leaves and drives us to the home of Senora Martinez where the boys in Tam-zunchale said we could get a room. Well! Here we are. It is about 4 P.M. We find the Senora and 3 merry daughters speak not one damn word of English. But we are staying a week anyway and exercising our foul Spanish on them. Anyway Jon got a garage for the car and I got bottles and supper for us, so we can't be too awful. Supper is over now and I'm finishing this in bed. This ends the log book for a while." And it did. Activities took over. It had taken them thirteen days to drive to Mexico City.

The narrative of Mexico continues in letters that both she and John wrote home, supplemented later in their stay by Jackson's *Mexican Interlude*. Since the Jacksons were a month behind them, John and Carol had Mexico City to themselves for their first few weeks. After one week of recovery at the "decayed gentility" of Senora Martinez's no-English-spoken casa, the two were "absolutely slug-nutty over the jernt" and frantic to find another place to live. They contacted folklorist Frances Toor and presented their letter of introduction. Toor rented apartments in an "ultra-moderne" building, and John and Carol moved into a vacant apartment with "Mexican furniture, linens, serapes for blankets and darling Mexican dishes and glassware," Carol reported. "This costs us $100.00 (pesos) a month. $27.00 to you, kiddo. And maid service thrown in. And do we save by being able to do our own cooking." Ever-thrifty Carol was pleased, even smug. Luxury and thrift in a single package. They had landed just off Paseo de la Reforma, one of the most fashionable streets in Mexico City.

Days passed with gentle harmony. During their first weeks alone in the city, the two had a long-delayed honeymoon of sorts, strolling down the Paseo, stopping by the consulate for letters, peeking into the Regis Hotel where, Carol reported, "the American bitches sit in the lobby and tear one another to pieces." They discovered a grocery store that sold American canned goods, cigarettes at three packs for nine cents, and local rum for sixty cents. Carol delighted in reporting the price of liquor and cigarettes to those back home, especially to Ed, drinker without parallel: Habanero "that's so-called rum" and crème de cacao, French, was one peso. "That is $.27." After cataloguing their drinks, she writes on the side of a letter home to all family and friends: "This is another general letter, but I guess not for mama this time. Use your judgment." Carol knew that her abstemious mother would scowl.

"We don't do much except walk around," John wrote to his uncle G. W. Hamilton. "Carol has walked two big blisters on her heels." He found it impossible to work, he said, because he was drawn to the windows, to the streets, watching the show. To Albee he wrote:

> The city is increasingly fascinating. We just stroll about the streets and get
> bathed in life. There has been too much death about us. This well of just pure
> life is charging us up again. We don't go to see things. The other day we saw
> some fine huge bronze doors and went inside. It was the National Museum.
> We're *not* getting material. Just getting life back in us and I'm beginning to lose
> the terrible dreams of constant death. Picture—Sentry in front of the national
> palace having to step over a peon asleep on the sidewalk every time he made his
> sentry go. If I ever write anything down here it will be called Dogs in Mexico.
> They are the most humorous dogs I've ever seen. They do funny things.
> Tomorrow we'll take a car to Xochomilco and hire a canoe and paddle around
> all afternoon. The policemen blow soft little whistles on their rounds at night.
> When it is late you can hear them all around. Met Diego Rivera the other day,
> a fine humorous human. Bit of a sophist but fine company. . . . Carol is terribly
> happy here. She loves it.

Immersed in the "well of just pure life," John and Carol recovered from the searing months of pure work. Their marriage had been defined by work, and now, five years married, they finally relaxed together. Although neither spoke Spanish well—John didn't learn the language until he took this trip— Carol relished any shopping trip that put her in contact with Mexicans, even when she stumbled with the language. She turned it all into an adventure. An early grocery expedition with the two maids was a "shambles. Anyway I have a stew on the stove. I asked for meat for *estofa* and got a large laugh. On looking it up, I find it is quilted stuff. Then I tried *estufa,* which is cook-stove. Oh, hell. Anyway, I have everything I went for, and then some, baby. They have long-stemmed lilies which look like water lilies at 5 cvos. Per bunch of about ten in the market." She couldn't resist the bargains or the variety: "Oh the fresh pineapples, papayas, mangoes, tunas (these are cactus fruit), oranges, limes, grapes, figs, everything! They are so colorful in the market that I go hog wild—and swell pastry shops."

Carol embraced delights and difficulties: "We moved today for the fourth time in two weeks," Carol wrote to George Albee in early October. "All except one in the same house. . . . Hard on us and harder on the maids. We did our own, but Madame [piano teacher] is sure getting her money worth out of two maids. They drive me mad though; it's like mice in the walls the way they titter and giggle just around the corner." But those maids, Candelaria and Appolonia, were often essential to her shopping trips and helped with the guests' rudimentary Spanish. John and Carol nicknamed them "Candy" and "Apple."

John and Carol's ebullient embrace of contemporary Mexico was supplemented by history books in Toor's large library, which both read avidly, and in their first month they "soaked up as much about the country as many people who have lived there for years," Jackson reported. Carol wrote to the Albees about their growing appreciation of the city and Mexican culture:

> Saw our first Jai Alai game Sunday. It is simple to grasp and grand to watch. The betting is the really complicated part of the game. Also went to a free symphony for workers . . . the crowd was thrilling—half in jeans, had come directly from work. The symphony is undramatized and rather inferior, but by god there was another far more thrilling symphony being played by that crowd.
>
> Every Sunday we join the promenade in the Paseo [de la Reforma]. Everyone is there, peons in guaraches and jeans, corriatos in black widows weeds and rich bastards in furs and silk. And the opposite walk is reserved for horsemen. The same democracy holds—rich land owners in rich charro costumes, Mexican versions of 'smart' English habits (executed in pink and green and orange!) and cute little English and American and French school boys valeted to their eyes.
> . . .
> What I like best in the whole city are the contradictions—a *modern* chromium and green marble apartment house with naked meters and fuses in the lobby and wood stoking bath heaters in the back yard (next door) and broken windows that aren't repaired for weeks. And lottery-ticket sellers on the steps of the Chapel of the virgin of Guadalupe—the holiest shrine in Mexico. And the maids in the most civilized houses cook on braziers and launder with stones— and are paid 10 to 20 pesos a month. Ours speak no English at all, but grin with delight when they grasp our Spanish (which is good enough so that I go to a store for rice, mutton and coffee and Rum).
>
> The names of the streets are swell! . . . One of our favorites is "Artielulo 123" and another is "Isabella la Catolica." I also like "Insurgentis" and "Abraham Gonzalis" Handy little gadgets to put on a visiting card. The brands of Tequila are also nice "Sangre de Cristo" "La Virgin Maria Santissima" "Corazon de Jesus" etc. Swell people—grand city. I love it. There is another street called "Calzada del Nino Perdido" Sad?

Carol's eye catches the contradictions and details that are also features of Steinbeck's prose: social inequities, the names of things. Their complementary vision is nowhere more evident than in these Mexican letters and in her journal. She wrote regularly to friends in Monterey, to Ed and to her sister and parents and friends, composing "general letters" because she couldn't describe the same things over and over—"there are too many new ones every hour." Indeed, her letters dart about as she and John must have—from purchases to crises back home (their boat was stolen) to "Oh, and we bought a lovely basket too. It is as big as a barrel, and God knows how we'll get it home."

> Must tell you about the coffee here, of all the bass-ackward things. They give you a cup of hot milk and a cruet of what looks exactly like soy sauce. You pour the soy sauce into the milk until its color suits you. That, my fraans, is what they call coffee. Detestable guck. . . .
>
> I saw some of the most beautiful roses I've ever seen in my life. They seem to be a curdled salmon-pink, like cream of tomato soup until you look close; then you see that they are finely veined with red.

After this John adds a note lauding Carol's observations: "Carol does our family proud in the matter of letters." Two eyes were one. As John rested from prose, Carol took up her pen, their roles seemingly interchangeable in this place of "pure life."

In late October, after the two finally got "bogged down from too much of our own company," they linked up with the Jacksons and Kitteridges. The Jacksons and the Steinbecks hit it off, getting "damn well boiled" together soon after they met—all but Charlotte, Carol noted in her letter home. "The Jacksons are swell. . . . They have a grand sense of humor, are near our own ages, like everything we do, adore Mexico, and swell company." November 1, the Day of the Dead Children, found the travelers in the large Toluca market, about thirty-five miles outside of Mexico City, "twice as full of people as usual," Jackson wrote, "and ten times as busy, yet no one pushed, no one was irritated, everyone took his time. . . . Country people [were] slow and courteous and ready to smile and make allowances for the strange *Norteamericanos* who did things all backwards." Carol concurred: "Everything was very gay. They set up a merry-go-round and pulque stands etc. in front of the cemetery." The Jacksons and the Steinbecks merrily bargained for goods, buying "embroidered belts and tablecloths and serapes"—the first in "red and black and white," Carol wrote. "Truly the loveliest thing I've ever seen. It was too expensive for us, but we fell in love, and what can you do?" Sometimes John would stand behind Carol or his bargaining friends, mouthing to the sellers: "muey burrito," too cheap! He couldn't resist giving coins to the beggars, who drew a bead on his generosity. In Toluca, the foursome feasted at a small cantina on vegetable soup and Mexican rice and chicken—all of them craving authentic Mexican food. John and Carol "would eat anything in Mexico," Charlotte Jackson later recalled. "Carol would just wash the fruit under the tap water. Never got sick although sometimes their companions did."

On November 2—the day when dead adults are honored—the four went in search of Day of the Dead paper toys, going to three markets. They bought "three golden skeletons and a paper funeral. It is eight skeleton priests carrying a little black coffin. Really sweet." They bought calaveras literarias, "political and social satire, poems and obituary notices of people they think should be dead even if they aren't. They are crime book items to say the least," Carol reported. In this vivid, tolerant country, her personality soared. She and John loved Mexico, and John loved watching her cut a swath through markets and streets. "Carol is having a marvelous time," he reported:

> The people like her and she them. Wherever she goes, howls of laughter follow. Yesterday in Toluca market, she wanted to fill out her collection of pottery animals. She went to a puesta and said I want a bull (quiero un toro). That means I want a stud, colloquially. The whole market roared. Most of her pottery animals have flowers painted on them. The rat, instead of being embarrassed pointed to me and said, Seguro, tengo un toro pero el no tiene flores en el estomago (sure I have a bull but he has no flowers on his stomach). Then the market just fell to pieces. You could hear the roars of laughter go down the street as each person was told the story. Half an hour later they were still laughing. And when Carol bargains, a crowd collects. Indians from the country stand with their mouths open. The thing goes from gentle to fury to sorrow to despair. And everyone loves it. The seller as much as anyone.

> My own bargaining yesterday was triumphant. The ordinary method is to run the product down, to be horrified at the badness of the work or the coarseness of the weave or the muddiness of the colors. But I reversed it. One serape priced at fifteen pesos I said was too beautiful . . . beyond any offer at all—by that time the duenno was nearly in tears. However I was a poor man and if ten pesos might be accepted, not as payment for the beautiful thing but as a token of esteem, I would take the thing and love it all my life. The method aroused

so much enthusiasm not only with the duenno but with the collected market crowd, that I got it for ten without even a squeak. That will be a story in the market too. I like what one market woman said to Carol. Carol said, I would like to buy this but I am not rich. And the market woman—you have shoes and a hat, of course you are rich.

As travelers and expatriates, the Steinbecks were in sync—eyes, sensibilities, techniques of bargaining, even prose style. For the first time as a married couple, they could spend money—and like two children, they gently indulged their fancies. Of course they were not rich, as John insisted to Albee: "the old standard of living stays right where it has always been." But neither were they impoverished. And in 1930s Mexico—not unlike 1920s Paris—the two expatriates saw their spending powers swell. They could easily purchase good food, exotic liquors, and vividly colored native arts.

The two rambled through Mexico City and beyond: to the canals of Xochimilco, to Michoacan (buying two fine masks), and to Cuernavaca and Acapulco. On the way to Pueblo, they ran into the Jacksons in the Huejotzingo market, where the four of them, reported Jackson, were "prayed for, very loudly and sincerely, by a gentleman who had never seen us before and would never see us again. That came to pass because of John, who has a talent for being the kind of person to whom utter strangers tell the story of their lives." Apparently the Mexican and his friend were only pleasantly drunk, "embriagado (not borracho which means completely drunk)" and wanted to sustain their "obviously desirable condition" through the next day, which was election day. John listened attentively to their plea for funds, gave them each a tostón (fifty-peso coin) and a cigarette, and was rewarded for his generosity by the orator's gratitude; he took all four Americans into the convento nearby and prayed not only for "the one whose kindness had been so remarkable but for the whole party, his patron's friends and companions. He rocked a trifle on his heels, but he knew what he was saying and he meant it. With the utmost caution he tiptoed down the aisle of that old, empty church, knelt before the altar, crossed himself and asked a blessing on us."

The only person of note that John and Carol sought out in Mexico, it seems, was Diego Rivera. The only letter of introduction they used was to Toor: "We don't use any of our letters of introduction," bragged John in a letter. "Prefer to go about among the Indians." Their interests tallied with the mid-1930s mood of the country itself, which was discovering native roots with postrevolutionary fervor, newly sensitive to experiences of indigenous peoples. "It is impossible for me to do much work here," John wrote home. "An insatiable curiosity keeps me on the streets or at the windows. Sometime I'll come back here to live I think." In Mexico, both he and Carol found a country that satisfied their own longings to bypass American cultural norms. It was not primitivism they sought—the goal of many modernist artists and intellectuals—but something more alluring to them, a full understanding and appreciation of a primary culture where people lived simply, embracing friends and family and home and church, a holistic embrace. The country matched their own sensibilities; the Mexican spirit diffused into the phalanx and shaped it in new ways—suggesting a solidarity of vision and economics, laughter and curiosity, appreciation and adaptation and a willingness to try almost anything.

They left because John couldn't write under such stimulating conditions. He needed his own space, a writing desk, and a measure of solitude. They made it home just in time for Thanksgiving at Carol's parents. But the desire to experience Mexico hardly waned. They would come back in 1940 on the Sea of Cortez to film *The Forgotten Village*. John would return to Mexico City and Cuernavaca with his second wife, Gwyn, in 1945 when researching *The Pearl* and in 1946, '47, and '48, when *The Pearl* was being filmed. Research for the film *Viva Zapata!* brought him to Mexico again in 1948 and 1949. His works about Mexico hardly glamorize the country or essentialize the peasants or fishermen he saw and talked to with his increasingly adept Spanish. In Mexico he found values of an older, more authentic culture that both he and Carol valued, a primary culture far more admirable in many ways than America's quest for things of the hand, not the heart.

A 1932 retablo by Diego Rivera's wife, Frieda Kahlo, depicts the Steinbecks' own feelings about Mexican and American values. Kahlo painted "Self Portrait on the borderline between Mexico and the United States" when she migrated north for a brief time, living in Detroit while Rivera completed a mural. A second miscarriage had left her feeling lonely and dispirited, missing her native country. In her retablo, typically a painting on tin of a divine image, she herself is at the center, not to inspire devotion but suggest division, her own sense of dualities. On Kahlo's left is the United States as a wasteland, painted in dark colors and represented by sharp-edged buildings, bulging machines, belching smokestacks, a blaring siren, electrical devices rooted by wires into the ground. On Kahlo's right is brightly hued Mexico, lit by both moon and sun. A Mayan pyramid sprawls on the horizon and pre-Columbian art objects are scattered on the foreground amid flowers with their roots deep in the soil. But underneath the figure of Kahlo, a single wire from the north penetrates into the south, bifurcates, and anastomoses with the roots of a flower. What direction do influences, beliefs, and values spread?

Kahlo's borderland is John and Carol's. They too yearned for the natural and authentic, a foot planted firmly in the soil of Mexico. A couple of weeks after Ed Ricketts died in 1948, John wrote to a friend that he felt "a little home sick for Mexico. There's an illogic there that I need." By that he meant a country where emergence was daily fare. The "illogic" that John found in Mexico suggests something similar to Kahlo's vision of her own country—although she would have chosen another word, to be sure: rootedness, spirituality, authenticity, spontaneity. Steinbeck wrote this to George Albee in 1932: "I think the error which amuses and infuriates me more than any other is the claim of our people to civilization. . . . 'We have autos and cars,' they say, 'We have telephones' and 99% of the people couldn't even smelt a piece of copper to make a hammer. . . . Our people haven't learned the first lesson of civilization, how to be happy."

Mexicans, he suspected, understood the superiority of happiness over "civilization." They lived nonteleologically, embracing what is. At their best, so did John and Carol. Together in Mexico, their first journey out of California, they were invigorated in a country where living well trumped earning well. Their Mexican sojourn sharpened their understanding of American values and Mexican "illogic," heightened the distinctions between an acquisitive culture and an appreciative one.

CHAPTER SEVEN

California Is a "Bomb Right Now . . . Highly Explosive"

Writing *The Grapes of Wrath*

MEXICO WAS A SEMINAL JOURNEY. In the spring of 1936, a refreshed Steinbeck sat down to write with a transformed sensibility. Both imaginatively and physically, he would leave his valley of the world and turn to the world at large, his focus changing from roots to routes (a distinction made by Paul Gilroy in his study of the African-American diaspora). Roots demand an attachment to a place based on history and deep connections, which is one way to describe all of Steinbeck's fiction through *Tortilla Flat*. But routes trace movement and involve fluid boundaries of identity, home, and place. Steinbeck's prose composed during the next five years—*Of Mice and Men*, "The Harvest Gypsies," "Starvation Under the Orange Trees," *The Grapes of Wrath*, and *Sea of Cortez*—all follow routes: of tramps in 1920s California, of Okies in the 1930s, of Steinbeck and Carol and Ricketts at sea in 1940.

That spring, while John hammered together a temporary writing room in Pacific Grove, Carol orchestrated their departure from the Monterey Peninsula and relocation to Los Gatos, about an hour north. With Ed Ricketts sixty miles away, Carol would become John's regular sparring partner and sounding board. There is no period in their lives where her identity slips so fully into his work, no period when so little of her distinctive voice is in evidence. But neither is his own voice, for that matter. He seems to have written fewer letters to Elizabeth Otis, his agent, to Pat Covici, his editor, and to old friends—at least fewer letters survive—and instead corresponded increasingly with partisan artists and activists. During this time, Steinbeck would run on overdrive, motoring through California's immense Central Valley, committing himself to the migrant cause, and working furiously to capture the story of the migrant journey to California. And he was married to a woman who "willed" his searing social commentaries into being, who willingly served as researcher, typist, editor, and title-maker for two novels that would become the signature works of the Great Depression, *Of Mice and Men* and *The Grapes of Wrath*.

Carol shadowed every step of this pilgrim's journey to partisan wrath and kept their reaction to social injustice turned on high. Her conscience was his, his wrath hers. Their indignation meshed, as they worked together on his "big book," *The Grapes of Wrath*. This novel is his most nuanced treatment of the constructive and destructive potentials of the phalanx, of its psychological as well as social implications: Tom Joad and Casy slowly keying into partisanship; the Joads joining other migrants moving west on Route 66; the California Farmers' Association (in reality the Associated Farmers) donning "hoods of hate . . . pulled down over the heads of men" in vigilante violence. Writing about California workers in both *Of Mice and Men* and *The Grapes of Wrath*, Steinbeck depicts those with the deepest roots as rigid and uncompromising—the Boss or Curley or Carlson, landowners or the Farmers' Association run by the "Bank of the West" (Bank of America). These fiercely rooted Californians resist change and furiously assert their right to maintain control. Confronting this bastion of the established are the "routed," like George and Lennie and the Joads, and all those whose fictional lives are fluid, liminal, pitched to survival, creative. The lives and emergent identities of wanderers were those that Carol and John set out to understand and record.

The town of Los Gatos was an "energetic place," John admitted soon after he and Carol arrived in May 1936. The choice of Los Gatos, at the southern end of the Santa Clara Valley, was largely Carol's idea, no doubt. She hated the foggy Pacific Grove summers, which inflamed her sinuses. Her spirit expanded in the sun, and, according to John, she needed sun more than food. And he agreed that summers in Pacific Grove were "lousy." Balmy Los Gatos, on the other hand, had endless days of summer sun, and a climate once celebrated as one of the two most ideal in the world (the other was Aswan, Egypt) in a 1905 article in the British medical journal *The Lancet*. In 1936, it was a charming town of thirty-five hundred nestled against the western slope of the Santa Cruz Mountains, with regal Victorian houses, a winery run by local priests, and a narrow-gauge railroad, the "Suntan Special," that chugged over the coastal mountains to the beach in Santa Cruz. Called the "Gem City" in Southern Pacific Railroad brochures, Los Gatos lured summer visitors from San Francisco to holiday homes and mountain lodges where riding trails meandered through oaks and madrones and redwoods. It was a prosperous little community of prune and almond growers, albeit "a little stuffy," one denizen admitted. The mayor bragged early in the decade that Los Gatos had "escaped the major force of the depression, both spiritually and commercially." A few years later, little had changed: in 1936, the local paper reported happily that "Everyone seems to have money" and in 1937 that "Christmas business experienced no recession here."

For Carol this was familiar turf. Her mother had driven "Betsy" through Los Gatos on the road north to Saratoga, where the Hennings had enjoyed picnics in the redwoods, or south, "over the hill," to Santa Cruz beaches on a winding two-lane road, paved in 1921. As a teenager, Carol undoubtedly rode on the San Jose–Los Gatos Interurban Railway from her downtown San Jose home to Los Gatos, where her closest high school friend spent summers. And any San Jose resident was familiar with the seasonal Blossom Trolley that looped through the Santa Clara Valley when apricot and plum blossoms burst forth in late February. Furthermore, Carol had roots nearby: Her great-great uncle had founded the village of Lexington, only two miles from Main Street in Los Gatos (now covered by a reservoir). The move was "natural," noted her sister. Carol had come home, a triumphant return. Her husband was a newly popular writer, she a proud wife, designing and decorating their first home.

There were other reasons for leaving the Monterey Peninsula. Monterey friends (Ricketts excepted, of course) envied John and Carol's newfound financial stability: "We were at a party at John Steinbeck's Saturday night," wrote one. "He is in clover but his poverty-stricken parties were better." John himself complained that if he brought rotgut liquor to a party, people called him cheap; if he brought a pricey bottle he was a snob. Furthermore, with Steinbeck's growing fame after *Tortilla Flat*, John and Carol were "too much in the public eye . . . pursued by Ella Winter etc.," wrote another Peninsula friend. Winter, Lincoln Steffens's wife, had published a biographical sketch on Steinbeck, and John was furious at having his privacy violated. A reputation, he thought, was a "horrible thing." Fame terrified him, because he felt that if he were recognized or lionized, he would be unable to write. In Los Gatos he hoped to hunker down, unknown once again.

Leaving Pacific Grove may have ended a brief and intense liaison between John and Evelyn Ott, Ed Ricketts's Jungian therapist, who was reputed to be deeply in love with John. John and Evelyn allegedly had an affair in the early months of 1936, while Carol was overseeing building of the Los Gatos house and John was camping out at Ricketts's lab "among the rats and snakes" (one snake, a pet, crawled out of the register whenever Ed turned on the heat). After John departed, Evelyn was said to have kept his letters by her bed and was buried with them; her relationship with John was the high point of her life. Evelyn suggests as much in one of her intimate letters to Ricketts: "One may evade an issue—go unconscious over it. That's what I have felt John did." Ricketts's letters to Evelyn also hint at a close relationship between the two. On John's side, his attachment to Evelyn may have echoed Carol's infatuation with Joseph Campbell. In fact, John and Carol's marriage rocked from intimacy to feelings of betrayal, and some of this was tolerated on both parts—though with bouts of anger and recrimination, particularly on Carol's side. Their bond may have tipped to the open side of sexual commitment. One friend insisted that John had "others" and that Carol's best friend, Tal, went after John "in a big way," although he resisted. Ed admitted that John was by no means "strait-laced about sexual matters with other women." And another lab group member commented that the general feeling was that when drunk, sexual indiscretions didn't count. "Steinbeck kept his infidelities secret and even after discovered refused to admit them, whereas he allowed Carol to be open, and then held them against her." But it's unlikely that she suspected any trysts in 1936, because John returned full hearted to her. On the cusp of the greatest writing of his career, he was committed to his marriage and his work. Another woman could not, at least at this point, drive a wedge.

Homebuilding turned out to be Carol's forte. Working with Los Gatos agent Effie Walton, she found a 1.6-acre parcel about a mile and a half above the picturesque village, on a wooded hill overlooking the broad Santa Clara Valley. The lot had "six varieties of oaks," John wrote Albee proudly, and manzanita and madrone. Nearby was one of the largest prune-bearing orchards in the world and a little farther north the vineyards of Paul Masson, where friend Martin Ray made a fine red wine. Carol had found a splendid location, a remote spot with a glorious view, where she helped design a house that did not scar the landscape—a topic she and Ed had discussed a few months earlier. Laurence Case, a reputable local builder, constructed the small, 1450-square-foot ranch-style house, built board-and-batten style like the Pacific Grove cottage, with porches front and back, painted white. There were two bedrooms, a dining room and kitchen that overlooked gnarled oaks and the broad valley lined with plum and apricot groves. Unlike the cramped quarters in Pacific Grove, the living room was spacious and rustic, with hand-rubbed white pine paneling and a beamed ceiling. Carol insisted on built-in bookcases, and they had a superb sound system set into the upper wall, built by Pol Verbek, a friend of Ricketts. Large speaker cabinets were constructed by Richard Albee and looked, Carol yelped, "like baby coffins." Carmel friend Francis Whitaker created a fireplace hood out of metal, modeled on the one John designed for the Pacific Grove cottage, and forged the ironwork for the house. Each door had handsome latches, and all cabinets closed with scalloped iron hinges. Carol knew how to assess good handiwork, and she called on her friends for the best. John first called it a "shack," probably because he needed to feel that as homeowners he and Carol were keeping things simple. Later he admitted it was "a cute little house."

By late June it was ready for occupancy, and after a brief vacation at Lake Tahoe, they became Los Gatos residents. "Deeply interested in Mexican things," Carol draped serapes over chairs, her color scheme all reds and whites, and unpacked her pottery-animal collection from the Mexican trip. She gardened furiously, allowing only John to help her with the weeding and heavy lifting, her realtor reported. They built a fishpond like the one John had constructed in Pacific Grove. Both before and after the move, she spent a good deal of time in her parents' backyard barn refinishing furniture she found in secondhand shops and then placing each piece carefully in the new house. Carol's homebuilding was deeply satisfying.

John's "little tiny" new workroom was at one end of the living area, facing the sloping front yard: "Just big enough for a bed and a desk and a gun rack [for the Winchester 30-30 carbine his father had given him when he was eleven and that he kept with him all his life] and little book case. I like to sleep in the room I work in." Carol claimed that he remained celibate when in a work frenzy, sequestering himself in monklike seclusion. In his six-by-six-foot study, he wrote on a "lovely little desk . . . high enough so that I can sit up almost straight." The "gun rack" was the room's exclamation point, signature of western pluck and his father's lessons: "I've been trying to shoot a quail for five years. . . . Every time I see one around the house I dash in and get the gun, and get it to my shoulder, and then I can't shoot. The minute I take a good look at a quail I can't kill it. They are such nice little birds." Steinbeck was not Hemingway, not a trophy man. Years later he clarified his love of fishing, saying that if you didn't bait the hook, even the fish would not bother you.

Secluded and quiet, the new house was paradise, the first time they had spent money without fear of insolvency. Carol wasn't entirely comfortable with the extravagant record player—too expensive, she thought, at seventy-five dollars—but like John, she relished music in their citadel, and it was a strong bond between them. Evenings with music and a big fire in the hooded fireplace were, John reported, very fine. They started seriously buying jazz records from a local store owned by Joe Levitt, who also sponsored a radio station. Carol was the jazz fan, telling one friend that "jazz let her forget herself," and she would listen for hours to the great blues singer Ma Rainey. She also liked "Frisco jazz, like Lou Waters—music performed by white people in café society," said Ricketts's son Ed Jr., also a jazz aficionado. Carol gave Ed Jr. copies of her favorite records: Billie Holiday's "Strange Fruit" and "Fine and Mellow" on Commodore; Eddie Condon and "Just Before Daybreak"; and Frankie Newton on the Blue Note label. John wrote a friend that while he disliked collecting of all kinds, he exempted "recorded music . . . mainly because it is good to have available. But outside of that I've never wanted to possess anything in my life. It is good to possess a horse because a horse with more than one rider makes a horse confused. But I can't afford that." He clung to the idea of their living modestly.

For a time, John and Carol were really quite alone, the way they wanted it. They didn't install a telephone for over a year. When invited to town functions, they usually declined. The secretary of the Los Gatos Chamber of Commerce and others thought Steinbeck a dangerous radical in their midst and left the couple alone. John wanted it that way, creating the impression that he wanted to "live a secluded life and has moved into the hills to get away from people," as the editor of the local newspaper noted after coming for an interview and finding Steinbeck polite but noncommittal. To ensure privacy, John had an eight-foot grape-stake fence constructed, necessary because a woman came up to his drive and pushed her little girl to "sing" for the famous man, hoping that Steinbeck could snag the child a Hollywood gig. Either he or sculptor Remo Scardigli carved a sign for the gate that read "Steinbeckia," later changed to "Arroyo del Ajo," Garlic Gulch, since a nearby Italian family made good wine and pasta. "Few people come here," he wrote a friend, "no casuals." He told Edward Weston that "directions for finding the place are so apt to fail and have failed so often that we just say to go to the Los Gatos taxi driver and he will lead you here—or go to the Western Union office and the boy will lead you here. If I described it you would just get lost anyway. Everyone does."

When the local paper had first reported that a celebrated author was moving to the town, Steinbeck had been heralded as celebrity—for Los Gatos considered itself a cultured town, not quite Carmel, but artsy. "Noted Author to Join Colony Here of Literary Folk," read a May 14, 1936, headline. Los Gatos was free of "artistic dilettantes," the article claimed, home to the discriminating. But Steinbeck shuddered at the notion of hobnobbing with literary folk: "Of one thing you may be absolutely sure. I shall never go to any literary gathering of any kind," he said in 1937. "I went to one some years ago and that finished it. There won't be any more even at the cost of 'temperament.'" Although other writers lived in the area, and he was aware of their presence, Steinbeck had little to do with polished and successful "authors."

In nearby Saratoga, novelist Kathleen Norris, sister-in-law of Frank Norris (*The Octopus, McTeague*), spent summers on a two-hundred-acre family ranch. During the 1930s, she was one of the best-selling and highest paid writers of fiction in the United States. She appeared on the cover of *Time* magazine in January 1935, and her name on a *Good Housekeeping* cover, said the editor, ensured fifty thousand copies sold. Dubbed by *Time* "the grandmother of the American sentimental novel" on her death at age eighty-five, she wrote over eighty novels of "good taste," sneered Steinbeck, several of them published during the 1930s, including *My California* (1933) and *My San Francisco* (1932). Her formulaic productivity may have irked John, but it was on his mind late in 1936 when he first envisioned a migrant novel: "Working on a devil of a long hard book," he wrote Carl Wilhelmson. "Having the same troubles as always—hesitations, suspicions, stage fright. I wish I could find a pattern and stick to it the way Kathleen Norris does." But *Grapes,* he knew at the outset, would resist novelistic formulas.

Another gracious author would figure more prominently in the Steinbeck orbit during the Los Gatos years, Ruth Comfort Mitchell. In her way, she was as iconic a westerner as Steinbeck—up at 7:00 A.M. for an hour's hike with her dogs, down to her writing from nine to one, and then off for horseback riding with her husband, a state senator. But she was John Steinbeck's creative opposite, politically and socially, and as soon as Steinbeck became aware of her residence in the area, he must have viewed her as a creative foil of sorts. In a 1933 review of one of her "light romantic tale[s]" set in the Santa Clara Valley, *The Legend of Susan Dane,* Joseph Henry Jackson struck a note that Steinbeck would echo a few years later: although Mitchell has an "all-embracing interest in anything and everything Californian," her view was unerringly "comfortable" and "bright."

Older by a generation, vivacious Mitchell was stamped with the Progressive Era social conservatism of Mrs. Henning and Mrs. Steinbeck, and she epitomized much that Steinbeck wrote against. She was a club woman, belonging to over thirteen. She counted among her friends Herbert Hoover and James Phelan (mayor of San Francisco until 1920, and who ran a campaign to "Keep California White"). She was a woman who sported many stylish hats: novelist, playwright, politician's wife, rancher, lover of California. There was much about Mitchell to admire—her energy, social activism, and love of California high on the list. Mitchell helped Chinese slave girls in San Francisco escape servitude. She acknowledged multiethnic California and was interested in Japanese culture in particular, writing melodramas with Asian characters early in the century—stereotypical, to be sure, but at least, like Steinbeck, noting the state's cultural diversity. Mitchell was also the author of sixteen novels about California, several books of verse, a few "cosy-comfy" melodramas, some short stories, and numerous scripts for the wildly popular Los Gatos pageants held throughout the 1930s. She was a teacher at the Christian Science Sunday school in town; a yearly guest speaker on the delights of poetry at the local high school; and most definitely a member of whatever salon formed around her, holding court either in Los Gatos or on her two-thousand-acre dairy ranch, Riverdale Ranch, twenty-five miles south of Fresno where she lived part of the year. When in Los Gatos, she and her husband lived in Yung See San Fong, a five-thousand-square-foot home inspired by Chinese architecture. Mitchell loved the color green—she dressed in green, decorated her house in green, drove a green car, and wrote on green paper with green ink. (In Steinbeck's final California novel, *Sweet Thursday*, another pretentious author writes on green paper in green ink; Joe Elegant is almost certainly an amalgam of Steinbeck's 1930s chief irritants, Mitchell and Joseph Campbell.) Mitchell's husband could be equally quirky. He had a pet fawn called Lo-Lo-Mi that, when he walked it on a leash daily, kicked Ruth whenever it could. Steinbeck sided with Lo-Lo-Mi. After publication of *The Grapes of Wrath*, Mitchell devoted her considerable energies to proving Steinbeck wrong, and in her 1940 novel *Of Human Kindness*, she told the "other side of the story" of California migrants. But she clearly recognized Steinbeck's stature, inscribing the copy she sent to him: "From a Los Gatos wild cat to a literary lion."

The Steinbecks found friends on their own end of the political spectrum. Los Gatos residents Charles Erskine Scott Wood and poet Sara Bard Field, a liberal and astute couple, became close friends. Their stately concrete mansion still stands on thirty-four acres atop a mountain south of town, the estate guarded on the highway by two large concrete cats, informal town mascots, sculpted by Robert Treat Paine. In Los Gatos and beyond, Wood was a legendary liberal. He had been a friend of Chief Joseph and Mark Twain, supporter of Margaret Sanger and Langston Hughes—an Indian fighter (a colonel in the army) and activist, artist and lawyer. Most of his career had been spent in Portland, Oregon, where, as lawyer and radical, he was an anonymous financial backer of Portland's IWW chapter and supporter of John

Reed. Wood was a passionate radical—opposed to World War I—and a social-ist, a supporter of Trotsky. He also wrote essays, poetry, and short stories. In his sixties, he left his wife and children in Portland. Lovely Sara, who had been married to a Methodist clergyman, left her family as well, and together they moved to California in 1925 and built their cement-block estate. Shortly thereafter he planted a vineyard—in part because winemaking intrigued him and in part to protest the Volstead Act—and spent his days writing, strolling his wooded hillside, and cultivating vines and friendships until his death at nearly ninety-three in 1944. Sara, who had studied poetry at Yale, contin-ued writing and publishing her verse and served as poetry editor for Carmel's left-leaning *Pacific Weekly* journal.

John and Carol probably met Wood and Field at Lincoln Steffens and Ella Winter's Carmel home. Wood often motored there to visit Steffens as well as Robinson Jeffers and Noel Sullivan, James Phelan's nephew and, like Phelan, a patron of the arts. (Sullivan was pro-labor, donating funds to striking work-ers; he counted Langston Hughes an occasional houseguest.) John and Carol owned a copy of Wood's trenchant and popular *Heavenly Discourse*, a col-lection of lively satiric dialogues between heavenly thinkers and lesser fig-ures inhabiting an unmannerly earth, "that little pill." Slightly irritated with earth, God—as well as Jesus, a few angels, Satan, and a smattering of phi-losophers—engage prominent earthly figures in timely topics: the wealth of William Randolph Hearst, birth control, and the trial of Sacco and Vanzetti among them. Both Steinbecks must have relished his broad parodies, his thrusts at bigotry and intolerance (In *Travels with Charley*, Steinbeck men-tions *Heavenly Discourse* and Wood. John and Carol might also have known Wood's *The Poet in the Desert* (1913), which has a section dedicated to Lincoln Steffens. The "Vagabonds' Song" begins: "I will sing a song to the loafers of the world, / The vagabonds, the bards, tellers of great tales." That could be an epigraph for the Junius Maltby story in *The Pastures of Heaven*, or the pai-sanos in *Tortilla Flat*.) Wood and Field were surely kindred spirits with John and Carol, and years later Sara attested to the power of their friendship: "John was a perfectly delightful person to have come into your home," she recalled "or to go into his home. It was the first money that he got, because he had been very poor, and he was so delighted he was like a child, and his wife too." John, in turn, was very respectful of Wood—he could treat people brusquely if he didn't respect their views.

Going to The Cats, the Wood-Field estate, was an adventure in aesthetics.

When Wood and Field had parties, the couple dressed in togas and were "a striking looking pair," noted a *San Francisco News* columnist. Field "had a face of extraordinary sweetness . . . and a light in her eyes that seemed to reflect an inner glow." The "merriest of men," the bearded colonel looked like "a rather elegant and benign Roman," remarked liberal lawyer and writer Carey McWilliams, or "like Zeus: fine eyes, commanding presence, incomparable whiskers, splendid head." Poet George Sterling seconded that description, calling Wood "the father of gods." Guests—perhaps feeling "strangely over-dressed and clothes-laden," as did Carey McWilliams when he stopped to see the couple in 1937—could hike along paths to benches carved with Field's and Wood's verses or attend readings or a play performed in the estate's small sunken theater. Visitors also quaffed Wood's Princess wine.

In a thank-you letter, Lincoln Steffens captures the magic of a visit to The Cats:

> When we drove home from The Cats Monday, I felt that I had been in a place of beauty, and I wondered why we didn't go oftener to you. The drive there is beautiful, the house, the hosts, the guests, the spirit of it all—the whole and every part are beautiful. Los Gatos is a work of art. A play of art. For one feels that the design is unconscious, as if it were a garden where beauty grew and became aware after the blooming. And to me, as a guest, it has the extraordinary effect of taking one in and making you also beautiful, as music and poetry do. You have a rare triumph in your continuous creation of The Cats, for it expresses you and Sara more completely than anything you two have ever written. . . . You are, both of you, each one of you, beautiful works of art.

Even in an age of extravagant thank-you notes, this missive stands out, testimony to the couple's impact. (Ed Ricketts came to a party or two at The Cats, once for lunch when Erskine called everyone to the table by blowing a ram's horn. Ed ended up sending shark's liver oil to Wood to help ease the pain of arthritis. When Wood ended up in the hospital a few months later, he wrote Ed to say he didn't blame the oil for his medical troubles.)

For the Steinbecks and many, many others who visited, The Cats was a respite from ordinary lives, from the strenuous task of writing a novel. "When we first knew him [Steinbeck] he had no desire for crowds at all," recalled Field, "and he was an awfully nice person to have up evenings for dinner or any social occasion, because he was an easy talker and a good one. I can remember him sitting on the floor at our house with a bottle of our good red wine next to him, and before the evening was over the whole bottle was consumed. He was a good Scandinavian in that he could take plenty of stimulant without seeming to feel it very badly."

The atmosphere of The Cats may, to some extent, have been a substitute for Ricketts's lab, a place that Steinbeck certainly must have missed. But here at The Cats, discussions gravitated toward politics, and the Steinbecks found themselves in a different world, both of ideas and people. Field and Wood were activists, she a suffragette, he a socialist and champion of labor. Sometimes the radical Wood spoke locally, and his salty opinions were circulated in Los Gatos and Saratoga papers: "The present condition of the country," notes a 1937 article about one lecture, "Colonel Wood compared to the 'brooding' period which prefaced the English and French revolutions." That was a position Steinbeck came to embrace. Wood also submitted an editorial to the *Los Gatos Mail-News* in May 1937 declaring that "the Russian political-economic experiment the greatest attempted by Man," which was certainly not the prevailing view in conservative Los Gatos. Wood's views on the Trotsky/Stalin standoff may well have shaped Steinbeck's own trip to the Soviet Union the same year, when Wood was denied a passport to attend the reception given in celebration of the new Russian Constitution.

Another close friend of the Steinbecks during their Los Gatos years, and a legend in his own right, was vintner Martin "Rusty" Ray. Carol had gone to school with his wife, Elsie, possibly with Ray as well, and undoubtedly their first dinner invitation came from that connection. The Rays lived about eight miles northwest of the Steinbeck home, in Saratoga, on an estate up another winding mountain road to what had been vintner Paul Masson's property, La Cresta. In the late nineteenth century, Masson had torn out chaparral and planted grapes for his "vineyards in the sky," also constructing a two-story stone chateau with a broad patio overlooking Santa Clara Valley. Just as the Steinbecks were planning their Los Gatos move in early 1936, Ray was purchasing from an aging Masson the famed Paul Masson Champagne Company and vineyards as well as the Saratoga winery. Ray's dream was to prove to the world the excellence of California wines, which, he believed, could equal French vintages. Ray was fanatical about bottling quality wines, and that passion alone would have fascinated the Steinbecks. In 1936 he produced a fine pinot noir, pinot blanc vrai, and others, all 100 percent varietals as labeled (as was not generally true of the California wine industry, which used only 51 percent of a varietal). The Steinbecks loved Ray's wine. "I don't drink often," Steinbeck wrote to a student who posed biographical questions in 1939, "but when I do, I try to drink to excess."

Rusty Ray was also a great storyteller and appreciated John's way of speaking "forcefully in a full throated sort of voice without any hesitancy." Both he and Steinbeck loved manual labor, and Ray's secretary, Daisy Haig, recalled the two working in the vineyards together for hours, shirts off and "bulging muscles" showing. But sometimes John worked too hard: "Yesterday I worked in the grapes and it proved how soft I am for the back hurt," he wrote in his journal in 1938. He would inscribe the limited edition *Nothing So Monstrous,* which came out in December 1936, "For Rusty & Elsie whose back rubbing has made me a little less monstrous than I have been."

When they visited the Rays, Carol stayed inside with forthright Elsie, who gave Carol suggestions on running a home—getting domestic help, for one, which Carol finally did. But not right away. She was too thrifty to waste good money on paying people to do what she herself, capable and energetic, could do.

These few but close friendships in Los Gatos provided the Steinbecks with food (and drink) for the mind and body, but they also affected the couple in a much broader sense by introducing them to a liberal network of influential people stretching from San Francisco to Steffens's home in Carmel— politicians, journalists, and artists. Among them was George West, editorial-page editor of the *San Francisco News* and also a Los Gatos resident, who met Steinbeck in spring 1936 at the Steffens home and commissioned him to write "The Harvest Gypsies," a series of articles on migrant housing. John and Carol's recent exposure to political engagement through Steffens, Winter, Wood, and Field was immeasurably important to Carol and John's own burgeoning partisanship and to what would become *The Grapes of Wrath.*

WHEN JOHN AND CAROL settled into the new house in May 1936, he was "two thirds done" with *Of Mice and Men,* "a study of the dreams and pleasures of everyone in the world." According to one friend, Lennie's character was based in part on a yarn that John recounted about a ranch hand he knew who would work furiously all day, then slick himself up "to beat hell," climb onto the plow horse, and gallop to a nearby farm to see two farm girls feeding the hogs. He would never move closer than about a hundred yards from the girls and yell, "Hey, think you are kinda pretty, don't you." That was it. Sometimes, said John, "he did not even have the nerve that far with the girls." He was a totally innocent character in John's mind, insisted the friend, and "he might be a symbol of humanity to John." By August 12 Steinbeck finished his play/novelette, a little study in humility, he said, "all experimental work." He worked hard at pitch-perfect dialogue: "For 2 weeks" while still living at Ricketts's lab, said one friend, "he beseeched all of us: 'What is the name of someone who swept out bunkhouse in 1910?' It was 'Swamper.' He knew the word existed." With that pure dialogue, he wanted to reach both a literary and playgoing public—a broad audience—since he intended that the novella be also a script for the stage. Originally entitled "Something That Happened," the manuscript became *Of Mice and Men* when Carol came up with the title from a poem by Robert Burns, "To a Mouse," which reads: "The best laid schemes o' mice an' men / Gang aft agley." In his modest novella, Steinbeck strikes Burns's eternal note of sadness.

Surely John's female characters capture some of Carol's insecurities and strengths: her aching need for home and acceptance and an equally compelling need for dramatic gestures, for whimsy and fun. Carol's language resembled a sailor's, no doubt, because she wanted to stand apart. That's not so far from Curley's wife's need for the men's attention. It's hardly accurate to describe John Steinbeck's female characters as stereotypical. Many of his fictional women are reflections of what males see in them—and hence they seem only silhouettes of women, silenced women, or, like Curley's wife, superficial women. The ranch hands believe she is "rat bait" because they cannot plumb her loneliness, cannot acknowledge her humanity. Only occasionally does a character listen to her—as does Lennie—and only the empathetic reader can measure her depths—or appreciate a lonely wife or a pregnant and frightened Rose of Sharon in *The Grapes of Wrath*. John Steinbeck certainly was aware of his own wife's complex needs: her bids for attention, her bravado, and a dark core she hid from nearly everyone but that erupted in anger.

The "little book," *Of Mice and Men*, was destined for success in print, on stage, and on film, making John Steinbeck a "household name" in America. Writing it helped him articulate the direction he wanted to go next: *Mice*, he wrote to his former publisher, Robert Ballou, is "mainly . . . an experiment in form—practice in a medium I hope to develop more completely. It's the best writing I've ever done but necessarily hasn't the content." At the height of his powers, and sensing that power, John Steinbeck needed a great story commensurate with his surging creativity. And he found his compelling drama, of course, in California's imbroglio of the 1930s, the migrant problem.

That problem had a complex history, waves of migration and expulsion that Steinbeck already knew from growing up in Salinas. Unlike factory workers, the farm laborers of California were plainly visible, stooped over in fields picking vegetables for the nation. Steinbeck had worked beside them. When he was a child and teen, fieldworkers were a mix of Chinese, Japanese, Filipino, and Mexican; by the mid-1920s, after the 1924 passage of the Johnson-Reed Immigration Act that capped the number of Asian immigrants to one hundred per year, Salinas Valley fieldworkers were increasingly Mexican and Filipino, the latter seen as a "third invasion from the Orient" by some nativists in the state (despite the fact that the Philippines was a US possession, achieving commonwealth status in 1935). By the early 1930s, the mostly single Filipino men who had immigrated to the United States a decade earlier had come to be viewed as oversexed and undesirable. In Watsonville, where Steinbeck's sister Esther lived, there were riots at a Filipino dance hall in 1930—erupting after years of tension over the fact that Filipinos dated white girls. Increasingly there were calls to cap immigration of "alien" Filipinos to fifty a year and repatriate workers living in the United States. Few were deported, but resentment toward Filipinos remained. At the same time, large numbers of Mexican migrant fieldworkers were sent home. Movement across the border between Mexico and California became more restrictive, with "over 400,000 Mexicans" repatriated from California and the Southwest during the early 1930s.

One of John's earliest short stories, "Fingers of Cloud," was set in a Filipino work camp of the 1920s. Working in the fields with Filipinos while in college, he knew well the prejudice of Californians.

It is against that background of hostility to ethnic workers that Steinbeck's migrant material must be considered. His focus was on a new wave, white workers entering California to work in the fields—for Steinbeck and for others, an old story with a critically different face. Refined during the next two years, Steinbeck's "thesis," as he termed it, was that California "agriculture could not carry on for one season without serf labor and that the present fight is to maintain the serf labor and to force the emigrants into a serfdom. That is not a popular thesis in CA." Indeed, it was not. Throughout the 1930s, migrants from the "dust bowl" states of Oklahoma, Kansas, Arizona, and Texas traveled west, with five hundred thousand crossing into California by the end of the decade. These displaced, broken farmers and their families, both sharecroppers and those who lost their farms in foreclosures, came with dreams of starting over in bountiful California—to find land, to work sixty acres, maybe eventually to own an orange grove. "In the growth of our country," Steinbeck said in a 1939 radio script, "new land" was always the "security symbol." But California was no wilderness waiting to be claimed. What the newcomers found instead was only irregular and low-paying field-work on vast agricultural tracts stretching for miles and owned by corporate farmers who were determined to treat dust bowl migrants in the same poor way they had the Chinese, Japanese, Filipino, and Mexican workers before them. Compounding the situation was the sheer number of potential work-ers entering the state. Unemployment soared. Housing was marginal or non-existent. East Salinas, called Alisal or sometimes Little Oklahoma, was home to thirty-five hundred Oklahoma migrants packed into tiny shacks. Farther south in Kern County, where most Southwest migrants entered the state, the situation was much worse: destitute families camped by the sides of roads, in ditches and fields. Relief was slow in coming, often too late to do any good.

Worst of all, resistance to the presence of feckless migrants, as they were perceived, was strong, resolute, and well organized, primarily by the well-heeled Associated Farmers. "Who Are the Associated Farmers?" read the ban-ner of a 1938 publication of the Simon J. Lubin Society, a group dedicated to helping migrants. The Associated Farmers was composed of big farmers: "I mean BIG," insisted the Lubin pamphlet, farmers who controlled "more than half of California's agricultural output." These men had "other interests besides—from banking to canning fish in Alaska, to running the Emporium Department Store," and they owned railroads and steamships and banks and controlled chambers of commerce across the state. "The Bank of America is the largest farmer in CA," Steinbeck noted wryly.

Formed in response to 1934 agricultural strikes around California, the Associated Farmers wanted to keep migrant labor cheap, accessible, and temporary—serfs in Steinbeck's mind—and they cried "Red" against anyone who opposed them. The Associated Farmers feared the presence of these new migrants, who would be drawn to labor unions as had the Mexicans and Fili-pinos before them. But under the surface they feared the new immigrants because they were white people bringing possessions and families to Califor-nia, clearly intending to settle.

Carey McWilliams, lawyer and journalist, and interested in Marxism in the 1930s—as so many were—published *Factories in the Fields* in July 1939, scarcely four months after *The Grapes of Wrath*. His nonfiction treatment of the migrant "problem" complemented Steinbeck's fiction, Paul Taylor's socio-logical studies, and the photographs of Taylor's wife, Dorothea Lange. They were all "witnesses to the struggle," as historian Anne Loftis terms the group of activists observing and recording the displaced families. McWilliams addresses the issue of "whiteness":

> Unlike the groups they replaced, these latest migratory farm workers were American citizens. They could not be deported or threatened with deportation. Moreover they were white, Protestant—just painfully Protestant—and of ancient Anglo-Saxon lineage. This was a dual embarrassment, first because the migrants, as primitive WASPs, should have been accepted with open arms by the established WASPs—but of course they weren't; and second, because the growers had long contended that only persons of a dark skin were willing, and able, to perform stoop-labor operations in the sun-drenched fields of the San Joaquin Valley.

McWilliams shared with other observant witnesses the belief that a new order was in the making and that a showdown was brewing between this new wave of white farmworkers and entrenched shippers and growers. There was an oncoming "war," said Steinbeck in the fall of 1936, an imminent "bloody fight," he declared by spring 1938. Steinbeck and Carol recognized early on the power of this emergent story, thrown into sharp relief against a "wall of background" that was the history of California's abominable treatment of ethnic workers. Asked in a 1939 radio program why he admired these dust bowl migrants, Steinbeck replied: "Because they are brave, because although the technique of their life is difficult and complicated, they meet it with increasing strength, because they are kind, humorous and wise, because their speech has the metaphor and flavor and imagery of poetry, because they can resist and fight back and because I believe that out of these qualities will grow a new system and a new life which will be better than the one we have had before." In the late 1930s, Steinbeck's views edged toward socialism. It's not whiteness that Steinbeck championed in the late 1930s but white workers who would prove—as the ethnic workers had not been permitted to—that fieldworkers were hardworking and admirable, to be accorded respect. Carol declared that he fell in love with the Okies, that his deepest interest in the migrant issue was not political but personal, the blasted lives of migrants. Since they came from an agrarian pattern and were "suddenly confronted with our capitalist industrialism," he noted, the "ridiculous thinking of that system is doubly apparent." These Southwest migrants would be the linchpin, to his mind, "a large determining factor in the imminent social change" as they clashed with the California industrial-agricultural complex, the juggernaut of the Associated Farmers. That was the big story that Steinbeck would take on.

Carol was fully in step with Steinbeck the partisan, choreographing his march towards activism. She had long been the more outgoing partner, the more politically engaged when they attended John Reed Club gatherings in Carmel, and when she fed and nurtured the Communist organizers who visited their Pacific Grove cottage. With her "great big heart," as one friend described it, and her quick study of the human character, she had "this great understanding of the relationship at that time between the farmer, shipper grower, people and the banks and . . . Pro-America and all that group on one side as opposed to the farm worker on the other side." Very much like Ricketts, "Carol seemed to have a terrific understanding of social relationships." Although John had long shared Carol's empathy for human foibles and passions, he broadened his sympathies during those years of social upheaval. Theirs was a joint cause—according justice and dignity to working people— and a shared passion, John's ability to capture the migrants' plight in their own words. Carol would certainly have agreed with her husband when he wrote to a student magazine at Berkeley that writers "capable of using their eyes and ears, capable of feeling the beat of the time, are frantic with material." By late fall of 1936, he certainly was, and she was there to help him realize the full potential of that material.

The first stage of Steinbeck's commitment to the migrant labor situation was reportorial, consisting of seven articles on migrant housing conditions for the pro–New Deal *San Francisco News*. The paper wanted to promote the federal government's camp program, started in 1935, a program to provide sanitary and safe migrant housing in the Central Valley. It was hoped that Steinbeck's imprimatur would help gain sympathy for the program and quell local resistance to the camps being located near Central Valley towns, which were seen as sites for union activity. In late August 1936, while Carol stayed behind in Los Gatos with their dog Toby, Steinbeck went on an investigative trip to gather material for the *News* articles, first driving to San Francisco to read background information at the office of the Resettlement Administration, and then on to Bakersfield in company with Eric Thomsen, a Resettlement Administration staff member. At the Arvin camp, four miles south of Bakersfield, he and Eric met Tom Collins, manager:

> The first time I saw [Tom Collins] it was evening, and it was raining. I drove into the migrant camp, the wheels of my car throwing muddy water. The lines of sodden, dripping tents stretched away from me in the darkness. The temporary office was crowded with damp men and women, just standing under a roof,

and sitting at a littered table was [Tom Collins], a little man in a damp, frayed white suit. The crowding people looked at him all the time. Just stood and looked at him. He had a small moustache, his graying, black hair stood up on his head like the quills of a frightened porcupine, and his large, dark eyes, tired beyond sleepiness, the kind of tired that won't let you sleep even if you have time and a bed.

Then and later, touring other makeshift "squatter camps" where the destitute huddled, Steinbeck and Collins "sat in the ditches with the migrant workers, lived and ate with them. . . . We ate fried dough and sow belly, worked with the sick and the hungry, listened to complaints and little triumphs."

Tom Collins would be Steinbeck's point person for the next two years, and he would come to share with Carol the dedication for *The Grapes of Wrath*: "To CAROL who willed this book. To TOM who lived it." Each played a significant role in the slowly emerging manuscript that became *The Grapes of Wrath*.

Collins lived with the migrants wholeheartedly, exhausting himself on their behalf. (At one point, Steinbeck "forced" Jonathan Garst, head of the Resettlement Administration Region IX in San Francisco, "to send Tom Collins an assistant because Tom hadn't slept for two weeks.") Collins spent the last half of the 1930s managing FSA "demonstration camps," sixteen permanent and nine mobile facilities eventually built in California and Arizona. Growers resisted because migrants settled in one place might be more easily ensnared by "Red" labor organizers. Communities resisted because Okie families would send children to school, use hospital services, strain tax rolls. Collins recorded the tensions. Each week, he sent the San Francisco office of the Resettlement Administration detailed accounts from Marysville (near Sacramento), the first camp, or from Arvin (near Bakersfield), the second, opened in January 1936. As director, Collins organized migrants into self-governing units and then provided recreational, sanitary, and child welfare programs to "re-Americanize" them, "building up of a morale and better citizenship and a feeling of better security and contentment and the like—with the subsistence farm as an integral part of the program here at Kern." As his Arvin camp drew national attention to the housing issue, he started a school to train other managers. Five new camps were soon scheduled after success at Arvin was demonstrated.

Steinbeck read Collins's finely tuned weekly reports, filled with statistics, commentary on wages and conditions, scraps of conversation, lyrics of Okie ballads, and "Migrant Wisdom": "We prays and shouts to git clos ter gawd, when we gits ahshouting and praying loudest and gits closest ter gawd the law int'rfeers or neibors kicks so we neber gits very clos." Those salty reports, Steinbeck's on-site tours with Collins around Kern County, and his own experience with growers and shippers in Salinas would form the backbone of the articles that appeared in the *San Francisco News* in October 1936.

Another disturbing event shadows his journalism as well as *The Grapes of Wrath*. On his way home from that first investigative trip to Bakersfield, Steinbeck may have pulled off Highway 101 in Salinas to witness a violent lettuce-packers strike. The mostly white lettuce packers, working in cold, wet, icy warehouses, had requested exclusive representation for the Fruit and Vegetable Workers union. Growers refused. For two weeks in early September, tensions mounted. Anticipating a strike, shippers had imported scab labor and consolidated behind one packing operation in Salinas, another in Watsonville, building ten-foot-high barbed-wire fences around each facility and guarding them with "a squad armed with tear gas, clubs and firearms." A national spotlight beamed on Salinas's labor problems—the "Battle of Salinas" declared headlines after a September 16th confrontation. As reported in newspapers across the United States, the lettuce strike pitted white migrants, "the red menace," against "embattled farmers." In reality, a well-financed cooperative effort united the powerful Grower-Shipper Vegetable Association of Central California (formed in 1930), a newly formed Citizens Association in Salinas, railroads, industrial interests, and the California Highway Patrol. Salinas became the "testing ground for a new technique of strike-breaking—the complete mobilization of rural and small town public opinion behind the grower-shippers' labor program." For the next two years, Steinbeck used his pen to sway public opinion in the other direction.

Years later, Steinbeck wrote about the ludicrous aspects of this showdown: A self-styled "coordinator" moved into downtown Salinas—Steinbeck dubbed him "the general"—who urged the Citizens Association to take up arms, declaring that this was war: "For a full fortnight the 'constituted authorities' of Salinas have been but the helpless pawns of sinister fascist forces which have operated from a barricaded hotel floor in the center of town," reported the *San Francisco Chronicle*. A "general" directing a town militia seems the stuff of comedy, a satiric parody—if reality hadn't been so deadly serious. "Now what happened would not be believable," wrote Steinbeck years later, "if it were not verified by the Salinas papers of the time." The "general" thought that San Francisco longshoremen, themselves on strike earlier, were marching toward

Salinas, their route marked by incendiary red flags on the road. These were later found to be survey flags put out by the highway department.

In 1936, however, Steinbeck was in no mood to see the situation as ludicrous: "There are riots in Salinas and killings in the streets of that dear little town where I was born. I shouldn't wonder if the thing had begun. I don't mean any general revolt but an active beginning aimed toward it, the smoldering." The Battle of Salinas shadowed the gestation and composition of *The Grapes of Wrath*.

"The thing" and "it" and "the smoldering." Steinbeck's language is inchoate as he struggles to find words to express the trauma of Salinas's violent standoff. Trauma, notes scholar Cathy Caruth, "brings us to the limits of our understanding," and that is where John Steinbeck stood in the fall of 1936, witness on the cusp of change, knowing that a writer might articulate what that "thing" was and show where "it" might lead. Although the details of exactly what that story would be, or how he would tell it, were not yet clear when he drove back home to Los Gatos from Salinas, his mission gradually crystallized: to give voice to the silenced and maligned in a story like that of George and Lennie but on an epic scale. It was at precisely this moment that Carol's vision fused with his own. She made him believe that he could fill the silences accorded the working man, could rewrite the official histories that condemned workers as "reds" and "radicals" and "sinister fascist forces." It was Carol who made John believe that from the cultural trauma of the Great Depression, and the localized venom that erupted in Salinas, he might hammer out a novel about those striking lettuce packers or about the destitute migrants huddled around Bakersfield.

With the big picture looming in the background, there was the series of newspaper articles to write. The next months were intense, and Steinbeck spent September on overdrive. First he thanked Tom for "one of the very fine experiences of a life" and suggested that the money enclosed with his letter be used to buy pigs for migrants to raise. He promised to send books for migrant children and a radio when he and Carol bought a new one, and he insisted that the FSA office in San Francisco send food and lard to famished migrants. He hoped that his articles would do "some good and no harm." Midway through writing, he went to San Francisco to select the Dorothea Lange photos that accompany each *News* article; a friend who ran into him there said he'd never seen him feel so deeply. In each of the seven pieces he wrote that September—his first journalistic assignment—Steinbeck engages readers in the bleak misery of people's hunger and hopelessness—and shows how the government camps ease some of that misery. With increasing urgency, these essays invite the reader to participate in the reality of migrant woe: "here" is "more filth . . . no toilet," he writes in one, and "here" in the faces of a migrant couple, "you begin to see . . . absolute terror of . . . starvation." The verbal snapshots, aimed at "you" the reader, are sharply focused, viscerally disturbing.

The October publication of "The Harvest Gypsies" in the *San Francisco News* (copies of which John and Carol didn't see immediately because the paper wasn't available in Los Gatos) brought John and Carol closer to the network of dreamers and radicals, socialists and journalists and activists who used New Deal opportunities to effect change. The two keyed into a phalanx of the empathetic. Dorothea Lange, whom they would not meet for another three years, sent them a "fine picture of a migrant." Tom Collins remained a friend, visiting in early October and sleeping much of the time. He sent the Steinbecks Tom Collins glasses as a house gift. John kept in touch with Eric Thomsen, the man who first took him to the migrant camp, and John and Carol sometimes went to dine with the Thomsens in Palo Alto, where they continued to explore the issues, including the Salinas strike, still smoldering in mid-October. Eric took the Steinbecks' old radio to Arvin. At home, their mailbox was "deluged with requests to speak all of which I am declining and referring to the Simon J. Lubin Society who should be able to furnish speakers." In the next two years, John also funneled money to the Lubin Society, an organization founded in 1937 by a fiery young government worker, Helen Hosmer, who launched the society to assist small farmers and workers— supplying food and gathering information on Associated Farmers. (Steinbeck used the society's files.) When Steinbeck first met Hosmer, she walked up to him and said: "'You know, I'd like to take those articles and make a pamphlet out of them and use the money to help the cause.' He said 'sure' most casual, nothing on paper." The reprint, entitled *Their Blood Is Strong*, sold for twenty-five cents. It took only a month to sell out the first edition, with the proceeds used to purchase food for workers.

Only a bad flu kept John and Carol from attending the Western Writers Congress in mid-November that drew many California radicals to San Francisco. It was dedicated to the memory of Lincoln Steffens, who had died in August. The program, organized by Carey McWilliams, lists Steinbeck as a sponsor. He had wanted to attend in order "to meet some people who might be able to kick through the migrant picture." But the fact that he lent his name to the event—his first public endorsement—is emblematic of his burgeoning partisanship. During the next two years, Steinbeck's allegiance to the farmworkers would be as broad as it was unwavering.

He would also miss another searing event that month. On November 25, a fire ripped through Cannery Row in Monterey, burning Ricketts's lab to the ground. "Lone Star Resort Hot Place Until Mayor's Arrival," wrote Ritchie Lovejoy in the *Monterey Herald*, noting how firemen saved Flora Woods's brothel—but not Ed's lab. Ricketts's many friends would gather around, giving solace and a library shower—the idea of Charles Erskine Scott Wood, who wanted everyone to donate books for a new personal library to replace some of the hundreds of scientific books and articles that had burned. For his part, John tried to raise his friend's spirits by giving him a new electric coffeemaker, eight-cup size, capable of brewing "enough coffee for him and me during one of our long confabs."

That may seem an odd gesture for one best friend to extend to another in the face of personal tragedy. Ed had lost everything. Undoubtedly John did more for Ed after the fire, probably investing in the lab, as he certainly did later, keeping Ed's business afloat for years. But the gift of a coffee pot also speaks to something deep in John's character: the tendency to become so immersed in a new project, new associations, a new "experiment," that he put old friends—and sometimes a wife as well—on hold. After completing *Grapes*, he wrote that "for the last couple of years, I've lived entirely for the book." Years later he would talk about his concentrated writing during that era, "a work dream . . . almost an unconscious state when one feels the story all over one's body and the details come flooding in like water." His obsession with the migrant material explains Carol's complaint that he had no time for sex when writing intensely. Friends were sidelined. He could be enormously selfish when he moved into that work dream, as he himself recognized. And the migrant "thesis" didn't include Ed at all.

After John had written only four of his own articles, he wrote Tom Collins to propose that he, John, would edit Collins's stunning reports—rewrite a bit, cut the figures, and highlight the "human stories" because "there is drama and immediacy in these things. I should reduce them almost to the form of a diary, iron out any roughness—write an explanatory preface and see to publication. It would make one of the greatest and most authentic and hopeful human documents I know of. Would you permit such a thing?" Once again, Steinbeck is appropriating another's material—and once again, he is doing so with full permission. He wrote again after Collins agreed to the project: "I hope you will be coming soon. It won't take long once we get started. Carol and I work very rapidly. . . . You will never know how complimented I am by the fact that you allow me to work with you on this material. I think it is one of the really great human documents. I only hope I can present it in a manner that is a tiny bit adequate to its importance."

Carol and John edited the Collins reports together: "We're going to stick close now for a while and do some work, no San Francisco, no meetings, no nothing," John wrote to Tom, as they attacked the project with messianic zeal.

Coediting weekly missives that ran to thirty pages provided the two with an overwhelming background in migrant experiences. In the May 30, 1936, memorandum, for instance, Collins writes that "some of the newly arrived groups were from Bakersfield's notorious squatter camp 'Hooverville.' May you never witness the terrible sights, the filthy human derelicts such as chugged to the camp from that hell hole. Honestly, even our own campers were amazed at the condition of these people. It was difficult to tell whether the newcomers were white or black." Collins offered the forlorn and destitute a sanctuary, sanitary units with toilets, tents. And each week, he recorded statistics: "Groups at Camp," "Number of illnesses," "Campers by states," "Campers by occupations," employment records, wages paid, resistance mounted by local growers—sometimes news clippings from the *Bakersfield Californian* about agricultural wages. Numbers were punctuated with observations: "Since the citrus and vegetable strikes to the South of us the corporation farmer prefers white labor to Mexican and oriental. We can readily see why Di Georgio plans importing the whites from Oklahoma and Arkansas" (July 11, 1936). He often included a "Picture of the Week" with accompanying story and recorded bits of "Migrant Humor" and included lyrics to ballads like "Eleven Cent Cotton and Forty Cent Meal" (September 5, 1936).

Like Steinbeck, Collins had a keen ear and a sharp eye for detail and social attitudes, and camp scenes and scraps of dialogue were recorded in weekly logs. When a box of clothes arrived from Berkeley during the week of July 11, 1936, they were catalogued, hung on racks, and placed in the community center. Collins describes the response: "We 'opened for business.' From 65 feminine throats came 'AHS'—'OHS'—'AINT EM PUTTY'—KAIN YER BEET IT'" A tussle for garments ensues: "There was shouting, tugs of war, hair pulling, hefty fists flew, shoes went through the air—foot ball tactics were used to tackle women and girls as they went out the community center door with the precious 'purty things.'" The women who came out empty-handed, the "aint gots" however, complained to camp officials. And when the women who had snagged the dresses wore them to dinner that night, the "aint gots" jeered:

"'Yer huzzy'—'yer theef' 'they aint yers' 'yer aint wuked for em'—'yer aint neber a-bin able ter buy sum fer yerself caus yer be too lazy and so's yer ole man.'" Ashamed, the "has gots," notes Collins, returned the dresses, and the Good Neighbors, the self-governing group of women at the camp, worked out a system whereby all the women sewed to earn clothes. "And so," Collins concludes, "'yer aint wuked fer it' once again becomes 'I dun wuked fer it.' Bless em, they are a grand bunch! Aint it so!!!"

Carol must have chortled at a song Collins noted was one of the men's favorites, "I've got no use for women." Collins writes: "Just why we have not been able to fathom as yet. Our experiences here show us that men DO have use for women. In fact they are quite dependent upon women. This is especially true during times of unemployment. At such times the women step in as 'master of the house.' During times of plenty the male recovers this prerogative." And in that, Steinbeck had the germ of Ma Joad's character and the arc of his great book that moves from patriarchy to matriarchy. Carol's own strengths and great endurance filled in his fictional Ma; they shared reliability, good sense, thrift, and courage—and adaptability, above all.

Refreshing details and meandering yarns are what John and Carol relished in the Collins reports, and it was the interpolated narratives that Steinbeck wished to enhance as he and Carol edited. In another letter to Collins, Steinbeck suggests that they include photographs, songs, and vignettes of the people:

I've worked out a plan for presenting his material, but it doesn't depart much from your plan. The dialect in this human side must be worked over because it is the hardest thing in the world to get over. . . . Above all we need songs, as many as we can get. For songs are the direct and true expression of a people. Maybe we can get them to bring them to us in their own spelling. That would be the best of all.

. . . We'll put the songs in and of course the histories. They are fine. Throughout the thing will be more on the human side than on any other. Then there is the one other thing I want to mention. In all of the stories there is no personal description. I have seen the people enough so that I could describe the speaker and it wouldn't be the real person who spoke but enough like him or her so that it would be essentially true. Do you think that is all right? But they do have to be described. If this works out as I hope it will I should like to include photographs of people, of the place of the activities.

If writing "The Harvest Gypsies" laid the groundwork for *The Grapes of Wrath*, this intense editing project enriched it as he and Carol hashed out ideas about structure and detail. Steinbeck was sociologist and historian, Carol his assistant, mastering the "wall of background" necessary to each chapter he wrote—the songs and the speech patterns, the images and histories and textures of lived experience. In noting that the reports needed the impact of documentary realism—photographs, music, dialogue—to make the people real, he speaks as a novelist, wanting to enhance character and contextualize basic ideas. The pair was engaged in what so many documentary artists and writers and photographers wrestled with during this decade: how to tell a story and also make a clear social statement. Documentary realism was, as William Howarth notes, "a didactic art that aims to look hard but feel soft, to affect an audience's emotions with ocular proof, the arrangement of apparently unselected scenes." Character and story, in short, mattered deeply.

By early January 1937, the two had completed the editing project—their most cooperative project to date—and sent it to Steinbeck's agents, McIntosh and Otis in New York City. A few days later, Annie Laurie Williams responded to both John and Carol that "the Tom Collins reports were so exciting that I started work immediately on them. . . . I am determined to find a publisher for these reports." Over a year later, she reported that "Norton wants the T. Collins book if he can get it in shape for publication." Nothing more came of it, however, and the Collins project fizzled. Steinbeck wrote to Collins that, after all, no publisher would touch the reports because, in the words of Pascal Covici, "they are sectional and not of general interest, second because to give them the completeness they would need to be of social significance . . . and third because no house could sell enough copies to break even."

This sounds straightforward enough, but since Covici knew that John himself had been working for over a year on the same "sectional" story, his reasoning seems disingenuous. It's more likely that by 1938 Covici was protecting his author (and himself, newly hired by Viking Press). Steinbeck's migrant book would be fresher and far more valuable if the Tom Collins book was not printed first. Undoubtedly Covici wanted no competition for a potential Steinbeck blockbuster. John probably wanted no competition either. Covici could easily have convinced him of that. And Carol wanted whatever was in John's best interest.

But it's also true that the editing project and the idea for a novel coalesced from the beginning. According to Carol, John "got so fascinated with these people, their salty quality; so native hard core Americans; so threadbare and so bloody respectable that he decided to write a book." It was the people themselves, she insisted, and not the politics, that inspired John. By December 1936, he had begun the "four pound book" called, in manuscript, "The Oklahomans." Later it became mostly "Carol's book" because it was she who recognized the potential of the Collins material, "saw at once," Sara Bard Field insisted, "with a very keen eye, that in these articles there was an excellent story to be extracted, and she urged him to do it. By his own admission, he was a lazy writer. He didn't rush at writing out of love of it; he had to be really engrossed by the subject. Evidently it was she who showed him how to become engrossed in the story from his experiences in writing these newspaper stories." *The Grapes of Wrath* was "Carol's book" because she insisted he write it.

For the next two years, she focused John's energies on the task of writing the migrant story, a Herculean effort from inception, or so it seemed to him. After a Christmas visit by Tom Collins and then New Year's in Monterey with old friends, John and Carol set up rules for early 1937: "no visitors except weekends," he told Collins, who probably knew that John was working on a novel based on the same material as his reports. The work "terrifies me," John wrote to his agent in December 1936; two weeks later, he acknowledged to Elizabeth Otis that "the new book comes along slowly but fairly satisfactorily. It will take a long time. It is a big book." The book "scares me to death," he repeated a month later, and in mid-February he wrote to Lawrence Clark Powell, his first biographer, that the "New book not going so well. Having a terrible time with it in fact." It was "raining like the duce. . . . What a wet winter." Little wonder the weather in the *Grapes* is so palpable from the first page, little wonder the pace so slow, reflecting the Joads' steady journey and his own. Carol mitigated that fear and his recurrent doubts about whether he was up to the task. She helped him pace his progress. Indeed, the gestation was long and painful. A few months into the year, John could report to his agent that "we've gone on the disciplinary system in which we work." Although written by John, *The Grapes of Wrath* was sustained week by week, month by month by Carol.

"We" never meant more in Steinbeck's career. The phalanx of art was "breaking thru," as Ricketts might say, to the highest expression of human experience.

The year 1937 was a time of consideration. John's progress on *Grapes* was interrupted by distractions that were, in the main, exhilarating, but also necessary, because he needed time for reflection. On February 6 *Of Mice and*

Men was published and became an immediate hit. Being a Book of the Month Club selection ensured large sales. By the end of March, publisher Covici-Friede announced that *Mice* was selling one thousand copies a day, on average, exclusive of Book of the Month Club editions. A month after publication, Annie Laurie Williams wrote: "I wish you could have been here and listened to the telephone calls that have poured in from enthusiastic playwrights who wanted to dramatize *Of Mice and Men,* including George Kaufman. As your motion picture and play representative I have been shining in your reflected glory. And everyone, thank goodness, has stopped talking about *Gone with the Wind* and is talking about *Of Mice and Men.*" The San Francisco Theater Union, a company formed in 1934 after the general strike to perform "revolutionary drama," gave the first performance of the book, staging it directly from the novel, as Steinbeck intended. Although John and Carol went to the city where he read *Of Mice and Men* aloud to actors, producer, and a female director before rehearsals began, they missed the production, which opened in late May 1937.

The two were steaming toward Europe when the play opened. As John wrote a friend, the "provincial rabbits" needed a break from nonstop work. Excursions cleared John's mind, and he was ever restless. So the two planned an ambitious vacation to Scandinavia and Russia, where both had dreamed of traveling once they could afford it. Carol was elated. She had never been on a ship, never been to New York City. John wrote to Joseph Henry Jackson: "Carol went shopping nuts in the afternoon and she had ants in her pants anyway about the boat. Still has. I bought two of those little trunks and left them to be initialed." They booked passage on the freighter *Sagebrush,* leaving San Francisco on March 23 and due in New York on April 15. The freighter was carrying a load of lumber that shifted, causing Carol some groggy days. But once in New York, the two frolicked, as they would throughout most of this trip. They booked rooms at the Bedford at 118 East Fortieth Street and took to the streets, Scott and Zelda style. At night, they went to Eddie Condon's jazz club. By day they raced through stores, up and down escalators: "In Macy's, they'd go up and down the escalator—every time he got to the sporting goods section he'd go over and touch a boat," reported his agent. It was the first time either had met Elizabeth Otis, Mavis McIntosh, and Annie Laurie Williams, his loyal agents. Carol went with Mavis McIntosh to lunch one day and then they had their palms read. The palmist asked Carol, "Why do you compete with your husband all the time? Why are you insisting on

competing with him when you can't compete against him? You have something else to do." Mavis felt that Carol was "kind of set back . . . she was trying
to write then."

The palmist spoke prophetically. While Carol was ever John's fierce
defender, at the same time she yearned for expression of her own. Her sharp
anger betrayed insecurities. Carol lacked John's monomaniacal drive, and her
talent was scattered in many directions. At this point in their marriage she
was writing a "seed book" (probably a book on gardening) that she submitted to John's editor Pascal Covici a few months later, and she was also seeing a publisher about a book of her poems and drawings. But her creative
outlets must have seemed like a miniature etching in the face of John's epic
scrawl. Competitive? Yes. But not because she wanted John's status or felt she
could match his talent. She simply wanted her expression to matter, to find
the right medium for her own creative bent. The palm reader intuited Carol's
deep need to make a mark. Although committed to John's career, she didn't
want to disappear into his words.

After two weeks in New York City, they sailed in May on a second-class
berth on the SS *Drottningholm,* an elegant Swedish trans-Atlantic ship that,
a dozen years earlier, brought Greta Garbo to the United States. John found
ocean travel tedious, "all sitting on a deck and while we needed some relaxing we didn't need that much of it. The only other things to do were to drink
scotch whisky and play bridge. I don't like scotch any better than I like bridge.
We sat and talked to the crew and then the master got jealous and wouldn't
let the crew talk to us any more." They landed in Denmark after ten days.
In Copenhagen, both saw a production of *Hamlet* at Elsinore. In Sweden,
they met Bo Beskow and his wife; Steinbeck had met the painter a few weeks
before in the McIntosh and Otis office, "sitting alone and lonesome." The
couples would become close friends, so close, in fact, that Steinbeck would
write to the painter after Ricketts's 1948 death that "now it's you." In frequent
letters during the 1940s, he often confided in Beskow, and the artist painted
three fine portraits of John, the first in 1937. "I like to paint his anger," Beskow later noted. Beskow also appreciated John's wit, noting that John did a
hilarious imitation of a seagull landing. And he found Carol to be winsome
and "very natural," her antics charming. When the three went to a Swedish
amusement park, Carol got separated from the others. They found her in the
hall of mirrors, squatting down in front of one waving surface and peeing
on the ground while "three horrified guards looked on." Another of Carol's

high jinks. In the late 1940s, years after Carol's divorce from John, Beskow wrote her that he couldn't "help telling you how much I liked you—and what your relationship meant to John and his work." And after that, in a sketch he wrote about John called "Of Wives and Man," he described Carol as "an outspoken girl from the west, with a hoarse voice and a loud laughter. No nonsense about her, she could shoot straight from the hip and love straight from the heart." Throughout her years with John, Carol drew creative people to her—they loved the warm, funny, outrageous, and clever side of Carol, her best self.

After Scandinavian hilarity, the two traveled to the Soviet Union. In all probability, either Lincoln Steffens or Charles Erskine Scott Wood or both were behind the Russian leg of the trip, even though Steffens had died a few months before the Steinbecks sailed. Perhaps Charlie Chaplin played a role, since he reported first meeting Steinbeck in 1936 when Chaplin lived briefly in Pebble Beach; he and Steinbeck discussed Russia. In the 1930s, many liberals were intoxicated by the possibilities of socialism. Steinbeck, however, felt he needed to cover his tracks. There is scant evidence of what he did in Russia. Wood had canceled his own 1937 attendance at the Moscow trials condemning former Trotskyites. Perhaps Steinbeck took his place. And Steffens must have often talked to John and Carol about conditions there. He himself had wanted to revisit the country: "Whatever you see will be changed to something better next year," he wrote to partisans contemplating a trip to Moscow in the mid-1930s. "If I went with you I'd concentrate on their intentions because, with privileged business out, they can have aims that can be realized."

Neither Steinbeck nor Carol, Steffens nor Wood knew the extent of Stalin's ruthlessness. By 1936, Stalin's purges were decimating families and erasing histories. But the world knew only what Stalin wished the world to know, not his purges of the "dying classes" and wealthier peasants, the kulaks. What was known to the outside world was that Moscow trials of 1936 and 1937 condemned former Trotskyites. And many Communist sympathizers thought the trials fair, the confessions of attempts to kill Stalin genuine. Stalin also purged the Red Army at this time, wanting to get rid of all who had been involved in the 1917 Revolution. It was an incendiary time to visit Russia.

Context is about all we know about this trip, since Steinbeck said next to nothing about why he was going and what happened when he was there. He did visit Moscow, he notes much later in *A Russian Journal* (1948), a book about a postwar visit to the Soviet Union. Only one or two opaque contemporary references exist: a March 1936 letter to Elizabeth Otis mentions that he might go to see the *New Masses* correspondent in Moscow, Joshua Kunitz, who was reporting on the Moscow treason trials: "The Russian thing hangs in the air. I'm supposed to write to Kunitz in Moscow and I . . ."—the extant letter breaks off. Nearly a year later, he responded to Cecil McKiddy, the strike organizer whose story was behind *In Dubious Battle*, who had asked him to write an article about sports: "We're going on a business trip. Going into Russia in a couple of weeks. . . . You know I'll do anything for this movement that makes sense. But for me to write about sports is insane." Only one comment remains: "I was thoroughly searched at the customs point, my suitcases were turned inside out, and I was even deprived of my American newspapers. This was during the Tukhachevsky period. However, I was totally aware of what was going on and came to no false conclusions." That scrap of information is as enigmatic as the trip itself. Carol and John went, one supposes, because both would do "anything for this movement that makes sense." They believed in the workers' future. When she returned, Carol joined the Communist Party—although perhaps only to irk Steinbeck's family.

What the trip to Moscow suggests, however, is that Steinbeck's commitment to the people's cause was not generic, was not solely artistic. He was a partisan—although the extent of his political engagement in 1937 and early 1938 is murky at best. He drew a curtain around his activism.

On August 12, the pair landed again on US soil, returning on a freighter from Stockholm to Albany, New York, that his college friend, Carl Wilhelmson, had recommended: "The little Wilhelmson boat was a joy. We played poker with the master and the steward all the way to New York," he wrote Beskow. The two also "devoured" pulp detective magazines. On landing, they were weary of travel and eager to buckle down to work again. When he gave an interview after landing, he responded, fairly typically, in the most noncommittal way he could and remain polite: "He reports that the Swedes are tired of hearing of their 'middle way' that the Russians are nice people, but talk a barbaric language, and that the Danes are the world's masters in the art of living. He neither read nor wrote books on his vacation, and is eager to return to the Santa Cruz Mountains, where the art of living is less developed, and there is more time." Clearly, he held his cards close, with the press and with many friends. Time to write was what he wanted. After a few days at Annie Laurie Williams's stone house in Connecticut, putting *Of Mice and Men* into play form with his agent's help, then working with George Kaufman at the Music Box Theater in New York City to further revise it for the stage, he and Carol headed west, driving much of the way on Route 66, and traveling on the last day "a thousand miles . . . without stopping," from Arizona to Los Gatos. Back to research for the "big book."

When he and Carol returned to California, John hit the road again immediately. In a green 1930 Model A truck, a bakery wagon purchased because he could travel without calling attention to himself, he first went to the Gridley migrant camp to pick fruit with migrants for two or three weeks and then, as he wrote to Lawrence Clark Powell, planned to head "south to pick a little cotton. . . . Migrants are going south now and I'll probably go along. I enjoy it a lot." But he cautioned Powell that this information was not for publication. Only Carol knew his schedule, perhaps not even she at times, for he went where situations dictated, always incognito. Knowing the incendiary nature of his subject, he drove around California drawing as little attention to himself as possible, gathering impressions, interviewing migrants. The fall and winter of 1937–38 were devoted to research, sometimes alone, sometimes with Carol, for a few weeks with a photographer, Harold Bristol. Perhaps Bristol went along on his second trip that fall, starting October 13 and returning on November 7; the two submitted an article to *Life* magazine, but *Life* refused to print the photo essay. Too incendiary.

Trips were as varied and veiled as his own writing. It's not clear how many trips he took to the Central Valley, or how many with Carol—certainly some. It's not clear if he went to Oklahoma in order to interview migrants there and travel back to California with them. Most say he didn't do that, but there is at least one letter claiming he did. He wrote fewer letters—or few survive— and all that is clear about these fall and winter months of research in 1937 and early 1938 is that he traveled and wrote. Carol typed draft after draft of preliminary scenes, hundreds of drafts he would later admit. He was "as busy as a rabbit on a skillet," a line that might have come from Tom Joad's mouth.

Details about their lives together are equally sketchy. When *Of Mice and Men* opened in New York City on November 23, 1937, John and Carol drove ten miles to a friend's house to receive Covici's reaction to the play; after that excursion, they decided to have a phone installed. Thanksgiving was spent with the Jacksons in Berkeley. At the end of November, the proofs arrived in the mail for Jack Kirkland's dramatization of *Tortilla Flat* for the Broadway stage. "We're going over it," Steinbeck wrote to Joseph Henry Jackson, "and Carol has the skitters and it makes her even more emotionally unstable than she ordinarily is." That was said tongue in check, in part at least, as both "howled with laughter" over the drama—initially—then declared their mutual dislike for the inauthenticity of the script. In November, Carol bought another dog to keep Toby company, a timid hunting dog they called "Judy Bouncefoot." "You ought to see them!" he wrote to Albee, who eventually became owner of the timid but wandering Judy. "While outside, Toby would go ahead and look back at Judy, and Judy would bounce ahead a little farther and look back at Toby. They would do this until they were on the rim of the property which is woods and then zoom! The dogs go and chase deer all over the mountains and I don't know if they will be home in a week or ever!" In mid-December, Carol threw a big party for John, with Toby the dog singing, trying to drown out the Steinbecks' hi-fi.

Christmas was spent with Carol's family in Los Gatos, New Year's in Monterey with John and Xenia Cage, Ritchie and Tal Lovejoy, and Ed Ricketts, a merry crew. Undoubtedly hungover, Carol stepped on a January 1 train for New York City, where she had Broadway tickets for *Tortilla Flat* and *Of Mice and Men*, her Christmas gift from John. She saw *Tortilla Flat* on January 13 and wrote home to John—in one of her daily letters to him—that it was "the worst thing" she ever saw. A few days later she attended the wildly successful production *Of Mice and Men* at the Music Box Theater, and her comments on the play testify, once again, to her intimate role in John's writing. She told a reporter for the *New York Post* that she "had such a curious reaction when finally I did see the play that it's almost impossible to explain. I had been so close to it while John was working on it, and had visualized it so many times, that the play was like a dream suddenly come to flesh and blood. Every time the audience laughed—and they laughed in the right places—I had a sense of outraged instruction. During the play I was brought back a number of times with a jolt; other people were seeing what I saw, too." Apparently, Carol helped Clare Luce visualize what she saw as well, lunching with the actress at 21. And she probably met Dorothy Parker on this trip.

John was pleased with Carol's reports: "I think Carol is having a marvelous time," he wrote to Joseph Henry Jackson in January. "She is so rushed that she can hardly breathe but in spite of that she gets off a letter nearly every day. I think she is taking New York and picking its bones. She is seeing everything and doing everything. We will be poor little provincials to her from now on. I'm really glad she went alone because I am prone to say oh to hell with it and not go the places I've wanted to go to," a comment suggesting something about how Carol's verve energized John throughout the marriage. Nearly everyone who met Carol testified to her radiant energy: "It is grand having her with us," Steinbeck's agent wrote him in late January, "and everyone likes her so much. She seems to be having a good time and I have been trying to do everything I could to help her see NY in the right way. She gets so much fun of going around that it is a joy to be with her. She is so good looking and clever and says and does such original things. I hope she hasn't worn herself out but I know her time is limited and we don't want her to miss any of the sights." When the sightseer returned to California in late January, John reported that she had visibly matured.

Another of Carol's New York contacts became vital to Steinbeck during the next two years, filmmaker Pare Lorentz, whom Carol met in Covici's office. Lorentz liked this "big, loud, lanky, cheerful female who reminded me of many competent and similarly loud girls I knew from the hills and mountains of West Virginia, so we had a comfortable meeting." Carol listened to Lorentz's proposal to make *In Dubious Battle* into a commercial film, a project he wanted to tackle because he had been moved by a "complete tragedy in which the land holders, the land users, and the land workers all lost." When Carol wired John about Lorentz's ideas for a script, Steinbeck immediately approved, and soon after that he met Lorentz in Los Gatos, taking him to San Francisco to meet the Jacksons at a tavern called John's Rendezvous.

When he came into Steinbeck's orbit, Lorentz had completed two successful documentaries for the Resettlement Administration, *The Plow That Broke the Plains*, about the Dust Bowl, "a record of the Land . . . of soil, rather than people" where visuals and Virgil Thomson's music tell the story of "Blues" and "Drought" and "Devastation"; and *The River*, about the Mississippi, which premiered in New Orleans in October 1937. He was working on another, never completed film that President Roosevelt wanted him to make about the steel industry—an "on the level" documentary that would counter the US Steel propaganda about "happy boys working in Pittsburgh." As a prelude to that project, he developed a radio script, "Ecce Homo," about four unemployed men from four regions of the United States." Lorentz's films were visually stunning, spare. "Ecce Homo" conveyed the "stupidity" of unemployment in a country with "gigantic industrial equipment" and arable land. Lorentz was another radical, another activist, another artist whose vision would impact *The Grapes of Wrath*. The novel's visual resonance owes something to Lorentz's films, as does the staccato beat of some interchapters, as does the novel's slow pace and the insistent message.

After Lorentz's Los Gatos visit, he and Steinbeck began to write each other throughout 1938, a significant epistolary bond for both. Months later, when

Steinbeck sat down for a fresh start on *Grapes,* he asked Lorentz to come to California and talk about the book, offered to pick him up in San Francisco. "I have a feeling that you and I could work together and I don't feel that way about anyone else," Steinbeck wrote. The activists that Steinbeck encountered in the late 1930s—men like Collins and Wood and Steffens, Garst and Thomsen and Lorentz—formed a phalanx of intellectual support that helped Steinbeck record the era. Such a network and the conversations with like-minded people were, as ever, the lifeblood of his work. The band of liberals surrounding Steinbeck is also a signifier for his political stance of the 1930s. *The Grapes of Wrath,* like *Of Mice and Men,* rejects the right-wing tropes of "fatherhood"—wise paternal decisions from the top down—and replaces them with the left-wing notion of "brotherhood"—friendship that extends laterally, not vertically. Camaraderie and Carol were the twin engines that propelled Steinbeck's art.

But first wrath. Shortly after the two met, Steinbeck turned to Lorentz for help in getting national syndication for a raw little piece that he wrote in February, "Starvation Under the Orange Trees," a far more incendiary essay than those he'd written fifteen months earlier under the title "The Harvest Gypsies." During a sodden trip to Visalia—that winter, like the winter before, rain drenched California—Steinbeck interviewed over fifty migrants, and came home in a "white rage," as one friend described his temper. In that mood, with day after day of rain pounding on the roof of his Los Gatos home, John penned a hard-hitting exposé. "I wish I could do more or better work for this," he wrote to Fred Soule, of the Regional Information Office for the FSA in San Francisco, asking Soule to send "Starvation Under the Orange Trees" to the newly launched (January 1, 1938) Communist daily in San Francisco, the *People's World,* and, if Soule wished, to enlist Lorentz's helping in getting national syndication for the piece. "But every time I get to it, I get angry again. The merchants who want to handle the relief and take ten percent. The Safeway stores who are fighting the surplus commodity distribution make me furious." In 1938, when Roosevelt's New Deal came under attack by powerful interests in the country, Steinbeck sided with the powerless, of course, connecting directly with the workers' network. National syndication for his raw and hard-hitting article meant that he might "make a few other people angry about" the suffering poor. But Lorentz had difficulty placing the piece nationally, as papers were wary of an incendiary pro-labor article. "The press and radio are so controlled that no information gets out at all," Steinbeck wrote to Lorentz. Even after editors agreed to publish the piece—the Scripps

Howard League was interested—the article didn't appear. Apparently a few national papers picked it up: in St. Louis and Des Moines (where Lorentz made contact with his former boss, now with the *Des Moines Register*), and it ran as well in the *San Francisco News* and in a small Monterey paper. But what is most important about "Starvation Under the Orange Trees" and the next project, "L'Affair Lettuceberg," a vicious satire that Steinbeck composed in April and May of 1938, is that neither was intended for a literary audience, neither was part of the "big book" that he had put on hold. He turned to invective to sway public opinion. "Every little bit that happens to make it more generally known what the set up is here is valuable," Steinbeck wrote to Lorentz.

Later Carol would tell a friend that it was an exhausting time. She would get up at 6:00 A.M. to type pages of manuscript. Sometimes she'd work until 1:00 or 2:00 A.M.. Both were under tremendous stress. By May, she had completed over four hundred pages of the "job" to be done, "L'Affair Lettuceberg." This manuscript was a "burlesque of strike breaking tactics told entirely from the employers viewpoint and tries to be funny," he told Lorentz. The seventy-thousand-word manuscript was "a vicious book, a mean book," he reported to his agent in mid-April. "I don't know whether it will be any good at all. It might well be very lousy but it has a lot of poison in it that I have to get out of my system and this is a good way to do it. Then if it is no good we can destroy it. . . . I feel so ferocious about the thing that I won't have much critical insight." The poison was directed at power brokers and vigilantes, and he wanted the message to hit hard, not wanting it to be a "good book" but rather to "do a job . . . to outrage the committees of seven and such because these men are never vigilantes. They just work out the methods by which the vigilantes are formed and kept steamed up. . . . The Vigilantes are clerks, and service station operators, and small shopkeepers and generally dopes. And it is to them I am writing. I want them to know they are being made suckers. For instance, if you were pumping gas in Salinas, and you didn't show the proper spirit about foreign agitators and take up a gun to defend America against a strike, then you would soon lose your job. I'm writing a common book. The burlesque is overdrawn, the points are underlined. I don't want any subtlety in it. It isn't for people who look for or understand subtleties. It is intended to hurt on the one side and to instruct on the other and it hasn't any intention of being literature."

But Carol hated the tone more and more with each day of typing. Finally she convinced John to scrap "L'Affair Lettuceberg." The title was terrible and the intent destructive. On May 18 Carol prevailed. He burned his diatribe against Salinas fat cats.

About the same time Carol's father found the couple new property to buy in the Santa Cruz Mountains, a forty-seven-acre ranch off Brush Road. Both agreed to abandon the Greenwood Lane house because noisy neighbors and cramped space had become intolerable to both. Mentally, physically, and emotionally John and Carol were clearing the decks. After he and Carol went to the Mother Lode country briefly, he returned to Los Gatos feeling "washed clean" and "able to go back to the other with enthusiasm and I think some force."

He started writing *The Grapes of Wrath* at about the same time that *Of Mice and Men* closed on Broadway. John was relieved because he felt "paradoxical" being a Broadway playwright, a liberal discussing the masses. He preferred having books in "25 cent editions. . . . I want to write for two bit people not for the three-thirty people."

And that he did. At the height of his creative and partisan powers, starting work that he must have known would be his best, John blocked off the world and hunkered down to complete the final draft of *The Grapes of Wrath* in one hundred working days. Turning again to his "big book" in late May 1938, he sat before an oversize ledger, purchased the year before on sale for one dollar, and wrote "New Start, Big Writing," reminding himself to resize his tiny handwriting so that Carol could better read each page. He set a pace of two thousand words a day, and kept a journal to map his progress. (The journals were later published as *Working Days: The Journals of the Grapes of Wrath*.)

After almost two years, most certainly with Carol's guidance, he found the structure for the final draft, a double helix. One strand is a family saga, the other a cultural manifesto. With the cadence of the Bible in his mind (he called the interchapters "biblical"), the revolutionary tenor and beat of the "Battle Hymn of the Republic" measuring his pace, and the scope of dispossession as his backdrop, Steinbeck's epic grasp was as mighty as Milton's, his subject the heaven and hell of contemporary life. The Joads were his angels: self-sufficient, honest, hardworking Americans, people of the soil; hell was the wasteland of Oklahoma and the forbidden orchards of California. Steinbeck had struggled long months to discover a way to tell this story—to meld the genres he had considered. *The Grapes of Wrath* is part journalistic and part fictive. Its dramatic roots can be traced in the book's participatory urgency. The satiric fire of the rejected "L'Affair Lettuceberg" seeps into its angriest passages. Tom Collins's reports are patched in. The photographic

stills became stoic Ma Joad, angry Tom, and disconsolate Casy. And the fabu-
lar turtle chapter reminds readers that this book is not a history of the Great
Depression—but rather a hybrid mix of genres, a tale told in many voices.
And in its mythic dimension, recasting the biblical story of Exodus, the novel
suggests that dispossession is hardly a story confined to one era. It has "five
layers" of meaning, Steinbeck insisted, layers that nudge readers from the
particular to the universal, from the 1930s to the twenty-first century.

Steinbeck's great achievement in this novel is not discovery of new subject
matter, for other documentary artists of the 1930s gave expression to poverty
in California and around the country: Dorothea Lange, Ben Shahn, Walker
Evans, and Harold Bristol in photography; Carey McWilliams in history;
John and Alan Lomax in music; Pare Lorentz in film. But perhaps more fully
than any other, Steinbeck, fully in sync with editor/assistant Carol, lent voice
and substance and a heart of humanity to the agony of marginalized immigrants in California through his blended narrative. For a public primed in
the late 1930s by journalistic reports of deprivation, by Pare Lorentz's documentary films for the Resettlement Administration, and by photo texts like
You Have Seen Their Faces, a 1937 collaboration by Margaret Bourke-White
and Erskine Caldwell, readers could relate to the material in Grapes and
"participate" in the experience of dispossession, as Steinbeck deeply hoped
they would.

The Grapes of Wrath is informed by all the genres documenting poverty
in the 1930s: photo stills, musical rhythms (John bought himself a guitar
shortly before he began the novel and taught himself a few chords), film
techniques—panoramic and close shots. John Steinbeck channeled genres as
fully as he did migrant voices. For example, the dialogue of Pare Lorentz's
1938 radio broadcast, Ecce Homo, to which both John and Carol listened with
rapt attention when they heard it with Joseph Henry Jackson, haunts that
opening scene with Muley, Casy, and Tom cooking rabbit and looking back-
ward and forward from a dismal present. "The new book will be utterly fine,"
wrote Ricketts to Evelyn Ott on June 30, 1938, after he heard John read part
of the early chapters. "Different form. No more fantasy. When he reads it I
am tearful; realism with the deepest poetry of beauty. . . . [Jon] seems to have
gone some way in accepting the hazards and values of an enlarged horizon
of consciousness." His best friend knew that Steinbeck had broken through to
new heights.

Carol knew it too. Her dedication to those new heights knew no bounds.
"Stay with the detail," she told him often as he wrote in his ledger book each

day. John told his third wife, Elaine, that Carol typed parts of the *Grapes* manuscript "over and over a thousand times." And in September 1938, he wrote his agent, Elizabeth Otis, that "Carol finally came through with a title that I think is swell," a flash of brilliance that occurred, appropriately enough, in Martin Ray's Saratoga winery. Her importance as John's collaborator was heightened by an empathy as fine-tuned as his own. Large-hearted, indefatigable, brilliant Carol was indispensable to John during those months of artistic challenge, when he struggled to convey with searing emotion the reality of migrant pain. In October 1938, nearly finished with *Grapes*, John responded to a letter from Pare Lorentz, agreeing to collaborate with Lorentz on a film of "Ecce Homo." "I want to learn something about pictures," John wrote, and "I regard you as the best man in the world" to work under. John didn't care about the money, he told Lorentz, but he did care about a couple of things: perhaps a credit on the film. And one other thing: "I should want Carol with me at least part of the time. We always go everywhere together. Not of course if the going were too tough. She's a wonderful steno and secretary and of course would pay her own expenses."

Perhaps that's the shadow dedication to *The Grapes of Wrath*. Through each page of writing, he was utterly dependent on her as partner, as editor.

He concluded his letter to Lorentz: "I do hope this god damn book is some good. It's been hard enough work." Together.

To Ed Ricketts, John and Carol's relationship looked like this as Steinbeck wrote *The Grapes of Wrath:* "Surprisingly, I am getting to like Carol more all the time; I feel that she loves me well, and I her. They seem to be about the same together. Maybe it's an armed truce, maybe it's a good relation. But mostly I think a mutual respect situation without much of the thing I call deep real love."

Marriages built on deep mutual respect are not shabby. The early Los Gatos years were "a time of great accord between them," said Jean Ariss, who visited the couple with Ed. "She so excited and happy about *Grapes*. They were comfortable, affectionate—which was a little bit rare for them, except in Ed's presence, when they were comfortable." John and Carol Steinbeck, like Granma and Grampa Joad, "loved and needed the fighting." And through 1938, they loved and needed each other.

CHAPTER EIGHT

Enter Gwen Conger

WHAT SETS THE LIFETIME OF A PHALANX? What allows the unit to frac-
ture and ultimately disintegrate can be as complex as the mixing of forces
that led to its creation. But in some cases the demise can be rather prosaic—
a spinning top running out of momentum can easily be tipped off axis. For
John and Carol, finishing *Grapes* finished them, leaving them physically and
emotionally drained and setting the stage for marital problems. Add to that
another woman, a younger woman unblemished by the years of struggle.
This mix would initiate the wobbling precession from which recovery would
be impossible.

Typing the final chapters of *Grapes* in September 1938, Carol wrote a
funny little note to Steinbeck's agent, Elizabeth Otis, urging her and husband
Larry Kiser to come to California to help them bring the book to completion:

> Please come, we want you to very much indeed. . . . I can repeat that until you'll
> come just to shut me off at the source. . . . Now just one more thing, I want
> Larry! Take that howsomever you will. Maybe he can incorporate it into a busi-
> ness trip if we promise to produce some interesting new designs for him. Pink
> elephants rampant on a field of stomach ulcers ought to make a nice Bigelow
> carpet. John says a trip to the Northwest and the Southwest—the Hopi coun-
> try—should prove valuable. I Hopi gets it . . .
>
> Honestly, it would mean an awful lot to John if you did come west now. He
> wants desperately to have somebody whose judgment he trusts read the ms.
> before it goes in. I'm too close to it now. . . . I've lost all sense of proportion, and
> am not fitted to judge it at all.

Through final edits, Carol kept up her vigilance. When the manuscript was
ready to post on December 12, 1938, it was she who wrote to Pat Covici ("Gad,
it is swell!!!!"). She asked Pat to help correct dialogue in the general chapters,
admitting that punctuating dialogue was difficult: "I have tried every known
expedient, in one chapter after another, to indicate generalized conversation,

and yet keep it clear from the conversation in the chapters dealing with the Joads." When the galleys arrived, Carol gave them a "tough reading," as John wrote Covici. "It's her book and she wants it right. I have to overcome a strong reluctance to read it at all. It's like unburying the dead."

And when Elizabeth Otis came to California in late December to read the galleys with John and Carol, the two women convinced him to omit unseemly words, those that "stopped the reader's mind," four versions of "f . . ." and five of "shit" (but he wouldn't budge on "shitheels," for "there is no term like it"). After changes were telegraphed to Viking in New York, Covici wrote to praise John and Carol's joint efforts in proofing the manuscript, offered Carol a job as a proofreader for Viking at any time, and thanked both them for their expediency, "unparaled [*sic*] in publishing history."

Toiling together, Carol and John meshed. In gratitude, John asked Covici to bind a copy for Carol in leather, and beneath the dedication he inscribed it to her in their private language:

Wan Carol eglit waren eleteer
Tri sogal ipi eglit meneseer
Su lapel aka sude seerondo
Wan Carol eglit ipi eglito

Sog John Steinbeck
Los Gatos in the evening.

But after the April 1939 publication (a little over two months after proofing was complete—Viking Press anticipated a blockbuster), their binding toil ceased. Old wounds festered; new ones erupted. Again, the story is achingly familiar, but for John and Carol it seems near tragic: the reach had been so lofty, the creation so nearly what they envisioned—John called it a symphony—and the fall so bitter. They were tossed on separate shores, exhausted, perplexed, and rich.

The first wedge was John's health. Soon after submitting the manuscript he fell gravely ill. He told his handyman at the ranch, Frank Rineri: "Shut the gate. Disconnect everything." An infected tooth triggered sciatica, shooting pains down his legs. Exhausted, he took to bed and left Carol to putter around in the garden, maybe planting the new Burpee double petunias as Covici suggested in a letter. To many, Carol remained "full of fun," recalled Rineri, certainly when outside in her beloved garden or busily canning fruits and jams and gallons of pickles, a task she loved. When John was able, he joined Carol in improving the house and grounds. He bought a cow for his new acreage, and Carol made butter and cheese. Later he purchased a one-eyed pig they named "Connolly" after the notorious gate crasher. He ordered Carol a special greenhouse for her bulbs, slips, and seedlings. He had a speaker built into the living room ceiling, "so the music could come right down as if it were out of heaven," said Sara Bard Field. He purchased a glorious new stove they named "Spencer Tracy"—the two loved to name things, cars, dogs, objects. He installed a swimming pool, tapping into a spring on the land, and the two eventually went swimming "thirty times a day."

The secluded forty-seven-acre ranch with all its animals and amenities gave both pleasure, and there were many serene and happy moments, as they recovered from the long haul of writing and editing *Grapes*. "Here I can lose the fanfare," he wrote a friend. "Here I become the little creature I really am. One cannot impress the forest." Appropriately enough for dream acres, his forest was enchanted, he thought, especially a spring that he was "frankly superstitious about." It fed a dark little pond, a tarn yoked with oaks and madrones, where, John told visitors, "You expect a witches Sabbath to meet." He called the eerie place an "earth birth," a spot not so different from the spring in *To a God Unknown*. When their beloved English setter, Toby, disappeared in April, John concluded that he "got to thinking too much and one day he just walked away and never came back. The Thoreau of the dog world, I guess." John swore he saw Toby float by in the sky, right over the spring. The bewitching pond and Edenic acres entranced all visitors, and there were many, famous and not so famous: Dorothea Lange and Paul Taylor, Lon Chaney Jr., Charlie Chaplin, George and Martha Ford, Joseph Henry Jackson, Burgess Meredith, Pare Lorentz, Ed Ricketts, and Spencer Tracy. From the outside, it seemed that life should be perfect: the book's publication brought fame, interesting friends, a large tract of land. Carol and John were on track to create another "Cats," the home of Charles Erskine Scott Wood and Sara Bard Field.

And some of John's letters read as if the Los Gatos ranch was, indeed, the Joads' visionary acres: "It's a beautiful morning and I am just sitting in it and enjoying it. Everything is ripe now apples, pears, grapes, walnuts. Carol has made pickles, and chutney, canned tomatoes. Prunes and raisins are on the drying trays. The cellar smells of apples and wine. The madrone berries are ripe and every bird in the country is here—slightly tipsy and very noisy. The frogs are singing about a rain coming but they can be wrong. It's nice."

But it was too beguiling. The money that purchased this "estate" and the cow and the pig became increasingly problematic. Poverty had bound the two; wealth unbound them. Carol saved each royalty check, "squirrel[ing] it away for the lean times that are surely coming." Thrift became an obsession at the same time that extravagant purchases marked their success. For John, as he admitted much later, the money was "bright stuff and I wanted to spread it around." He gave his Pulitzer Prize money for *Grapes* to Ritchie Lovejoy and offered Ricketts's son and Carlton Sheffield education funds (and for Carlton, an education plan as well—first to Oxford or Cambridge for a masters and then to the University of London for a doctorate). He gave Carol a star sapphire ring for her birthday, and both wore cashmere coats. He purchased two buff Packard convertibles, a 180 for himself and a 160 for Carol. These were the signs they had made it, Carol said later. When John married Carol, he had promised to swath her in furs, build her a swimming pool—a lap pool fed by spring water—and have her name up in neon lights: those pledges he fulfilled. But gifts could not bind the two as artistic creation had.

Only half of their hearts beat as one. He and Carol played parts in a script that had lost its center. "I sit up on this beautiful ranch in this comfortable chair with a perfect servant, a beautiful dog and I think I'm more homesick than ever," John wrote to Tom Collins. He yearned for roots—physical and psychic—for renewed artistic energy, and for a sharp sense of self. Their old selves, both his and Carol's, were shaped by privation, the flinty ground of creation, and the struggle for survival that he thought so essential to art. On fecund earth, where was he? And who was she?

Other projects enticed John, particularly filmmaking, since collaborative projects gave him an excuse to escape *Grapes* fanfare. But collaborating with others sidelined Carol. In April 1939, John went to Chicago to work with Pare Lorentz for a month on a government-sponsored film addressing the need for a comprehensive health bill, *The Fight for Life*. In June he went alone to Los Angeles—ostensibly to help with the LA production of *Of Mice and Men* and the film that Lewis Milestone was making from the book. Away from home, he dodged the intense publicity and the calls and telegrams that, he complained, came "all day long—speak . . . speak . . . speak, like hungry birds. . . . The telephone is a thing of horror."

Friends recognized the marital strain. According to Francis Whitaker, who made the metalwork for both the Greenwood Lane house and the Brush Road ranch, Carol and John were happy in the first house, not in the second. John became withdrawn and, Whitaker insisted, quite a different person. Publication of *Grapes* was the beginning of "a great deal of sadness" between them, noted Sara Bard Field, and in her eyes the root cause was that "Holly-wood grabbed" John, and the two no longer lived a "simple life. She thought John made life "pretty hard" for Carol, bringing Hollywood people to dinner at the last minute. "She had no help," Field recalled. "His associations for him were easy and for her they were pretty difficult. . . . John had so many people in the Hollywood life that he just grew away from her."

His escape to Hollywood left Carol sequestered on the ranch. For weeks, she would field calls, becoming Steinbeck's mouthpiece. She opened mail on her own, "fifty to seventy-five letters a day," John reported. Alone she went to see the Broadway production of *Of Mice and Men* in San Francisco. The headline in the *San Francisco Chronicle* read: "Mrs. Steinbeck Enjoys Her Husband's Play." She was John's public voice: "Mrs. Steinbeck saw the play twice with the NY cast but she feels the local production is just about the tops, too," and in some ways better since "San Francisco knows the Salinas valley and 'gets' more of the play." But being John's publicity agent was hardly fulfilling. "Carol was alone," a visiting friend recalled about the post-*Grapes* period, "and they were getting about 300 horrible letters: 'we will rape your wife,' 'we will de-ball you. . . . She had a little Filipino guy helping out; she wasn't scared, but she was not very easy in her mind about all these threats. . . . The letters . . . were just awful." Feeling abandoned a couple of months after the novel's release played on Carol's deepest fears. As a child, Carol had been the "important one in family until Idell came along and she felt left out." And in her marriage, Carol had been used to having all the attention, Mar-jory Lloyd insisted. If you met John and Carol, it was Carol you noticed. And then "suddenly John becomes nationally famous, and Carol not the attrac-tion. John became so sure of himself after Grapes." And Carol shrank. When John returned from Los Angeles, he wrote a friend that "hysterical" Carol had been "pushed beyond endurance."

The public outrage over *The Grapes of Wrath* bewildered them, and they drowned in human voices that continued throughout 1939. Responses to *Grapes* ranged from partisan fervor to rabid condemnation that, in fact, frightened Steinbeck—"the rolling might of this damned thing," he wrote his publisher, "a kind of hysteria about the book." For a man who hated publicity and feared that fame would sap his creative powers, the *Grapes* firestorm was fearsome. He hunkered down and let others carry on the fight (although he donated fifteen leather-bound copies of *Grapes* to a Hollywood auction rais-ing money for migrants, each with a page tipped in: "At the request of John Steinbeck fifteen numbered and signed copies of this book were especially bound for the Steinbeck Migrant Organization"). At the Commonwealth Club in San Francisco, Carey McWilliams and Philip Bancroft, president of the Associated Farmers, went toe to toe, Bancroft claiming that the novel "built up class hatred, contempt for officers of the law and contempt for religion." Anti-American, in short. McWilliams whipped back that the only "sordid" pages were found "in the transcript of the La Follette committee investigating agricultural conditions and not in *The Grapes of Wrath*." California novelist Gertrude Atherton declared that "Landholders of California!" were "on the spot," because *Grapes* was another *Uncle Tom's Cabin*. She urged landowners to "divide up their immense holdings" and give the dispossessed "life" and "land."

Powerful forces in Oklahoma and California hammered the book's veracity, political slant, and language. Ruth Comfort Mitchell, his novelist neighbor, vowed to tell the "other side of the story," and prove that Californians were not mean-spirited, wealthy land barons. *The Grapes of Wrath*, she told a Los Gatos reporter, had "excessive use of profanity," which "offends many people who would otherwise read the book." Speaking on the eve of an Associated Farmers December 1939 convention in Stockton, she told an attentive audience of fifteen hundred: "The question is whether or not our citizens are willing to sit calmly by and see state socialism, accompanied by certain Communistic elements under the guise of 'production for Need' introduced within the framework of a state whose industries are maintained and whose taxes are paid under the profit system." She and others saw *The Grapes of Wrath*, with its eloquent defense of the people, as a socialist tract.

After the largest gathering of agriculturists in California history had ended, Mitchell started her novel *Of Human Kindness*, about genteel small farmers in California, one family accepting one Okie as an equal—once he is taught hygiene, manners, and grammar. Her voice represented many in the Associated Farmers camp, who defended themselves against Steinbeck's characterization of them as greedy and vicious and hateful. Migrants were "Okie Dokie," insisted the Bakersfield secretary of the chamber of commerce, Emory Gay Hoffman. And John Steinbeck definitely was not. Hoffman produced "Plums of Plenty," a six-thousand-word manuscript (lost) and also a propaganda film used by News of the Day and shown at the San Francisco World Exposition in 1939. Like others, Hoffman set out to prove that Steinbeck lied about labor conditions in sunny California.

Unleashed vitriol damaged John and Carol in different ways, he hating the public glare and she hating the glare that put her in the shadows. With the spotlight solely on John as author, her role in the book's construction was erased, and, not surprisingly, she felt blotted out. Warm-hearted Carol shrank. More and more often the brazen woman swamped the breezy one. Her "strange side that was masculine, a bully," as her sister Idell termed it, surfaced more frequently, and friends and family felt wary because they "never knew which one was coming out," the funny, warm Carol or the angry, vindictive Carol. Her barbs were "stronger than ever," insisted Louis Paul, and "she forgot who her friends were." Helen Hosmer, director of the Simon J. Lubin Society, visited the couple after *Grapes* was published and thought Carol "underwent a deep sea change in this period. She had taken her piano and painted it shocking pink and she was doing crazy things and talking about the big times they had." One day Carol bought a bright red coat, a purchase John thought was crazy. Sometimes she would go alone to the Lyndon Hotel bar in downtown Los Gatos to drink and emote. On one occasion, a friend drove her into Los Gatos for cigarettes, and she picked up a couple of policemen she knew and, at 11:00 P.M., brought them up to the house. John was furious, as one policeman tried to convince everyone present that it was he who had composed the music for "When the Swallows Come Back to Capistrano." Erratic behavior. Bullying. Attention-grabbing ploys. All betray an unhappy woman. Undoubtedly Carol wanted to needle John—and he her as well. "They tried to irritate one another," a friend said.

Documentary filmmaker Pare Lorentz, who spent time with both during this period, put their problems in context: "Over and over I've known professors, scientists, and senators who were very poor . . . having to work very hard. They marry their college sweetheart, one who typed for nothing. When the character receives distinction, the wife becomes self-conscious, jealous—feels cut off from the charmed circles. . . . I've been in houses with successful men talking—and the women do something to call attention to themselves." The last time he visited Carol and John in the Los Gatos house, John was trying to open a bottle of wine and kept breaking the cork. Carol put Beethoven's Ninth on the record player and turned up the volume as loud as it would go. She had a drink. "Turn the god-damned volume down," said John. "I can't hear." Carol turned it off, ran out the door, fell down the hill, and screamed at the bottom. She had sprained her ankle.

Rusty Ray provided another astute view of their crumbling marriage:

> We went to school with her and remember her as not in any way limited by class restrictions. . . . She was hurt somewhere along the line and she is today

still suffering from a feeling of inferiority, which accounts for her often being misunderstood. She speaks out very boldly and sometimes not delicately in the presence of people just met and in groups which she has just entered and sometimes the things she says are not very nice. She shocks people and they think she is brazen but underneath she is really frightened.

John is bigger than she is and his success in a way has hurt her. She doesn't like the way people shower their attention on him and pay little attention to her. . . . Understand, she is healthy, attractive and pleasant. Actually she is a very good sort. It was she who joined the Communist Party and if there is a left wing to the family, it is Carol rather than John. . . . It is naturally difficult to have all this attention pushed at one all of a sudden and to be making money hand over fist after all those lean years. . . .

John doesn't care about money, he leaves all that to Carol. . . . Now John and Carol have made many new friends and the effect of this material and intellectual wealth has naturally become noticeable. It has made John a bigger and a better man and I believe it has had the opposite affect [sic] upon his wife. [John] is terribly strong willed and yet I think his wife can do almost anything with him just as he would make any sacrifice for a friend. You will gather I am very fond of John. I think he is a great person. I like his wife and understand something about her, but she is not a person I can reach for she is always somebody else rather than herself, furthermore, she doesn't drink well.

Carol was a nasty drunk—accusatory, angry, loud. In July 1939, she went with John to Los Angeles and they ended up in one of the worst fights of their marriage. Carol slugged John and stormed out of a party given by Robert Benchley, then left LA and returned to the ranch. Witnesses said it was a wrenching public confrontation; John admitted that she was "hysterical and pulled out." For a few weeks the two were separated, cooling off, but realized that they needed each other. Carol's dependency was sharper. She needed to be needed, to feel that she was an essential part of John's life and creative work. With John not writing in 1939, she had no job, other than gardening and partying and answering mail. They had no shared purpose, which left Carol empty. And John couldn't minister to her because he couldn't minister to himself. He was as tense and unhappy as she.

The separation drove Carol "very close if not over the edge of insanity," John admitted. She raged in frustration at things she could not control. In 1939 those things were John's affections, her own failures, and finding purposeful work.

Carol's alienation called for great understanding, something John could give only intermittently, if at all, since he was as depressed as she. In a long and revealing letter to Toby Street that John wrote during this same period, he admits to a "profound physical and spiritual disappointment that things turned out the way I knew they would," and suggests that his depression is inherited:

You know, my father was a morose man and had been a morose child. His mother explained it by saying that when he was a baby the soldiers' funerals went by the house in Florida all day every day. It is strange the explanations. I think he was disappointed in the same way. And my mother's father was a brilliant and beautiful man. He married a stupid religious woman and all his life he had to pretend things. And because or contingent with his pretenses, he had a family of neurotics, all expecting the life he projected for his own protections. Then I came along, probably as neurotic as the rest only I learn a trick. I learn to throw all the neuroses in one direction and holding it there. And that's the books. And the books have become more and I less. So that finally when there isn't a book either being written or planned, I have very little life left, feel a little like a shortage of oxygen. And this time I worked too hard and too long and actually strained some kind of mental ligament, so that my resources or resistances are down. And then I realize that in spite of all the effort and training and straining, it isn't much of a book. But that's not the worst. The worst is that it is the best I can do. . . .

This is a morose letter. It is caused by the conviction that I have no home. Never did have but I always thought I might have and now I know I never will have, and that makes for a continued longing for extinction and that is not healthy nor real nor wise. But it slides in like water under my spring box and it is like a dampness which is there all the time. And I'm more afraid of it than of anything else.

Despair "like a dampness" dogged Steinbeck all his life. He finally saw a therapist when he married his third wife and moved to New York City in the 1950s. In 1939 success was hollow, writing nonexistent, roots severed. For Steinbeck homesickness was the absence of a skein of associations linking place, artistic creation, companionship, and security. And a grounded phalanx. A deep vein in Steinbeck's fiction, as in his life, is the significance of home, and again and again he explores the kaleidoscopic meanings of homes lost, gained, imagined, and replaced. That he and Carol seemed unable to create a loving home, even when artistic success, financial security, fruitful land, and a new house were theirs, was beyond comprehension for him. He had failed at the one endeavor that for him was a biological and ethical necessity—sanctuary.

Sensing John's dark mood that June when he holed up in the Aloha Arms Apartments, off Sunset Boulevard in Hollywood, a childhood friend who worked in Hollywood, Max Wagner, found a woman to distract him. Gwendolyn Conger, age twenty to John's thirty-seven, would provide everything but the support that John needed to get back on track with Carol.

One story has it—this from Gwen's mother—that John heard Gwen sing on a Los Angeles radio station, her throaty voice crooning a song his father had loved, "Peg in the Little Black Cart," with husky suggestiveness. Another version has it that Max told Gwen to bring his ailing friend chicken soup and John fell for the woman behind the bowl. Gwen Conger was lovely, with golden hair, milky skin, and winsome ways. She had "sex appeal," noted Charlotte Jackson. "She was the aphrodisiac," said Burgess Meredith. That first June night, according to Gwen's own account, "was pure chemistry . . . I fed him his soup, I washed him, I bathed him, and I rubbed his back and legs . . . never in my life had I seen varicosities of the legs into the groin such as he had. . . . Whatever I was able to provide was something he needed." What chance did Carol have?

Perhaps the relationship with Gwen was not sexual on that first trip—both John and Gwen said it wasn't. But with the bathing and back rubs and eying his groin and instant chemistry, that's a hard yarn to swallow. He visited Gwen daily during that June 1939 visit to LA. During their first dinner out together, they rubbed knees under the table. He held her hand and looked at her breasts. Several friends had noted the sexual tensions in John and Carol's marriage, from Ed Ricketts to painter Ellwood Graham, who insisted that in Los Gatos John was "lonely and miserable because he needed a woman and he needed a good one, and he had a hard time finding one." Gwen's attention and youth, her femininity and curves, fit the bill. She was young, impressionable, eager, funny, and pliable. She "reminded you of the bedroom," noted one friend. She was "marvelous, a very female woman . . . soft, agreeable," said Dan James, driver for Charlie Chaplin.

Gwen's aura was in sharp contrast to Carol's swashbuckling stride, which, by 1939, had trampled and unmanned John, claimed Lewis Milestone, who was working with John on the screenplay for *Of Mice and Men* that summer: "He began to feel castrated by this strong woman. And the reason he fell for Gwen was because suddenly he found out that he was not impotent, it was just the woman who was making him like that. When he met Gwen, she restored his confidence and his masculinity." The powerful magnetism that was Gwen Conger could hardly be resisted, his health and identity restored.

And the timing was impeccable on both sides. Born in Chicago on October 25, 1919, Gwen had recently moved to LA with her mother and grandmother and plunged into the promise of California. What Gwen wanted, like so many others newly arrived in Hollywood, was a good time in the California sun. To make that happen, she took "every job [she] could get" in Hollywood, "anything to earn a buck": staff singer with Columbia Broadcasting Studios as well as waitress at Brittingham's Radio Center restaurant; small parts in films; a spot on a chorus line. She was a version of Faye Greener in Nathanael West's *Day of the Locust*, a yearner and a dreamer and an alluring prize for the right man, the right script—one that John was willing to write for her, he as leading man. He cast her as heroine in a real-time movie, offered a ticket to the glittering show. He called her "an earth woman," and Gwen replied to his remark, "I guess I am," not having any idea what he meant. Steinbeck was her knight—older, successful, and well connected, the man with the "Svengali eyes," as Gwen wrote of his gaze on her. She was his rescued virgin—so very young, sexy, willing to be purloined. The plot was irresistible for both director and ingénue.

In the first of his many love poems to Gwen, written months after the June introduction, John describes her, in Robert DeMott's words, as the "eternal woman, a fantastic and impossible-to-attain combination of goddess and muse."

> I will speak to you always young,
> Young, milk-skinned
> Smelling of sweetness that has
> No simile;
> Smell of warm, young, clean skin,
> Smell of the unknown house
> And a dear home.
> I will address you always
> Although your name change
> And your sister sit
> In the seat you made warm.

In letters he addressed her as "Floppet, Doxie, Wimbleton, Queen of the May . . . Mother Mouse." If Gwen came to mean home to the unhomed John, what chance did Carol ever have in this subplot to their marriage?

On that first meeting in June and on many subsequent visits, Gwen and John had rollicking good times. Together they "broke out of the box," as one friend described it. Gwen was "sharp and funny," though her wit less razor-sharp than Carol's. Frank and Lynn Loesser became LA pals, as did Gwen's voice coach (also Lynn's), Sandy Oliver, who said that Gwen liked to sing but she wasn't too serious about a professional career. "It was play time for John and Gwen," said Oliver. Whenever John was in Hollywood, Frank and Lynn joined in the fun, and the foursome behaved "like a bunch of young-sters," admitted Lynn—going to seedy bars, singing in taxis, concocting off-beat schemes. Their joint humor "was never mean. It was never cruel . . . but it was always inventive and slightly juvenile." They drank endless martinis.

When back in Los Gatos, John drank heavily with Carol as well. How-ever smitten with Gwen, he was also committed to his marriage. In the late summer and fall of 1939 through mid-1940, he worked on having fun with Carol. That summer the couple went often to the Golden Gate International Exposition in San Francisco, the first time with his sister Beth, Charlotte and Joe Jackson, and Paul de Kruif. "I'm nuts about fairs even County fairs. Just an extension of steam shovel watching and no one ever watched an excavation with more energy than I." The San Francisco exposition helped take his mind off his troubles, literary and personal.

Who in the San Francisco Bay Area—or far away for that matter—didn't long to go again and again in the summers of 1939 and 1940? The exposi-tion had been discussed and anticipated for years. It was a celebration of San Francisco's two new bridges, the Golden Gate and the Bay Bridge, completed in 1936 and 1937, and its recovery from the 1906 earthquake. The phoenix had risen—almost literally, in this case. In the shallowest, most treacher-ous point of the bay, engineers had constructed a wall from a depth of sixty feet to the surface, filled it with dredged sea bottom and iced it with topsoil. From the bay rose Treasure Island, the world's largest manufactured island at that time, one mile long by three-quarters mile wide. Architects constructed buildings, gardens, fountains, and statuary to celebrate the "Pageant of the Pacific"—ships coming from Asia into San Francisco, and a new Pan Ameri-can flight linking San Francisco to Asia. San Francisco became the gateway to the Far East, and the fair celebrated that glorious potential. Constructed on the island was a temporary city that had an exotic air, with motifs from

Cambodian, Mayan, and Incan civilizations. The four-hundred-foot Tower of the Sun dominated the island, surrounded by statues representing Science, Agriculture, Industry, and Art. There was a Court of the Moon and Courts of Flowers and Reflections. Port of the Trade Winds drew visitors to see sloops, sampans, and seaplanes. In cavernous proto-hangars—after the fair the island was to be used as an airport, and was until 1942, when it became a naval station—were artistic and cultural exhibits.

It's hard to imagine John and Carol not attending one of the fair's several flesh shows, Sally Rand's Nude Ranch being the most notorious. Women clad in cowboy hats, gun belts, and boots sashayed lasciviously on stage for a mixed audience of men and women who, in attending a flesh show, could allow themselves to "feel devilish," as a local paper noted. Just up Carol's alley. The two must have taken in other Gateway attractions: the cyclone coaster, the rocket ship, the giant crane. They definitely rode in the many rickshaws, racing each other around the streets of the fair.

In the summer of 1940, Gwen had a gig singing at the fair, and amid all the brilliance the golden girl must have shown ever more brightly. Carol didn't have much of a chance during these months, when she probably didn't know about Gwen but sensed John's diverted gaze.

That fall, John and Carol tried other escapes, first to Seattle and Vancouver, later to Chicago. On the car trip north, they had no plans. They meandered through the redwoods, to Oregon, Washington, wanting, no doubt, to recapture the magic of their earlier years. In Seattle they visited John Cage and his wife Xenia, Tal Lovejoy's sister. Back home again, they took off almost immediately to Chicago on a second trip to work with Lorentz; it was Carol's first time on a plane. "Right now I run around like a bug," John told his sister.

Although John's commitment to the marriage was real enough, that didn't dilute his attraction to Gwen. He couldn't banish her. In October 1939, she visited Monterey for the first time and John introduced her to Ed, whom she took a shine to: "the best time I had was during those moments with you," she wrote him. "And John told me as much, when he said I should meet you. Another bestseller for John." When John first brought her to the lab, he turned to Jean Ariss and said, "Watch when she walks in here. Every woman will hate her because she is so beautiful." She had a gold net over her hair, Jean remembered, and "looked like a medieval princess." She was naïve, and "that would have fascinated John," Jean said. When John's friends in Monterey and Los Gatos eventually found out what he was up to, some thought Gwen a floozy, out to snag John and set up a literary salon with herself at the center. One found her "shallow." Another "hard," lacking in gracious manners. Some hated "the other woman." And some, including Ed Ricketts, simply enjoyed her festive ways. Indeed, Ed served as a go-between of sorts, and later John would enlist Ed to write Gwen about his marital situation, a weird blending of identities, lover and surrogate lover.

Marriages in decline are depressingly similar. The poignancy of John and Carol's marital collapse is the steady spiral downward after the success of *Grapes*, a book dedicated with such evident love and gratitude to Carol. John knew his wife was a gem—at her best, kind and funny and warm. A survivor. Indeed, his awareness of female strength and adaptability is one the central threads in *The Grapes of Wrath*. Confronted with social upheaval, men attempt, without success, to "figure" out a solution. Displaced heads of households use rationality to understand their dispossession—men drawing figures with a stick in the soil is a repeated trope in the book. Women like Ma Joad cope. In one of her most famous speeches, voiced right after her son Tom has left the family, Ma tells a mournful Pa, who has lost his grounding, his farm, his identity: "Man, he lives in jerks—baby born an' a man dies, an' that's a jerk—gets a farm an' loses his farm, an' that's a jerk. Woman, it's all one flow, like a stream, little eddies, little waterfalls, but the river, it goes right on. Woman looks at it like that." Women's survival quotient is strong, Steinbeck acknowledged. The first chapter of the book concludes by marking gender difference, and the symbolic final chapter magnifies that difference. Rose of Sharon has learned from her mother that she must put aside pain and resolutely face what life brings.

The Grapes of Wrath pays homage to women, writ large, and to Carol, who inspired that large-hearted vision. The adaptability and courage, in essence a chivalric loyalty, that Carol brought to the relationship for ten-plus years indelibly stamped Steinbeck's masterpiece and his life. He believed in Carol's virtues as much as in his own. He relied on her vision as well as his own. Their phalanx had produced his best work. He couldn't shed her without also shedding a vital part of his own character: honorable action, loyalty, and truth. Without Carol, his own chivalric soul would be—and was—mortally wounded.

To John in Los Angeles, Gwen may have seemed exactly what he needed, perhaps nothing more than a pleasant diversion from what had come to ail him. But she would give the final push that toppled the gyroscopic whirlwind that had given rise to *The Grapes of Wrath*.

I have a little driedel. I made it of clay.
When it's dry and ready, then dreidel I shall play.
It has a lovely body, with legs so short and thin.
When it gets all tired, it drops and then I win!
My dreidel's always playful. It loves to dance and spin.
A happy game of dreidel, come play now let's begin.

Yiddish children's song (lyrics by Samuel S. Grossman)

CHAPTER NINE

On the Sea of Cortez

A FEW YEARS after the 1940 voyage that Steinbeck, Ricketts, and Carol took to the Sea of Cortez, Carol and a friend were on a fishing boat on Monterey Bay, watching the sunset. Suddenly Carol exclaimed that the scene reminded her of Baja: "Oh what a time we had. That was the happiest time of my entire life." There were tears in her eyes. It was the only occasion when Viola Franklin, Carol's friend for over forty years, ever saw her cry.

Carol's recollection might seem baffling, since the six-week trip to the Sea of Cortez in March and April of 1940 was an unsettled time in her marriage—surely not, one would suppose, the happiest time for either partner. While Carol may not have known about Gwen, she must have recognized the unsteadiness in their marriage, the hollow intimacy. Evidence enough is that she and John slept in separate berths throughout the trip, she in the stateroom, he with the crew in a common cabin. (Although this may have been something John would have wanted to do in any case; he would not have wanted to be off in an exalted stateroom.) John was often quiet, while Carol was unpredictable, wild and flirtatious with the crew. But if marital bonds were frayed, intellectual ties remained strong. For six weeks, Carol, Ed, and John, each emotionally fragile when the *Western Flyer* sailed out of Monterey Bay, revitalized the creative phalanx. Collecting marine invertebrates created a colony of workers on and off the boat, friends and crew bound to a common purpose. And sailing through the little-known Gulf of California was palliative—a place where, as Steinbeck wrote in *Sea of Cortez*, "the very air . . . is miraculous, and outlines of reality change with the moment. A dream hangs over the whole region, a brooding kind of hallucination." John, Carol, and Ed took themselves out of time.

So Carol's nostalgia was not far off the mark. Near the end of the voyage, John wrote to his agents that "Carol is beginning to be homesick for her garden. But she has been marvelous on this trip. I don't know any other woman who could have done it." Captain Tony Berry concurred: "She was good on the trip, seventy five percent well behaved." Perhaps the journey was life-altering for both, helping each recover psychic balance—despite a doomed marriage. Years later John insisted that *Sea of Cortez* was his favorite among all the books he'd written. And a perceptive reviewer, Lewis Gannett, wrote in the *New York Herald Tribune* that the haunting and thoughtful *Sea of Cortez* contains "more of the whole man" than in "any of his novels . . . the best of Steinbeck is in it." It remains the seminal text for appreciating his mind—the holistic and ecological sensibilities that he and Ed Ricketts shared. For a writer who spent the 1930s cultivating a "detached" stance, writing this personal, idiosyncratic text was transformative. Conversations structure *Sea of Cortez*, as Ed noted after publication: it reads, he said, as "a Jon-Ed sit by the fire."

But of course Carol was there too, joining those conversations, a part of the phalanx.

The trip had a brief gestation period. In part because John and Carol were restless in the fall of 1939, at marital loose ends, they planned a Christmas collecting trip with Ed Ricketts to take advantage of a "minus tide of unusual depth," north of San Francisco to Olema, near Point Reyes, and then to Duxbury Reef and Tomales Point—places where Ricketts had often worked in the intertidal. For John, study of marine invertebrates was liberating: "the two most important [things] I suppose—at least they seem so to me," John wrote to Carlton Sheffield, "are freedom from respectability and most important—freedom from the necessity of being consistent." To move from social problems to scientific inquiry was, in his mind, to broaden his world outlook immeasurably. After writing *Grapes,* he wrote a long letter to his uncle Joe Hamilton, explaining this shift from partisan to scientist:

> The new work must jump to include other species beside the human. That is why my interest in biology and ecology have become so sharpened. . . . The bio-ecological pattern having at its conception base and immeasurable lengthened time sequence, does not admit the emphasis of such crises as human unemployment, except insofar as they vitally threaten the existence of the species. I have little doubt that the species is so threatened, but, if it is, it is because human psychic mutation has given it a tendency toward extinction, just as the saurian tendency toward skeletal mutation condemned it to extinction. . . . I live in and of my work. When I lengthened the time sense and spread the picture, I made it nearly impossible to narrow it again. . . . What I am trying to say is this. By changing the world picture, all proportions were changed. And with this

change (in me) unemployment and its concomitants ceased to be an emergency and the war ceased to be a destruction of civilization and both of them became phases neither good nor bad, completely nonteleological in the life history of a fairly complicated, highly variable species.

In this letter, written as much to himself as to his uncle Joe, whom he had seen when in Chicago working with Pare Lorentz, he explains his necessary shift to an expanded ecological vision and acknowledges biological, historical, and social connectivity. Human migrations and suffering, however terrible, are one part of this wider horizon. In the introduction to *Sea of Cortez* he expresses his complex convictions far more simply: "None of it is important or all of it is."

As part of this broadened perspective, an ambitious project gradually took shape that fall. He and Ed decided to collaborate on a "tide pool hand book" of San Francisco Bay. Almost immediately that collaborative project morphed into a book about the Mexican intertidal as well, initially envisioned as a car trip down the Baja Peninsula.

Indeed, John and Ed's mutual commitment to marine invertebrates was momentous for both. Ed documented the genesis of these projects in his private journal. His description conveys some sense of their tight bond, how the two "sparked" each other in conversation:

Jon has been saying that his time of pure fiction is over, that he'd like next to portray the tidepools, that [his] next work will be factual. He came down this time depressed and unconfident, heading for a long walk or a bus ride. He said that in Feb. he and Crl would go to Mexico. I said if they'd wait until Mch I'd go along and that I wanted to go, that I'd rather go with someone who knew the ropes and that I'd rather go with them. He said "Fine, then maybe too we could get in a little collecting." I said if I had any gumption I'd get busy first and get well started on the a/c of SF Bay Reg. Mar. Invertebrates that [] suggested I should do. Then John said, why don't we do that book together. We talked it over a while and it began to seem to me quite feasible. So we began to lay plans for it, work to start immediately. Then some how or other we got to talking about the Mex trip, it changed around more and more from the idea of a motor trip down to Mexico City, to the idea of, primarily, a Gulf of Calif. collecting trip (Jon said "If you have an objective, like collecting specimens, it put so much more direction into a trip, made it more interesting"). Then he said "We'll do a book about it that'll more than pay the expenses of the trip" and as we considered it we got more and more enthusiastic about the whole thing.

We started at once to lay out plans, to write down lists of things to do, to get, to take, to plan our itinerary and activities and went down to Chev. that next morning (Wed. Nov. 29) to look up a station wagon. There happened to be one coming in and Jon just about closed with him that same day. Then the idea of the book loomed up more and more as the significant feature of the whole thing. We both became quite sure that it could be a great thing, maybe very great "modern Odyssey."

Their great "Iliad and odyssey," however, was meant to rescue not Helen but themselves.

Everyone involved needed to sever landed pursuits—true for John, Carol, and Ed in equal measure. John had spent the months since *Grapes'* April 1939 publication "busily fencing out the forces and people who would take my life and work over for their own ends." With bravado he declared that "the novel, as we know it, is dead" and that a new form would emerge from scientific inquiry; he sought a "new basic picture."

To work as a marine biologist with Ed Ricketts must have seemed a soothing prospect. Scientific research turns one's gaze to an objective external, not the internal; the project would be collaborative rather than solitary; and in the remote Sea of Cortez he could escape from everything—publicity and correspondence and expectations from readers and a well-meaning editor who wanted him to write another fictional blockbuster. Furthermore, Mexico might offer the time for "Salvations to be worked out . . . mine and ours," he wrote in early January 1940. "Maybe this is wrong or right [for the marriage]. That it is so is more important than either. But the work is to be done and I must do it. Things are slipping. I can't stand firm unless there is something to stand on and I am attempting to find the foundation of some new discipline in this book." That confused utterance reflects his mind. The only way out of this uncertainty was to lay new foundations—artistic, ecological, and domestic. Perhaps locating his marriage in this larger framework would allow non-teleological acceptance: "it is so."

Carol also must have relished the chance to sever stateside distractions, to escape memories of the grim months after publication of *The Grapes of Wrath*. She may have suspected that John's affections were sidelined, and if so then to have him to herself—or nearly so—must have seemed a perfect antidote to his detachment. Furthermore, like John and Ed, she had also completed a manuscript, a gardening or "seed book" that she sent off to a New York publisher in mid-January 1940. There's no draft of that book, no record about whether or not it was a revision of an earlier manuscript, but we know she wrote a book on gardening, her passion during the Los Gatos years.

For Ed the timing was equally fortuitous and salvational. After years of delays and missteps by Stanford University Press, his own book on Monterey Bay invertebrates, *Between Pacific Tides*, was finally published in 1939. Even if few reviewers appreciated the book's departure from the standard intertidal texts of the day, the publication was cause for satisfaction. Ed's innovative approach organized the world of invertebrates by habitat and communities and relationships, rather than by a taxonomic grouping—kingdom, phyla, class, order, family, genus, species. Ed's vision was relational and stressed the connections between and among species as well as connections with environmental features, such as wave shock. The book was to become a classic in marine ecology.

But publication of this daring new work did little to lift the despair that settled on Ed in midsummer 1939. Since 1936, he had been passionately involved with a married woman, Jean Ariss, the "love of his life," admitted Toni Jackson, his common-law wife in the 1940s. In 1939 the liaison was at its nadir, and he spent much of that year in a deep depression, dreaming that Jean would leave her husband and child and live with him. The thought obsessed him. "Don't have any morale for work. Well one reason is that the only work is of the future or past type, nothing coming in now, and the present financial situation and the prognosis for the future is so discouraging that it also probably affects my morale." In his private journal, his pain is palpable: "I correspond with almost no beauty at all right now because my whole horizon . . . is blocked out with just one thing, my obsession, my possessiveness with reference to the Jean-Ed relation." In December 1939, he wrote to Joseph Campbell in the same vein, saying that only recently had he "got my morale up to the point of working on a new scientific library. . . . I have had more suffering in the past year than in all my life up to that point."

In the Sea of Cortez, fantasies of Jean might be banished. Certainly all the elaborate plans and preparations, reading scientific articles, and anticipating the pleasure of collecting and sorting specimens were distractions perfectly fitted for the energetic, productive (perhaps manic) side of Ed. In agreeing to finance the trip, John gave his friend the gift of forgetfulness. He had never been Jean's champion, feeling that the much younger woman was using Ed. A scientific expedition would almost certainly bring his friend back to life—as Ed admitted it might: "And Monday we'll be off for west coast of Mexico," he writes in his journal. "As tho I were starting new life."

All three longed for adventure, collaborative work, research, and the excitement of acquiring knowledge of unfamiliar intertidal species, focusing on "common forms . . . the ubiquitous and economically important forms" and not on the spectacular or curious types. This and more drew them together. Although Carol may have been only tentatively enlisted in the actual writing or cataloguing, she was an energetic participant in the adventure. As John writes in the opening section of *Sea of Cortez*, collecting specimens was, for all, "only part of the truth" for setting forth. "We were curious." In that quality, John, Ed, and Carol were soul mates.

January and February of 1940 were spent hastily organizing this "make-shift expedition," which had evolved from a car trip to Baja to a voyage of nearly four thousand miles to the Gulf and back. In the opening chapter of *Sea of Cortez*, John carefully explains what went into those frantic weeks, modeling his narrative on Thoreau's *Walden*, where "Economy" is the initial concern. Philosophical speculation is grounded in the prudential. Steinbeck lays out trip essentials: groceries bought, equipment sorted, books read, "what books were available about the Gulf." He ordered scientific books from Covici, W. C. Allee's *Animal Aggregations* (undoubtedly Ed's own copy of his professor's text burned in the fire), and texts in invertebrate biology. Carol, a willing participant, might have perused the Jesuit priest Clavigero's account of the Gulf or learned names of invertebrates. Certainly she would have surveyed the charter, laughed at the permits (she pasted one in her scrapbook). Her sly voice surfaces, perhaps, in a reference to the charter: "it took us several hours to get over the solemn feeling the charter put on us. We thought we might live better lives and pay our debts, and one at least of us contemplated for one holy, horrified moment a vow of chastity." That sounds like Carol's wit.

During one of those California winters when it rained "hard and constantly," there was a lot of drinking on the side, Ricketts reported. (One memorable day was spent consuming all the wine in the Steinbecks' house and then continuing the revelry at the lab with Robert Benchley's secretary.) Leave-taking was occasion for one last shoreside hurrah. Carol and John would have attended the huge barbecue on the end of the pier on the day before they sailed, March 11, 1940. The occasion was the annual sardine festival in Monterey, where fishermen and friends crowded the pier to eat fish and pasta and drink wine. All the crew dipped into the "medicine"—alcohol—intended for the trip before sailing, waving woozily in the good-bye photos: "The moment or hour of leave-taking is one of the pleasantest times in human experience," Steinbeck writes, "for it has in it a warm sadness without loss. People who don't ordinarily like you very well are overcome with affection at leave-taking. We said good-by again and again and still could not bring ourselves to cast off the lines and start the engines. It would be good to live in a perpetual state of leave-taking, never to go nor to stay, but to remain suspended in that golden emotion of love and longing: to be missed without being gone; to be loved without satiety. How beautiful one is and how desirable; for in a few moments one will have ceased to exist." Reflections punctuate this narrative, gently lifting observations from time-bound to timelessness.

That poignant departure must have been exhilarating for all—certainly for Carol, now part of an active whole, seven people launching an expedition. "Sea-gulls flew around and around but did not land. There was no room for them—too many people were seeing us off." As the purse seiner that John had secured for the voyage, the *Western Flyer*, rounded Point Joe, near Asilomar Beach, "we were all a little sentimental." Carol's sentiments, however, must have been fleetingly voiced since Ed notes in his personal log that she "was sick until well into the night." Pacific swells unsettle weak stomachs.

Eight months after the *Western Flyer* sailed past Point Joe at the south end of Asilomar Beach, John sat down to write *Sea of Cortez* in his sister's Asilomar cottage. For over six weeks he wrestled with how to structure his travel narrative, "very slowly feeling" his way in December 1940 because "it is something of a new form not only for me, but I want it new in every sense. And it is genuinely worth doing." *Sea of Cortez* was another in a series of experiments in form throughout his career (*Of Mice and Men*, the play-novelette, another). But in 1940, more than his art hung in the balance: so did his marriage and his ability to write an extended piece of nonfiction much more challenging than "The Harvest Gypsy" articles four years earlier. Another six weeks passed and he was still worrying about the opening chapters: "Hard things beginnings—very hard," he admitted in his journal. One difficulty was voice. The first page calls attention to a shift from a personal to collective voice. The first sentence reads: "The design of a book is the pattern of a reality controlled and shaped by the mind of the writer." The second paragraph qualifies that design: "*We* have a book to write about the Gulf of California." Although he carves personalities for Tony Berry, the captain, and each of the crew—Tiny Colletto, Sparky Enea, and Tex Travis—he does not name himself, Ed, or Carol. Their presence is embedded in the narrative, in collective conversations, reactions, conclusions, discoveries. Ricketts would be a coauthor of *Sea of Cortez*, but Carol simply faded into the "we."

This "we" serves Steinbeck well. As noted on their application to the Mexican government, this odyssey was undertaken "to evaluate and consider the way marine invertebrate animals occur along shore—their interlocking associations or societies in their relations to each other and to the environmental factors." As summed up for friends in Monterey, the trip to the Sea of Cortez was undertaken to observe how invertebrates "get along together." Everything about the trip was focused on connectivity, both human and invertebrate.

There is no escape on a small boat, so the trip was, of necessity, a collective endeavor. Berths and the galley on a purse seiner are cramped—the main deck and wheelhouse deck draw all. Solitude is at a premium, and meals and drinks and conversation are shared. *Sea of Cortez* is as much about the crew and the planners getting along together as it is about intertidal associations. It is as much about human cooperation as it is about cooperation and survivability among intertidal animals. And for Ricketts, being in Mexico reinforced the importance of friendship: "the whole non-western character" of Mexico, he writes in his journal, "emphasizes the spiritual values of real friendship between men for instance, as against the European-American insistence on material values." The "we" that includes the crew models what the book is all about.

And yet the narrative "we" excludes Carol. The crew is mentioned often—Captain Tony, Sparky, Tiny and Tex—so readers assume they are present when "we" reach conclusions. John is author of *Sea of Cortez*, so he is part of the "we." Ed is coauthor, responsible for the phyletic catalogue in *Sea of Cortez*, so he is included. But Carol remains the unnamed sailor, an out-of-focus member of a group photograph. Why this is so has mystified many, and the tendency is to blame the male author whose "we" seems decidedly male.

Tony Berry's explanation about Carol's absence in the text is the most straightforward: "We didn't count Carol because she couldn't steer." But John's reasoning was undoubtedly more complex. Certainly when he began composition in December 1940, he was intimately involved with Gwen Conger, the woman who would become his second wife. But Carol's omission was not vindictive, insisted Toni Jackson, Ed Ricketts's companion and Steinbeck's typist for the manuscript. Toni worked closely with John throughout composition, typing, and proofreading the manuscript, and she didn't believe for a moment that the reason John failed to mention Carol was because their marriage was in difficulty. Carol sort of went along for the ride. . . . John was the one in the doghouse, really. He was having this big affair with Gwyn [Gwen later changed the spelling of her name] and he was the one who wanted the breakup; he really felt sorry for Carol and felt bad about the whole thing. If anything, he would have (as he did in other ways) bent over backwards to "do the right thing" by Carol.

My speculation about why he didn't mention her is that they were using a sardine boat and a sardine boat crew and those fellows wouldn't ordinarily dream . . . (well, yes, of course they might) of having a woman aboard. Bad luck, etc. They were mostly Sicilians I think. This was a very male sort of thing, science and the sea as far as the doing and as far as the writing. . . . I can imagine that bringing her into the picture would complicate things from a writing standpoint.

For Steinbeck, the "writing standpoint" was central, always. His account was part of a long tradition of books about brotherly camaraderie on the high seas—an account of an expedition, he insisted to Covici, and definitely not an "adventure story except as an adventure of the mind." Hence the "we" and Carol's disappearance into that voice. Her participation in the trip must be reconstructed by disentangling threads of actions and reactions, and relying on Ricketts's occasional references to her in his own "Verbatim Transcript of Notes of Gulf of California Trip, March–April 1940."

On their first night out, discussion turned to the Old Man of the Sea—a mythic narrative surfacing from watery depths. This conversation sets the tone for all of the book's narrative flights, which begin in the concrete and individual and move to the abstract and collective. Tiny may have started the discussion, since his own relative, Captain Sal Colletto, cruising on the family purse seiner, the *Dante Alighieri*, had seen the ghostly "Old Man of the Bay" three times in ten years, the local paper reported in 1938 (probably an elephant seal gliding through the water). The legendary "Old Man" suggests far more profound truths about the human spirit, Steinbeck writes: "the preponderantly aquatic symbols in the individual unconscious might well be indications of a group psyche-memory which is the foundation of the whole unconscious."

Sea of Cortez comes again and again to such notions and symbols that cross cultures, burrow deep in the waters of the human psyche, and suggest "a pattern of his whole species"—race consciousness, Steinbeck and Ricketts termed it. During the crew's first stop in the Gulf, Cabo San Lucas, they hear a story about a cross marking the spot where a man died after failing to reach home one night. In that tale, Steinbeck sees the stories of countless failed pilgrimages. Later in the trip, the statue of Our Lady of Loreto reminds Steinbeck that all cultures long for altars "on which to pour their force." At another point in *Sea of Cortez,* he notes that the "sound symbols of wild doves" play, as do visual images, in the unconscious. Such universalizing moments in the narrative "break through," in Ricketts's terminology, from physical to metaphysical. Discussions of racial memories must have intrigued Carol, for her mind, like John's and Ed's, moved fluidly from the physical and specific to the abstract and universal. It was she, after all, who first put her finger on the implications of Robinson Jeffers's notion that humanity was the crust to break through, thus recognizing the poet's embrace of the physical and spiritual in "Roan Stallion."

This travel narrative, like the others he wrote (*A Russian Journal, Travels with Charley*) traces movement that is both physical and intellectual. The *Western Flyer* sailed to a mapped place with precise coordinates designating each stop, as indicated in Captain Berry's nautical manual, *Coast Pilot,* which was frequently consulted and occasionally referenced in the narrative. But the Steinbeck/Ricketts expedition was not a voyage of exploration, not an attempt to plant flags of discovery on an "unknown" peninsula. Throughout, Steinbeck considers the Indians and priests, mappers and explorers who preceded them. Their own voyage was more loosely defined, a holistic grasp of the peninsula that includes names of intertidal organisms, description of natural landmarks, consideration of historical context, and speculation on any lopped-off thought that comes up in conversation. From any coordinate on the physical map, be it Cabo San Lucas or the island of Cayo, the text moves readers to a more nuanced sense of place that embraces a vertical axis that is historical, impressionistic, speculative. The book, like the trip, is and was a heady mixture of ideas and activities, work and relaxation: only in "laziness," Steinbeck reminds readers, "can one achieve a state of contemplation which is a balancing of values, a weighing of oneself against the world and the world against itself."

Laziness sometimes involved sampling "2160 individuals of two species of beer" on board. Undoubtedly Carol drank on this trip—probably like the others, "just enough, and we refuse to profane a good little time of mild inebriety with that slurring phrase 'over-indulgence.'" Tony Berry reported that she never got drunk on the boat, even with a stocked "medicine chest" for emergencies—tequila and rum. For John, as for Carol, alcohol was a "warmer of the soul, a strengthener of muscle and spirit." But when Carol did overindulge in wine, which was her drink of choice, she acted with a spunky kind of abandon that struck others as excessive. Sparky Enea, who ended up as cook, vividly recalled Carol's first indiscretion, which tapped into another weakness, being tight-fisted. She had not purchased enough groceries, and when the captain told Tiny to buy an additional eight hundred dollars worth of food, Carol "hit the ceiling." She then refused to cook, which caused a row among the crew and embarrassed John. "Carol was supposed to be the cook for the trip but I had cooked every meal since we started," Enea recalled, and Captain Berry kept telling him to cook when Carol wouldn't. He made breakfast daily and spaghetti with sardines on Thursdays and Sundays, "a tradition among Sicilians," he boasted. According to Enea, Carol kept telling him that she would make everyone chicken cacciatore, but she never did, managing only one dinner of chicken and dumplings, and one dessert, a delicious lemon meringue pie.

An unhappy woman, a seasick woman, or a woman drinking with gusto might well slough off all responsibilities for cooking, if indeed her "assigned" role was "ship's cook," as reported in the local paper. Steinbeck, however, writes that "we carried no cook and dishwasher; it had been understood that we would all help." Furthermore, on chartered boats a cook is typically a crew member, and with Tiny Colletto signed on as an extra crew member, perhaps Carol opted for a role as collector and scientist. As a woman who had always been a full participant in her husband's work, time on deck and shore must have been far preferable to hours in the tight, dark galley. Tony Berry reported that Carol was a good sailor, willing to mop out the galley and help around the boat in general, and that she was the first to get into their skiff, *Baby Flyer*, when they went ashore to collect. Carol was a stalwart sea comrade—she probably embraced "laziness" as heartily as anyone else during the hours they were not collecting.

And she must have been determined to play her part as the loyal wife when the occasion demanded. One curious moment occurred a few days after leaving Monterey, when the boat "sneaked" into the port of San Diego. A reporter came on board and, missing John, who was shopping for an admiral's hat, interviewed Carol. Once again, Carol served as John's mouthpiece. When the reporter's questions turned to the Soviet Union, she defended his liberalism, expressing "scorn" for the "dialectic" rationalization of Marxist theories, and recalled her husband's widely quoted remark on the Russian aggression: "I am for racial minorities whenever they appear to be in danger." And while Carol agreed with the reporter that the "perfidious" actions of Russia in joining Nazi Germany's aggression was a "set-back" for the liberal movement in the United States, she believed that what would emerge would be a "truly American liberalism based on fundamental principles understood and endorsed by a freedom and justice-loving people." Carol did not allow the reporter to slap on John the label "Marxist".

It took four days running night and day to arrive in Cabo San Lucas, then merely a tuna cannery, a cantina, and a few houses on a lonely beach. With permits in hand, everyone on the boat first headed to the sad little cantina—anxious to hit land after nearly ninety hours on the rolling Pacific. After drinking coffee with the Mexican officials who cleared them for landing, Carol, John, and Ed pulled on their boots, stuffed pockets with glass tubes, loaded the skiff with quart jars, and started for the rocks at low tide, a place "ferocious with life." All three felt the urgency of the moment, for with only six weeks to collect in as many Gulf locations as possible, they collected "furiously" at each spot, "spent every low-tide moment on the rocks, even at night." That first day they poked in the intertidal until "the afternoon surf began to beat on the littoral and covered it over again," filling their jars with snails, worms, starfish. After the day's work, "the killing and relaxing and preserving took us until dark, and even after dark we sat and made the labels to go into the tubes." Collecting was tiring and all-consuming work.

Here and at other stops, Carol worked hard at collecting and sorting specimens. She went on "every trip to pick up specimens. Didn't miss a one," Tony Berry recalled. They would take two or three buckets with them, Carol always carrying her load. On the run from Cabo San Lucas to La Paz, Tiny Colletto notes, "Ricketts, Steinbeck and Carol were getting anxious to start collecting the specimens. She knew the Latin names of many animals." And Ricketts's journal also mentions her collecting skills: In San Lucas Cove, Carol "got a large male Uca and several fleshy tubes which are apparently Enteropneusta," and she worked on Enteropneusta "that we had found at San Lucas Cove and at Angeles Bay." She caught a horned shark at San Francisquito Bay. And in Guaymas, Ricketts returned to the boat for a dip net after Carol spotted "several swimming crabs" in the water. Carol was an intrepid scientist. When work was called for, she plunged in one hundred percent.

If John, Ed, and Carol's central focus was collecting and sorting, stops at Gulf towns were opportunities to study Mexican culture. The *Western Flyer* docked in three ports on the Baja California peninsula: Cabo San Lucas, La Paz, and Loreto, as well as in Guaymas on the Sonoran coast. Carol poked around with delight in towns that were, in 1940, little changed from centuries of sun-baked living. If Cabo San Lucas was a forlorn place, La Paz, their next stop, was anything but. La Paz seemed a magical, legendary place to Steinbeck: "a cloud of delight hangs over the distant city from the time when it was the great pearl center of the world. The robes of the Spanish kings and the stoles of bishops in Rome were stiff with the pearls from La Paz. There's a magic-carpet sound to the name." Ricketts concurred, writing in his journal that it was a "beautiful town," with "lush, palm trees, white buildings with contrasting roofs, houses with inside gardens, kids everywhere to guide you. . . . La Paz has many poor people," he continued, "kind and loving, with no work and simply frantic for money. . . . By being a little careless with tips, we have supported several families for several weeks by our two or three-day stay here." Carol must have felt equal pleasure in the city: One afternoon, the courtly customs agent "squired" her around. Another day everyone on the boat attended a Good Friday service at the stately church, where a "fine earnest priest, black eyes blazing, good voice," said Mass punctuated by "old Spanish chants like madrigals."

And Carol must have loved stately Loreto, the third community they visited and famous as the first in the chain of successful Baja missions, the town where, in 1779, Father Junipero Serra started overland to Alta California. At this spot of layered histories, Steinbeck offers one of his most resonant explanations of ecological holism, moving from particular to universal at this holy spot. Our Lady of Loreto, he notes, was

> one of the strong ecological factors of the town of Loreto, and not to know
> her and her strength is to fail to know Loreto. One could not ignore a granite
> monolith in the path of waves. Such a rock, breaking the rushing waters, would
> have an effect on animal distribution radiating in circles like a dropped stone in
> a pool. So had this plaster Lady a powerful effect on the deep black water of the
> human spirit. She may disappear and her name be lost, as the Magna Mater, as
> Isis, have disappeared. But something very like her will take her place, and the
> longings which created her will find somewhere in the world a similar altar on
> which to pour their force. No matter what her name is, Artemis, or Venus, or a
> girl behind a Woolworth counter vaguely remembered, she is as eternal as our
> species, and we will continue to manufacture her as long as we survive.

Steinbeck may have been thinking of Gwen as he wrote this. Or perhaps Carol and her great strength of purpose. Perhaps he reworked this passage when he wrote *Cannery Row;* Doc's vision of the drowned girl in the intertidal suggests the "deep black water of the human spirit." Woman as monolith—Ma Joad or Juana in *The Pearl* or even shape-shifting Margie in his final novel, *The Winter of Our Discontent*—is a repeated trope in Steinbeck's work, and life.

The main thrust of this journey was scientific, to be sure, but also deeply personal, and Steinbeck's structure reminds readers that this is so. The text embraces *all* of life, giving each part of the journey weight and significance: the animals of the intertidal, the people of the Gulf and their customs, and the yearning for spiritual connection at the core of life. The meandering conversations, the zealous collecting, the forays into sleepy Gulf towns, the haunting landscapes—all melded to make this the memorable trip that Carol fondly recalled.

Nearly fifty years after the *Western Flyer* sailed out of Monterey Bay, the only surviving crew member, Captain Tony Berry, remembered the trip in nearly the same way that Carol had: it was a harmonious journey. "There were no enemies on board," he recalled, and the crew didn't gossip about one another. "You pick your men before you go and know who you're taking." Nor did Carol and John argue. Only once did Tony get mad at Carol and only once at John, whom he saw as the "backbone of the voyage," the main push— not Ed. Ed was more relaxed and had a habit of taking long soaks in the tub on deck; he wouldn't swim, only soak for hours and he didn't care who saw him naked. But "everybody took one another at face value," Tony said. Carol's habit was to perch on the side of the boat. She was a "good passenger." She ate with everyone, and she didn't dominate the conversation. "The guys enjoyed her all the way. They would talk to Carol. It broke the monotony. She'd talk about the day, the weather, the local news. She could carry a conversation." John was also at his conversational best, according to Tony. He talked about "war, fish, the stars. He had binoculars and used them." And it was John who kept Tony to their schedule. "Be here by such and such a time," he would say. "He had a lot of determination."

Undoubtedly, however, there were rough spots. Sometimes the central relationship, at least as reported in Ricketts's own journal (John didn't keep one, relying on Ed's), seems to have been the one between him and John, as the two of them followed their own collecting whims. That must have rankled Carol at times, and so, in typical fashion, she acted out to get attention. As Tony Berry put it, she was "75 percent good and 15 percent bad." That 15 percent was unbridled. In La Paz she jumped overboard, nearly ruining a gold watch that John bought her, inscribed "Carol Steinbeck." Later, he would fix it for her, writing Mavis McIntosh that the watch "was ruined by the rust and . . . I am having new works put in at the factory and will send it just as soon as gets back." Frequently she took her top off to bathe, and that disconcerted the crew. Everyone stared except John. And she flirted with both Tiny and Ed—and, according to Tony, "could make love to everybody." Sometimes she went off with one of the crew, Tiny or Sparky (never Tony or Tex). In his journal, Ricketts hints at some sexual antics between Carol and Tiny at Puerto Escondido, a stop after La Paz, when he and John went hunting with local ranchers: "Crl and Tiny went out the following morning, when Jr. and I were up on the mountain." After John and Ed's two-day hunting trip, Ed reports that "the mices was playing, as Jon says. A little scurrilous drinking got done." Carol and Tiny may have had a dalliance or two on shore, but that was the only time for the two of them, Tony said. If Carol felt abandoned, she would undoubtedly have flirted with Tiny.

And with Ricketts, perhaps. She had a "yen" for Ricketts, said Tony. Certainly Ed went to Carol's stateroom often, and it's not hard to imagine that the two were together, simply to enjoy sex. Ed would have sex with any woman—he had no scruples on that score. On at least one occasion she had one of her frequent nightmares, awakening screaming, and Ed calmed her. But he did more than that; he empathized with her situation. Tony claimed that Ed paid more attention to Carol than John did. And Ed later told Toni Jackson that he had a hard time seeing Carol so upset and not saying to her: "Yes of course; you're right. You have a very good reason for feeling as you do. Your intuition is quite correct." He wanted to tell her that he had been in much the same situation years before—counselor to the aggrieved—when John was disturbed and angry but didn't know why. At that time it was John's intuition about Joseph Campbell and Carol. Everyone went to Ed with tales of woe.

On the whole, however, it seems that John and Carol coped and made the best of things on the voyage. In Ricketts's notes, as in Sea of Cortez, there is a sense of common purpose. He reports fulsomely about the crew's two days in Guaymas, the fourth port on their trip, where, according to Tony, "everyone got smashed." On April 5, anchoring in Guaymas Bay on the Sonoran coast, Ed "went ashore at once with Crl, Sparky, and Tiny. Jon followed later on." Guaymas offered gay diversions—one with two waitresses, Soccoro and Virginia, from a local restaurant, the Mitla. After several shots of tequila, no doubt, Ed passed out on the boat, "puking drunk," and all others followed suit. Ed's hangover was cured by five beers the following morning, and Carol's by a leap into the sea, fully clothed, "starting a rumor inshore (so it was reported) that she fell overboard," Ricketts reported. Tony was surprised as well, since "she had a nice spring dress on, a straw hat." This party, however, left John in a "deep post-alcohol depression, feeling very low, not wanting to go in town." So Ed, Carol, and Tiny—he having lost a fight with a local boxer the night before—went again into Guaymas for an evening frolic. They first discussed "the salutary disciplinary effect of defeat. Seemed to me," wrote Ricketts, "that if Tiny hadn't known defeat before, which is a common concomitant of life, it was high time he was meeting it." At their favorite restaurant, Mitla, the "Orchestra in the restaurant played "Crls' 'Mi Partita' several times." Then Ed, Carol, and Tiny "took a pleasant walk along the waterfront to oyster shuck-ing place (fisherman co-op) and back through the whorehouse Yankee-town section. . . . District lacked the usual severe segregation of prostitution. There were children all about." Then the party went to a saloon for High Life beers, where Sparky joined them, and the orchestra again played "Mi Partita" for Carol. And after they went to the Municipal Dance briefly, and Ed tried and failed to locate a water taxi to take them back to the boat. They didn't succeed in getting back to the boat until 2:30 or 3:00 A.M.—"Jon very low."

Guaymas had been jolly for everyone except John, it seems. Was he miss-ing Gwen? Or did he dread leaving the hallucinatory dream of the Gulf and facing the reality of Gwen at home?

If the distance between John and Carol contracted during most of the expedition, it widened after Guaymas. The trip home along the Pacific coast was difficult, the *Western Flyer* sailing into constant wind with waves up to fifteen feet high, and there were two particularly bad days of rough weather before they reached San Diego. Carol was sick all the way back. John was increasingly fidgety, probably because he wasn't writing, maybe because he had decided, finally, that he'd had enough of expansive Carol. In San Diego, Ed got off the boat and headed back to Monterey by car. The boat hit more bad weather off Point Sur. The little group fell apart long before reaching Monterey.

The *Western Flyer* docked at the Monterey Wharf on April 21, 1940, with about fifty people there to greet the boat. Carol claimed that Gwen was among them, this being the first time she met her. When the boat tied up at the wharf, Carol, under great pressure, yelled: "No pictures, No pictures." Evidently she was serious, evidently on edge.

The final months of Carol and John's relationship were characterized by slow drift and shifting tides: uncertainty and guilt, respect and need, commitment and resistance. Perhaps John embedded the complexities of the human heart in what he said was a four-layered *Sea of Cortez.*

After publication, Ed noted that John "built it carefully," moving from humorous to reflective, descriptive to narrative, intertidal catalogues to abstract thoughts, historical to contemporary issues. One critic called the book a "cioppino," a stew of narrative tropes. Another metaphor might be the intertidal itself. Each chapter of *Sea of Cortez* is a tiny tide pool, teeming with life and ideas. Another metaphor might be the very activity of collecting. On Espiritu Santo, their third site, "the boulders on this beach were almost a perfect turning over size—heavy enough to protect the animals under them from grinding by the waves, and light enough to be lifted." Metaphoric boulder-turning is at the book's core, each paragraph rounded and complete, something to turn over and see what lies in layers beneath. "And so we'll let the book fall as it may," Steinbeck writes at the beginning, as if replacing intertidal rocks. *Sea of Cortez* concludes with the image of rock turning: "Our fingers turned over the stones, and we saw life that was like our life."

Considering the delicate balance that John and Carol were maintaining in their relationship at this time, certain passages in this boulder-turning book take on personal resonance. "With marine fauna, as with humans, priority and possession appear to be vastly important to survival and dominance. But sometimes it is found that the very success of an animal is its downfall. There are examples where the available food supply is so exhausted by the rapid and successful reproduction that the animal must migrate or die. Sometimes, also, the very by-products of the animals' own bodies prove poisonous to a too great concentration of their own species." Is Steinbeck thinking of his own condition and crumbling marriage, as well as a scientific principle?

"It is difficult, when watching the little beasts, not to trace human parallels. . . . The dominant human, in his security, grows soft and fearful." Is he voicing his and Carol's fear of wealth and status? On a softer note, he muses after the crew goes to church on Good Friday in La Paz: "For it is through struggle and sorrow that people are able to participate in one another—the heartlessness of the healthy, well-fed, and unsorrowful person has in it an infinite smugness." Both John and Carol knew, on some level, that struggle and sorrow forged their relationship. When "well fed," the two collapsed, and even the waves of the Sea of Cortez could not shock them out of that trajectory.

And perhaps *Sea of Cortez* comments on a marriage atrophied: "When a hypothesis is deeply accepted it becomes a growth which only a kind of surgery can amputate. Thus, beliefs persist long after their factual bases have been removed, and practices based on beliefs are often carried on even when the beliefs which stimulated them have been forgotten. The practice must follow the belief." John had ceased to believe.

Even the long "Easter Sunday Sermon," essentially written by Ricketts and included in the book as chapter 14, a "center" as Ed noted, testifies to the importance of nonteleological thinking and stands as an eerie testament to John and Carol's future. There was no "why" to explain the breakup—the end simply was a fact, the complex product of a long, convoluted history. "Nonteleological methods more than any other seem capable of great tenderness, of an all-embracingness which is rare otherwise. Consider, for instance, the fact that, once a given situation is deeply understood, no apologies are required. There are ample difficulties even to understanding conditions 'as is.' Once that has been accomplished, the 'why' of it (known now to be simply a relation, though probably a near and important one) seems no longer to be preponderantly important. It needn't be condoned or extenuated, it just 'is.'"

Ed insisted that the book was truly a collaborative venture. A few months before publication, he wrote to Toni: "I have just been reading what Jon wrote today. It's so damn beautiful I can hardly stand it. He takes my own words and gives them a little twist, and puts in some of his own beauty of concept and expression and the whole thing is so lovely you can't stand it." Later he wrote to a friend: "However much it seems otherwise 'Sea of Cortez' is truly a compilation. Jon worked at the collecting and sorting of animals and looked over some of the literature, including the specialist literature, and I had a hand even in the narrative, although the planning and architecture of the first part of course is entirely his, as the planning of the scientific section is entirely mine. But much of the detail of the narrative is based on a journal I kept during the trip. . . . Some of the text derives from it and from unpublished [essays] of mine."

Carol's name was not on the title page, nor included in a dedication, as in *Grapes*. But her role, erased publically, was intact privately: as collector, commentator, and, once again, if faintly, muse. John wrote Covici in July that the book had "four levels of statement in it and I think very few will follow it down to the fourth." But Carol could, and had, through layers and layers of his prose. That she was no longer his first reader and editor and auditor was, in fact, the sad end of the marriage.

Ed's new girlfriend, Toni Jackson, assumed Carol's role, typing the manuscript and proofing the galleys. But some of the zest for life that Carol shared with Ed and John seeped into the text, a vicarious contribution. In

the glossary definitions, Toni said, there were "some wonderful little jokes
. . . that got put in while we were going over galleys. *Proctofilius Wincelli* is
one—I think it is the name of a new species of something or other that lives
in the anus of a sea cucumber and the Wincelli is, of course, Walter whom Ed
and John abominated. Another has to do with the aquarium—a second one
because the first was such that the fish could see but we couldn't see in. These
crept in because the copy editor at Viking—a very excellent and meticulous
man—we thought carried meticulousness a little too far. We named him
Sadistic Sadow and wrote naughty little things next to his polite queries and
some of them John marked 'stet.' We really half expected to be sued over the
Wincelli bit, but nobody picked it up or if they did, was of like mind."

If editing the glossary was a rollicking task, the writing was not. John was
in pain throughout, because by this point, 1941, he and Carol had separated.
John commissioned his friend Ellwood Graham to paint his portrait, since
Covici had requested a new photo for the new book and Steinbeck hated to be
photographed. It is the only painting of Steinbeck at work. "John didn't want
a conventional study," said Graham, "so I had him come to my Huckleberry
Hill studio. For at least a month, I guess, he sat at a table on a model stand,
where he peculiarly gripped his pen between his index and forefinger and
wrote . . . from Ed Ricketts's notes. John . . . was in turmoil, and this is what I
showed in my sketches and . . . in the painting." Ellwood Graham's sad portrait of John Steinbeck is a study in ferocious concentration—that death grip
on his pen—and utter despair, depicting a face contorted with pain. Ricketts
was one of the few who thought the tormented portrait was "a very good job
in its own right, one of the best, the only good portrait of John. . . . Distorted
and nasty or I guess agonized. . . . But so very fine."

Graham's Steinbeck Agonistes conveys torment of a marriage on the
rocks. Ricketts added a postscript to the unraveling union that, in his mind,
had never been "true." A few months after the Sea of Cortez trip, Carol tried
to tell Ed "what a beautiful relation" that she and John "had had," but Ed was
not convinced. Carol had "never really loved anyone" in a participatory, deep
sense, he wrote to Toni Jackson. "Jon is a far more consequential, deeper person," he continued, who lived on a "level higher (to me) than hers." Then
again,

> Gwen, who seems better adapted at the moment or at least with whom he gets
> along well at the moment, is also a less person than Jon. Probably less than Crl.
> But in addition to Crl being less than Jon, there is bad blood between them, and

I think it's truly on both sides despite Crl's claim that she became what she has become—a hard, brittle sophisticated wise-cracking inward hiding woman—in response to what Jon said he wanted; and the circle is going around the wrong way. With Gwen, who is maybe even less a person (but more malleable in a womanly way, more womanly, more earthy) the circle is going round right . . . even tho [Carol] may be a greater person. And when on top of that you see that Crl is hard to get along with and herself needing training and a strong loving hand, it's easy to see what a strain it would be on Jon who himself needs loving tolerance and firmness, not criticisms and abjectness.

And there you have it. A loyal friend. A discerning eye. A union severed.

CHAPTER TEN

Life in Fragments

WHEN CAROL LOST JOHN, she lost her life's narrative. It was difficult, nearly impossible, for her to find another that sustained. John cut Carol adrift. The marriage lasted a year, almost to the day, after the *Western Flyer* docked in Monterey in late April 1940. John spent that year on overdrive, working on *Sea of Cortez*, a Mexican film, and a film of *The Red Pony* with Lewis Milestone, as well as a project with Lorentz and an introduction for the second edition of Ricketts's *Between Pacific Tides*.

As the marriage frayed, he worked on a documentary film, *The Forgotten Village*. His first original script, it focuses on a remote Mexican community where the village well is tainted and children are dying of cholera. Only modern medicine can save them, and only the village teacher and one local boy, Juan Diego (also the name of the central figure in the legendary story of the Virgin of Guadalupe), recognize that fact. In the end, Juan Diego goes to medical school to learn skills that will serve his country. The film is largely propaganda—Steinbeck wished to shore up the recently elected Mexican government in their efforts to provide medical services to indigenous populations.

Carol was involved in the project, though to what extent is not clear. She went with John to Mexico in May 1940, but he went alone in September, while she stayed in Los Gatos. Around the same time, John consulted with Lewis Milestone in Los Angeles, who planned to turn *The Red Pony* into a film. He also worked sporadically on a new manuscript, "God in the Pipes," which would eventually become *Cannery Row*. Between trips to Mexico and Los Angeles, he worried about writing *Sea of Cortez*: "When this work is done," he wrote to Covici, when he was finally well into the project in June 1941, "I will have finished a cycle of work that has been biting me for many years and it is simply the careful statement of the thesis of work to be done in the future."

Sea of Cortez was pivotal to his career, an end and a beginning. So many of the ideas in that book appear as well in *The Grapes of Wrath:* species cooperation, "survivability," nonteleological thinking, holistic "levels" of appreciation, participation, emergence. And those ideas appear again in *Cannery Row*—and in books throughout his career. Steinbeck was always interested in the relationship between the individual and a family, a community, a nation. Throughout most of 1940 he was on a cusp, professionally and personally. Working frantically helped ease him through borderlands—between women, between writing projects, between theories of art.

By September 1940, Carol, not surprisingly, felt more and more "lone and lost" as John wrestled with his projects and his demons: loyalty to Carol kept him bound to the ranch, fascination with Gwen carried him forth. He took up flying lessons to cope with his uncertainties, to escape from his "messy" life and to fly to San Francisco to see Gwen, who was singing daily at the Exposition ("There's something so god damned remote and beautiful and detached about being way to hell and gone up on a little yellow leaf"). Carol told pregnant Tal Lovejoy that she would give their baby "a scholarship in the school of hard knocks," testimony to how she felt as Steinbeck flew away from her— bruised and angry. She had no outlet for her sadness and insecurity, other than raucous parties at the Los Gatos ranch, continued gardening, and too much drinking. She was emotionally marooned, and her escapes turned out to be the final blows to the marriage: drink, for one, sharp anger, for another. (According to Gwen, Toby Street warned Gwen's mother to keep her daughter away from John, telling her that "once Carol had been a sweet girl too but John made her into a monster.") Another escape was to leave town. In February 1941 John sent Carol off on the *Lurline* to Hawaii to see her sister for six weeks, ostensibly so that she would relax and recover from the debilitating flu that both came down with around Christmas. While she was basking in the sun with Idell, John "hid out" with Gwen in a little cottage near Asilomar Beach on the Monterey Peninsula owned by his sister Esther and composed *Sea of Cortez.* He planned to ask Carol for a divorce upon her return.

Carol and John's marriage was officially over on April 27, 1941, the day they separated. In a series of letters to Mavis McIntosh, agent and friend, Steinbeck recorded the painful weeks before and after the split, each missive scrawled in his tiniest handwriting, as if his nerves, "cracked to pieces," and his mind, shriveled by pain, could shrink into nothing. The letters chart a course of despair and recovery, with Mavis serving as sounding board, counselor, conscience, and witness. He wrote letters for Mavis's "ears . . . and [hers] alone." Undoubtedly he chose Mavis because she visited California in

March 1941, met Gwen, knew Carol, understood the situation, and served as his emissary. John pressed Mavis into going to LA to talk to Gwen for him and "explain to G that Carol wasn't well and that J would straighten everything out." Faithful Mavis, willing go-between, saw Gwen several times in Los Angeles, talked to John frequently on the phone, and from him heard the story that Carol was pregnant: "Later I heard that G also claimed to be pregnant but the fact was that neither of them was." What a mess.

That false pregnancy marks Carol's woe. She told her sister Idell that she was pregnant by a man she met on the ship to Hawaii. She called Sara Bard Field "in a very mysterious manner" and said "very excitedly that she was going to have a baby. I think it was just wishful thinking. . . . She had been in Hawaii, and I think she may have had an affair, and felt she was going to have a child. But it was not so. And that's the very last I ever heard of Carol. . . . I really loved her. She was a very lovable girl then, and I think her heart was broken." It was. Claiming she was pregnant was not revenge; she yearned for motherhood—and to keep John.

A nasty scene marked the nadir of the breakup, an April confrontation in the Eardley Street cottage in Pacific Grove, a little house John bought after the Sea of Cortez trip. When John finally told her, with Gwen present, "how deeply involved I was and how little was left," Carol snarled that she "wanted what was left and was going to fight," and at that point lashed out with the pregnancy news. According to Gwen, Carol said these words to her when John left the two women alone to hash things out (bad idea on his part): "You don't want him. You don't love him. I love him terribly, but he hasn't slept with me in three years. I have to masturbate all the time and that's why I sleep with lesbians. . . . He is a jealous, nasty man and if you get him, I am going to take him for every goddam, fucking cent. I'll kill you if I can, because I want him, and I know he is going to be famous. After all the years that I've lived with him, I won't let this happen." Gwen's account must be taken with some salt, of course, but the bitterness rings true—and familiar in crumbling relationships. Carol's sense of betrayal would stay with her for years.

Although John stayed by Carol's side after that mid-April blowup, hers was a Pyrrhic victory. She got the "outside," John wrote, and Gwen the "inside." Ten days later, however, Gwen got the outside as well. John left Carol. She was completely adrift, uncertain who she was, what she wanted, where she would land.

Almost immediately after the official separation, Carol landed in New York City because it was a "busy place where she could keep busy." City life would distract her. John counted on that too and encouraged her escape, hoping she would recover her equanimity—something the guilty party always wants. "Please be very kind and patient with her," John wrote Mavis, who seems to have been mired in the breakup. "Listen to what she says. She will need some help but she must learn to stand on her own feet a little." He thought Carol wanted a father figure. She "has not grown up and she must." But in addition to analyzing Carol's weaknesses, he wanted Mavis to listen to his side of the story: "Whatever Carol may believe now, we have never been easy together. It was nobody's fault but it was just so. I thought that was the way everyone was. It was a very shocking thing to find that it was not a part of living with a woman to be in a state of constant hostility with her." This, of course, was written by a man newly smitten with a much younger, seemingly more tractable woman, a man whose sex life, he reported, was "prodigious and I take strength rather than depletion from it." And it shows how hard it is to ever measure a marriage. Certainly not by comments made immediately after a separation by either party.

Without a doubt, John and Carol had been deliriously happy together at one point. Certainly they had argued fiercely, but they relished the scraps for years. By 1941, however, the marriage had shriveled to what John declared it was all along—a "constant state of hostility." Carol accused John of beating her, of having affairs. John wrote Mavis that he should have beaten her to keep her in line. He wrote Elizabeth Otis about Carol's "basic violence" and his fear of her "vindictiveness." Carol craved limits "put on her behavior," he wrote to Mavis, "wants limits, but keeps defying them." Again and again he wrote to Elizabeth or his main confidant, Mavis, about Carol's nature: she was immature, combative; she was miserly and argumentative, angry and accusative, inhospitable. But some were also traits he had cherished, had accepted. In trying to assuage his guilt, understand himself, and distance himself from Carol—all stages that divorced parties pass through—he painted Carol in somber hues: "a most frustrated and unhappy girl ever since I first knew her." He was convinced that Carol "has forgotten how utterly unhappy she was with me. Strange unhappy girl."

An acute observer who understood his wife's character, John pinpointed her faults for Mavis with grim precision. He understood her anger and vulnerability since some of her darkness tallied with his. For the moment, Gwen soothed John's demons. Carol had no such savior.

While John never thought it was a temporary separation, Carol convinced herself that it was, or might be, or could be if she threw her considerable will into luring John back. Carol was a fighter. And John was so fearful of the backlash that he kept from her the reality that the separation was permanent. Part of Carol's strategy in agreeing to an interview with a New York City journalist, no doubt, was to win public sympathy. In an August article that was reprinted in papers around the country, "Mrs. John Steinbeck Fights for Her Man," Carol declared that John simply needed space. "I want to see it through. . . . This is something all men go through," Carol told the reporter, revealing her pain as well. "I had the chance at other experiences, but I didn't take them. I was smug in my own happiness. I even told others how to be successfully married. Then came the break. . . . I supposed every woman yearns over man the way she would a child." The interview puzzled John, who, like others, found Carol enigmatic:

> The newspaper splurge bothered me mostly because I know how badly C must have felt when she saw it. She sent me a copy of it saying she had been tricked. But she needn't have sent it since it was represented in every paper out here. . . . Also it bothered me some because while it was true it was also untrue. C was not a promising writer. I tried to get her to do something, and all that. She didn't support me for five years. She had a job for about six months. She didn't submerge herself in me, she resented me like the devil and told me so regularly. She impressed me all the time with the information that I was ruining her life. And there is an undercurrent of revenge in these words of hers that worries me. She has more sense than to think you can talk confidently to a columnist. I'm desperately sorry she did it. . . . The poor darling is so clumsy. That's why I feel sick about it. . . . It seems so out of character in her to let the world in on finances—unless unconsciously she does want to destroy herself and me. But I get such pain out of her pain which would force her to do a thing like this.

John did not snip his bond to Carol without regret; Carol did not sever ties to John without alternating waves of anger and equanimity: at times she wrote him letters "full of goodness and sweetness and they help a lot" and at other times she raged about money and women and betrayal—and of course in desperation talked to the press and then regretted that she did so. Carol rocked from acceptance to fury; John felt guilty. For two years, he had lusted after Gwen, idealized her, relished her wit, danced the streets with her in hand. But Carol had been his rock for a dozen years—even though their marital problems were real enough: Carol's tightness with money, her drunken wrath, her critical voice (all evidence of her own insecurity, as John knew). However much one might want to blame John the wife deserter, it's clear that he suffered nearly as much as Carol. He had loved his sassy, unconventional mate. He was not a vindictive man. And he could not shed guilt about leaving the woman who had stood by him for so long, and who arguably had made his career. "I'm desperately sorry about Carol," he wrote to his sister Esther. "It was a horrible thing to do. . . . Every appearance is against me and that's as it should be. I'll bet Salinas is having a field day."

Carol's anger caught up with her after the interview—or she simply didn't know what do to with herself next. On September 20, 1941, she boarded the SS *President Van Buren* out of New York and sailed back to San Francisco, arriving October 5. She listed her address as South Sixteenth Street, San Jose—her parents' home. Carol was returning home because she really had no other place to go, the ranch having been sold. She threatened to move into the Eardley Street house in Pacific Grove, purchased by John in 1940, where John and Gwen now lived. In early November Ed Ricketts wrote a long letter to John, now on the East Coast himself, detailing how Carol was making a "vindictive ass of herself. . . . I think . . . that Crl, whether or not she's getting better, is and probably always has been a little off her head." At that point she was.

Working out details wasn't easy. John sold his Packard—Carol kept hers. That worked. But talks about financial settlements were rocky, since the subject of money was a charged topic for Carol, weighted down with a sense of unfairness she'd inherited from her childhood. Money meant security. It meant equity and respect. So in letters she queried John about past loans— one to his sister Beth, a widow raising three children alone—and counted interest on bonds so she wouldn't get shortchanged. Money became the battleground, as Carol pressed John for every penny. She wrote him that she didn't think she could live on the interest on $100,000, and that she didn't think she could get a job because she was too old—thirty-five. John was disgusted, of course, and remained guilty—he had given her a thousand dollars a month to live on as soon as she arrived in New York City, and he had asked Toby Street, his lawyer and Carol's as well, to split assets evenly. Blind to the larger picture and Gwen's character, he wrote Mavis that "Gwen is as generous as Carol is not."

As the twelve months of separation drew to a close and the interlocutory degree was to be granted, however, John withdrew from Gwen into dark moods and "tense" days, as Gwen admitted to Toby Street on Valentine's Day

1942. Gwen used Toby as her sounding board (as did, in different ways, John and Carol):

> He is going thru the "weighing" period. By that I mean, he is weighing his life
> with me & his past with Carol. I'm sure that all of us must go thru this, but I
> hope it won't last forever. If forever & a day he will be saying to himself "this is
> what I could have had with Carol" it is not going to make existing [sic] pleasant
> for me. . . . The actual impact of the divorce papers were a little shock to me, but
> a great one to Jon. I suppose, unconsciously, we thought it would never come
> about. And now that its [sic] here, I wonder if its [sic] what Jon really wants? . . .
> It is fortunate I love him more than he does me, otherwise I don't know how I
> could gotten thru these past few days. For I see him walk around in a dazed way,
> with the memory of the past twelve years imprinted in his face.

With the divorce looming, John admitted to Mavis that he got "the horrors about Carol with great regularity." At the same time, Gwen told Toby that Carol "has become the 'poor little thing' in his mind. And he is defending her strongly." Clearly, Gwen wanted to nudge Toby over to her side, telling him how deeply she loved John while trying to nudge Carol out: "if she is as brilliant and beautiful as Jon says she is, he would never been able to have eyes for me."

Gwen's letters seem insincere, self-dramatizing—traits that would later become abundantly evident. She tried to convince Toby, and herself one suspects, of her devotion. The words seem hollow: "His work must come first," she wrote Toby ten days after her first appeal. "I like to think that God put me here just to love, and take care of Jon. And that I think is to be my life's work. . . . Sometimes I wish I could tell Jon the thrill I get every time I see him. When he is gone for a few hours in the day I go crazy with loneliness. I actually miss him. When he comes home I can't keep my hands off of him, or do enough for him." She concludes: "This has been a wacky letter, but I don't want you, of all people, [to] think I am a shitheel." Gwen didn't want to think of herself as a shitheel either.

One of Carol's parting shots to John was that she found him a "bad Don Byrne and left him a good writer." The dig would bother John for years to come, since critics came to echo the sentiment. Starting in the early 1940s, not only critics but also friends and readers said over and over that John Steinbeck wrote his best work in the 1930s, that he needed tough Carol by his side as editor. But it's probably also true, as John wrote to Mavis McIntosh, that "Carol has a kind of king-making side and she wouldn't like me to do good work without her." He would do good work—*Sea of Cortez*, one of the finest books of his career, came out in December 1941—but recovery would take time, for both of them.

After Carol returned to California and moved to Carmel in the fall of 1941—across the Peninsula from her former life—she experienced a kind of release, relieved to be out of the marriage "as if she were out of jail," said one friend. She took up sculpting more seriously. She had told the New York City reporter that she was working on clay sculptures: "All caricatures, aren't they? I see things that way. I always could, even in my poems and sketches. . . . I work all day in the clay . . . till midnight." That was one emotional outlet, as it had long been, seeing the world with an askew eye. That fall she wrote John that she felt happier than she had ever been with her work, and John felt she was recovering, finding "genuine joy" in clay. Her clothing changed. Throughout her time with John she'd favored slacks or jeans or pantsuits; in New York City, she switched to dresses, wore hats. She was, literally and figuratively, donning a new identity

At her postdivorce best she stepped firmly and judiciously from the set-tlement—and moved forward with a good deal of sensibleness about her money from the divorce. On her return to the Peninsula, she immediately started buying rental property in Carmel, at least two cottages in 1941 and three more in 1942 (Dimity for $4,900, Next Door for $4,625, and Green Gables for $3,500), and finally one for herself overlooking the ocean in 1942 or early '43, Sea Wolf. She rented them to military officers, charging top dol-lar, and after the war sold them to returning officers for healthy profits. After the divorce was final in March 1943, she bought stock in railroads: Northern Pacific, Southern Pacific, and Illinois Central.

She settled into wartime Carmel with the determination to move ahead. She was thirty-five at the time of separation, a whole life ahead of her. Although she remained angry and vengeful—as the spurned can be—she also retained the incredible vitality that drew people to her. Who could resist a woman who, shortly after her return to the Peninsula, had a pair of for-est green Robin Hood shoes made for her by a Carmel cobbler, the better to stride around the town? Or a woman who marched her Robin Hood shoes into the Del Monte Lodge, the Peninsula's most elegant destination, and without hesitation asked that her sloppily dressed self be seated for dinner among those in evening dresses, caring not a whit that everyone stared. Or who, on another occasion, wore fishnet stockings and her Red Cross uniform into the elegant Hotel Del Monte, ordered martinis, and talked rough with service people. Or who met a *Monterey Herald* writer, Ted Durain, on Ocean Ave and said with characteristic zest, "Hi Ted, you old son of a bitch." Perhaps it was a studied exuberance, but it was a pose that drew many to her. Carol made friends with ease, and divorce from John initially sent her on a whirlwind of activity. For Carol, it was time to play after spending her twenties married, poor, and typing John's manuscripts.

One new friend who came into her life that fall was teacher Viola Franklin, and the first weeks of their friendship show Carol at her best. Viola taught eighth grade at Bay View Elementary School in Monterey, and her sister Dorothea, a nurse, had been living in Carmel since early 1941. One night Dorothea and Viola were on their way north on Highway 1 to a high school reunion. An old man in an ancient automobile turned onto the highway from the left—he couldn't stop because his car had no brakes. The terrible crash left him dead and Dorothea seriously injured, hospitalized for weeks. When she came home in December, she was catatonic. All day Dorothea sat at home, staring at the wall, while Viola went to teach. Dorothea refused to move, to go out, to recover.

After a few weeks, Carol burst into Dorothea's sickroom. Since the bombing of Pearl Harbor, Carol had been determined to help with the war effort by starting a nurse's aide program in Monterey. Carol had heard that Dorothea was a nurse and thought she could teach the nurses' aides, and so came to recruit the ailing Dorothea. But Dorothea didn't budge: "I can't do that, I'm too sick." Carol tossed her head back and told Dorothea, "Of course you're well enough. You've got to get a hold of yourself." To effect Dorothea's recovery, Carol came to see her daily, bolstering her, telling her stories, feeding her. "You're the only one who can do it, Dorothea, train those nurses' aides," Carol assured her over and over. Within three weeks, Dorothea was up—and eventually passed her overseas examination and went to the Philippines as a war nurse.

Of course Viola was enormously grateful to this green-eyed woman who revived her sister, and the two became close. Viola relished Carol's friendship, as did many women. Carol refused to take credit, for example, for her energetic ministrations to Dorothea: "You liar," she'd say to Viola. "I never did that." Even years later, when Viola wrote a book on Africa that Carol edited, Carol again refused plaudits for her many valuable editorial suggestions. "What are you thanking me for?" she asked Viola. "I didn't do anything." "That was Carol," said Viola, "modest about what she'd done for me, for Dorothea, for John with *Grapes*."

The war changed Monterey, and Carol, Viola, and others changed with it. In the late 1930s, the army expanded facilities and landholdings off Highway 1 near Seaside, long a training ground for Presidio troops. In 1940, Fort Ord became a major army installation, "mobilization buildings" were constructed, and thousands of troops moved in to train and to protect Monterey Bay, deemed vulnerable to enemy attack. When troops were deployed overseas, new faces appeared, opening fresh opportunities for friendships. Jobs were plentiful, as were parties and men. Viola quit teaching to become a fish and game warden on Cannery Row, which delighted Carol—she loved Viola's official hat and overalls. She introduced Viola to her old friends, Beth Ingels and her partner Peg. The four women cruised the Peninsula. They formed the CIC Club (Christ I'm Confused), whose members signed a long scroll in order to belong. It was a raucous, liberal, and hard-drinking crowd—not unlike Carol's female buddies a dozen years earlier in Eagle Rock. Beth "drank like a fish" and loved to go on pub crawls after her work as a journalist. Peg saw to it she got home. Some nights the CICs would troll the Carmel bars and come out singing hymns up and down Ocean Avenue—Viola was a minister's daughter and knew them all. Every Wednesday night, Carol and Viola would go to a local bar where the Lions Club met in the late afternoon. Carol's avowed purpose was "to collect burs out of the lion's claws." Men loved her, Viola recalled, because she was so much fun. On one occasion Carol stole a local liquor store's statue of an "Old Crow" and placed the wooden statue in the doorway at a party so that everyone stepped over Old Crow coming in. "What's the matter with you, got syphilis," snapped Carol as a friend came in. "What's this crow doing here?" said the new arrival. "What crow?" said everyone else at the party. No one admitted there was any crow at all, all night long.

But sometimes Carol's flip side emerged—the desperate neediness, the unpredictable behavior. She could turn on a dime. If she were flirting with a GI in those days, he was hers for the night—or not. She might get mad at him, order the car to stop, and jump out. And if the rejected soldier turned his attention to another woman, then Carol's wrath fell on her rival: "Oh yes, you went back into the hotel with old liver lips." Carol's words cut deeply, not only with those she didn't like, but often with friends. "So and so has now exceeded her own stupidity" is something Carol might say to a friend—reducing anyone to jelly. She could be haughty and domineering. These qualities, of course, made many men wary. And although Carol craved men's company, she often had poor judgment about GIs in Monterey—at least according to

Viola's tastes. Carol yearned for center stage, and sometimes it didn't seem to matter who served as audience.

On March 16, 1942, Carol filed a divorce petition, claiming that the cause of the separation was the plaintiff's "extreme cruelty," which caused her "to suffer great mental anguish and physical pain and suffering." The final divorce was granted on March 18, 1943. When Viola met Carol in 1941, "she was still so emotionally disturbed about it all, she couldn't and wouldn't discuss it." That was true later as well—Carol didn't open up to many about what her marriage had really meant to her, how the divorce seared her. Although she invested in Carmel property and enjoyed the hilarity she helped generate there, she didn't know quite what to do with herself in the long term. Shortly after the petition was filed, she thought of moving to Denver with her sister, as Ed Ricketts wrote to John. John responded: "I hope it works but, between you and me—Idell is a chiseller and Carol is the world's greatest resenter of chiseling." That move never came to pass. Instead, she went to Colorado for an extended stay with old friends, the Kitteridges, as Toby Street reported to John. "Carol will have a very good time with the Kitteridges," John wrote back:

> She likes Bob. One night she was drunk and mad at me in NY and she ran away and was gone all night with Bob and I looked for her in police stations and morgues and then she was madder at me. And another time when she was mad at me she told me she had spent the night trying to make up her mind whether to run away with him or not, that is for good. Oh, I had fun in my time. I wouldn't be much surprised if Carol sometime settled in Arizona. No income tax there or if there is it very small one. And she likes high mountains and things like that.

In fact, many of John and Carol's old friends on the Peninsula were reporting to John, assessing the marriage. Ed Ricketts's epitaph for the marriage was included in a letter to his daughter Nancy. He wrote her that it was a good thing that John and Carol parted. "They never did get along very well. . . . Jn could never tell what he was going to do, probably didn't even know, without having a cue from Carol, and Carol was sometimes a bit power driven." Everyone in the area was watching and assessing Carol. Most liked her, but they were also wary, never sure what she might do next.

By September of 1942, Carol's life was more even-keeled, and she seemed determined to stay in Carmel, immersing herself in community activities.

She was on the rationing board. She helped organize a soldiers' art exhibit, recognizing the talents of many of the men stationed at Fort Ord. She finished courses for the Nurse's Aide Corps, Carmel-by-the-Sea Chapter. In October, she completed the course in staff assistance at the American Red Cross, and by November she was working in the community hospital as a nurse's aide, a vocation that would keep her busy during the war. (Her ID card included statistics: five feet seven inches, 145 pounds, green eyes, brown hair, banana birthmark on nose.) She spent much of her time during the war as a nurse's aide, giving blood when she could. In 1945, Ed Ricketts wrote to friends that he had "met the MD under whom she works at Ft. Ord Hospital and he says she's a very good nurse." Carol told Viola that she had always wanted to be a doctor, a surgeon, and only settled for nurse's aide because there was a war. But Carol was given to exaggerations: she might never have considered medicine, and was only trying out the statement for effect. That was part of her coping strategy—try on a new self just to see what might happen. Because she still didn't have a plan.

In another era, Carol might have run a small company, taken on the world, shaped something larger than John into a force for good. But she could not, or would not, imagine great things for herself, only small victories. And even those didn't satisfy—nursing, for example. In 1943, she also went to school to become a car mechanic, attending classes at Fort Ord Motor School—Training Automotive Maintenance and Repair, completing the course at the top of her class on March 26, 1943, earning an "Excellent" recommendation. Although she excelled at her work as a "Trainee, Auto Mechanic Helper," she quit the Ordinance Service Command Shop on April 22, scarcely a month after she began, because the "job promised me was not forthcoming." Imperious Carol. "She probably wanted to run the fort," noted one friend. Or maybe she didn't want to work as hard as she had in the past. Or maybe what surfaced, once again, was the old fury at being slighted, her merits not given their due. "Trainee" and a "Helper" didn't cut the mustard.

On the other hand, when she was recognized for real artistic talents—her sculpting, for example—she would make light of her skills. She continued to work with clay and, in 1942, was voted into the Carmel Art Association, organized in 1920. She exhibited seven of her delicate female statues. She wouldn't allow herself to be called an artist, however: "I'm only a student making cartoons in clay," the local paper reported her saying. "Down in her cottage at Casanova and Seventh, she works on a card table. As tools she uses a tongue depressor, a nail file, a broken towel rack, a large crochet hook, a swizzle stick from Hotel Brevoort, and three ordinary modeling implements." At home she kept her most playful pieces: a winged elephant named Jimmy and three mermans, one taking a seal for a walk and another playing an accordion. "There is something deeply satisfying about mud work," she said. But she didn't take it all that seriously. She didn't consider herself primarily an artist. She didn't consider herself primarily anything.

After she purchased her own cottage in January 1943, Sea Wolf on Scenic Drive, a street that curved along the Pacific, she started hosting garden parties. Friends remember her knowing the names of birds very well. But she wouldn't answer anyone's questions about a particular species without responding, "Well, I'll have to go get my bird hat," a Swiss hat with the feather, and then she began her discourse. She loved the limelight. She adored hats. And she was adept at grand gestures.

Loren Alanson Howard came into her life in 1942. Born in Duluth, Minnesota, he had gone to the University of Washington for two years, married, divorced, and become a wholesale and retail jeweler in Spokane, Washington. In March 1941, he enlisted in the army and was sent to Fort Ord to train in field artillery; he started active duty in 1942 and listed his specialty as an intelligence officer. He was younger than Carol by three years, handsome and smooth, six feet one and 185 pounds, a hunk. Loren was a ladies' man, even if "kind of prissy." Carol was smitten and probably charmed by the fact that they shared a birthday, March 15. That coincidence may have helped Loren win her hand, since Carol was needy and, at that point in her life, had poor judgment in men. Not one of her friends liked him. Loren was "a fake," snorted one, "vain" and "dull" noted another. In front of Carol's nose he made passes at both Viola and her sister, Dorothea, and had an affair with a chaplain's wife while still living in Monterey, and another with Dorothea when the two were posted overseas. "A pants rabbit," Carol would come to admit. Even worse, most people who knew Carol thought Loren was nothing but a gold digger, interested in the former Mrs. Steinbeck for her name and her money.

But Carol needed a male companion, if only to prove something to John; he had snagged a sexy woman, so she would hook a sexy man. Most friends thought that was the reason Carol stayed with a man everyone else found dull and vain. When Loren transferred from Fort Ord to Camp Roberts, one hundred miles south of Carmel, Carol went with him to Paso Robles. On July 4, 1943, three months after John married Gwen Conger, Carol married Loren Howard in an army chapel on the base. The ceremony, sniped one guest, was "a circus." Elizabeth Cass, head of the Carmel Art Association and another of Carol's new friends, was a reluctant matron of honor. Right before the wedding, Loren was found in his East Garrison room staring at their marriage notice in *Time* magazine, "absolutely fascinated" with notice of his nuptials—undoubtedly evidence of his narcissism. At the ceremony, military trucks surrounded a Camp Roberts chapel, and a band played with brassy energy. After tying the knot, Carol and Loren drove around the post in the back of a truck, rolled out of town for a five-day Lake Tahoe honeymoon, and then settled in Paso Robles. Carol would list "grape raising" as her occupation on her 1943 tax returns.

Life on a remote Paso Robles farm bored Carol. During the war years there were some vineyards, a few herds of cattle, and the college Cal Poly down the highway in San Luis Obispo, but Paso Robles was a very remote place. Carol often escaped north to her Carmel friends. Jerry Hastings, whom she'd met a year earlier, was a favorite; he was divorced, too small to enlist (to his humiliation), and as much in need of a pal as she was. He adored her and remembered rollicking times. One day Carol picked up Jerry and drove him to Monterey, then to Salinas—her old haunts—and then all the way back south on 101 to her Paso Robles farmhouse. The next morning she tossed him a tie and told him they were going to the local bank run by Mr. Derryberry and Mr. Stufflebeam, two Dutch bankers, both "little round almond growers." It seemed that the main purpose of her outing had been to bring Jerry two hours south of Carmel just to meet those remarkable bankers.

Another day Carol came looking for Viola, who was then working for the USO and also stationed in Paso Robles. There was a knock at the office door, and Viola looked up to see at the window a hat covered with little daisies, all on wires, swaying gently as the head beneath bowed and tipped. Underneath was Carol, making faces at the window. It was early December, five months into her marriage, and Carol was ready for an adventure. "The only thing I need," Carol told Viola as they drove north on Highway 101, heading toward Carmel shops for Christmas gifts, "is a pair of great horny owls. I have no owls." As a farm matron, she had started collecting pairs of animals, as if she were Noah. By December she had several sets, including two hogs, Tristan and Isolde, and twin peacocks. Right after she voiced her need for two owls, there on the road appeared an enormous owl, nearly two feet high. "Do you see what I see?" Carol squealed, slamming on the breaks. "It's very dangerous," offered Viola. Carol put on her gloves and was tugging them over her fingers when Fish and Game drove by. "What are you girls doing?" Carol told the official, "I want that owl. I'll get him well." That was apparently a solid enough response for Fish and Game, and they picked up the completely passive owl and put him in Carol's car. For the next hour, Viola and Carol crooned, "Owl see you in my dreams." Reaching Salinas, they stopped in a veterinarian's office and he took X-rays. "That's a sick owl you've got." Carol agreed: "Sure, he's dying, but we're going to take him with us." When they got to Carmel, there was still plenty of time to shop, and Carol thought that the owl would enjoy the outing. So she perched it on her shoulder, where it loomed high above her head, and off they went. That afternoon, Carol was the town's pied piper. Kids followed. Adults stared. They went into a bar where the owl peered out at the world complacently. They went to Beth and Peg's and perched the owl on their mantle. Still it made no move. (Beth wrote up the story for the local paper.)

Soon enough, Carol and Loren left their Paso Robles ranch. He was transferred back to Fort Ord and then shipped to the Philippines. Carol moved back into her beloved Sea Wolf in Carmel, where she went back to hobnobbing with friends: Beth and Peg, Jerry Hastings, Libby Cass, director of the Carmel Art Gallery, and Virginia Miculak, a "crazy blond."

In Loren's absence, Jerry became her steady companion, and the two of them went to parties and to the Mission Ranch for dinners and dancing. Theirs was a partnership that worked well—slight and sweet-tempered Jerry hobnobbing with tall, energetic, and bossy Carol, who orchestrated their movements. Jerry loved Carol's zaniness. "I knew she was lonely and wanted to be loved. . . . She knew I loved her; I was happier with Carol than with anybody." She treated him a bit like a son—she would later write him letters addressed to "my son, my man-child." And he, recently divorced and terribly broken up, was willing to be coddled a bit. He ignored—and also understood—her occasional cruelty. "Mostly she would kill with her tongue," but "one time she kicked me in the shins. It hurt!" And she said something like, "You stupid bastard." He sighed, "She didn't get mad often." Most of the time she simply told Jerry what to do. He built her a goldfish pond in her yard and stocked it from the Carmel River with a lamprey and some crawdads—Japanese koi were not available during the war. That didn't satisfy Carol, so she had Jerry go to a park in Carmel to get goldfish. While Jerry was netting the goldfish, the Carmel police came to investigate the heist; but when they saw that the fish were not doing too well in the park, they drove Jerry, Carol, and the fish to Carol's pond, apparently recovery waters.

On another occasion, Carol parked her car in a Carmel loading zone, and a policeman came over and said she could not park there. "If you think I'm not loaded you're crazy." Those one-liners.

For those who loved her, as John had once, Carol's self-dramatization was unforgettable—a vivid pose or outrageous dress or a quip. During the war, a colonel gave Carol and Jerry a "7 rib standing roast" one day, a highly illegal gesture. So Jerry and Carol celebrated their good fortune during times of thrift. Carol put on a cowgirl outfit—leather jacket, leather skirt. Jerry was her beef bearer, and the two strolled haughtily around Carmel with the roast.

Another day Jerry came to Carol's from the post office and brought her a long package. She opened it before the two went into her house and studied it thoughtfully: "Damn. Somebody sent me a fucking machine."

Carol gave Jerry cooking lessons: "Put the steak in a pan with only salt, no grease," she instructed him. One rollicking night she made blue corn tortillas: "Frisbie them to the ceiling," she called out gaily. "If they stick to the ceiling, they're not ready." Or she might say to Jerry, "I haven't had any abalone for a while," and then send a friend out in the ocean to get her some. If parties at her house went on too long, Jerry recalled, Carol would count bodies and pitch sleeping bags on the living room floor. Without John, without Loren, she needed people around her—Jerry to nurture, others to entertain. They got her through the war.

As did her dogs. The first was "Concertina Dalmation God damned Dog," Tina, "a beauty but dumb!" Tina jumped out of the car traveling at thirty-five miles per hour and damaged nerves in her legs. And Tina dug up her garden. So Carol gave Tina to Noel Sullivan, patron of the arts and also a new resident in the area. He'd moved to Carmel Valley in 1939 and bought Hollow Hills Farm, where he raised dogs, sheep, and goats and directed the Carmel Music society. The next dog was Antonine, a poodle, her "dream dog," she wrote Jerry, who had left the Peninsula, "a large French Poodle who *loves* me! He is ex-coast guard, and verry tough. It keeps kids out of the yard, no end."

Husband Loren was missed, but more as an idea than a real person. He was the group's absent soldier, so they sent him the same kind of crazy letters that John and Carol had generated when Ritchie and Tal were in Alaska. One night Carol hooked up with her old group—which she saw much less often now that she lived in Carmel—Ritchie and Tal and Ed Ricketts and Beth, Xenia—and all contributed witty verses for Loren from "Robles Del Rio [a community south of Carmel River], July 4." Here's what Loren received in the Philippines:

"Mrs James Joyce, nee Ricketts, a fugitive from erotica, told a usually reli-
able authority today that she was through with sex. When asked by reports to
explain her statement, she said: 'Fuck you!'"
MORE 6:06 . . .
BULLETIN
Carmel, July 4, it was reliably reported today by a traveler returning from Car-
mel Valley that there are no more gold fish to be had.
The traveler said the gold fish shortage was caused by meat rationing.
More 6:32 . . .
HERE WE GO READY?
False rumors that goldfish had been rationed are due to an erronious [sic]
report that Mrs. Ricketts-Dali-Joyce discovered a hereto unknown aphrodisiac
in goldfish oil.
Unfounded, overoptimistic and unscientific, says Ricketts.
Flash (Correction)
Tail is being rationed,—not fish.
FLUSH!
Unexplained fish shortage in Carmel Municipal Fish Pond.
Flash—No shortage in Howard pool.
Flash—add shortage
Carmel, July 4, Reports of a fish shortage are erroneous, an expert said today.
The expert was Dr. Ed. Ricketts who told correspondents that ever if there were
a fish shortage, "Who cares."
More 6:56
FLASH
Mrs. Salvador Dali, who disappeared two weeks ago, in company with a low-
slung rakish Cadillac coupe, was found today, under the wrecked car, covered
with gardenias. [A reference to the 1942 Dali party at the Hotel Del Monte.] On
being questioned, Mrs. Dali asserted in very positive terms, "Salvador taught
me to love 'the different.'"
Oh, rock it to me. . . .
Dali to Howard.
Add xxx As he struck her for the 29th time she lost count said, "That's 30 for
tonight folks."

. . .

Flash: Mrs. Salvador Dali, having heard that Salvador had just made a dance floor of clams Rockefeller was alleged to say: I'm just one of the Dali Sisters". Unquote.

Xenia . . .

Dear dear Loren,

On our heppu july 4, we are thinking of you.

Love, Beth

BULLETIN

Robles Del Rio, Calif. July 4—Two Indians, one 14, the other 18, riding along in a canoe today came across the sleeping body of a woman, dressed in white slacks, local police announced.

The woman, who was taken to Carmel hospital, was later identified as Mrs. Carol Howard, who told authorities upon questioning, "I wanted to sit in mud." Police did not say wheter [sic] charges would be pressed.

Loren absent was more fun than Loren present.

During the war, few were stationary on the Peninsula. Viola went to San Francisco to work. Jerry left. That left Carol rich and unfettered and lonely. Her sister thought that she hated being wealthy, "despised it" in fact, because Carol needed something to struggle against and to see herself as outside the dominant culture. While Carol was a "perfect pioneer woman," in Idell's mind, she was an improbable Carmel matron—too loud, too crazy, at bottom too unsure of herself. In Carmel, she was no longer a bum. A weekly poker game was only a mild diversion: "Costs about as much as a movie, and less than a Carmel Music Society Clambake, and much more fun, to boot," she wrote Jerry. Resolutely she hosted parties and continued with her art and corresponded with absent friends: "I'm sitting in a perfectly boiling sun, drinking iced tea and trying to catch up on the thousand letters I owe—getting six or seven a week off to Loren takes just about my entire budget of writing time." But she wrote Jerry that she was "blue and bored . . . very low in the mind" and "weeping big salty tears because I have a telegraph blank for overseas messages, and all that canned sentiment seemed so pitiful all of a sudden that I just boiled over." She tells Jerry of days giving blood, going to see the dog she gave to Noel Sullivan, gardening. But the letter cycles back to her misery: "Chickie, I miss you. I'm blue and bored, and my heart is mixed up with my shoe-laces. I hear very seldom from Loren. Maybe that has something to do with it."

Jerky and sorrowful, meandering and listless, Carol's letter sinks like her spirit. She might not have adored Loren, but his lack of interest was bruising. How much John's work and his need for her had sustained Carol is contained in those scattershot lines. In the early 1940s, she was woman without a cause.

When the war ended, Loren came home, released from service on February 18, 1946. Carol had heard from him irregularly throughout the war, and the homecoming must have been strained. He returned decorated with the Philippine Liberation Medal, but it was presented to any service member who participated in the liberation of the Philippine Islands. His was not glorious service, and his return was hardly triumphant. Even before being shipped overseas, he had calculated how he would spend Carol's money: a three-hundred-acre chicken ranch in Carmel Valley. It was probably a good investment, if not for the chickens then definitely for the land. But Carol, prickly about money, was not pleased. By 1946 her stock and real estate investments had done well, and she was in no mood to allow Loren to drain her resources. Not only that, but his philandering became more and more apparent, even to Carol. To heal their relationship, they took a two-month summer trip through the Pacific Northwest with poodle Antoine, "who was mistaken for a black bear several times when they were driving through the bear country." The trip did not mend the relationship, and Carol filed for divorce on March 15, 1947—their mutual birthday. She was bored with him, said her sister, and that's why she divorced him.

A year and a half after Carol's divorce, John Steinbeck moved back to the Peninsula after his final break with Gwen. In 1941 Steinbeck had gloried in his release from Carol's "sharp" control of money and "tight resistance" and fights and "competition" and her accusations of his "dominating" her, as he had confided to Mavis McIntosh. But he had, in fact, jumped from the frying pan into another, much hotter, fire. Living with Gwen felt "easy" at first; he told Mavis that it had been "so long since I have lived in an easy house." In 1941, John had wanted peace, and for a few months, that's what he got. But when he went overseas in the fall of 1943, only a few months after marrying Gwen, that relationship shifted—at least in Steinbeck's eyes. The war changed everyone. When he and Gwen separated five years later, John wrote his beloved sister Mary, trying once again to figure out his failed second marriage:

> I don't want you to think this is all Gwyn's fault. [Gwen changed the spelling of her name after her marriage.] If I have lost twice in exactly the same way it must be for one of two reasons or a combination of both. Either I am attracted to and marry the same kind of women or I drive wives crazy. I think the first is

the truth but it is probably blended with the second. But I would do anything to reform that if I could. I do have to work and it is my work that finally seems to destroy marriages. So maybe I will have no more wives. I can't cut the work off because that is all I am and incidentally that is why they want to marry me in the first place. I can't figure it out. I've tried for years.

Maybe he also tried to puzzle out the failure with Carol present. In 1948, John and Carol were once more drawn to each other, their meetings probably brought about by remembered love, nostalgia, and mutual pain. Perhaps he asked her to marry him again, as Carol claimed. Probably not. Bo Beskow, who was always solidly in Carol's camp, said that John had written him to say that all the bitterness of the past was gone. John admitted that he'd seen a "good deal" of Carol, but added that she was still unhappy, still tended to blame others for her problems. He would not go back to her, he told Beskow.

But living on their separate sides of the Peninsula, John in the Eleventh Street cottage, Carol in her little house overlooking Carmel Bay, both mourned the lost phalanx. Both sensed that their partnership had, in many ways, defined their lives. In 1948, depressed and alone, unable to write, he wrote this in a notebook: "Where then does this despair come in? Why does it come in? Perhaps it might be like this. A few times I have in work heard the thundering and seen the flash which must have been the universe at work. In that participation there was a glory that shadows everything else and that makes me seem like a grey and grizzled animal now. It never happened often and usually it happened when outward things were either terrible or sad." "Participation." The keying of the phalanx, catalyst of creativity.

The terrible and sad times, which might have swamped others, had buoyed their union.

Coda

CAROL MET BILL BROWN DURING THE WAR, when mutual friends introduced them, and he attended parties at Carol's house. After her divorce from Loren, they renewed their acquaintance at Carmel's Mission Inn in the early 1950s, where he was manager and bartender. (He had been resident manager of the Palace Hotel in San Francisco and of the Moana Hotel in Honolulu as well.) On January 19, 1952, Judge Ray Baugh of Monterey married the couple at Carol's home on San Antonio and Twelfth in Carmel. Bill was thirty-nine to Carol's forty-five.

Carol's third husband was a refuge for Carol. It was a "good marriage," said Congressman Fred Farr, Bill's cousin. Son of a prominent San Francisco family, Bill had a "good name" that Carol appreciated. He was interested in politics and engaged in the community, as was she. He knew everybody, was gregarious and outgoing. In his later years, he was devoted to the volunteer fire department. Bill was a rock, a "happy, outgoing human being" and a "traveling encyclopedia of sports information." And he "worshipped Carol in a motherly way," said a friend who knew the couple well. In fact, Carol was a lot like Bill's mother, who was "quite a gal." Carol brought life and color to Bill's life—and he brought stability to hers for thirty years. In the 1950s, Carol bought a vacation home in Tahoe and another home by the Carmel River, about four miles up Carmel Valley, not far from where John had envisioned living with Gwen, near the "green cliff up the Carmel River," a place "deeply burned" into his "memory treasure," as he wrote Mary in 1944, anticipating his return to the Monterey Peninsula with Gwen. (The rock-lined pool is the scene of the frog hunt in *Cannery Row*.) While John never realized his dream of living by that lovely little river, Carol did. In her house overlooking the river, Bill and Carol entertained together and Carol swam laps in their pool. She gardened. She cooked curries and paella, Mexican food, creative dishes.

A year into their marriage, Carol was interviewed by the local paper and confessed to five interests: "Cooking is one, and her artist's collection of herbs is another. Of the remaining three, her long-time work as public information director of the Carmel chapter of the American Red Cross is her only continuing contact with the public these days. Her other two interests are both concerned with her home."

Being loyal to Bill.

She remained a fascinating woman, "ageless in conversation" said a younger friend. "She always knew what was going on. Took three to four newspapers and read them all": the *San Francisco Chronicle,* the *New York Times,* the *Monterey Herald,* and the *Los Angeles Times.* As ever, Carol kept up with the world.

And she continued to delight friends with her wit. One time the "P" from her Pontiac station wagon fell off, and she went to a gas station to have it fixed. "I'd like you to fix my P," she told the owner. The wordplay went on for some time. "What's wrong with your P?" said the owner. "Let me take a P," said Carol.

But the demons remained, perhaps because life was simply too comfortable, perhaps because she was so obviously still in love with John, as friends attested. With Bill, "she was the boss," perhaps because she wouldn't allow herself to be vulnerable, to be hurt again. Perhaps because she never found a way to heal that ancient hurt—her mother's rejection, her furious insecurity. Sometimes she and Bill had "horrible fights," often over politics. She would flip her cigarette and sneer, "You don't know what you're talking about." She belittled Bill, who, as an insurance agent, was far from wealthy and living largely on her money. And Carol was never settled in her own mind about Bill's role as provider: she did want him to work and yet she didn't. It can't have been easy for him to fully understand Carol, to defend her, to love her, particularly with John Steinbeck "always in the background." In front of Bill, Carol often verbally remembered John.

At one point when the couple was living in Los Gatos at 90 Highlands Avenue in the mid-1950s, Bill had Carol committed to Agnews State Hospital for seventy-two hours after she attacked him, hitting him over the head with a bottle. Drinking and dissatisfaction with the way her life turned out sometimes left her unmanageable. Carol "never forgave" Bill for having her committed. She was often sarcastic with him and hurt him quite consciously. These were some of the traits that doomed her first marriage—although John made only veiled references to her rages in letters. With the passing years, the anger must have intensified. Certainly the drinking did.

Carol relied on alcohol to ease the pain of arthritis as well as her own deep dissatisfaction. One drinking buddy was old friend Beth Ingels; but there again, the two had terrible fights, physical and verbal. One friend thought that Carol argued fiercely with Beth because she cared so much for her—as she had for John, as she did Bill. At her worst, Carol wounded those she loved. At one point she said to Tal Lovejoy, her friend of decades: "Listen you're a stupid bitch, you're a cow. I'm not going to have anything to do with you." To some extent, these barbs were Carol's way. On the rationing board during the war, lines would form and listen to Carol's booming voice, "Listen you stupid fools, don't try to get anything else." She whipped people into shape, demanding that the world live up to her standards. But as years passed, she became less tolerant. Carol had a "high moral expectation of people," mused Jean Ariss. "That sounds contradictory. There were a lot of contradictions in her. She could get indignant in the way people acted . . . judgmental in a moral sense. She was not moral about sex or drinking—but hers was a deep morality. She was a deeply moral person and the demands she made were not often lived up to on the part of other people. She was fiercely engaged in her own concepts of things. . . . Carol wanted to change people into her version of what they should be."

One story captures much about this complex woman, who was demanding, creative, jealous, exacting. From 1969 to 1972, Carol's sister-in-law was also named Carol Brown. The two were married to brothers. Both couples lived on the Monterey Peninsula, and both women were artists, although Carol Steinbeck Brown was not a professional artist. The city of Monterey commissioned Carol Brown, a sculptor, to make a bust of John to be placed in Steinbeck Plaza on Cannery Row. Carol Steinbeck Brown thought this a terrific idea, and she came to see her sister-in-law weekly to check on the progress of the bust. She brought photos of John from her scrapbook and would critique the bust that Carol was carving: "the son of a bitch's nose was big," she would bark to Carol. "Make his goddamn head larger." The sculptor raged inside but did as Carol Steinbeck Brown bid, adding more and more clay. And the bust collapsed. She had to start all over again. Carol Brown, artist, was more and more frustrated with the visits of Carol Brown, critic, which weren't helping her complete the bust. "Please God," she would say, looking to the heavens. "Keep her away." Carol kept coming, kept "god-damming" clay John, kept bringing photos to make sure the likeness was true. Carol Steinbeck Brown wanted an accurate bust of the "son of a bitch." At the end of the project, she also wanted her name on the bust, for she felt it was a collaborative project, that her suggestions were as much a part of the bust as was

Carol's work in clay. She "was really grieving when we collaborated," sculptor Carol mused years later, after she had recovered from Carol's high-handed assumption of artistic control. "I was the sounding board. I got both sides, the sentimental and the bitter. She talked about John's writing. She felt so utterly confident in editing or interpreting." Carol Steinbeck Brown felt she had collaborated with John and had given him very good advice—she was secure in that knowledge. And she felt that she had collaborated with her sister-in-law on the bust. But "I had failed her," Carol Brown recalled. Just as John had failed her, failed to appreciate her criticism, failed to stick by her.

Carol Steinbeck Brown's obituary notes that this bust was one of her accomplishments.

After the bust was finished, Carol walked around it twice and said, "You old fucker you." That meant she liked it. She liked it and she hated it. She had the same mixture of feelings about John. And yet, when he was awarded the Nobel Prize in 1962, she wrote to congratulate him, and he wrote back to say that he had expected her note. He knew she was still in his camp, in the way that counted most, his art.

Carol died in February 1983 at age seventy-six, estranged from her sister, Idell, cherished by her husband. Idell resented Carol's drinking, thought Carol snubbed her when Carol was prosperous, resented the way that Carol favored one of Idell's daughters over the other. Bill, on the other hand, was bereft, and asked Viola Franklin, author of a book on Africa and Carol's lifelong friend, to write Carol's biography. To Bill, Carol was a magnificent woman, whose life with John Steinbeck had never been fully told. To his mind, she was John's backbone.

Her sister's and her husband's assessments are the measure of Carol's complexity. To the end, the lamb and wolf in Carol's nature wrangled.

At her funeral, held at her beloved Carmel Valley home, one friend commented that she'd "never met so many varied people in her life." At the end of the reception, a helicopter flew over the house and scattered Carol's ashes over the Carmel River.

This poem is one of the last pasted in a scrapbook Carol assembled.

Poltergeist
And when at last I join the myriad dead,
I prey you, no tall candles burn,
Nor weep till your beloved eyes are red,
But rest assured in knowing I'll return.

No solemn spectre, I, in winding-sheet
And musty grave clothes, trailing through the halls,
I shall not howl forlornly in the sleet,
Nor make portentous rappings in your walls.

But if your lights should suddenly go dim,
And raucous, ribald laughter fill the room,
You'll know it is no haunter sour and grim,
But only I, returning from the tomb.

And if I'm very sure that you still care,
I'll come to you from out the depths of hell,
The sheet and pillow-case I wear
Will bear a label reading "Grand Hotel."

Successor there may be, and simply grand,
But when you start to tenderly enfold her,
Just remember, kid, I'll be on hand,
Leering at her over your left shoulder.

                    Carol Steinbeck

John also wrote an epitaph, of sorts, a decade before he died: "I know now that I am never going to be the best writer in the world," he told his sister Mary in 1958, "but I'm a good one and I love my work. I'll probably have a pencil in my hand when they lay me out. I hope so."

Both sketched their own ghosts, the wit and the writer. Maybe the two are leering and peering over our left shoulders, wrangling still.

Notes

Interviews and letters are cited in the notes, as are newspaper articles contained in archives. The first time a letter to a recipient is cited, I indicate the archive. Since Steinbeck did not date most of his early letters, I have not included notes for letters when the recipient is clear in the text and when no further information can be given. If a Steinbeck letter is included in *A Life in Letters*, I cite only the page number in that text (*LL*). Letters from John Steinbeck to his sister Mary Dekker are from the Dekker archive and are quoted with permission from Toni Heyler. Letters and notebooks of Edward F. Ricketts in the Ed Ricketts Jr. collection are quoted by permission of Ed Ricketts Jr. The material attributed to Joseph Campbell's journals comes from an unpublished manuscript for a work of fiction developed by Campbell and is quoted under license by the Joseph Campbell Foundation. When an interviewer is not identified, the interview is by me. For these I have included the name of the person interviewed, if not identified in the text, and the date(s) of the interview only the first time the person is quoted. All interviews conducted by others are identified as such. These are generally from two sources: Benson interviews housed at Stanford University Special Collections, and the Pauline Pearson/George Robinson interviews housed at the National Steinbeck Center, Salinas.

Material quoted is from the following archives, identified briefly in the notes as follows. I wish to thank each library, as well as Steinbeck's literary agents, McIntosh and Otis, and his longtime publisher, Viking Penguin, for permission to quote from published and unpublished material.

Bancroft: Bancroft Library, University of California, Berkeley
    Albee Papers: George Sumner Albee Papers, BANC MSS C-H 120
    Jackson Papers: J. H. Jackson Papers, BANC MSS C-H 40
    Steinbeck: John Steinbeck Letters and Manuscripts, 1938–1963, BANC
        MSS 70/124
CB archive: Carol Henning Brown archive, Center for Steinbeck Studies,
        San Jose State University
CSS: Center for Steinbeck Studies, San Jose State University

Morgan: Pierpont Morgan Library Department of Literary and Historical
      Manuscripts
NSC: National Steinbeck Center, Salinas
Powell Papers: Lawrence Clark Powell Papers Concerning John Steinbeck,
      1935–1941, Houghton Library, Harvard University
Ransom: Harry Ransom Center Book Collection, University of Texas at Aus-
      tin, John Steinbeck Collection, 1926–1977. HCR, MS, Steinbeck, John
Small: Papers of John Steinbeck, MS 6239, Albert and Shirley Small
      Special Collections Library, University of Virginia
Stanford: Department of Special Collections, Stanford University Libraries
      Wells Fargo: Wells Fargo Steinbeck Collection, M1063
      JS: John Steinbeck Collection, M0263
      S-A: Steinbeck-Ainsworth collection, M0263
      ER Papers: Edward Flanders Ricketts Papers, M0291
      JJB: Jackson J. Benson, *True Adventures of John Steinbeck, Writer* research
      materials, 1935–1980, M0522
Williams: Annie Laurie Williams Collection, Rare Book and Manu-
      script Library, Butler Library, Columbia University
Wulf: William A. Wulf historical papers, private collection

ABBREVIATIONS

AA:	*America and Americans and Selected Nonfiction*
ER:	Edward Ricketts
GOW:	*The Grapes of Wrath*
JS:	John Steinbeck
LL:	*A Life in Letters*
LSOC:	*Log from the Sea of Cortez*
LVL:	Long Valley Ledger
TC:	Tom Collins

INTRODUCTION

1   "had a blockbuster": Viking files.

1   "purchase it for circulation": French, *Companion,* 130.

1   "wrathy": Frank Taylor, "California's 'Grapes,'" 232.

1   "line must be drawn somewhere": Bob Work, "Editorially Speaking," *Spartan
      Daily,* May 29, 1939, 2.

1   "unfit for patrons": "'Grapes of Wrath' Under Library's Ban at San Jose,"
      San Jose Mercury News, June 29, 1939, Carol Henning Brown archive

(uncatalogued), Martha Heasley Cox Center for Steinbeck Studies, San Jose State University (hereafter cited as CB archive).

1   "letter to the Kansas City school board": See Rick Wartzman, *Obscene in the Extreme,* 10.

2   "distorted mind": French, *Companion,* 125, 126.

2   "what I am going to do": JS to Tom Collins, n.d. JJB, author's files (hereafter cited as JS to TC; letters from 1936 to 1939 are not dated).

2   "period of my research": JS, *LL,* 202.

2   "Migrant John": Tom Cameron, "'Grapes of Wrath' Author Guards Self from Threats at Moody Gulch: Dust Bowl Book Brings Trouble," *Los Angeles Times,* July 9, 1939, in Fensch, *Conversations,* 18–20.

2   "Carol's book": JS, *LL,* 180.

4   "rather than to undergo it": Weinstein, *Nobody's Home,* 146.

4   "rejection slips": W. J. Weatherby, "From Monterey: John Steinbeck Writes as He Talks—Painfully, Simply, and with Love," *Guardian* (London), October 13, 1959, n.p.

4   "fearless": Idell Budd, telephone interviews, June 3, 1990; July 26, 1990; August 1, 1990; September 7, 1990; November 14, 1990; March 23, 1991; November 12, 1992. In addition, Idell agreed to interviews by her daughters, Carla Budd and Nikki Tugwell, August 3–4, 1994, and at other times, and transcripts were sent to the author.

4   "violent, passionate, stimulating": Jean Ariss, interviews, May 1989; July 24, 1990; April 17, 1991; March 3, 1994; and numerous joint presentations for Pebble Beach Company.

4   "rebellion in an individual": JS to Carl Wilhelmson, summer 1924, box 7, folder 6, JS, Stanford.

5   "soul will take care of itself": Bennett, *Wrath of John Steinbeck.*

5   "I certainly do hate expediency": CB archive.

5   "ego bolstering": Toni Jackson Volconi, interview by Benson.

5   "great sensitivity": Robert Sears, interview by Benson.

6   "I care not what the world thinks": Paul, *Hallelujah,* 83.

6   "inhibitions Mr. Scatterbing": Paul, *Hallelujah,* 56.

7   "man at twice its natural size": Virginia Woolf, "A Room of One's Own."

7   "see me that way": Carol Brown, interview by Benson.

7   "equal fervor": Jean Ariss, interview.

7   "common cause": Francis Whitaker, interview, February 1991.

7   "of matter and of life": JS, *LL,* 80.

8   "meanings I am interested in": JS, *LL,* 94.

8   "fluid necessary to his life": JS, *LL,* 81.

8   "shameless magpie": JS, *LL*, 95.

8   "springs all the other things": JS, *LL*, 93.

8   "history of his people": JS to Harry Moore, August 25, 1937, CSS.

8   "completely ignored": JS to Bill Gage, December 1, 1936, author's collection.

CHAPTER ONE | RENEGADES

10   "stranger there from birth": JS to Mary Dekker, April 3, 1959, Dekker archive.

10   "demure" . . . "receptive": Idell Budd.

11   "great fury": "Conversation with Bo Beskow and Bo Holmstrom," August 12, 1962.

11   "when we were broke": Steinbeck, "Always Something to Do in Salinas," in *AA*, 5.

11   "seemed to be painted": Qtd. in Quaide, "Early History."

12   "nice place to grow up": Randy [last name unknown], interview, October 19, 1993.

13   "sunshine, minerals": Benjamin Gilbert, *Pioneers*, 88, 89.

13   "smart as all hell" . . . "going on": Maggie O'Keefe, interviews, 1990 and 1991.

13   "brick buildings, spilled outward": JS, "Always Something," in *AA*, 4.

13   baby Carol inside: Maggie O'Keefe, interview.

14   "great wealth": Maggie O'Keefe, interview.

14   "unless it included his house": Ledger, box 18, JS, Stanford.

14   "taste, beauty, and restraint": Starr, "Sunset."

14   "jolly alert smile": Nellie Henning scrapbook, CB archive.

15   "straining at the leash": Beth Ainsworth, interview by Benson.

15   "being free": JS to Beth Ainsworth, 1959, S-A, Stanford.

15   "women rarely walked on that side": Sallee, "Reconceptualizing," 360.

15   "what you shouldn't": Beth Ainsworth, interview by Benson.

16   Großsteinbecks in Holy Land: Perry, "John Steinbeck's Roots," 48.

16   *Horn's Overland Guide:* Wulf, papers on the Henning family.

17   "make him his heir": Henning family papers, Nikki Tugwell.

18   "while crossing the plains": Richard Albee.

18   "drowned in the reservoir": Dick Barrett, "Share It with Barrett: Lost Nell of the Sierra," *San Jose Mercury News*, June 5, 1960, 8E, Wulf papers.

18   "tension around her mother": Sharon Brown Bacon, interview, November 11, 1994; January 5, 1995; and subsequent questions answered.

19   "full vocalization": Madge Craig, interview, 1990.

19   "star lit *outer space*: Nellie Henning scrapbook, CB archive.

20   "fancy dictates": Nellie Henning scrapbook, CB archive.

21   "extrovert like her daughter Carol" . . . "flock to her": Maggie O'Keefe, interview.

21   "bounce the burly prowler": May 29, 1913, Nellie Henning scrapbook, CB archive.

22   "what he told me": Dean Storey, interview by Benson.

22   "gauzy beauty": JS to Mary Dekker, February 13, 1957, Dekker archive.

23   *Million Dollar Mystery:* JS to Mary Dekker, September 9, 1958, Dekker archive.

23   "individual and society": Cederstrom, "The 'Great Mother,'" 78.

23   See Gladstein, "Missing Women."

23–24   "steady one" . . . "content within themselves": Toni Heyler, interview, May 1994, and other dates.

24   "shame to our parents": JS to Esther and Beth, January 26, 1965, J-A, Stanford.

24   "The Salinas Saga": box 4, folder 109, Wells Fargo, Stanford.

25   "sometimes stern": Beth Ainsworth, interview by Benson.

25   "sure crop every year": Mr. Steinbeck to Esther, box 1, folder 38, Wells Fargo, Stanford.

25   "work he wanted to do": JS to Elizabeth Bailey, June 1935, box 1, folder 1, NSC.

26   "competitive jealousy": Person, "Steinbeck's Queer Ecology," 8.

26   "a doll": Harriet Eels Meyer, interviews, October 19, 1989, and May 27, 1994.

26–27   *deepwater port:* "Sequels: Deep Water Port Still San Jose Dream, and Wilbur Henning Still Hoping," Carl Heintze, *SJ Mercury News,* n.d., and "SJ's Deep Water Port Dream Revives," Stanley Waldorf, *San Francisco Examiner,* April 19, 1953, Nellie Henning scrapbook, CB archive.

27   "business world": Harriet Eels Meyer, interview.

27   "stayed in an unhappy marriage": JS to Mavis McIntosh, n.d., Small, Virginia.

28   "sometimes thought": "The Winter of Our Discontent," ms., Morgan.

28   "sharp and penetrating" . . . "very much": JS, *LL,* 18, 20.

30   "very independent": Randy[last name unknown], interview.

31   "so charitable of em" . . . "Thekops": Carol Henning to Harriet Eels, n.d., author's collection.

32   "closed between 12:00 Noon and 1 PM.": Schilling Spice: http://www .allelementsdesign.com/schilling/company/spices/65years.html.

33   "knock me down": JS, *LL,* 218.

CHAPTER TWO | MAKE IT NEW

34   "intellectual and sexual freedom": "The New Woman," www.library.csi .cuny.edu/dept/history/lavender/386/newwoman.html.

34   "thirteenth glass of cognac": Robert Cathcart, interview, July 25, 2001, and several interviews in 2007.

34   "ecological sensibilities": Owens, "Ways Out of the Waste Land," 16.

34   "pleasure in the work": JS to Amasa Miller, 1931, box 2, folder 2, JS, Stanford.

34   "cold and heartless" . . . "beaten the pants off me": JS, "Making of a New Yorker," in *AA*, 36.

35   "whole earth affords": Twain, *Roughing It*, chap. 22.

35   "frightfully bad taste": JS to folks, 1926, box 1, folder 90, Wells Fargo, Stanford.

35   "add shortening": JS to folks, November 1, 1926, box 1, folder 91, Wells Fargo, Stanford.

36   "button holes": JS to folks, November 11, 1926, box 1, folder 92, Wells Fargo, Stanford.

36   headlines and comics: JS to folks, December 14, 1926, box 1, folder 97, Wells Fargo, Stanford.

36   "increasingly good as I go on": JS to folks, March 22, 1927, box 1, folder 99, Wells Fargo, Stanford.

36   "not a dressy place": Lisa Butler, "Summer Splendor: the Lure of Lake Tahoe, Part Two," http://www.stylemg.com/El-Dorado-County-Foothills/July-2011/Summer-Splendor/.

36   "take a trip": Idell Budd.

37   "get on my nerves": JS to folks, April 21, 1928, box 2, folder 61, Wells Fargo, Stanford.

37   tourists through the hatchery: Delbert H. West, interview by Benson.

37   "interesting work": JS, in *AA*, 327.

37   "what have you published?": Idell Budd, interview by Benson.

38   "kinship of sex with poetry": Paul, *Hallelujah*, 56.

38   "pleased him": Sheffield, *Steinbeck*, 20.

38   "has no words": JS, *Travels with Charley*, 106.

39   Truckee: Guy Coates, "How Truckee Survived Prohibition" and "Truckee Was Once the Film Mecca of the Sierras," http://truckeehistory.org/historyArticles/history5.htm.

39   Bucket of Blood: Lloyd Shebley, interview by Benson.

39   "dirt on her nose": Sheffield, *Steinbeck*, 140.

39   "enjoying it tremendously": JS to folks, July 2, 1928, box 2, folder 64, Wells Fargo, Stanford.

39   "nor continuity": Sheffield, *Steinbeck*, 78.

40   "mouse in woodpile": Robert Cathcart, interview.

40   resident mermaid: JS, "E Pluribus Unum," in *AA*, 328–29.

40   Omar and the garbage bear: JS to George Albee, 1932, Albee Papers, Bancroft.

40   "one-legged babysitter": Robert Cathcart, interview.

40   "He was a ham": Toby Street, interview by Benson.

40   "fond of Mary": Robert Cathcart, interview by Benson.

40   "ghost of Mr. Brigham": Robert Cathcart, interview.

40   Hermetica: Robert Cathcart, interview.

41   "piece he had been reading": Sheffield, *Steinbeck*, 30–31.

41   "bled from him": Robert Sears, interview by Benson.

41   "belly laugh": Toby Street, interview by Benson.

42   "a patron or a guardian": JS to folks, 1926, box 1, folder 90, Wells Fargo, Stanford.

42   "fulfilled the first": "Some Thoughts," *Saturday Review*, May 28, 1955, 22.

42   "plus the moods of other persons present": JS, *LL*, 18.

43   "writer does the work": JS, "Conversation with Bo Beskow."

43   "to be able to write": Burl Ives, interview by Benson.

43–44   "band of Archangels" . . . "before I ever went there" . . . "cave in North Beach": JS, "The Golden Handcuff," in *AA*, 14.

44   "50 cents": JS, "The Golden Handcuff," in *AA*, 14.

44   trout almadine, her favorite meal: Robert Cathcart, interview.

44   "public place": Amasa Miller, interview by Benson.

45   "growing rapidly": Benson, *True Adventures*, 151.

46   "finest writer alive": Benson, *True Adventures*, 156.

46   "best prose in America": DeMott, *Steinbeck's Reading*, 24.

46   "symbiotic relationship": Amasa Miller, interview by Benson.

46   "understood as being separate I do not know": Ledger, box 18, JS, Stanford.

47   "John was not a nurturer": Toni Jackson Volconi, correspondence with author, June 15, 1994; and interviews: June 3, 1994, and December 7, 2000.

48   "some given experience": Benson, *True Adventures*, 126.

48   "mind my poverty in the least": Benson, *True Adventures*, 142.

48   "a distant look": Sheffield, *Steinbeck*, 152.

48   "various combinations, and hamburger": Sheffield, *Steinbeck*, 150.

49   "roof where cats fought": JS to Elizabeth Otis, May 8, 1931, box 2, folder 6, JS, Stanford.

49   "important as his work": Qtd. in JS to Kate Beswick, 1929, box 1, folder 8, JS, Stanford.

50   "warm relaxed person": Margaret Ringnalda, letters to author, 1989–93.

50   "and never could be": JS, *LL*, 13.

50   "with a rock": JS to folks, April 12, 1927, box 1, folder 4, Wells Fargo, Stanford.

51   sits in front of a mouse hole all night: JS to Carl Wilhelmson, October 20, 1930, box 7, folder 7, JS, Stanford.

51   "our Oscar": Margaret Ringnalda, letter to author, May 24, 1990.

51   suffering poetic type: Jean Ariss, interview.

51   "Tartar eyes" . . . elegant ballerina . . . "wild bunch of girls": Jean Ariss, interview.

51   "witty and intellectual": Toni Jackson Volconi, interview.

51   "contribute to a very worthy cause": JS, "Conversation with Bo Beskow."

52   "remarkable fidelity": Sheffield, *Steinbeck*, 175.

52   novel potions and such: Sheffield, *Steinbeck*, 159–64.

52   "most discussed books of the past year": "John Steinbeck, Jr. Weds San Jose Girl," *Salinas Index*, January 16, 1930.

52   "so there you are . . . evil advertising": JS to folks, January 18, 1930, box 2, folder 65, Wells Fargo, Stanford.

53   "fifty-fifty basis": JS to Kate Beswick, box 1, folder 8, JS, Stanford.

53   "mental states, and the like": Sheffield, *Steinbeck*, 177.

53   "very good for her": JS to Kate Beswick, box 1, folder 8, JS, Stanford.

53   "see their underwear": Carlton Sheffield, interview, October 1988.

54   "Diego Rivera and Orosco": Margaret Ringnalda, letter to author, November 19, 1993.

54   "intershot with moments of unreal romance": JS to Ted Miller, 1930, box 2, folder 2, JS, Stanford.

54   "stolen avocados": JS, *LL*, 20.

54   "throughout our house": Sheffield, *Steinbeck*, 166.

54   "informality in the house": Carlton Sheffield, interview.

55   "seen in hair before": Sheffield, *Steinbeck*, 182.

55   "a small renaissance": Ringnalda, *Joy Laughed*, 44.

55   "and unzipped": Alice Cohee, letter to Margaret Ringnalda, July 24, 1989, author's collection.

55   "listened to the black singer Leadbelly . . . and zaniness": Margaret Ringnalda, letter to author, September 12, 1990.

55   "attention to anyone else": Margaret Ringnalda, letter to author, February 1, 1991.

56   "at least noticed": Margaret Ringnalda, letter to author, February 1, 1991.

56   "tumbled down house": JS, *LL*, 20.

56   "busy as a birddog": JS to folks, January 18, 1930, box 2, folder 65, Wells Fargo, Stanford.

57   "skating around in sandboxes": Carlton Sheffield, interview by Benson.

57   "now it is entrancing": JS to folks, January 18, 1930, box 2, folder 65, Wells Fargo, Stanford.

57   "proper flowers": JS to Amasa Miller, 1930, box 2, folder 1, JS, Stanford.

57   "good influence" on his work: JS, *LL*, 22.

57   "bluebird love . . . Dogface": Richard Albee.

57   "Mounting Police Dog": Benson, *True Adventures*, 170.

58   "and their characters injustice": JS to Amasa Miller, 1930, box 2, folder 1, JS, Stanford.

58   "milk bags a swingin'": Martin Biddle to Carol, n.d., author's collection.

58–59   "taut wire . . . pursue further": Margaret Ringnalda, letter to author, July 11, 1989.

CHAPTER THREE | HOME IN PACIFIC GROVE

60   "sleep there": JS to Mary Dekker, January 26, 1955, Dekker archive.

60   marooned . . . "no companionship of any kind": JS, *LL*, 50.

60   "nothing happens": JS to Amasa Miller, December 1931, box 2, folder 1, JS, Stanford.

60   William Millis, "Early Retreat Still Mainly Residential: Old American Strain Is Dominant in Daily Life of City," *Monterey Herald*, May 28, 1941, 1. This and other clippings and pamphlets on the town and Julia Platt are from the Pacific Grove Library historical files.

61   "here and there": Red Williams, interview, April 18, 1993.

62   clear shouting voices: "Mizpah" in Ledger, box 18, JS, Stanford.

62   "twinning legs": Sheffield, *Steinbeck*, 67.

62   play tag: JS to Maryon Sheffield, July 7, 1923, box 5, folder 15, JS, Stanford.

63   "it's just ugly": Qtd. in Toni Jackson, "Julia Platt, Lady Watchdog," *What's Doing*, December 1946, 48, Pacific Grove Library historical files.

63   See "Julia B. Platt (1857–1935): Pioneer Comparative Embryologist and Neuroscientist," *Brain Behavior and Evolution* 43 (1994): 92–106, Pacific Grove Library historical files.

64   "large part of its charm": JS to George Albee, 1930, Albee Papers, Bancroft.

65   "building very much": JS to George Albee, 1930, Albee Papers, Bancroft.

65   "beautiful gardener": Anna Merkel tape, Ed Ricketts Jr. collection.

65   "alive with nasturtiums": JS, *LL*, 45.

65   "very cheap": "The Wizzard," CSS.

66   "broke us": JS, *LL*, 33.

66   "delicious gravy": "A Primer on the '30s," in *AA*, 22.

66   really did struggle: Sara Bard Field, "Poet and Suffragist," 568.

66   "sleep very well" . . . "served on toast": Carlton Sheffield to Art Ring, April 14, 1982, Art Ring private collection.

66   "so potent is it": JS to George Albee, late 1931, Albee Papers, Bancroft.

66   "101 Ways to Cook Hamburger": Virginia Scardigli, interviews, April 1989; May 1, 1990; April 4, 1991; April 11, 1991; December 3, 1994; May 1, 1996. And sessions at the Steinbeck Festival and Asilomar Conference Grounds.

66   the "Goon": Richard Albee, October 21, 1976, NSC.

66   Carol stuffed the clams down her bra: Bonnie Gartshore, note to author, n.d.

66   "neighborly interest" . . . "very exciting": JS to Amasa Miller, October 24, 1930, box 2, folder 1, JS, Stanford.

66   "didn't kill us": JS, "A Primer on the '30s," in *AA*, 22.

67   "French bread": Edith Hamlin, interview by Loftis, May 7, 1982, author's collection.

67   "pass for the whole thing": JS to George Albee, 1930, Albee Papers, Bancroft.

67   "Zena": Toby Street, interview by Benson.

67   "eat up winter evenings": JS, *LL*, 50.

67   Jack French, "Orientals in OTR: A Preliminary Survey," *The Illustrated Press* (of the Old Time Radio Club) 248 (May 1997): www.otrr.org/FILES/Magz _pdf/Illustrated%20Press/IP_97_05_248.pdf.

68   "tall talk": Qtd. in Paul Wells, "'Where Everybody Knows Your Name': Open Convictions and Closed Contexts in American Situation Comedy," *Because I Tell a Joke or Two: Comedy, Politics, and Social Difference*, ed. Stephen Wagg, 178–99. Taylor and Francis e-library, http://books.google.com /books?id=1m9qjn52ZZUC&pg=PA182&dq=%22Vic+and+Sade%22&hl=e n&ei=Q2YGTonKEfLYiAK92tDRDQ&sa=X&oi=book_result&ct=result& resnum=4&ved=0CEUQ6AEwAzgK#v=onepage&q=%22Vic%20and%20 Sade%22&f=false.

68   "same thing—vanilla": Wells, "Where Everybody," 182.

68   "powerful but prickly woman": JS, n.d.

68   "invention went into our pleasures": JS, "A Primer on the '30s," in *AA*, 21.

68   "into the hills": JS to Amasa Miller, February 6, 1931, box 2, folder 2, JS, Stanford.

68   "around the dinner table": Esther Rogers, interview by Benson.

69   "flaming with flowers": JS to George Albee, 1931, Albee Papers, Bancroft.

69   "darling little Airedale": JS to George Albee, 1931, Albee Papers, Bancroft.

69   "affectionate": ER to Ed Ricketts Jr., March 23, 1944, box 10, folder 8, ER Papers, Stanford.

69   dog to dominate: Amasa Miller, interview by Benson.

69   "ashamed to be seen with her": JS, *LL*, 46.

69   "ordinarily volatile disposition": JS to Amasa Miller, December 1931, box 2, folder 1, JS, Stanford.

70   "amusement quota for this month" . . . "luxurious ducks": JS, *LL*, 48–49.

70   "even of wind": JS to George Albee, 1931, Albee Papers, Bancroft.

70   "copulating with a Mexican woman": Dean Storey, interview by Benson.

70   amazing wit—if also caustic: Marjory Lloyd, interview, March 1990.

70   poke fun at friends: Marjory Lloyd, interview, August 1990.

71   "I see things that way": Helen Worden, "Mrs. John Steinbeck Fights for Her Man," *San Francisco Chronicle*, August 12, 1941.

71   "burlesque tone": JS, *LL*, 32.

71   "my own children": JS, *LL*, 35.

71   "living without her now": JS, *LL*, 28.

71   "loneliness and lostness": JS to Carl Wilhelmson, October 1, 1931, box 7, folder 7, JS, Stanford.

71   "of course": JS, *LL*, 38.

72   "we ride the clouds": JS, *LL*, 29.

72   group of artists: Edith Hamlin, interview by Loftis, author's collection.

72   "anti-feminist propaganda" . . . "extensive experience": JS to Amasa Miller, January 7, 1931, box 2, folder 1, JS, Stanford.

72   "hated to go to church": Harold Ingels, interview, April 2, 1989, and April 17, 1991. All quotations from Beth's manuscripts are from Harold Ingels's files, by permission. See also John Thompson, "The Mysterious Trunk," Secret History 12, *Coast Weekly*, 1990.

72   "kookie dry" wit: Idell Budd.

72   "caustic": Viola Franklin, interview, March 1990; November 11, 1990.

74   sue her older brother: Beth Ainsworth, interview by Benson.

74   "told him local tales": Glen Graves, interview by Benson.

74   would become "Johnny Bear": George Mors, interview by Benson.

74   "write this some time": JS, *Working Days*, 30.

74–75   John Taliaferro, e-mail, June 6, 2002, and Montana Memory Project, http://cdm16013.contentdm.oclc.org/cdm/compoundobject/collection /p267301coll2/id/208/rec/19.

75   "a little lazy": Evelyn Larson, interview, April 26, 1994.

76   "shameless magpie": JS, *LL*, 95.

76   "every place and from everybody": Richard Albee.

76   "cagey cribber": Qtd. in Harold Bloom, ed., *John Steinbeck: Bloom's Modern Critical Views* (Chelsea House, 2008), 62.

77   "broke up in hatred": JS to Amasa Miller, 1931, box 2, folder 1, JS, Stanford.

77   "write them like John did": Viola Franklin, interview.

77   "interested John very intensely": Frances Strong to Joel Hedgpeth, May 3, 1970, Ed Ricketts Jr. collection.

77   "creative matrix of life": Qtd. in Smith, "Mutualism," 37.

77   "a lot of fun": JS to Amasa Miller, January 7, 1931, box 2, folder 1, JS, Stanford.

78   "an early example of the leisure community": Qtd. in Starr, *Made in California*, 77.

78   "surprising place": *Carmel 1931*, author's collection. All quotations are taken from this unnumbered text.

79   "To Carmel" poem: CB archive.

80   "maybe they do" JS to Wilhelmson, June 16, 1931, Box 7, Folder 7, JS Stanford

80   "if she were": JS, *LL*, 37.

81   "things you don't put down": JS to Mary Dekker, July 20, 1946, Dekker archive.

81   "at least too little": Webster Street journal, February 4, 1931, author's collection.

81   "encourage unknown writers": Margaret Ringnalda to Clint Williams, June 5, 1989, author's collection.

81   "a perfect Pisces": Elaine Steinbeck, interview by Benson.

82   "army cot": JS to George Albee, 1931, Albee Papers, Bancroft.

82   "in each other's way": JS to George Albee, 1931, Albee Papers, Bancroft.

82   "quite pleased with": JS to George Albee, late 1931, Albee Papers, Bancroft.

82   "for that reason": Qtd. in Karman, *Robinson Jeffers*, 45.

82   "same emotions": JS, *LL*, 85.

83   "22 rifle, a little beauty": JS to George Albee, late 1931, Albee Papers, Bancroft.

83   "so much": *LVL*, CSS.

83   "she was unabashed by anything": Marjory Lloyd, interview, August 31, 1990.

CHAPTER FOUR | AT ED RICKETTS'S LAB

85   "fun is one of them": letter ms., December 22, 1942, box 10, ER Papers, Stanford.

85   "a genius for human relationships": Toni Jackson Volconi to Joel Hedgpeth, n.d., Ed Ricketts Jr. collection.

85   "a haven": Jean Ariss, interview.

85   including Carol: Virginia Scardigli, interview by Benson.

85   "took under his wing" . . . philosophical discussions: Jean Ariss, interview.

85   "feeling better": Rolf Bolin, interview by Benson.

85   "hand them glass of wine": Robert Cathcart, interview by Benson.

85   "fun and games, with music": Toni Jackson Volconi, interview.

86   "talk about when they're young" . . . "fetishes": Webster Street, "John Steinbeck: A Reminiscence," 37.

86   "own horizons had advanced": Nancy Ricketts, "Edward Flanders Ricketts," 11.

86   "thought of it that way": Frances Strong to Joel Hedgpeth, May 3, 1970, Ed Ricketts Jr. collection.

86   "an emergent": ER to Campbell, 1940, ER, *Renaissance Man*, 169.

86   "first love": Frances Strong, Ed Ricketts Jr. collection.

86   On Ricketts and Allee, see Kelly, "Ed Ricketts," 16, and Rodger, introduction to ER, *Breaking Through*, 4–5.

87   "Wave Shock": box 12, folder 3, ER Papers, Stanford.

87   "controlling environmental factors": ER, *Renaissance Man*, 240.

87   standard invertebrate texts: see Kelly, "Ed Ricketts," 16.

88   "efficacy in arthritis and asthma": ER, *Renaissance Man*, 5, 7.

88   "the signs of depletion are serious": ER, *Renaissance Man*, 35.

88   "Good long ones too": ER, *Renaissance Man*, 228.

88   "mind has no horizons": JS, "About Ed Ricketts," in *AA*, 188.

88   "complicated affair": JS to [] Hartog, June 3, 1948, Ed Ricketts Jr. collection.

88   "there are spurts":ER to Xenia Cage, August 1944, ER, *Renaissance Man*, 205.

88   "on graph paper": Carol Brown to Joel Hedgpeth, October 1971, Ed Ricketts Jr. collection.

89   "refutation of reason and of its possibilities": ER, *Renaissance Man*, 146.

89   "Black Marigolds" into his journal: Ricketts, Post Fire Notebook, Ed Ricketts Jr. collection.

89   "that is good": Virginia Scardigli, interview by Benson.

89   Mozart's Piano Concerto no. 20: Ed Ricketts Jr., interview.

89   "listening to music": ER to Xenia Cage, 1940, box 9, folder 15, ER Papers, Stanford.

89   "Beethoven's music" . . . "THE GREAT CONTINUITY": ER, "Notes from a 3 day pass," box 10, folder 36, ER Papers, Stanford.

89   "old sung music": ER to Gretchen Schoeninger Corazzo, February 23, 1939, box 9, folder 19, ER Papers, Stanford.

90   "mathematics of music" . . . "my books": JS to Merle Armitage, February 17, 1939, Small, Virginia.

90   "sounds, movements, background": Carlton Sheffield, interview, NSC.

90   "the notion of relation being significant": ER, *Breaking Through*, 86.

90   discuss books and writing: Carol Brown, interview by Benson.

90   "this during Prohibition": Carol Brown.

90   "nothing but selling": JS to Richard Albee, 1931, Steinbeck, Bancroft.

90   "father confessor": Carol Brown.

91   "more than hell": Crunden, *American Salons*, 4.

91   "interested in the Russian experiment": Marjory Lloyd, interview, March 1990.

92   "brought up": Burgess Meredith, interview by Benson.

92   "divine geometry": ER to Gilbert and Margaret Neiman, box 10, folder 1, ER Papers, Stanford.

92   "intensity and magnitude": Lannestock, "Vilhelm Moberg," 180–81.

92   "melodious, sympathetic": Beth Ainsworth, interview by Benson.

93   sorts of trouble: Nancy Ricketts, "Early Days: Nicknames and Such," ER, *Breaking Through*, 336.

93   "constantly witty": Frances Strong to Joel Hedgpeth, May 3, 1970, Ed Ricketts Jr. collection.

93   "little pieces of spontaneous wit": Frances Strong, interview by Benson.

93   "old fashioned giggles": Idell Budd.

93   "isn't a word for it": Toni Jackson Volconi, interview by Benson.

93   "furious cats demand": box 10, folder 10, ER Papers, Stanford.

93   false noses . . . plaster masks: Jackson, "The Introverts," ms., author's collection.

93   "outhouse and fell in": Ed Ricketts Jr., interview.

93   "death of some sow bugs": ER to Gwyn Conger, November 1941, "about Sunday or Monday 3rd or 4th," ER, *Renaissance Man*, 123.

94   "pretty good time": ER Papers, Stanford.

94   naked "for hours": ER to Evelyn Ott, July 31, 1938, box 10, folder 3, ER Papers, Stanford.

94   "rest and quiet": ER, Carmel notebook, Ed Ricketts Jr. collection.

94   first philosophical friend: Beth Ainsworth to Jackson Benson.

94   "Jon's regard": ER Papers, box 11, folder 9, ER Papers, Stanford.

94   "interest in truth": ER, Post Fire Notebook III, 72, Ed Ricketts Jr. collection.

178   "sparked one another": Frances Strong to Joel Hedgpeth, May 3, 1970, Ed Ricketts Jr. collection.

95   "third entity": Toni Jackson, interview by Benson.

95   "become lacking:" Sheffield, Steinbec, 205–06

95   "an integrated growth": box 11, folder 18, ER Papers, Stanford.

96   "fight the war:" Sheffield, Steinbeck, 201.

97   "jungle I guess": Carol Brown.

97   two rattlesnakes and about 200 white rats: JS, *LL*, 59.

97   "And he said 'nope'": Carol Brown.

98   "great giver . . . to the poor": Red Williams, interview, August 18, 1993.

98   "advertising purposes": Ted Durain, interview, 1990.

98   "I'll cut your throat": Ted Durain, interview, 1990.

98   "really high class joint": Ted Durain, interview, 1990.

99   "sometimes shows, occasionally jazz": Jean Ariss, interview, and Jake Stock, interview by Pearson.

99   "clients on the street": Carol Brown.

100   "still floating around": Carol Brown.

100   rare cheeses for parties: Ellwood Graham.

100   "foreskin of a whale": Ellwood Graham.

100   "balloon smuggler": Carol Brown.

100   name in lights: David Tollerton, interview by Benson.

100   "Carol's Place": Ed Ricketts Jr., interview.

101   "she says of that sort": ER, notebook, 1931, Ed Ricketts Jr. collection.

101   "superior type" . . . "devoted": Bruce and Jean Ariss, interview, March 3, 1994.

101   "spirit of the depths" . . . "and the world" . . . "destroy emotions": ER, Post Fire Notebook IV, 1939, Ed Ricketts Jr. collection.

102   "pathologically or more or less secretly": ER, Post Fire Notebook IV, 1939, Ed Ricketts Jr. collection.

102   "Ideas on Psychological Types": box 11, folder 22, ER Papers, Stanford.

103   "composing a life": See Bateson, *Composing a Life.*

104   written each other . . . sent her books: Idell Budd.

104   "straightforwardness about her": Larson and Larson, *Fire in the Mind,* 165–66.

104   "door squeak": Joseph Campbell.

104   seeing myself: Larsen and Larsen, *Fire in the Mind,* 167.

104   local butcher shop: Joseph Campbell, tape.

105   "whole thing in my mind": Larsens, 179

105   "above pity" Joseph Campbell, interview by Benson.

105   "endlessly of Knightly tales": Idell Budd.

105   "racial memories": Robert Cathcart, interview.

105   with Eckerman: Joseph Campbell, interview by Benson.

106   "so happy": Joseph Campbell interview by Winston Elstob

106   "happy, happy time": Joseph Campbell, interview by Robinson.

106   "our year of crazy beginnings": Campbell to ER, September 14, 1939, box 9, folder 17, ER Papers, Stanford.

106   "deep thing": "Notes from a Three Day Pass—GC and Deep Thing," box 10, folder 36, ER Papers, Stanford.

106   "was the mystical": Toni Jackson Volconi, interview.

106   generator of myth: Campbell, interview by Benson.

106   "the unconscious": JS to Wilbur Needham, April 4, 1934, Small, Virginia. The letter continues: "This volume which simply attempts to show some sense of how the unconscious impinges and in some cases crosses into the conscious, was immediately branded mystical. It had never occurred to the critic that all the devils in the world and all the mysticism and all the religious symbology in the world were children of the generalized unconscious."

106   "synthesis of Jung and Spengler": Campbell to ER, August 22, 1939, box 9, folder 17, ER Papers, Stanford.

107   "Jons *vade mecum*": ER to Lucille Elliot, February 8, 1937, box 9, folder 23, ER Papers, Stanford.

107   "unreal quality": JS to Bennett Cerf, March 22, 1938, Williams, Columbia.

107   Una Jeffers read *To a God Unknown:* CB archive.

107   "message of 'Roan Stallion'": Larsen and Larsen, *Fire in the Mind.*

108   "things which are": ER, "The Philosophy of 'Breaking Through,'" in ER, *Breaking Through,* 95.

108   "apperception of the whole": ER to Toni Jackson, February 4, 1948, Ed Ricketts Jr. collection.

108   ER, "A Spiritual Morphology of Poetry," in ER, *Breaking Through,* 106–18.

109   "is perfect to me": *Publishers' Weekly,* July 1935.

109   "should have the Nobel": JS to Powell, February 14, 1937, Powell Papers, Harvard.

109 "Tower beyond Tragedy": Danford, "Questionnaire" at end of "A Critical Survey of John Steinbeck."

109 "one thing is all things": ER to Jewell F. Stevens, March 26, 1942, box 10, folder 18, ER Papers, Stanford.

109 "cosmic world feeling": Campbell, Grampus journal, 1932.

109 "Golden Mean": Campbell, Grampus journal, 1932.

110 "feathers . . . all over the place": Anna Ricketts, March 25, 1984, audiotape, Ed Ricketts Jr. collection.

110 "too thick" . . . "knew no one" . . . "any subject": Idell Budd.

111 "'It is. It is, by God,' I said": Larsen and Larsen, *Fire in the Mind*, 183–85.

111 "mutual admiration society": Idell Budd.

112 "meant to have married": Larsen and Larsen, *Fire in the Mind*, 186.

112 "This is outside me" . . . "I'm in love with": Campbell, Grampus journal, 1932.

112 "harmony that I found here": Larsen and Larsen, *Fire in the Mind*, 192.

113 "perfectly marvelous friendship": Campbell, Grampus journal, 1932.

113 "point of a gun": Jack Calvin, interview by Benson.

113 "magnanimous and wise": Campbell, Grampus journal, June 27, 1932, 61–62.

113 "little bit on me": Qtd. in Al Goodman, "Scholar Recalls Friendship with Steinbeck: One of the Group in the Old Days of Depression-Era Cannery Row," *Monterey Peninsula Herald*, December 4, 1983, B:3.

114 "full of fun": Campbell.

114 "different as two people could be": Campbell.

114 "Carol has been jipped" . . . "high tragedy" . . . "John and Carol adventure": Campbell, Grampus journal, 1932, 64b.

115 "Worth remembering concepts": box 11, folder 34, ER Papers, Stanford.

115 "source of [my] enlightenment": Campbell to Ricketts, box 9, folder 17, ER Papers, Stanford.

115 "not quite a guru": Tamm, *Beyond the Outer Shores*, 17.

116 "thoughts are acts": box 11, folder 2, ER Papers, Stanford.

116 "problems facing us": box 11, folder 3, ER Papers, Stanford.

116 "become one unit": JS, "Discussion of Hybrid Form of Prose Writing," Williams, Columbia.

116 "interesting thing in the world": box 11, folder 23, ER Papers, Stanford.

117 hit by the car on Jean Ariss's birthday: Jean Ariss, interview.

117 "just remember me": ER, handwritten will, NSC.

117 "which was which": JS to Richie and Tal Lovejoy, May 27, 1948, Steinbeck, Bancroft.

117 "a valuable thing": JS to Mr. Hartog, May 24, 1948, author's collection.

CHAPTER FIVE | WAVE SHOCK, 1932–35

119   "I never knew anyone": JS to Carlton Sheffield, July 1940, box 5, folder 9, JS, Stanford.

119   "plenty" . . . "soft": JS, "Dear Adlai," in *AA*, 108.

120   "opposition to work against": JS to agents, n.d., Williams, Columbia.

120   "literary conscience": Tony Jackson to Joel Hedgpeth, n.d., Ed Ricketts Jr. collection.

120   "makes a writer": JS to Paul Adair, May 3, 1948, Small, Virginia.

120   burned seventy old stories: JS to George Albee, May 1932, Albee Papers, Bancroft.

120   "dying earth": Ledger, box 18, JS, Stanford.

122   "had a shell" . . . "show empathy": Marjory Lloyd, interview, March 1990.

122   "a cue from Carol": ER, *Renaissance Man*, 139.

122–27   "urge to clip and save": Carol Steinbeck's scrapbooks, CB archive.

125   "human frailities": Peter Stackpole interview, 1994.

127   "wrapped up in each other, happy": Carlton Sheffield, interview.

127   "forever and forever, amen": Carol Steinbeck's scrapbooks, CB archive.

128   "gasoline any more": JS, *LL*, 70.

128   John in bathtub: Richard Albee.

128   "trifle seasick": "Quake Terrors Told by Local Girl at Beach Home," *San Jose Mercury News* ("So Mrs. John Steinbeck, formerly Carol Henning. . . . Describes the earthquake in S CA a week ago as she felt it in her home in Laguna Beach") CB archive.

128   "static things are heartbreaking": "Noted Author Sees Hope in Roosevelt," Laguna Beach, CA, CB archive.

129   "irons them": JS, *LL*, 82–83.

129   "good discipline": JS, *LL*, 72.

129   "out of the boy's mind": JS, *LL*, 71.

129   "whirling like sparks out of bonfire": JS, *LL*, 80.

129   "huger" . . . "larger" . . . "worth it": JS to George Albee, 1933, Albee Papers, Bancroft.

130   "none of these memories": JS to Sheffield, *LL*, 75.

130   *"three were gathered together"* . . . "third person" . . . "and of life": JS, *LL*, 80.

130   "emotion which is I": LVL, CSS.

130   "Jody was the eyes": LVL, CSS.

131   "known and unknown": Cobb, *Ecology of Imagination*, 27–28.

131   "take their ghosts": LVL, CSS.

131   "Carol thought the story described her": Carol Brown, interview by Benson.

132   "was Tortilla Flat": Carol to Joel Hedgepath January 19, 1971, Ed Ricketts Jr. collection.

132   Danny was Sue's neighbor: Evelyn Larson, interview.

132   Hattie told Steinbeck *Tortilla Flat* stories: Bertha D. Hellem note to author, February 15, 1991.

132   "borrowing": Evelyn Larson, interview.

132   "remittance man": Carol to Joel Hedgpeth, January 19, 1971, Ed Ricketts Jr. collection.

133   cold as marbles: JS to George Albee, n.d., Albee Papers, Bancroft.

133   pink testicle warmer: Toni Jackson to Joel Hedgpeth, n.d., Ed Ricketts Jr. collection.

133   "A Slim Volume": CB archive.

133   "intrinsically flawed": Miller, "Making Love Modern," 764.

133   "the joke is staged": Miller, "Making Love Modern," 769.

134   "saving each issue": Mrs. Wilhelsom, interview by Benson.

137   "thought the poems were swell": On February 25, 1934, Steinbeck wrote to George Albee that "Carol's book of poems is getting popular and she is swamped with demands for copies" (JS, *LL*, 91).

138   because it's good: Worden, "Mrs. John Steinbeck Fights for Her Man."

138   "poems were published under": On January 5, 1934, the *Monterey Beacon* published four of Carol's poems; on January 26, four more; on February 2, a final poem.

138   "pumping out the words": JS to Hugh Miller, box 1, folder B2, NSC.

139   "com[ing] up to surface": JS, *LL*, 193.

139   "little security": JS, *LL*, 55, 56.

139   "more expensive market": LVL, CSS.

139   "golden age": Timmerman, *Dramatic Landscape*, 35.

139–40   "color of realities" . . . "endurance": LVL, CSS.

140   "something happens": LVL, CSS.

140   "same emotions": JS, *LL*, 85.

140   "think of Carol": JS, *LL*, 93–94.

140   "hunk of protoplasm": Caroline Decker, interview, 1989.

141   equality of humanity: Francis Whitaker, interview.

141   See Benson and Loftis, "John Steinbeck and Farm Labor Unionization."

141   "exception of the Ku Klux Klan": Pichardo, "Power Elite," 25.

141   "system for the unemployed": http://www.sfmuseum.org/hist1/sinclair.html.

142   "the opportunity to work": http://www.ssa.gov/history/epic.html.

142   "products of the depression": http://www.ssa.gov/history/epic.html.

143   "Overthrow Government": Loftis, *Witnesses to the Struggle*, 85.

143   "lead it": Steffens, *Letters*, 2:934.

144   "typical punk": Dan James, interview by Benson.

144 "when their eyes are opened": Steffens, *Letters*, 2:983.

144 "third degree": Porter Chafee, qtd. in letter from Anne Loftis to Jackson Benson, March 9, 1977, Loftis files.

145 "leaving out any conclusion": JS, *LL*, 98–99.

145 "about the vigilantes": Steffens to Sam Darcy, February 25, 1936, Steffens, *Letters*, 2:1015.

145 "rabies than babies": Jean Ariss, interview.

145 books are children: Marjory Lloyd, interview, August 31, 1990.

146 "never stopped": Peggy Coogin, interview, April 24, 1994.

146 "knowledgeable women": Margaret Ringnalda, letter to author.

146 "scared of them": Anna Merkel, qtd. in Detro, "Carol Steinbeck—the Woman Behind the Author," 6.

146 "true or wishful thinking": Carol Crow, interview, August 1995.

147 "Quit talking. Do it": Jean Ariss, interview.

CHAPTER SIX | "VIVA MEXICO"

148 "all our talk": JS, *LL*, 213.

148 "mind of its community": JS to Elizabeth Otis, October 2, 1932, box 2, folder 6, JS, Stanford.

149 "forgotten by all world planners": JS to George Albee, 1934, Albee Papers, Bancroft.

149 "banditry and backwardness": Berger, "Drink Between Friends," 16.

150 "cultural pilgrims": Delpar, *Enormous Vogue*, 15.

150 "vogue of things Mexican": Qtd. in Delpar, *Enormous Vogue*, 55.

150 "no doubts about the moral": Jackson, *Mexican Interlude*, 123.

150 "complete human being": www.insidemex.com/people/people/frances-paca-toor-and-mexican-folkways.

150–51 businessmen and politicians . . . "most spectacular highway in the world": Rippy, "Inter-American Highway," 287.

151–55 "Her logbook sparkles": Carol's Mexican logbook, CB archives.

152 "bothered much about Americans": Jackson, *Mexican Interlude*, 36.

153 "strange insects": Jackson, *Mexican Interlude*, 45

155 "bank to bank": Jackson, *Mexican Interlude*, 50.

155 "Neck of Death": Jackson, *Mexican Interlude*, 55.

155 fallen rocks: Jackson, *Mexican Interlude*, 64.

155 "rocks rolling down": JS to George Albee, 1935, Albee Papers, Bancroft.

156 thirteen days: Steinbeck to G. W. Hamilton, 1935, NSC.

156 "do our own cooking": CB archive.

156 "tear one another to pieces": CB archive.

156 "use your judgment": CB archive.

157   "She loves it": JS to George Albee, 1935, Albee Papers, Bancroft.

157   John didn't know Spanish until he took this trip: Carol Brown, interview by Benson.

157   "swell pastry shops": CB archive.

158   "giggle just around the corner": Carol to Albees, October 11, 1935, Albee Papers, Bancroft.

158   "Candy" and "Apple": Jackson, *Mexican Interlude*, 83.

158   "people who have lived there for years": Jackson, *Mexican Interlude*, 83.

158   "Calzada del Nino Perdido Sad?": Carol to Albees, October 11, 1935, Albee Papers, Bancroft.

159   "too much of our own company": JS to George Albee, 1935, Albee Papers, Bancroft.

159   "things all backwards": Jackson, *Mexican Interlude*, 89.

159   "embroidered belts and tablecloths": Jackson, *Mexican Interlude*, 91.

160   "companions did": Charlotte Jackson, interview by Benson.

161   "of course you are rich" . . . "always been": JS to George Albee, 1935, Albee Papers, Bancroft.

161   "tell the story of their lives" . . . "desirable condition": Jackson, *Mexican Interlude*, 192.

161   "asked a blessing on us": Jackson, *Mexican Interlude*, 196.

161   "among the Indians": JS to George Albee, Albee Papers, Bancroft.

163   "illogic there that I need": JS to Lovejoys, May 27, 1948, box 1, folder C3, NSC.

163   "how to be happy": JS to George Albee, 1932, Albee Papers, Bancroft.

CHAPTER SEVEN | CALIFORNIA IS A "BOMB RIGHT NOW
. . . HIGHLY EXPLOSIVE"

164   "highly explosive": JS to George Albee, fall 1936, Albee Papers, Bancroft.

164   "roots to routes": See Gilroy, *Black Atlantic*.

165   "over the heads of men": LVL, CSS.

165   "an energetic place": JS to George Albee, 1936, Albee Papers, Bancroft.

165   sun more than food: JS, *Working Days*, 124.

165   "lousy": JS to George Albee, 1935, Albee Papers, Bancroft.

165   "a little stuffy": Eddie Goulart, Los Gatos authors file, Los Gatos library.

165   "spiritually and commercially": Conaway, *Los Gatos*, 93.

166   "to have money": *Los Gatos Mail-News*, December 14, 1936, Los Gatos Library historical files.

166   "no recession here": *Los Gatos Mail-News*, December 1937, Los Gatos Library historical files.

166   "poverty-stricken parties": Frank Lloyd to mother and father, February 24, 1936, author's collection.

166 "Ella Winter, etc.": Marjory Lloyd to grandma, July 23, 1936, author's collection.

166 "horrible thing": LVL, CSS.

166 Evelyn in love with John: Jean Ariss, interview.

166 "among the rats and snakes": JS to Elizabeth Otis, n.d., Williams, Columbia.

167 "felt John did": Evelyn Ott to ER, August 7, 1938, box 10, folder 3, ER Papers, Stanford.

167 "with other women": ER, *Renaissance Man*, 78.

167 "held them against her": "Small notes, Misc file," n.d..

168 "a cute little house": JS to Elizabeth Otis, 1936, Williams, Columbia.

168 "Mexican things": Sara Bard Field, "Poet and Suffragist," 569.

168 "room I work in": JS, *LL*, 133.

168 "almost straight": LVL, CSS.

168 "nice little birds": "More a Mouse Than a Man, Steinbeck Faces Reporters," *New York World Telegram*, April 23, 1937, in Fensch, *Conversations*, 6–7.

169 "jazz let her forget herself": Jack Stock.

169 blues singer Ma Rainey: Sharon Brown Bacon, interview.

169 "can't afford that": JS to F. B. Adams Jr., January 27, 1937, Morgan.

169 "away from people": Danford, "Critical Survey," 6.

169 "no casuals": JS, *LL*, 131.

169 "Everyone does": JS to Edward Weston, n.d., NSC.

170 "cost of 'temperament'": JS to F. B. Adams Jr., January 27, 1937, Morgan.

170 "grandmother of the sentimental novel": *Time*, January 28, 1966.

170 "good taste": DeMott, *Steinbeck's Reading*, 85.

170 "Kathleen Norris does": JS to Carl Wilhelmson, December 2, 1936, JS, Stanford.

170 "unerringly 'comfortable' and 'bright'": *San Francisco Chronicle*, March 7, 1933, n.p.

171 "Christian Science Sunday school in town": John Baggerly, interview. See also Joan Barriga, "Ruth Comfort Mitchell: A View from the Window," paper, February 1989, Los Gatos Library files, and Stella Haverland, "Ruth Comfort Mitchell," Ruth Comfort Mitchell Papers, California History Room, Martin Luther King Jr. Library, SJSU.

171 the "other side of the story" of California migrants: *Los Gatos Mail-News*, March 22, 1940.

171 "Los Gatos wild cat to a literary lion": Ruth Comfort Mitchell to JS, book in Eleventh Street cottage, Pacific Grove.

172 "like a child, and his wife too": Sara Bard Field, "Poet and Suffragist," 567.

173 "reflect an inner glow": Loftis, "Celestial Gatherings," 6.

173 "the merriest of men": Bingham and Barnes, *Wood Works*, 265.

173 "splendid head": "Southern Writer Tells of Visit to 'The Cats,' Here," *Los Gatos Mail-News and Saratoga Star*, January 21, 1937.

173   "the father of the gods": Loftis, "Celestial Gatherings," 6.

173   "beautiful works of art": Steffens to C.E.S Wood, February 13, 1929, Steffens, *Letters*, 2:828.

174   "feel it very badly": Sara Bard Fields, "Poet and Suffragist," 569.

174   "English and French revolutions": *Los Gatos/Saratoga Star*, May 20, 1937.

175   "I try to drink to excess": Qtd. in Danford, "Critical Survey," 2.

175   "forcefully . . . without any hesitancy": Marinacci, *"The Grapes of Wrath,"* 7.

175   "bulging muscles": Marinacci, *"The Grapes of Wrath,"* 6.

175   "for the back hurt": JS, *Working Days*, 78.

175   "monstrous than I have been": Marinacci, *"The Grapes of Wrath,"* 6.

175   "two thirds done": *LVL*, CSS.

176   "humanity for John": Richard Albee, February 23, 1975.

176   "It was 'Swamper'": Virginia Scardigli, interview.

176   "household name": Press books for *Of Mice and Men* and *The Grapes of Wrath*, CSS.

176   "hasn't the content": JS to Robert Ballou, January 25, 1937, Small, Virginia.

177   nativists in the state: Ngai, *Impossible Subjects*, 109.

177   "over 400,000": Ngai, *Impossible Subjects*, 136.

177   "not a popular thesis in CA": JS to Pare Lorentz, April 23, 1938, Morgan.

178   "security symbol": JS script for 1939 radio interview, Jackson Papers, Bancroft.

178   "Who Are the Associated Farmers?": Simon Lubin Society publication, author's collection.

178   "largest farmer in CA": JS to Pare Lorentz, April 23, 1938, Morgan.

178   "Marxism in the 1930s—as so many were": Qtd. in Loftis, *Witnesses to the Struggle*, 74.

179   "San Joaquin Valley": McWilliams, *"A Man, a Place and a Time."* 8. See also Rose C. Field, "Behind 'The Grapes of Wrath'" 'Factories in the Field,' by Carey McWilliams, Is a Forceful and Admirable Complement to John Steinbeck's Novel," *New York Times Book Review*, July 30, 1939, 4, 18.

179   on coming "war": JS to George Albee, late fall 1936, Albee Papers, Bancroft.

179   "bloody fight": JS to Pare Lorentz, n.d., Morgan.

179   "better than the one we have had before": JS script for 1939 radio interview, Jackson Papers, Bancroft.

179   "deepest interest . . . personal": Carol Brown, interview by Benson.

179   "imminent social change": JS to Hadley, Los Gatos, n.d., author's collection.

180   "understanding of social relationships": Frank Lloyd, interview by Benson.

180   "frantic with material": JS radio interview, 1938.

181   "time and a bed": "Tom Collins," in *AA*, 215.

181   "little triumphs": "Tom Collins," in *AA*, 216.

181   "slept for two weeks": JS to Pare Lorentz, n.d., Morgan.

181   "here at Kern": Tom Collins reports, CSS.

182   "tear gas, clubs and firearms": For all information on the Salinas Lettuce Strike, see Lamb, "Industrial Relations."

182   "labor program": Lamb, "Industrial Relations," 3.

182   "hotel floor in the center of town": Qtd. in Starr, *Endangered Dreams*, 187–88.

182   "Salinas papers of the time": JS, "Always Something to Do in Salinas," in *AA*, 11.

183   "the smoldering": JS, *LL*, 132.

183   "limits of our understanding": Caruth, Trauma, 4

183   "very fine experiences of a life": JS to TC, author's collection.

183   "some good and no harm": JS to TC, author's collection.

183   never seen him feel so deeply: Robert Cathcart, interview by Benson.

184   "fine picture of a migrant": JS to TC, author's collection.

184   "radio to Arvin": Thomsen, "Eric H. Thomsen," *Steinbeck Newsletter*, Summer 1990.

184   "furnish speakers": JS to TC, author's collection.

184   "said 'sure' most casual, nothing on paper": Helen Hosmer, interview by Benson.

184   "kick through the migrant picture": JS to TC, author's collection.

185   "new personal library": Jean Ariss, interview.

185   one of our long confabs: ER to Thayer and Evelyn Ricketts, February 8, 1937, box 10, folder 11, ER Papers, Stanford.

185   "lived entirely for the book": Thomsen, "Eric H. Thomsen," 3.

185   "come flooding in like water": JS, Wayward Bus Ledger, Morgan.

185   "edit Collins's stunning reports": Copies of the Tom Collins reports are at the Center for Steinbeck Studies.

188   "apparently unselected scenes": Howarth, "Mother of Literature," 55.

188   "publisher for these reports": Annie Laurie Williams to JS, January 9, 1937, Williams, Columbia.

188   "in shape for publication": Annie Laurie Williams to JS, July 5, 1938, Williams, Columbia.

188   "break even": Pat Covici to JS, n.d., Viking files.

189   "decided to write a book": "Estate on the Summit," Los Gatos Library files.

189   "four pound book": Annie Laurie Williams to JS, January 9, 1937, Williams, Columbia.

189   "these newspaper stories": Sara Bard Field, "Poet and Suffragist," 568.

189   "terrifies me": Annie Laurie Williams, December 2, 1936, Williams, Columbia.

189   "big book": JS to Elizabeth Otis, December 15, 1936, Williams, Columbia.

189   "scares me to death": JS to Elizabeth Otis, January 15, 1937, box 2, folder 7, JS, Stanford.

189   "What a wet winter": JS to Lawrence Clark Powell, February 14, 1937, Powell Papers, Harvard.

189   "system in which we work": JS to Annie Laurie Williams, July 9, 1937, Williams, Columbia.

190   "taking about *Of Mice and Men*": Annie Laurie Williams to JS, March 10, 1937, Williams, Columbia. See also John Barry, "Ways of the World: Triumph for the San Francisco Theater Union: First Night of a Play by John Steinbeck, a Notable Achievement Founded on His Novel 'Of Mice and Men,'" Monday, May 1937, CSS.

190   "provincial rabbits": JS, *LL*, 134.

190   "left them to be initialed": n.d., Jackson Papers, Bancroft.

190   "touch a boat": Mavis McIntosh, interview by Benson.

191   something else to do" . . . "trying to write then": Mavis McIntosh, interview by Benson.

191   "talk to us any more": JS to Esther and Beth, JS, Stanford.

191   "sitting alone and lonesome": JS, "Conversation with Bo Beskow," 3.

191   "now it's you": "Notes from meeting with Bo Beskow, May 23, 1981," by Donald Coers, author's collection.

191   "paint his anger": JS, "Conversation with Bo Beskow," 3.

191   "horrified guards looked on": Don Coers, interview, 1991.

191   "straight from the heart": "Of Wives and Men," Don Coers collection.

192   "aims that can be realized": Steffens, *Letters*, 2:1003.

193   "sports is insane": JS to Cecil McKiddy, May 3, 1937, NSC.

193   "no false conclusions": Stojko and Serhiychuk, "John Steinbeck," 71.

193   "all the way to New York": JS to Beskow.

193   "there is more time": *Buffalo Times*, September 3, 1937, CB archive.

194   "without stopping": JS to Annie Laurie Williams, September 14, 1937, Williams, Columbia.

194   "I enjoy it a lot": JS to Lawrence Clark Powell, 1937, n.d., Powell Papers, Harvard.

194   "as busy as a rabbit on a skillet": JS to Lawrence Clark Powell, n.d., Los Gatos, 1938, Powell Papers, Harvard.

195   Steinbecks' hi-fi: David Tollerton, interview by Benson.

195   "worst thing she ever saw": JS to Joseph Henry Jackson, January 1938, Jackson Papers, Bancroft.

195   "seeing what I saw, too": May Cameron, *New York Post*, n.d., CB archive.

196   "any of the sights": Mavis McIntosh to JS, January 21, 1938, Small, Virginia.

196   "comfortable meeting": Pare Lorentz, *FDR's Moviemaker*, 108

196   "land workers all lost": Pare Lorentz to JS, n.d., Morgan.

196   "happy boys working in Pittsburgh": Pare Lorentz to JS, March 1, 1938, Morgan.

197   "I don't feel that way about anyone else": JS to Pare Lorentz, May 24, 1938, Morgan.

197 "white rage": Fred R. Soule, Regional Information Officer, San Francisco, to John Fischer, Acting Director, Division of Information, Farm Security Administration, Washington DC, February 28, 1938, Morgan.

197 "make me furious": JS to F. R. Soule, February 24, 1938, Morgan.

197 "no information gets out at all": JS to Pare Lorentz, March 22, 1938, Morgan.

198 "set up is here is valuable": JS to Lorentz, April 24, 1938, Morgan.

198 "employers viewpoint and tries to be funny": JS to Pare Lorentz, April 1938, Morgan.

198 "critical insight": JS to Annie Laurie Williams, April 20, 1938, Williams, Columbia.

198 "hasn't any intention of being literature": JS to Elizabeth Otis, May 1938, box 9, folder 2, JS, Stanford.

199 "some force": JS to Pare Lorentz, May 1938, Morgan.

199 "three-thirty people": JS to Pare Lorentz, n.d. (May 1938), Morgan.

199 interchapters "biblical": Robert Cathcart, interview by Benson.

200 *Ecce Homo:* Joseph Henry Jackson, interview by Benson.

200 "Stay with the detail": JS, *Working Days*, 39.

201 "over and over a thousand times": Elaine Steinbeck to Carol Brown.

201 "I think is swell": JS to Elizabeth Otis, September 6, 1938, box 9, folder 2, JS, Stanford.

201 "It's been hard enough work": JS to Lorentz, October 17, 1938, Morgan.

201 "I call deep real love": Ed Ricketts to Evelyn Ott, June 30, 1938, box 10, folder 3, ER Papers, Stanford.

201 "they were comfortable": Jean Ariss, interview.

CHAPTER EIGHT | ENTER GWEN CONGER

202 "judge it at all": Carol to Elizabeth Otis, September 1938, Viking files.

202 "Gad, it is swell" . . . "dealing with the Joads": Carol to Pat Covici, December 12, 1938, Viking files.

203 "like unburying the dead": JS to Pat Covici, January 31, 1939, Viking files.

203 "stopped the reader's mind": JS to Pat Covici, 1939, n.d., Viking files.

203 five of "shit": "Changes in The Grapes of Wrath," Viking files.

203 "proofreader . . . at any time": Pat Covici to JS, February 1, 1939, Viking files.

203 "unparalled [sic] in publishing history": Pat Covici to JS, February 14, 1939, Viking files.

203 dedication copy bound in leather: Pat Covici to JS, May 25, 1939, Viking files.

203 John called it a symphony: JS to Merle Armitage, February 17, 1939, Small, Virginia.

203 "Disconnect everything": Frank Rineri, interview by Pearson.

204 "as if it were out of heaven": Sara Bard Field, "Poet and Suffragist," 569–70.

204   cars, dogs, objects: Mrs. Carl Wilhelmson, interview by Benson.

204   "frankly superstitious about": Roger Condon, interview by Benson.

204   "witches Sabbath" . . . "earth birth": Richard Albee.

204   "Thoreau of the dog world, I guess": JS, *LL*, 184.

204   Toby float by: Mrs. J. H. Jackson, interview by Benson.

204   "It's nice": JS, *LL*, 189.

205   "lean times that are surely coming": JS, *LL*, 182.

205   "to spread it around": JS to Maryon Sheffield, July 14, 1961, box 5, folder 16, JS, Stanford.

205   cashmere coats . . . signs they had made it: Peggy Coogin, interview.

205   "thing of horror": JS, *LL*, 183.

206   "grew away from her": Sara Bard Field, "Poet and Suffragist," 453.

206   "fifty to seventy-five letters day": JS, *LL*, 185.

206   "more of the play": *San Francisco Chronicle*, May 4, 1939, "Mrs. Steinbeck Enjoys Her Husband's Play," CB archive.

206   "were just awful": Polly Teas, interview by Benson.

206   "sure of himself after Grapes": Marjory Lloyd, interview.

206   "pushed beyond endurance": JS, *LL*, 185.

206   "hysteria about the book": JS, *LL*, 188.

207   "Steinbeck Migrant Organization": Pat Covici to JS, May 25, 1939, Viking files.

207   McWilliams, Bancroft Debate *Grapes* at Commonwealth Club: See "Farm Life of Nation Eyes Stockton: Associated Farmers' Convention Program Holds Wide Interest," *Stockton Record,* December 6, 1939, 1, 17.

207   "life" and "land": Gertrude Atherton, clipping, CB archive.

207   "other side of the story": See Shillinglaw, "California Answers the Grapes of Wrath," in Heavilin, *Critical Response*, 183–99.

207   "otherwise read the book": *Los Gatos Mail-News,* June 30, 1939.

207   "under the profit system": *Stockton Record,* December 6, 1939.

207   "Plums of Plenty": Schamberger, *Steinbeck and the Migrants,* 64–65.

208   "forgot who her friends were": Louis Paul, interview by Benson.

208   "painted it a shocking pink": Helen Hosmer, interview by Benson.

208   "tried to irritate one another": Robert Cathcart, interview by Benson.

208   "call attention to herself": Pare Lorentz, interview.

209   "she doesn't drink well": Martin Ray, qtd. in Barbara Marinacci, "*The Grapes of Wrath.*"

209   "hysterical and pulled out": JS to Elizabeth Otis, August 20, 1939, JS, Stanford.

209   "edge of insanity": JS to Elizabeth Otis, August 28, 1939, JS, Stanford.

210   "man of anything else": JS to Toby Street, 1939, author's collection.

211   "Peg in the Little Black Cart": Mrs. Hewitt, interview by Benson

211 "sex appeal": Charlotte Jackson, interview by Benson.

211 "the aphrodisiac": Burgess Meredith, interview by Benson.

211 "was pure chemistry": Gwen Steinbeck, qtd. in Halladay, "Closest Witness," 2.

211 "something he needed": Halladay, "Closest Witness," 37–38.

211 "he had a hard time finding one": Ellwood Graham, interview by Benson.

211 "soft, agreeable": Dan James, interview by Benson.

211 "confidence and his masculinity": Milestone, interview by Benson.

212 "anything to earn a buck": Halladay, "Closest Witness," 33, 34.

212 "I guess I am": Gwen Steinbeck, qtd. in Halladay, "Closest Witness," 3.

212 "combination of goddess and muse": DeMott, "After *The Grapes of Wrath*," 25.

213 "broke out of the box": Lynn Loesser, interview by Benson.

213 "play time for John and Gwyn": Sandy Oliver, interview by Benson.

213–14 San Francisco exposition: http://www.sfmuseum.org/hist1.

214 "run around like a bug": JS to Esther, September 17, 1939, S-A, Stanford.

214 "Another bestseller for John": Gwen to ER, October 11, 1939, ER Papers, Stanford.

215 One found her "shallow": Ellwood Graham, interview.

215 another "hard": Charlotte Jackson, interview by Benson.

CHAPTER NINE | ON THE SEA OF CORTEZ

217 "happiest time of my entire life": Viola Franklin, interview.

217 "slept in separate rooms": Tony Berry, interview, August 25, 1994.

217 "kind of hallucination": JS, *LSOC*, 68.

217 "could have done it": JS, *LL*, 201–2.

218 "seventy five percent well behaved": Tony Berry, interview.

218 "*Sea of Cortez* was his favorite": Elaine Steinbeck, interview, November 6, 1998.

218 "the best of Steinbeck is in it": book dust jacket.

218 "a jon/Ed sit by the fire": ER to Toni Jackson, February 11, 1942, box 10, folder 17, ER Papers, Stanford.

218 "minus tide of unusual depth": Carol to Joel Hedgpeth, n.d., Ed Ricketts Jr. collection.

218 "of being consistent": Sheffield, "Steinbeck," 230.

219 "variable species": JS to Joe Hamilton, October 23, 1939, box 2, folder 70, Wells Fargo, Stanford.

220 "great 'modern Odyssey'": ER, Post Fire Notebook III (Thurs Sept 28, 1939. First part of 1940 MX trip), Ed Ricketts Jr. collection.

220 "for their own ends": JS, *Working Days*, 108.

220 "new basic picture": JS, *LL*, 193.

220   "discipline in this book": JS, *Working Days*, 110.

221   "love of his life": Toni Jackson Volconi, interview by Benson.

221   "affects my morale": ER, Post Fire Notebook V, Ed Ricketts Jr. collection.

221   "reference to the Jean-Ed relation": Post Fire Notebook V, October 5, 1939, Ed Ricketts Jr. collection.

221   "all my life up to that point": ER, *Renaissance Man*, 54.

221   "starting new life": Post Fire Notebook II, Ed Ricketts Jr. collection.

222   "We were curious": JS, *LSOC*, 1.

222   "vow of chastity": JS, *LSOC*, 9.

222   rained constantly: JS to Pat Covici, February 29, 1940, Ransom.

223   "ceased to exist": JS, *LSOC*, 25.

223   "seeing us off": JS, *LSOC*, 25.

223   "a little sentimental": JS, *LSOC*, 26.

223   "sick until well into the night": ER, "Verbatim Transcription," ER, *Breaking Through*, 136.

223   "genuinely worth doing": JS to Pat Covici, December 2, 1940, Williams, Columbia.

223   "Hard things beginnings—very hard": JS, *Working Days*, 125.

224   "the environmental factors": Jimmy Costello, "Steinbeck, Ricketts Embark on Cruise," *Monterey Herald*, March 1940.

224   "get along together": "Steinbeck to Pry into Sea's Social Life," *Monterey Peninsula Herald*, March 11, 1940.

224   about human cooperation: "cooperation which in tidepool animals is perhaps as important as the competition, the struggle for existence, about which we've been hearing nothing else since Darwin was popularly misinterpreted"; ER to Arie and Lockie, May 20, 1944, box 10, folder 21, ER Papers, Stanford.

224   "insistence on material values": "Verbatim Transcription," in ER, *Breaking Through*, 161.

225   "from a writing standpoint": Tony Volconi to Joel Hedgpeth, n.d., Ed Ricketts Jr. collection.

225   "an adventure of the mind": JS to Pat Covici, April 18, 1941, Williams, Columbia.

225   discussed the Old Man and the Sea": JS, *LSOC*, 27.

225   "paper reported in 1938": *Monterey Peninsula Herald*, October 21, 1938.

225   "foundation of the whole unconscious": JS, *LSOC*, 28.

226   "failing to reach home": JS, *LSOC*, 59.

226   "pour their force": JS, *LSOC*, 145.

226   "sound symbols of wild doves": JS, *LSOC*, 152.

226   "world against itself": JS, *LSOC*, 150–51.

226   "2160 individuals of two species of beer": JS, *LSOC*, 139.

226   "over-indulgence": JS, *LSOC*, 163.

226 "a strengthener of muscle and spirit": JS, *LSOC*, 163.

227 "Carol hit the ceiling": Tony Berry, interview by Benson.

227 embarrassed John: Tiny Colletto, interview by Benson.

227 cook on the trip to the Sea of Cortez: Enea and Lynch, *With Steinbeck in the Sea of Cortez*, 18.

227 "'assigned' role was as 'ship's cook'": "Steinbeck to Pry . . . ," *Monterey Peninsula Herald*, Marcy 11, 1940.

227 "we would all help": JS, *LSOC*, 69.

227 good sailor . . . help around the boat: Tony Berry, interview by Benson.

228 "justice-loving people": CB archive.

228 "moment on the rocks, even at night": JS, *LSOC*, 52.

228 "go into the tubes": JS, *LSOC*, 67.

228 "Latin names of many animals": Tiny Colleto, interview by Benson.

228 "apparently Enteropneusta": ER, *Breaking Through*, 165.

228 "and at Angeles Bay": "Verbatim Transcription," in ER, *Breaking Through*, 185.

228 "several swimming crabs": "Verbatim Transcription," in ER, *Breaking Through*, 172]

229 "magic-carpet sound to the name": JS, *LSOC*, 85.

229 "everywhere to guide you" . . . "two or three-day stay here": "Verbatim Transcription," in ER, *Breaking Through*, 146, 150–51.

229 "chants like madrigals": "Verbatim Transcription," in ER, *Breaking Through*, 150.

229 "as long as we survive": JS, *LSOC*, 145.

230 "didn't care who saw him naked": Tex Travis, interview by Benson.

230 "no enemies on board" . . . "carry a conversation" . . . had binoculars": Tony Berry, interview.

231 "bathe, and that disconcerted the crew": Tony Berry, interview by Benson.

231 "could make love to everybody": Tony Berry, interview.

231 "up on the mountain": "Verbatim Transcription," in ER, *Breaking Through*, 155.

231 "drinking got done": "Verbatim Transcription," in ER, *Breaking Through*, 156.

231 "had a 'yen' for Ricketts": Tony Berry, interview.

231 "quite correct": ER to Toni Jackson, box 10, folder 17, ER Papers, Stanford.

231 "everyone got smashed": Tony Berry, interview.

231 "Jon followed later on": "Verbatim Transcription," in ER, *Breaking Through*, 172; and account of time in Guaymas.

232 "a nice spring dress on, a straw hat": Tony Berry, interview.

232 "No pictures, no pictures": Fred Strong, December 24, 1983, Ed Ricketts Jr. collection.

233 "built it carefully": ER to Campbell, 1941, ER, *Renaissance Man*, 135.

233 "called the book a 'cioppino'": *San Francisco Chronicle*, December 14, 1941; *This World* magazine, 26; McElrath, Crisler, and Shillinglaw, John Steinbeck: The Contemporary Reviews, 207.

233   "light enough to be lifted": JS, *LSOC*, 77.

233   "let the book fall as it may": JS, *LSOC*, 58.

233   "like our life": JS, *LSOC*, 223.

233   "their own species": JS, *LSOC*, 78–79.

233   "grows soft and fearful": JS, *LSOC*, 79

233   "infinite smugness": JS, *LSOC*, 85.

234   "follow the belief": JS, *LSOC*, 151.

234   "extenuated, it just 'is'": JS, *LSOC*, 12.

234   "can't stand it": ER to Toni Jackson, February 25, 1941, box 10, folder 15, ER Papers, Stanford.

234   "unpublished [essays] of mine": ER to Joel Hedgpeth, November 18, 1941, ER, *Renaissance Man*, 131.

234   "follow it down to the fourth": JS to Pat Covici, July 4, 1941, Williams, Columbia.

235   "of like mind": Toni Jackson Volconi, interview by Benson.

235   "in the painting": Ellwood Graham, interview.

235   "But so very fine": ER to Virginia Scardigli, n.d., box 10, folder 15, ER Papers, Stanford.

236   "criticisms and abjectness": ER, *Renaissance Man*, 77–78.

CHAPTER TEN | LIFE IN FRAGMENTS

237   spent that year on overdrive: JS, *Working Days*, 123.

237   "work to be done in the future": JS to Pat Covici, June 9, 1941, Ransom.

238   "lone and lost": JS, *Working Days*, 121.

238   "messy life": Benson, *True Adventures*, 467.

238   "little yellow leaf": Benson, *True Adventures*, 463.

238   school of hard knocks: ER to Herb Kline, August 17, 1940, box 9, folder 33, ER Papers, Stanford.

238   "Carol had been a sweet girl too": Halladay, "Closest Witness," 57.

238   "and [hers] alone": JS to Mavis McIntosh, April 16, 1941, Small, Virginia.

239   "neither of them was": Mavis McIntosh to Mr. Flemming, March 27, 1974, Small, Virginia.

239   "her heart was broken": Sara Bard Field, "Poet and Suffragist," 570.

239   "I won't let this happen": Halladay, "Closest Witness." 47-8

240   "vindictiveness": JS to Elizabeth Otis, July 13, 1941, box 9, folder 5, JS, Stanford.

241   "do a thing like this": JS to Mavis McIntosh, n.d., Small, Virginia.

241   "they help a lot": JS to Elizabeth Otis, June 24, 1941, box 9, folder 5, JS, Stanford.

242   "Salinas is having a field day": JS to Esther Rodgers, November 21, 1941, box 2, folder 74, Wells Fargo, Stanford.

242   "little off her head": ER, *Renaissance Man*, 130.

243   "imprinted in his face": Gwen to Toby Street, February 14, 1942, box 7, folder 44, JS, Stanford.

243   "eyes for me" . . . "shitheel": Gwen to Toby Street, February 24, 1942, box 7, folder 44, JS, Stanford.

244   "as if she were out of jail": Viola Franklin, interview.

244   "in the clay, till midnight": Worden, "Mrs. John Steinbeck Fights for Her Man."

245   "talked rough with service people": Peggy Coogin, interview.

245   "son of a bitch": Ted Durain, interview.

245   "get a hold of yourself": Viola Franklin, interview.

246   "in order to belong": Viola Franklin to Bill Brown, June 15, 1984, CB archive.

246   "drank like a fish": Evelyn Larson, interview.

246   "crow at all, all night long": Evelyn Larson, interview.

246   "hotel with old liver lips": Viola Franklin, interview.

247   "physical pain and suffering": Steinbeck divorce decree, NSC.

247   "wouldn't discuss it": Viola Franklin to Bill Brown, June 2, 1984, CB archive.

247   "high mountains and things like that": JS to Toby Street May 12, 1942, box 7, folder 44, JS, Stanford.

247   "a bit power driven": ER, *Renaissance Man*, 139.

248   "a very good nurse": ER to Cohees, May 22, 1945, box 9, folder 19, ER Papers, Stanford.

248   "giving blood when she could": Viola Franklin, interview.

248   "probably wanted to run the fort": Jerry Hastings, interview, July 24, 1990.

249   "modeling implements": CB archive.

249   "go get my bird hat": Jerry Hastings, interview.

249   "kind of prissy": Evelyn Larson, interview.

249   "Loren was 'a fake'": Evelyn Larson, interview.

249   "vain and dull": Jerry Hastings, interview.

250   "a circus": Jerry Hastings, interview.

250   "absolutely fascinated": Jerry Hastings, interview.

250   "little round almond growers": Jerry Hastings, interview.

250   "Tristan and Isolda": Viola Franklin, interview.

250   owl story: Viola Franklin, interview.

251–52   "Carol than any body" . . . through the war: Jerry Hastings, interview.

252   "kids out of the yard, no end": Carol Howard to Jerry Hastings, author's collection.

254   "wheter [sic] charges would be pressed": CB archive.

255   "driving through the bear country": *Carmel Pine Cone*, August 9, 1946, CB archive.

256   "I've tried for years": JS to Mary Dekker, August 26, 1948, Dekker archive.

256   seen a "good deal" of Carol: JS to George Albee, December 19, 1950, Albee Papers, Bancroft.

256   "either terrible or sad": JS, Wayward Bus notebook, Morgan.

CODA

257   "good marriage" . . . "gregarious and outgoing": Fred Farr, interview, April 11, 1994.

257   "good name": Peggy Coogin, interview.

257   "encyclopedia of sports information": "William Beresford Brown," CB archive.

257   "in a motherly way" . . . "quite a gal": Peggy Coogin, interview.

257   "memory treasure": JS to Mary Dekker, November 29, 1944, Dekker archive.

258   "with her home": "Fun with Food," *Monterey Peninsula Herald*, December 27, 1953.

258   "read them all" . . . "fix my P": Peggy Coogin, interview.

258   "was the boss" . . . "horrible fights": Peggy Coogin, interview.

258   "don't know what you're talking about": Sharon Brown Bacon, interview.

258   "always in the background": Peggy Coogin, interview.

258   "never forgave him": Peggy Coogin, interview.

259   "anything to do with you": Evelyn Larson, interview.

259   "what they should be": Jean Ariss, interview.

259   "make his goddamn head larger": Carol Crow, interview.

260   "You old fucker you. That meant she liked it": Fred Farr, interview.

260   "so many varied people in her life": Peggy Coogin, interview.

260   "Poltergeist": CB archive.

261   "I hope so": JS to Mary Dekker, September 12, 1958, Dekker archive.

Selected Bibliography

Albee, George. George Sumner Albee papers: BANC MSS C-H 120. Bancroft Library, University of California, Berkeley.

Alpern, Sara, Joyce Antler, Elisabeth Israels Perry, and Ingrid Winther Scobie, eds. *The Challenge of Feminist Biography: Writing the Lives of Modern American Women.* Urbana: University of Illinois Press, 1992.

Arbuckle, Clyde. *Clyde Arbuckle's History of San Jose.* San Jose, CA: Smith and McKay, 1985.

Astro, Richard. *John Steinbeck and Edward F. Ricketts: The Shaping of a Novelist.* 1973. Reprint, Hemet, CA: Western Flyer Publishing, 2002.

Astro, Richard, and Tetsumaro Hayashi, eds. *Steinbeck: The Man and His Work.* Corvallis: Oregon State University Press, 1971.

Bateson, Mary Catherine. *Composing a Life.* New York: Penguin, 1990.

Beegel, Susan F., Susan Shillinglaw, and Wesley N. Tiffney, eds. *Steinbeck and the Environment: Interdisciplinary Approaches.* Tuscaloosa: University of Alabama Press, 1997.

Bennett, Melba Berry. *The Stone Mason of Tor House: The Life and Work of Robinson Jeffers.* Los Angeles: Ward Ritchie Press, 1966.

Bennett, Robert. *The Wrath of John Steinbeck: or, St. John Goes to Church.* Los Angeles: Albertson Press, 1939.

Benson, Jackson J. *The True Adventures of John Steinbeck, Writer.* New York: Viking, 1984.

———. *True Adventures of John Steinbeck, Writer* research materials, 1935–1980. Stanford: Department of Special Collections, Stanford University Libraries.

Benson, Jackson J., and Anne Loftis. "John Steinbeck and Farm Labor Unionization: The Background of *In Dubious Battle.*" *American Literature* 52 (1980): 194–223.

Berger, Dina. "A Drink Between Friends: Mexican and American Pleasure Seekers in 1940s Mexico City." In *Adventures into Mexico: American Tourism Beyond the Border,* edited by Nicholas Dagen Bloom, 16–29. Oxford: Rowman and Littlefield, 2006.

Bick, Sally. "Of Mice and Men: Copland, Hollywood, and American Musical Modernism." *American Music* 23 (2005): 426–72.

Bingham, Edwin, and Tim Barnes. *Wood Works: The Life and Writing of Charles Erskine Scott Wood*. Corvallis: Oregon State University Press, 1997.

Blew, Mary Clearman, Susanne George Bloomfield, Melody Graulich, and Judy Nolte Temple. "Writing Women's Biographies: Processes, Challenges, Rewards." *Western Literature* 43, no. 2 (Summer 2008): 179–203.

Boas, Nancy. *Society of Six: California Colorists*. Berkeley: University of California Press, 1988.

Bracher, Frederick. "Steinbeck and the Biological View of Man." *Pacific Spectator* 2, no. 1 (1948): 14–29.

Brown, Carol Henning. Archive, Martha Heasley Cox Center for Steinbeck Studies, San Jose State University.

California/Pacific Grove: On Monterey Bay. California History Room, Monterey Public Library, ca. 1920.

Campbell, Joseph. Grampus Journal, 1932.

Caruth, Cathy. *Trauma: Explorations in Memory*. Baltimore: Johns Hopkins University Press, 1995.

Caughey, John W., with Norris Hundley Jr. *California: History of a Remarkable State*. Englewood Cliffs, NJ: Prentice-Hall, 1982.

Cederstrom, Lorelei. "Beyond the Boundaries of Sexism: The Archetypal Feminine versus Anima Women in Steinbeck's Novels." In *Beyond Boundaries*, edited by Susan Shillinglaw and Kevin Hearle, 189–204. Tuscaloosa: University of Alabama Press, 2002.

———. "The Great Mother in *The Grapes of Wrath*." In *Steinbeck and the Environment*, edited by Susan F. Beegel, Susan Shillinglaw, and Wesley N. Tiffney Jr., 76–91. Tuscaloosa: University of Alabama Press, 1997.

Chaplin, Charles. *My Autobiography*. New York: Simon and Schuster, 1964.

Cobb, Edith. *The Ecology of Imagination in Childhood*. Putnam, CT: Spring Publications, 1977.

Coers, Donald V., Paul D. Ruffin, and Robert J. DeMott, eds. *After "The Grapes of Wrath": Essays on John Steinbeck in Honor of Tetsumaro Hayashi*. Athens: Ohio University Press, 1995.

Collins, Tom. Collins/JS correspondence. Author's collection.

———. Weekly reports from Arvin. California State Archives and Center for Steinbeck Studies, San Jose State University.

Combs, Virgil E. "The Joad Family in Kern County." With a foreword by Lee A. Stone, MD. Ms. Fresno County Free Library Reference Department. January 1940.

Conaway, Peggy. *Los Gatos*. Images of America. Charleston, SC: Arcadia, 2004.

Crunden, Robert M. *American Salons: Encounters with European Modernism, 1885–1917*. New York: Oxford University Press, 1993.

Cruz, Frank Eugene. "'In Between a Past and Future Town': Home, the Unhomely, and *The Grapes of Wrath*." *Steinbeck Review* 4, no. 2 (2007): 53–75.

Danford, Merle. "A Critical Survey of John Steinbeck: His Life and the Development of His Writings." Master's thesis, Ohio University, 1939.

Davison, Richard Allan. "*Of Mice and Men* and *McTeague*: Steinbeck, Fitzgerald, and Frank Norris." *Studies in American Fiction* 17 (1989): 219–26.

Dekker, Mary Steinbeck. Dekker/JS correspondence, Toni Heyler collection.

Delpar, Helen. *The Enormous Vogue of Things Mexican: Cultural Relations Between the United States and Mexico, 1920–1935*. Tuscaloosa: University of Alabama Press, 1992.

DeMott, Robert. "After *The Grapes of Wrath*: A Speculative Essay on John Steinbeck's Suite of Love Poems for Gwyn, 'The Girl of the Air.'" In *John Steinbeck: The Years of Greatness, 1936–1939*, edited by Tetsumaro Hayashi, 20–45. Tuscaloosa: University of Alabama Press, 1993.

——. Introduction to *To a God Unknown*. New York: Penguin, 1995.

——. *Steinbeck's Reading: A Catalogue of Books Owned and Borrowed*. New York: Garland, 1984.

De Roos, Robert. "Stanford Greats: Edith Mirrielees." *Stanford Observer*, October 1988: 21-23.

Detro, Gene. "Carol Steinbeck: Victor of a Dubious Battle." *Monterey Life*, January 1985, 83–87.

——. "Carol Steinbeck—the Woman Behind the Man." *Herald Weekend Magazine*, June 10, 1984, 3–6.

——. "Carol Steinbeck and the Round Table." *Herald Weekend Magazine*, July 31, 1988, 16, 18.

——. "The Truth about Steinbeck (Carol and John)." *Creative States Quarterly* 2 (1985): 12–13, 16.

Dickstein, Morris. *Dancing in the Dark: A Cultural History of the Great Depression*. New York: Norton, 2009.

Diepenbrock, David. "Florence Wycoff, Helen Hosmer, and San Francisco's Liberal Network in the 1930s." http://userwww.sfsu.edu/epf/journal_archive/volume_III,_no._2_-_sp._1994/diepenbrock_d.pdf.

Dourgarian, James. "Collecting John Steinbeck." *Firsts: The Book Collector's Magazine* 17, no. 1 (2007): 22–51.

Elstob, Winston. "The Meeting of 3 Minds." *Alta Vista Magazine*, July 1, 1990, 16–17.

Enea, Sparky, as told to Audry Lynch. *With Steinbeck in the Sea of Cortez*. Los Osos, CA: Sand River Press, 1991.

Fensch, Thomas, ed. *Conversations with John Steinbeck*. Jackson: University Press of Mississippi, 1988.

———. *Steinbeck and Covici: The Story of a Friendship.* Woodlands, TX: New Century Books, 1979.

Field, Sara Bard. "Poet and Suffragist." Interview by Amerlia R. Fry. Suffragists Oral History Project. Regional Oral History Office, Bancroft Library, University of California, Berkeley, 1969. http://texts.cdlib.org/view?docId=kt1p3001n1&doc .view=entire_text.

French, Warren. *A Companion to "The Grapes of Wrath."* New York: Viking/ Penguin, 1963.

Gilbert, Benjamin Franklin. *Pioneers for One Hundred Years: San Jose State College, 1857–1957.* San Jose State College, San Jose, CA, 1957.

Gilbert, Lauren Miranda, and Bob Johnson. *San Jose's Historic Downtown.* Images of America. Charleston, SC: Arcadia, 1995.

Gilroy, Paul. *The Black Atlantic: Modernity and Double Consciousness.* Cambridge: Harvard University Press, 1995.

Gladstein, Mimi Reisel. "Missing Women: The Inexplicable Disparity Between Women in Steinbeck's Life and Those in His Fiction." In *The Steinbeck Question: New Essays in Criticism,* edited by Donald Noble, 84–98. Troy, NY: Whitston, 1993.

Greathead, Estelle. *The Story of an Inspiring Past and Historical Sketch of the San Jose State Teachers College from 1862–1928.* Special Collections, San Jose State University.

Hadella, Charlotte. *"Of Mice and Men": A Kinship of Powerlessness.* New York: Twayne, 1995.

———. "Steinbeck's Cloistered Women." In *The Steinbeck Question: New Essays in Criticism,* edited by Donald Noble, 51–70. Troy, NY: Whitston, 1993.

Halladay, Terry Grant. "'The Closest Witness': The Autobiographical Reminiscences of Gwyndolyn Conger Steinbeck." Master's thesis, Stephen F. Austin State University, 1979.

Harrel, William. "The Banning of *The Grapes of Wrath* in Kern County." Kern County Historical Collection.

Hayashi, Tetsumaro, ed. *John Steinbeck: The Years of Greatness, 1936–1939.* Tuscaloosa: University of Alabama Press, 1993.

Heavilin, Barbara A. *The Critical Response to John Steinbeck's "The Grapes of Wrath."* Westport, CT: Greenwood Press, 2000.

Helfand, Jessica. *Scrapbooks: An American History.* New Haven, CT: Yale University Press, 2008.

Hennig, Calvin. *James Fitzgerald.* Rockland, ME: William A. Farnsworth Library and Art Museum, 1984.

Henning, Nellie, comp. "Carol's Book: Scenes and Memories," 1906 to 1951. Henning Archive, Center for Steinbeck Studies, San Jose State University.

Historic Monterey and Surroundings. California History Room, Monterey Public Library. Ca. 1910.

Holman, Zena. *My Monterey.* Monterey, CA: Lee Printing, 1973.

Hoover, Mildred Brooke, and H. E. and E. G. Rensch. Revised by Ruth Teiser. *Historic Spots in California.* Stanford, CA: Stanford University Press, 1948.

"Hopkins Marine Life Refuge and Pacific Grove Marine Life Station," May 13, 1937. WPA Report. Archives of Hopkins Marine Station of Stanford University.

Hovde, Carl F. "The Dag Hammarskjöld—John Steinbeck Correspondence." *Development Dialogue: The Journal of the Dag Hammarskjöld Foundation* 1 (1997): 97–129.

Howarth, William. "The Mother of Literature: Journalism and *The Grapes of Wrath*." In *Literary Journalism in the Twentieth Century,* edited by Norman Sims, 53–81. New York: Oxford University Press, 1990.

Ingels, Beth. Papers. "Parody of dog stories"; "Romance on Tortilla Flat"; "Cannery Row; Stories" "Series of tales about C.D.T. [Corral de Tierra] and country childhood." Author's collection, copied with permission of Harold Ingels.

Ingels, Beth, and Carol Steinbeck. *Carmel.* 1931.

Jackson, Joseph Henry. *Mexican Interlude.* New York: Macmillan, 1936.

———. "Why Steinbeck Wrote *The Grapes of Wrath*." *Booklets for Bookmen,* 1. New York: Limited Editions Club, 1940.

Jackson, Toni. "Julia Platt—Lady Watchdog." *What's Doing,* December 1946.

Jochmus, A. C. *The Circle of Enchantment.* Pacific Grove Historical Society files.

———. *Pacific Grove California and the Monterey Pennisula.* Pacific Grove Chamber of Commerce, 1928. Pacific Grove Historical Society files.

Kaplan, Amy. *The Anarchy of Empire in the Making of U.S. Culture.* Cambridge: Harvard University Press, 2002.

Kappel, Tim. "Trampling Out the Vineyards—Kern County's Ban on *The Grapes of Wrath*." *California History* 61, no. 3 (Fall 1982): 210–21.

Karman, James. *Robinson Jeffers, Poet of California.* Ashland, OR: Story Line Press, 2001.

Kelly, James C. "Ed Ricketts, Ecologist." *Steinbeck Newsletter* 9 (1995): 15–17.

Lamb, Helen Boyden. "Industrial Relations in the Western Lettuce Industry." PhD diss., Radcliffe College, 1942.

Lannestock, Gustaf. "Vilhelm Moberg in California: Personal Recollections and Impressions." Ms. Author's collection.

Larsen, Stephen, and Robin Larsen. *A Fire in the Mind: The Life of Joseph Campbell.* New York: Doubleday, 1991.

Loftis, Anne. "Celestial Gatherings." *Steinbeck Newsletter* 8 (1995): 5–8.

———. "Three Aspects of Advocacy: The Dust Bowl Migrants and California's Federal Camps as Viewed by Paul Schuster Taylor, John Steinbeck, and Carey McWilliams." Anne Loftis files.

———. *Witnesses to the Struggle: Imaging the 1930s California Labor Movement.* Reno: University of Nevada Press, 1998.

Lorentz, Pare. *FDR's Moviemaker: Memoirs and Scripts.* Reno: University of Nevada Press, 1992.

Lovejoy, John. "The Man Who Became a Steinbeck Footnote." *Steinbeck Review* 5 (2008): 59–84.

Lydon, Sandy. *Chinese Gold: The Chinese in the Monterey Bay Region.* Capitola, CA: Capitola Book Company, 1985.

Madison, Charles A. "The Friendship of Covici and Steinbeck." *Chicago Jewish Forum* 24 (1966): 293–96.

Marinacci, Barbara. "*The Grapes of Wrath* and the Wrath of Grapes: The Friendship of John Steinbeck and Martin Ray." *Wayward Tendrils Quarterly* 22, no. 1 (2012): 1–12. Part 2 in *Wayward Tendrils Quarterly* 22, no. 2 (2012): 29–39.

Marinaccio, Rocco. "George Oppen's "'I've Seen America' Book': *Discrete Series* and the Thirties Road Narrative." *American Literature* 74, no. 3 (2002): 539–63.

McCosker, John E. "Ed Ricketts: A Role Model for California Biologists." *Steinbeck Newsletter* 9 (1995): 12–14.

McElrath, Joseph R., Jesse Crisler, and Susan Shillinglaw. *John Steinbeck: The Contemporary Reviews.* New York: Cambridge University Press, 1996.

McIntosh, Mavis. Letters from JS. Papers of John Steinbeck, Albert and Shirley Small Special Collections Library, University of Virginia.

McLoughlin, William G. "Julia Ward Howe: The Battle Hymn of the Republic, 1861." In *An American Primer,* edited by Daniel J. Boorstin. New York: Meridian, 1985.

McWilliams, Carey. "A Man, a Place, and a Time: John Steinbeck and the Long Agony of the Great Valley in an Age of Depression, Oppression, Frustration, and Hope." *American West* 7 (1970): 4–8, 38–40, 62.

Mead, Marion. *The Portable Dorothy Parker.* New York: Penguin, 2006.

Merchant, Carolyn. "Women and Ecology." In *Feminisms,* edited by Sandra Kemp and Judith Squires, 472–73. Oxford University Press, 1997.

Miller, Nina. "Making Love Modern: Dorothy Parker and Her Public." *American Literature* 64 (1992): 763–84.

Mitchell, Ruth Comfort. Ruth Comfort Mitchell Papers. California History Room, Martin Luther King Jr. Library, San Jose State University.

Monterey Peninsula. American Guide Series. Stanford University, 1946.

Ngai, Mae M. *Impossible Subjects: Illegal Aliens and the Making of Modern America.* Princeton, NJ: Princeton University Press, 2004.

Orey, Cal. "Travels with Charley (and Omar, Bruga, Tillie, Toby Dog, Judy, Willie and Angel)." *Dog World,* December 1987: 22, 54–60.

Owens, Louis. *John Steinbeck's Re-Vision of America.* Athens: University of Georgia Press, 1985.

———. "Ways Out of the Waste Land: Steinbeck and Modernism, or Lighting Out for the Twenty-First Century Ahead of the Rest." *Steinbeck Studies* 13, no. 2 (2001): 12–17.

———. "Where Things Can Happen: California and Writing." *Western Literature* 34 (1999): 150–55.

"Pacific Grove." In *Pacific Coast Assembly,* Session June 30 to July 13, 1892. Hopkins Marine Station of Stanford University archives.

Pacific Grove's Architectural Heritage Guide. Centennial Edition. Heritage Society of Pacific Grove, 1975.

Parini, Jay. *John Steinbeck: A Biography.* London: Heinemann, 1994.

Paul, Louis. *Hallelujah, I'm a Bum!* London: Methuen, 1937.

Perry, Yaron. "John Steinbeck's Roots in Nineteenth-Century Palestine." *Steinbeck Studies* 15 (2004): 47–72.

Person, Leland. "*Of Mice and Men:* Steinbeck's Speculations in Manhood." *Steinbeck Newsletter* 8 (1995): 1–4.

———. "Steinbeck's Queer Ecology: Sweet Comradeship in the Monterey Novels." *Steinbeck Studies* 15 (2004): 7–21.

Pichardo, Nelson A. "The Power Elite and Elite-Driven Countermovements: The Associated Farmers of California During the 1930s." *Sociological Forum* 10, no. 1 (1995): 21–49.

Price, C. W. "Charles Erskine Scott Wood: The Development of an American Radical." Bachelor's thesis, Rutgers University, 1963.

Prose, Francine. *The Lives of the Muses: Nine Women and the Artists They Inspired.* New York: Harper Collins, 2002.

Quaide, Rustin. "Early History." National Parks Service, Santa Clara County: California's Historic Silicon Valley. June 5, 2011. http://www.nps.gov/nr/travel/santaclara/history.htm.

A Ramble Through Monterey County. California History Room, Monterey Public Library, ca. 1920.

Rathmell, George. "The Spice Boys." *Nob Hill Gazette,* September 2001.

Ricketts, Anna. "Recollections." Interview with Ed Ricketts Jr., Mill Valley, California, July 4, 1984.

Ricketts, Edward F. *Breaking Through: Essays, Journals, and Travelogues of Edward F. Ricketts,* edited by Katharine A. Rodger. Berkeley: University of California Press, 2006.

———. Edward Flanders Ricketts Papers. Stanford: Department of Special Collections, Stanford University Libraries, Stanford University.

———. Post Fire Notebook III. Post Separation Notebook II. Started Thurs. Sept 28, 1939. First Part of 1940 Mex. Trip. Post Fire Notebook IV; "Notes and observations, mostly ecological, resulting from northern Pacific collecting trips chiefly in southeastern Alaska, with special reference to wave shock as a factor in littoral ecology." Letters. Collection of Edward Ricketts Jr.

———. *Renaissance Man of Cannery Row: The Life and Letters of Edward F. Ricketts*, edited by Katharine A. Rodger. Tuscaloosa: University of Alabama Press, 2002.

Ricketts, Nancy. "Edward Flanders Ricketts: Four Perspectives, 'in the sense that . . .'" *Steinbeck Newsletter* 9, no. 1 (1995): 11.

Riley, Glenda. "Wimmin Is Everywhere": Conserving and Feminizing Western Landscapes, 1870 to 1940." *Western Historical Quarterly* 29, no. 1 (1998): 4–23.

Ringnalda, Margaret B. *Joy Laughed in His Bones: An Anecdotal Biography of Carlyle Ferren MacIntyre*. South Yarmouth, MA: Allen D. Bragdon Publishers, 1991.

Rippy, J. Fred. "The Inter-American Highway." *Pacific Historical Review* 24, no. 3 (1995): 287–98.

Rudnick, Lois Palken. *Mabel Dodge Luhan: New Woman, New Worlds*. Albuquerque: University of New Mexico Press, 1984.

Sallee, Denis. "Reconceptualizing Women's History: Anne Hadden and the California County Library System." *Libraries and Culture* 27, no. 4 (1992): 351–77.

Schaible, Daniel, Patrick Chapman, and Brian Chilcott. "Camp Curry Historic District Cultural Landscape Report, 2010." http://www.nps.gov/history/history/online_books/yose/camp_curry_clr.pdf.

Schamberger, John. "Steinbeck and the Migrants: A Study of *The Grapes of Wrath*." Master's thesis, University of Colorado, 1960.

Sheffield, Carlton A. *Steinbeck: The Good Companion*. Portola Valley, CA: American Lives Endowment, 1983.

Shillinglaw, Susan. *A Journey into Steinbeck's California*. Berkeley: Roaring Forties Press, 2006.

———. "The Wrath of a Nation: Reading *The Grapes of Wrath*, 1939–2007." In *Homer from Salinas: John Steinbeck's Enduring Voice for California*, edited by William A. Nericcio, 155–81. San Diego: San Diego State University Press, 2009.

Smith, Andy. "Mutualism and Group Selection in *The Grapes of Wrath*." *Steinbeck Review* 7, no. 1 (2010): 35–48.

Starr, Kevin. *Endangered Dreams: The Great Depression in California*. New York: Oxford University Press, 1996.

———. "Sunset Magazine and the Phenomenon of the Far West." http://sunset-magazine.stanford.edu/html/influences_1.html.

Steffens, Lincoln. *The Autobiography of Lincoln Steffens*. New York: Harcourt Brace, 1931.

———. *The Letters of Lincoln Steffens*. Vol. 2, *1920–1936*. New York: Harcourt, Brace, 1938.

Steinbeck, John. *American and Americans and Selected Nonfiction*. Edited by Susan Shillinglaw and Jackson Benson. New York: Penguin, 2002.

——. "Brief Outline of Play 'Of Mice and Men.'" Columbia University Library, New York City.

——. *Cannery Row.* New York: Penguin, 1994.

——. "Conversation with Bo Beskow and Bo Holmstrom." August 12, 1962. Jackson J. Benson *True Adventures of John Steinbeck, Writer* research materials, Department of Special Collections, Stanford University.

——. *The Grapes of Wrath:* New York: Penguin, 2006.

——. *In Dubious Battle.* New York: Penguin, 1996.

——. John Steinbeck Papers, Wells Fargo Collection, and John Steinbeck Collection. Stanford: Department of Special Collections, Stanford University Libraries, Stanford University.

——. *The Log from the Sea of Cortez.* New York: Penguin, 1995.

——. *The Long Valley.* New York: Penguin, 1995.

——. Long Valley Ledger. Center for Steinbeck Studies, San Jose State University.

——. *Of Mice and Men.* New York: Penguin, 1994.

——. *The Pastures of Heaven.* New York: Penguin, 1995.

——. "Some Thoughts on Juvenile Delinquency." *Saturday Review,* May 28, 1955, 22.

——. "Steinbeck: I Want to Be Understood Today." *Polityka* 46 (November 16, 1963), Warsaw. Jackson J. Benson *True Adventures of John Steinbeck, Writer* research materials, Department of Special Collections, Stanford University.

——. *Steinbeck: A Life in Letters.* Edited by Elaine Steinbeck and Robert Wallsten. New York: Viking, 1975.

——. *To a God Unknown.* New York: Penguin, 1995.

——. *Travels with Charley: In Search of America.* New York: Penguin, 1997.

——. *Working Days: The Journals of 'The Grapes of Wrath.'* Edited by Robert DeMott. New York: Penguin, 1989.

Stojko, Wolodymyr, and Volodymyr Serhiychuk. "John Steinbeck in Ukraine: What the Secret Soviet Archives Reveal." *Ukrainian Quarterly* 51, no. 1 (1995): 62–76.

Stott, William. *Documentary Expression and Thirties America.* New York: Oxford University Press, 1973.

Street, Richard Steven. "The Economist as Humanist—The Career of Paul S. Taylor." *California History* 4 (1978/80): 350–61.

Street, Webster. "John Steinbeck: A Reminiscence." In *Steinbeck: The Man and His Work,* edited by Richard Astro and Tetsumaro Hayashi. Corvallis: Oregon State University Press, 1971.

"Sunset Magazine: A Century of Western Living, 1898–1998: Historical Portraits and Bibliography." Stanford, CA: Stanford University Libraries, 1998. http://sunset-magazine.stanford.edu.

Tamm, Eric. *Beyond the Outer Shores: The Untold Odyssey of Ed Ricketts, the Pioneering Ecologist Who Inspired John Steinbeck and Joseph Campbell.* New York: Four Walls Eight Windows, 2004.

Taylor, Frank. "California's Grapes of Wrath." *The Forum, November 1939,* 232–38.

Taylor, Paul. *On the Ground in the Thirties.* Salt Lake City: Gibbs M. Smith, 1983.

Taylor, Ted M. "Ellwood Graham: Painter Laureate of Cannery Row." *Fine Arts Quarterly,* Winter/Spring 1991, 16A–19A.

Thomsen, Alice Barnard. "Eric H. Thomsen and John Steinbeck." *Steinbeck Newsletter* 3, no. 2 (1990): 1–3.

Timmerman, John. *The Dramatic Landscape of Steinbeck's Short Stories.* Norman: University of Oklahoma Press, 1990.

Valjean, Nelson. *John Steinbeck, The Errant Knight: An Intimate Biography of His California Years.* San Francisco: Chronicle Books, 1975.

Van Noy, Rick. *Surveying the Interior: Literary Cartographers and the Sense of Place.* Reno: University of Nevada Press, 2003.

"Viking's 'Grapes of Wrath' Campaign." *Publishers' Weekly,* February 17, 1940.

"Viking's Guessing Contest on Steinbeck Shipments." *Publishers Weekly,* May 20, 1939.

Walton, Effie. *Two for the Show.* New York: Vantage Press, 1964.

Wartzman, Rick. *Obscene in the Extreme: The Burning and Banning of John Steinbeck's "The Grapes of Wrath."* New York: Public Affairs, 2008.

Weinstein, Arnold. *Nobody's Home: Speech, Self, and Place in American Fiction from Hawthorne to DeLillo.* New York: Oxford University Press, 1993.

"Who Are the Associated Farmers?" *The Rural Observer* 2, no. 4. Published by the Simon J. Lubin Society of California, 25 California Street, San Francisco, September/October 1938.

Wulf, William A. Historical papers, private collection.

Index

6–7, 8, 23, 41, 45–48, 82, 243–44;
fraught relationship with mother, 10,
18–19, 21, 22; humor and wit of, 70,
125, 137, 258; 1928 Lake Tahoe trip and
meeting of John, 36–41; Los Gatos
homemaking, 167–68, 203–4; love
of dogs, 69, 252; love of jazz, 168–69;
marriage to Bill Brown, 257–58; marriage to Loren Howard, 249–50, 252,
254, 255; marriage to John Steinbeck
(*see* Steinbeck-Henning relationship/
marriage); Mexican experiences and
reflections (*see* Mexico); money issues
and thrift, 48, 242; nightmares suffered
by, 127; personality and appearance, 4,
5, 38, 55, 58–59, 83, 103, 104, 109–10,
114–15, 121, 122, 191–92, 195–96, 246–
47, 259; poetry of, 5, 79, 133–39, 143,
260–61; political views and activities,
140–45, 180, 184–85, 193; Ed Ricketts
and, 90–94, 97–98, 99–100, 231, 235–
36, 242; role in *Grapes of Wrath*, 2–3,
165, 183, 189, 201, 202–3; scrapbooks
created by, 122–27; Sea of Cortez trip
and, 217–34 passim; Steinbeck family
and, 68–69, 129, 139; wartime years in
Carmel, 244–49, 251–54
Steinbeck, Esther, 15, 23
Steinbeck, John Adolph (Johann Großsteinbeck), 16
Steinbeck, John Ernst: on adolescence, 28;
attitudes toward and fictional portray-
als of women, 23–25, 47–48, 132, 176,
187, 211–12, 215, 230; Joseph Campbell
and, 104–6, 112, 113, 119; Carol's role as
muse to, 6–7, 8, 23, 41, 45–48, 82, 243–
44; childhood and family background,
11, 14, 15–16, 22–26, 43; Gwen Conger
and (*see* Conger, Gwen); creative
breakthroughs during mother's illness,
129–33; creative inspiration and "use"
of others' material, 74–77; decision not
to have children and Carol's probable
abortions, 145–47; depression of, 81,
210; difficult adjustment to post-
Grapes period, 203, 205–6, 210, 220;

on dogs, 69; early literary influences,
46; ecological vision/holism of, 8, 23,
25–26, 46, 218–19, 229; on fathers and
fatherhood, 27–28; female characters
based on Carol, 47–48, 131–32, 176;
friendship and collaboration with
Ed Ricketts, 8, 77, 88, 90–97, 106,
116, 117, 185, 219–20, 225–26, 234;
importance of friendship to, 25–26,
95–96, 197, 224; importance of home
and homemaking to, 56–57, 64–65,
210–11; infidelities, 166–67 (*see also*
Conger, Gwen); influence of Salinas
on, 10–11, 57–58; interest in the occult,
40, 106; involvement in filmmaking, 201, 205; journalism of, 180–82,
183–84; Lake Tahoe years, 35–36, 37,
38, 42; marriage to Carol Henning
(*see* Steinbeck-Henning relationship/
marriage); Mexican experiences and
reflections (*see* Mexico); migrant
worker situation and (*see* migrant
workers); nostalgia for Pacific Grove,
60, 61–62; personality and appearance, 4, 5–6, 38, 39–40, 70, 81, 103,
185; phalanx theory and (*see* phalanx
theory); political views and activities,
140–45, 180, 184–85, 193; prose style
of, 46, 68; on public reaction to *Grapes
of Wrath*, 2, 206; relationship with
mother, 15, 18, 22, 43; Sea of Cortez
trip and, 218–35 passim; separation
and divorce from Carol, 237–44, 247;
views and reflections on marriage, 96,
99, 255–56; on writing and himself as
a writer, 7–8, 34, 43, 80–81, 82–83,
89–90, 120, 166, 169–70, 185, 210,
256, 261; writing process and habits of,
40–41, 81–82, 139, 168
Steinbeck, John Ernst (father), 16, 25–26,
68–69
Steinbeck, Mary, 15, 22–24
Steinbeck, Olive, 15, 18, 22, 68, 128–29, 138
Steinbeck-Henning relationship/mar-
riage: Carol's "dalliance" with Joseph
Campbell, 109–15, 119; Carol's